INDIGENOUS WOMEN AND WORK

Indigenous Women and Work

From Labor to Activism

Edited by

CAROL WILLIAMS

UNIVERSITY OF ILLINOIS PRESS
URBANA, CHICAGO, AND SPRINGFIELD

Supported by the Research Office, Trent University.

Library of Congress Cataloging-in-Publication Data
Indigenous women and work: from labor to activism /
edited by Carol Williams.
p.   cm.
Includes index.
ISBN 978-0-252-03715-3 (cloth)
ISBN 978-0-252-07868-2 (pbk.)
ISBN978-0-252-09426-2 (e-book)
1. Indigenous women—Employment.
I. Williams, Carol, 1956–
HQ1381.I42   2012
331.1089—dc23   2012016757

CONTENTS

List of Illustrations   *vii*

Preface   *ix*
　　Marlene Brant Castellano

Acknowledgments   *xiii*

Introduction   *1*
　　Carol Williams

1.　Aboriginal Women and Work across the 49th Parallel:
　　Historical Antecedents and New Challenges   *27*
　　Joan Sangster

2.　Making a Living: Anishinaabe Women in Michigan's
　　Changing Economy   *46*
　　Alice Littlefield

3.　Procuring Passage: Southern Australian Aboriginal Women
　　and the Early Maritime Industry of Sealing   *60*
　　Lynette Russell

4.　The Contours of Agency: Women's Work, Race, and Queensland's
　　Indentured Labor Trade   *73*
　　Tracey Banivanua Mar

5.　From "Superabundance" to Dependency:
　　Women Agriculturalists and the Negotiation of Colonialism
　　and Capitalism for Reservation-era Lummi   *88*
　　Chris Friday

6.　"We Were Real Skookum Women": The shíshálh Economy
　　and the Logging Industry on the Pacific Northwest Coast   *104*
　　Susan Roy and Ruth Taylor

7.　Unraveling the Narratives of Nostalgia: Navajo Weavers
　　and Globalization   *120*
　　Kathy M'Closkey

8. Labor and Leisure in the "Enchanted Summer Land":
   Anishinaabe Women's Work and the Growth of Wisconsin
   Tourism, 1900–1940   *136*
     Melissa Rohde

9. Nimble Fingers and Strong Backs: First Nations and Métis Women
   in Fur Trade and Rural Economies   *148*
     Sherry Farrell Racette

10. Northfork Mono Women's Agricultural Work, "Productive
    Coexistence," and Social Well-Being in the San Joaquin Valley,
    California, circa 1850–1950   *163*
      Heather A. Howard

11. Diverted Mothering among American Indian Domestic
    Servants, 1920–1940   *179*
      Margaret D. Jacobs

12. Charity or Industry? American Indian Women and Work Relief
    in the New Deal Era   *193*
      Colleen O'Neill

13. "An Indian Teacher among Indians": Native Women
    As Federal Employees   *210*
      Cathleen D. Cahill

14. "Assaulting the Ears of Government": The Indian
    Homemakers' Clubs and the Maori Women's Welfare League
    in Their Formative Years   *225*
      Aroha Harris and Mary Jane Logan McCallum

15. Politically Purposeful Work: Ojibwe Women's Labor
    and Leadership in Postwar Minneapolis   *240*
      Brenda J. Child

16. Maori Sovereignty, Black Feminism, and the New Zealand
    Trade Union Movement   *254*
      Cybèle Locke

17. Beading Lesson   *268*
      Beth H. Piatote

Contributors   *271*

Index   *279*

LIST OF ILLUSTRATIONS

Figure 3.1   Southeastern Australia Sealing Grounds map.   *62*

Figure 4.1   Kanakas—Bundaberg District, circa 1897.   *73*

Figure 4.2   South Sea Islander women planting sugar cane by hand at Bingera, Queensland, circa 1897.   *76*

Figure 4.3   Kanaka women working in the sugar cane.   *77*

Figure 4.4   Group of South Sea Islander workers on a property in Cairns, circa 1890.   *77*

Figure 5.1   Thomas Jefferson and family at Lummi Indian Reservation home place.   *93*

Figure 5.2   George Boone and three women working Boone's farm at Neptune Beach.   *94*

Figure 5.3   Solomon Balch and August Martin behind a group of women at a Lummi Fair spud-peeling contest.   *95*

Figure 5.4   Brown family of five posing for picture outside their home at Gooseberry Point.   *97*

Figure 6.1   Mary Joe, Violet Jeffries, Mary Anne Jeffries, Carrie Joe, and Madeline Joe rolling cedar sections, 1939.   *105*

Figure 6.2   Ellen Paul, Christine Julian, Janet Louie, and Mary Anne Jeffries, with a young boy, Val August, demonstrate cedar-root basket weaving, 1940.   *106*

Figure 6.3   Map of shíshálh territory within British Columbia, 2009.   *109*

Figure 6.4   Johnny Joe Dixon felling a tree, 1940.   *116*

Figure 7.1   Weaver Grace Joe, Red Valley, Arizona, October 1992.   *121*

Figure 7.2   "Pound" handspun and aniline-dyed wool rug produced circa 1905. Photograph taken in 1988.   *123*

Figure 9.1   Wally Dion, "Nurse Tracy," 2005. Acrylic on wood panel, 48 × 38¾ inches.   *148*

Figure 9.2   Sealskin boots made by "Good Mrs. Lane" for Sir William
              MacGregor, 1907.   *158*

Figure 9.3   Fur coat with bone/ivory toggles made by "Good Mrs. Lane"
              for Sir William MacGregor, 1907.   *158*

Figure 9.4   (Unidentified) Indian women and children picking rocks
              near Davidson, Saskatchewan.   *160*

Figure 10.1   Susan Benedict, Ida Carmen, and Susie Walker working
              at the Minturn Vineyard Company/Sierra Vista Vineyards,
              circa 1910.   *170*

Figure 12.1   An unidentified Navajo woman working at a WPA mattress-
              making project in Shiprock, New Mexico, 1940.   *193*

Figure 12.2   Navajo CCC workers build a diversion, Navajo Nation,
              Tuba City, Arizona.   *195*

Figure 12.3   Interior view of the Milwaukee Sewing Project.   *198*

Figure 12.4   Blackfeet women from the Browning WPA Sewing Group
              wearing garments they "renovated out of CCC clothing."   *201*

Figure 13.1   Retirement card of Julia DeCora Lukecart (Winnebago/French).
              Lukecart's career spanned from 1892 to 1932, and she was
              one of the few Native employees to receive a pension.   *215*

Figure 13.2   Civil service photograph of Katie Loulin Brewer.   *221*

Tyendinaga Mohawk Territory

Marlene Brant Castellano

The chapters in this volume explore Indigenous women's work in Canada, the United States, New Zealand, Australia, and the western Pacific islands. The lens employed is historical, in close focus on the experience of small groups and societies, with a broader sweep in comparative analysis of events and relationships in four principal nation-states. The studies emphasize the importance of situating records, observations, and commentary in time and place.

It seems appropriate, then, to identify the space and times from which my perceptions originate. I am a Mohawk woman, a mother and grandmother embedded in traditional relations, which is to say my community of origin in southern Ontario. I have been a witness to and participant in a half-century of astounding change, as an academic in Indigenous Studies for much of that time. Popular assumptions about the "vanishing Redman" have been laid to rest, though the view that Indians are a problem to be solved, rather than peoples to be respected, persists.

In Canada, Aboriginal rights grounded in prior occupation of lands, along with rights flowing from historic treaties and contemporary land claims settlements, have been accorded protection in the *Constitution Act* of 1982. The Supreme Court has given substance to some of these rights in a series of decisions. A precedent-setting decision in *Delgamuukw v. British Columbia* (1997) affirmed that oral history must be given equal weight with documentary evidence in the adjudication of claims.

Traditional homelands of Dene, Inuit, Cree, and other Indigenous peoples have been mapped and numerous precolonial names of villages, waterways, and mountains have been restored. Historical and social science research has shed new light on settler-Indigenous relations and, in the case of residential schools, substantiated claims for redress that led to a Settlement Agreement and an apology from the Prime Minister on behalf of the Government of Canada in 2008.

Legal and historical research has been central to revisioning Canada's past and breaking new ground in settler-Indigenous relations. Charting the path to more equitable and just relations remains a work in progress.

In parallel with political change that has looked outward to relations with Canadian society and governments, First Nations, Inuit, and Métis peoples in Canada have been engaged in profound social change within their communities. Part of their energies have been focused on coping with the stresses of resource deple-tion, isolation, unemployment, and social disorder stemming from the disruption of their traditional community and family structures. A very significant part of their energies has been, and continues to be, devoted to reestablishing links with their past—the stories that were deliberately suppressed in colonialist attempts to solve "the Indian problem" by erasing Indigenous histories and identities.

Elders have been reinstated as knowledge-keepers and mentors; ceremonies, no longer banned, are celebrated openly; artifacts and human remains are being retrieved from distant museums; languages still at risk of erosion and disappear-ance are being taught in classrooms and explored for insights into philosophy and ecology.

Responding to the practical demands of social and economic survival and the spiritual imperative to know and honor one's roots are the dual challenges taken up by increasing numbers of Indigenous scholars. Some are located in university departments of Indigenous Studies. Some are pursuing advanced degrees and research in faculties of health sciences or humanities. Some are serving their communities directly as local partners in community-based research initiatives.

Indigenous scholarship consciously engages with knowledge creation and elaboration within a paradigm of Indigenous ways of knowing and Indigenous perceptions of reality. Contemporary Indigenous research is not, however, carried out in isolation from intercultural experience.

Rich insights are stimulated in the dialogue between non-Indigenous col-leagues from various disciplines, who bring their specialized skills and tools, and Indigenous researchers whose questions often originate from personal experience and observation. The outcome of collaborative effort can have utility in society at large as well as the Indigenous community.

In the same vein, international discourse on Indigenous rights and exchanges between Indigenous scholars have gained momentum, highlighting common experience and regional distinctiveness and creating common cause across na-tional boundaries.

Emphasis on political development on the larger stage has been essential to create space for the complementary work of cultural renewal and personal heal-ing from loss and trauma. Indigenous women do not hesitate to claim primacy in this personal domain, just as they do not hesitate to pick up the tools and the burdens of making a living in the forest, on lakes and seashore, or in the city.

We know that we are resilient and that this is our inheritance from mothers and grandmothers who were the anchors of family and community through years much harsher than we have known.

The authors of papers in this volume make a welcome and valuable contri-bution to documenting the continuity and adaptability of Indigenous women's work as wave after wave of change swept through their communities. Weaving fragments from stories with different emphasis, gathering new accounts, revisiting documents and photos, they enable us to see, with fresh vision, vignettes of personalities and communities. And, with historians' perceptiveness, they reveal the unthinking cruelty of the economic enterprises and civilizing mission that are lauded in the official stories of the liberal democracies that frame the volume.

ACKNOWLEDGMENTS

Gratitude is extended to University of Illinois Press senior editor Laurie Matheson to whom I proposed this manuscript in 2007. She has sustained a firm commitment and confidence throughout the many stages of our project. I also thank Ned Blackhawk, Devon Mihesuah, Jennifer Nez Denetdale, Kate Ellinghaus, Angela Wanhalla, and Joan Sangster who responded to my search for names of individual scholars during the early development of the manuscript. In August 2008, Joan Sangster and I coorganized a workshop at Trent University, generously funded by the Social Science and Humanities Research Council of Canada, to assemble the contributors. Joan secured additional funds from Trent's Frost Centre for Canadian and Indigenous Studies; Canadian Studies Department; President's N.I.N.D. fund; Indigenous Studies Department and the History Department for extraordinary expenses. Thank you, Joan, for this valuable work and commitment to the project. Trent's Research Office headed by Dean James Parker and administered by Cathy Smith provided ongoing support between 2008 and 2011 as well as a generous subvention to support photographic reproductions in the publication. Support for student research assistance, travel, and some printing expenses for the workshop was provided by The Canada Research Chair Program as well as by Dean Christopher Nicol in the Faculty of Arts and Science at the University of Lethbridge (AB); the University of Lethbridge's Students' Union; and the Copy Centre at the University of Lethbridge.

All of the contributors who attended the 2008 workshop have remained loyal to the project. I appreciate the hard work and avid commitment of all the contributors despite many disruptions caused by my itinerancy across the continent over the course of three years. Marlene Brant Castellano, Sarah Carter, Sandra Fairman-Silva, and Beth Piatote provided valuable commentary on the presentations at the workshop and they deserve our collective acknowledgment for their efforts. Shirley Williams offered her ceremonial blessings at that time. Miigwech, Shirley, you set us off in the right direction!

Although we had never met, I had frequently seen the work of Faye HeavyShield in exhibition and subsequently invited her to permit us to feature a reproduction of one of her works on the book's cover. Don Gill provided services in kind to generate a beautiful reproduction of Faye holding her beaded book. The book, and Faye's explanation of it, offered a doorway into my introduction. Don

Gill, Sarah Williams, Heidi MacDonald, Tracy McNab, Dee McArthur, Glenda Bonifacio, Colleen O'Manique, Caroline Langill, Marlene Brant Castellano, Faye HeavyShield, Beth Piatote, Margaret Jacobs, Leanne Simpson, Wanda Nanibush, and Susan Roy all significantly influenced my conceptual thinking about this project. I would like to particularly acknowledge the individual anonymous reviewers because they were so generous with their close reading of our manuscript in draft. I hope I may reciprocate in some way in the future.

My work on the manuscript would not have been possible without the collegial support of faculty and staff in the Women's and Gender Studies Department and Indigenous Studies at Trent and in the Women and Gender Studies and History Departments at the University of Lethbridge. I am particularly in debt to Dean Chris Nicol in the Faculty of Arts and Science at University of Lethbridge; his sustained commitment to my professional activity and to Women and Gender Studies has been invaluable. Graduate and undergraduate student research assistants put considerable effort and time into this manuscript at both development and editing stages. Therefore, this volume is dedicated to Kelly Pineault, Daisy Raphael, Thera Body, Lynette Schick, Michelle Bennison, William Knight, and Christine Sy. Their delightful company, whether extended or momentary, was enthusiastic and inspired. May your intellectual and community labor be enriched by all the contemporary and historical women you encounter.

INDIGENOUS WOMEN AND WORK

Introduction

Carol Williams

The essays of *Indigenous Women and Work: From Labor to Activism* are set within the historical context of four settler nations—Canada, Australia, the United States, and Aotearoa/New Zealand—covering a broad span of time from the 1830s to the late 1980s. In each of these nations, the state overextended its bureaucratic reach into the intimate, conceivably "private," and working "public," lives of women.[1] Scholars have been necessarily vigilant in exposing the blunt instrumentality of modern state statutory formations in contouring and disfiguring Indigenous women's experiences, and this volume participates in that analysis (Borrows 1994; McGrath and Stevenson 1996; Robert 2001; Lawrence 2003; Ellinghaus 2002; Barker 2006; Jacobs 2007; Russell 2007; Simpson 2008; Wanhalla 2008; Perley-Dutcher and Dutcher 2010). Clearly identity—or subjectivity—for Indigenous male and female constituents under the rule of settler nations has been neither straightforward nor biologically "natural" or, for that matter, decisively cleaved into gendered domains of private and public. Identifications such as "Indian," "black," "colored," or "Aborigine" emerge not from sovereign identities based on fundamental relationships with tradition, ceremony, land, kin, the peoples of other Indigenous nations, or the "natural" environment but rather from an artificial morass of state legislation and bureaucratic programs, much specifically targeting women and unashamedly designed to assimilate and subordinate. These exceptional conditions distinguish the histories of Indigenous women's labor of the modern era from the histories of other women of settler colonies. Nevertheless, while secondary sources on Indigenous women's labor exist by scholars (including some written by scholars in this volume), a more dedicated focus on Aboriginal, Maori, Native American, Métis, or Inuit women as workers, waged or unwaged, is surely needed. *Indigenous Women and Work* aspires toward that end, and to prevent continued neglect of Indigenous women's contributions as modern workers.

Since the late 1980s, the discipline of Women's History applied the analytic category of gender intersectionally with other sociocultural categories such as work, class, citizenship, sexuality, ability, age, race, religion, nation, and ethnicity to understand how these variants, or intersecting inequalities, shape the experiences, consciousness, and perceptions of divergent groups of women (Bennett 2006). The intersectional approach arrived on the wake of critiques as Stasiulis explains: "Within some settler societies, divisions between different feminist and women's politics have followed the schisms in power relations, worldviews, and living conditions between Indigenous peoples and the colonial settlers/immigrants . . . the women's politics of those previously on the margins of feminist politics in settler societies—Indigenous women, women of colour, and ethnically non-dominant immigrant women—have increasingly called attention to the injustice of differential, racist, and sexist citizenship" (1999: 185). Hoskins summarizes from a Maori perspective:

> Western feminist tradition has for a long time posited gender as the primary and universal site of oppression, while largely ignoring factors of class and race . . . this position is untenable because it fails to expose/own/acknowledge not only white Pakeha[2] women as beneficiaries of Maori women's dispossession through colonization, but also their implication in these relations in a post-colonial Aotearoa. Our status as *tangata whenua* [first peoples], our culture and shared experience of colonization (with Maori men) situates Maori women in a much larger reality than that of "women's rights" (2000: 43).

Dissecting how and why certain dominant interpretations and certain speakers historically prevail is a prerequisite to see or meaningfully comprehend Indigenous women's experiences.

Just as Indigenous women and women of color have criticized the universal assumptions of Women's History, Indigenous Studies and critical Indigenous scholarship dispute "mainstream history," fruitfully testing the interpretative monopoly of Eurocentric *cognitive imperialisms* (Battiste 2005). Other counterstrategies, in particular the incorporation of Indigenous intellectual traditions, artistic processes, and philosophies as well as the critical reevaluation of a range of data, including visual and material culture, oral interviews and life histories, fiction, and song are deployed. Are "traditional historical forms such as song, dance, and stories" more "valid than published forms," as pondered by McGrath and Stevenson (1996: 38)? Indigenous "traditional knowledge" is an entirely distinct "knowledge system with its own concepts of epistemology and its own scientific and logical validity" (Battiste 2005) considering "all kinds of scientific, agricultural, technical and ecological knowledge, including cultigens, medicines and the rational use of flora and fauna" (Daes 1993 in Battiste). Eurocentric knowledge practices espouse a reliance on preexisting scholarly authority or published literature and might even be characterized as cannibalistic by so doing; in the aim toward "objectivity" is there a willful detachment from rooted, or embodied, relationships with specific communities of alternative knowledge holders, or with one's homeland, its flora or fauna? Are the two systems entirely diametric? To be sure, within the academy Eurocentric systems of knowing are granted inflated credibility over Indigenous knowledge systems and practices, and within academia the value and credibility of elder and "community" knowledge is often called into question. This hierarchy taxes hybrid scholars who confront "profound cultural differences in the ways in which truth, knowledge and wisdom are constructed" (Monture-Angus 1995: 28). To work in close collaboration and consultation with one's community of origin or ancestry has long been a priority among Indigenous scholars, and in Canada is presupposed as the ethical responsibility of any scholarly interaction within First Nations' communities.[3]

The research in this volume implicitly converses with these overarching methodological, political, and practical questions of historical method and interpretation. Faye HeavyShield's creamy, multipaged, glass-bead book titled *hours* graces the cover of *Indigenous Women and Work*. Beth Piatote's short fictional story, "Beading Lesson" featuring an aunt's tutorial serves as finale. While creative works are unconventional bookends to a manuscript of historical research and analysis, these choices are purposeful. HeavyShield's cover is a constitutive part of the book as is Piatote's fiction. They reinforce the theoretical threads about the legibility, or illegibility, of Indigenous women's lives and history shot through the collection. As shown by the innovative interpretative approaches pursued by the respective authors, the breadth of women's labor may be teased from interviews, life histories, oral narrative, visual culture, or even, as Piatote shows, from fiction derived from fact. The preface, by senior scholar, and Professor Emerita Marlene Brant Castellano reinforces the distinct commitment to building community relationships that many scholars utilize as an entry point for research. As she notes, "responding to the practical demands of social and economic survival and the spiritual imperative to know and honor one's roots are the dual challenges taken up by increasing numbers of Indigenous scholars." Indigenous scholars particularly have illuminated the path toward meaningful reciprocity in the process of knowledge production and exchange.

This manuscript emerges from a wide network of consultation. Development began in 2007 when I approached Laurie Matheson, a senior editor at the University of Illinois Press. I felt there was a large gap in the literature on women's labor history; subsequently, I consulted a number of Indigenous and non-Indigenous scholars across the United States, Canada, Aotearoa/New Zealand, and Australia casting a wide call for participants through personal communication. Those who were unable to participate were invited to recommend others whose work harmonized with the themes and content. I sought a range of scholars, Indigenous and non-Indigenous, senior and junior. The endeavor to stimulate a transnational conversation made selection all the more difficult; decisions in terms of scale were crucial to ensure that the manuscript was economically accessible. When I moved from a university in western Canada to another in southern Ontario, historian

Joan Sangster and I jointly applied for external, and internal, funding covering travel and accommodation to assemble the invited scholars, commentators, and student assistants. Once gathered, the proposed contributions were considered in workshop, with each short paper made available in advance to all participants to allow for interaction between contributors.

I enter this transnational dialogue as a non-Indigenous cultural historian actively interested in the complex histories of cross-cultural relations between Indigenous and non-Indigenous populations and that between Indigenous and visible minority immigrants in settler colonies. As a teacher of Indigenous students in Women and Gender Studies and within Indigenous Studies programs, my scholarship and practice is influenced by the major resurgence of contemporary and critical Indigenous scholarship across North America, Australia, and Aotearoa/New Zealand, and not just knowledge issued, or authorized, by academia. My comprehension of the histories of settler colonialism has been radically deepened by the insights of scholars such as Audra Simpson, John Borrows, Dian Million, Leanne Simpson, Renya Ramirez, Patricia Monture, J. Kehaulani Kauanui, Devon Mihesuah, Paula Sherman, Jackie Huggins, Jennifer Denetdale, Marlene Brant Castellano, Margaret Jacobs, Angella Wanhalla, Radhika Mohanram, Ann McGrath, Manulani Aluli Meyer, Victoria Haskins, Nancy Shoemaker, Kate Ellinghaus, Lynette Russell, Patricia Grimshaw, and Sherry Farrell Racette, as well as by the scholarship and policy analysis conducted by activist community groups and their leadership as represented by the Native Women's Association of Canada, the Ontario Native Women's Association, the Quebec Native Women's Association, and cultural professional organizations such as ImagineNATIVE, NAPT, the Aboriginal Curatorial Collective and the Native American and Indigenous Studies Association, among others. As a scholar and teacher who benefits from all of this production, I do not make judgmental distinctions between "community"-produced knowledge and "academic" production; both critically inform my research and pedagogy. A non-Indigenous scholar aware of the privileges and access I bear as a highly educated woman of Anglo-Celtic ancestry, I am committed to building ethical collaborative relationships with Indigenous and immigrant scholars in cooperation with other politically engaged individuals and communities.

This introduction first maps the logic for the unconventional inclusions of HeavyShield and Piatote. Thereafter, the introduction forms a portal to the extraordinary set of essays nesting between the covers of HeavyShield and Piatote by sampling some key concerns for a transnational history of Indigenous women's labor. Although not clearly scored between chapters nor among sectors of work, the book is organized both chronologically and relative to various sectors of labor discussed by the respective authors. Starting with examinations of women's resources or manual labor (Russell, Roy and Taylor, Banivanua Mar, Farrell Racette), the analysis moves to variations on rural, agricultural- or land-based labor (Friday, Howard, Banivanua Mar, M'Closkey); turns to reproductive and/ or domestic "service" or labor within arenas such as women's social networks or "clubs" (Jacobs, O'Neill, Farrell Racette, Harris and McCallum, Piatote); focuses on entrepreneurial and creative initiatives and the professional opportunities that evolve according to external market demands (M'Closkey, Littlefield, Rohde, Cahill); and concludes by looking at women's labor and their compounding social capital as they transition into advocacy, activism, education, or administration (Harris and McCallum, Child, Cahill, Locke). Readers will notice that some chapters afford "long" histories and others are more regionally specific. Nonetheless, on all fronts, the writers critically account for the cultural and political context that distinguishes Indigenous women's history as laborers. Joan Sangster, in Chapter 1, selectively reviews debates across the 49th Parallel, thus steadying the reader in the fertile discursive terrain introduced by recent secondary literature.

Beading Literacy

In the cover photograph HeavyShield holds her beaded book *hours* as if reading. Contemplate the precision needed to uniformly bind tiny glass seed beads, with thread alone into a multipage book; the cream-colored beads are glossy and tremble or roll at touch. Imagine the book's heft. These qualities—conceptual simplicity, tactile physicality, weight, density—viscerally evoke the hand and intellect of the maker and testify to the effort, time, and thought she expended in production of the material object.

Without text or surface design, *hours* harbors minimal clues for those dependent on Eurocentric notions of legibility. HeavyShield's book pages are blank; no geometric or floral ornamentation is evident. *hours* disappoints museological expectations. It is neither functional nor ceremonial; it is not a bag, embellished cuffs, moccasins, leggings, a dress, or a cradle board. *hours* is curiously mute. As Birgit Brander Rasmussen convincingly demonstrates, alphabetic-based writing, or literacy, was not hegemonic during early contact. Wampum, for example, affords a beaded "narrative and documentary tradition" crucial to Iroquoian diplomacy across generations (Rasmussen 2007: 445). Nevertheless, "pen and ink work," as one eighteenth-century Iroquoian speaker apparently described the white man's writing, "came to signify reason" with epistemological distinctions increasingly drawn between the divergent forms of expression (446). Alphabet-based writing, ultimately, was equated with literacy and civility thus "mak[ing] dialogic study of the [Euro and Indigenous] encounter impossible, and [it] leaves uncontested the monologues of colonial agents." Increasingly, encounters between "civilized" and "savage" peoples were respectively "marked . . . by literacy and illiteracy" (446).

Written archives still configure contemporary knowledge and legal procedure. The intellectual dependency on archival written sources for the interpretation of history and knowledge production is limiting as the misrepresentations of the colonial past are potentially recycled into the present (Ganter 1999; Smith 2004). If postcontact treaties, for example, arose from extended oral *negotiations* between European newcomers with the representatives of resident Indigenous peoples, the resulting records, or written accords, structurally and economically favored settler society.

The recycling of these inequities from the colonial past across multiple generations to the present becomes apparent in contemporary legal challenges. In Aotearoa/New Zealand, "until 1985 the land rights of Indigenous people carried no weight in the courts unless backed by Pakeha documents. Legal rulings and government legislations . . . made it impossible to enforce against the Crown 'Maori customary' or aboriginal title to land. . . . Grievances about the loss of tribal lands and other *taonga* (prized property) were to large extent ignored" (Macdonald 1990: 4). Only the displacement of the hegemonic power of writing and of the primacy of alphabetic script will enable recognition of distinct, or competing, literacies. Rasmussen calls for more equitable understandings of intercultural textual reciprocity in order to recover Indigenous records, and agency, from obscurity (446).

HeavyShield's *hours* alludes to this friction, or historical incommensurability, between Indigenous and non-Indigenous textual epistemologies. *hours* tests the hegemony of alphabetic writing as sole or primary measure of literacy, or "civility"; the viewer must search beyond the seemingly mute surface. Moreover, when the title *hours* is juxtaposed with the embedded possessive pronoun "ours," a long-embattled history of outsider territorial, cultural, and linguistic appropriation, theft, or dispossession is signified (HeavyShield correspondence 2010).

As a fusion of visual and cultural ideas, beadwork was not a minor byproduct of male-dominated trade relations as conventional approaches to histories of decorative or functional goods might construe. Nomadic, the portable object possesses an existence detached from the maker. Exchanged, the object absorbs "nicks, scratches, deteriorations, and repairs" embedding signs of communal use and value (Nicolson cited in Williams et al. 2005: 155). On the northwestern plains of North America, traders introduced manufactured glass seed beads prior to the "journey of discovery" along the Missouri and Columbia Rivers undertaken by Meriwether Lewis and William Clark from 1804 to 1806. Beaders of the western plains selectively incorporated or innovated eastern styles just as easterners, northerners, or southerners surely adapted designs and aesthetics as beaded objects traveled with makers or consumers. Naxaxalhts'i Albert (Sonny) McHalsie recollects how his grandfather dried extra Fraser River salmon to trade with interior Okanagan people who exchanged dried berries, buckskin, and elkskins as well as "gauntlet gloves with all kinds of beadwork or embroidery on them" (McHalsie in Miller 2007: 102). Design and application surely evolved depending on custom, the function of the object or garment, the skills and mobility of the individual beadworker, and the regional availability of resources. The resulting handiwork, whether political, functional, decorative, or any combination therein, illuminates the expertise of the producer on the one hand and the breadth of communication and trade among linguistically and culturally diverse networks of tribally and trade-linked peoples on the other (Duncan 1996).

If contemporary Kwakwaka'wakw artist Marianne Nicolson yearns for objects to "inform us of the great events that have worn away at their surfaces," *hours* accommodates this request quietly (Nicolson in Williams 2005: 155). It is tribute to a profound history of Indigenous women's beading literacy and cultural innovation heralding their part in continent wide inter- and intracultural diplomacy and trade. *hours* also represents, for HeavyShield, the companionship of family and women; as the process of beading consumed many months "[*hours*] came to be another visitor and so to me it felt that all the talk and often laughter was woven into the work. True, a part of the concept does have to do with (historically) opposing perspectives but I would have to say the community outweighed the political aspect" (HeavyShield correspondence 2011).

As with all beaded objects, the interpretation of *hours* demands creative thinking to fathom its purpose and political or cultural reach. HeavyShield conceptually binds past to present, reminding contemporary viewers of colonialism's history of cultural theft and appropriation but also of the ongoing relevance, and joy, of community.

"Beading Lesson" likewise honors women's cultural labor and community. Piatote, a historically informed literary critic and a storyteller, intuitively reveals how and why women's "unorganized" or ancillary labor eludes standard historical interpretation. The personality, labor, and history of Piatote's narrator in the story unfold almost incidentally. Fiction, unlike much detail-driven "history" writing, opens breathing space in its narrative style. Piatote conveys an affectionate and reciprocal exchange between female relations; the primary speaker, unidentified by name, gently addresses or instructs a seemingly attentive younger, university-aged recipient. The narrator possesses a unique and practiced skill in beadwork and design, which, clues hint, is formidable. Her monologue, if spare, navigates vast terrain: family, social, and cultural history; community activism; and even colonial effects. She mentions work among American Indians incarcerated at a local prison. Succinctly imparted is something, too, of her economy of survival: "Most everything I make I give away, but people pay me to make special things. And they are always askin' for my work at the gift shop. My beadwork has got me through some hard times, some years of livin' skinny" (Piatote). While the broader social context of women's circumstances or labor is perhaps only incrementally grasped from these episodic exchanges, the elder woman's guidance as gentle educator is vivid. This scenario invokes a pedagogical tradition whereby younger women are tutored, or nudged, by elders with youth "discovering through trial and error" (Duncan 1996: 115). In "Beading Lesson," a sister's daughter is mentored, and not exclusively about beading. Metaphorically braiding relationships across generations, communities, and culture, "Beading Lesson," like *hours*, underscores the persistence of cultural relationships over time, history, and generation to highlight the exchange, or relational, value of beading despite the invasive ruptures exacted and expected by colonialism (Piatote, correspondence).

hours and "Beading Lesson" clearly indicate that personal narratives of survival and economic adaptation entwine with, but are not dependent on, the narratives of the settler nation. Yet whereas Indigenous history afforded women respect as storytellers, the documentation of their labor is consistently minimized in colonial records. Settler nation histories thrive on parliament, politics, commerce, and war to privilege a record of men's public work and nation-building (Lake 2007). As Joan Sangster emphasizes in Chapter 1, following from Knack and Littlefield, the mystification of Indigenous women's labor as *unproductive* or *ancillary* within a capitalist society, and within nation-building narratives, reinforces the disregard or devaluation of women's contributions. Sangster observes innovative approaches adopted to rectify this invisibility and to chart new directions.

The Invisibility of Colonized Labor within History

As Hoskins asserts, earlier generations mistakenly universalized the category of *women* with the claim "they"—implying settler women primarily—were "outside" the domain of national stories. Euro-American women, in fact, were not consistently "outside" settler histories but often endorsed, or enabled, the imperial or colonial enterprise, whether as missionaries, educators, maternal feminists, agriculturalists, social reformers, or community boosters. Women settlers, shut out of governance by Euro-American men, felt duty-bound to exploit their procreative duties in allegiance to the nation (Sinha 2004). By elevating their "demographic" identities as mothers patriotically in service as "reproducers of the race," white women marshaled a degree of status, privilege, and power within increasingly racialized and classed regimes. While not full recipients of the nation's bounty or governance, by the turn of the nineteenth century, settler women and feminists of this era strove toward political enfranchisement. Endeavoring to gain male-defined equity, elite and educated white women conceived themselves, their bodies, and social mores as more righteously deserving of the settler nation's rights, privileges, and citizenship than other women (Sinha 2004). Lower-class or racially marked women were conscripted as indentured or *colonized* manual laborers, at the extremes of political or social marginality as they toiled in settler fields or in households managed by wealthier, and lighter-skinned, women. Thus some women subscribed to, rather than challenged, the stratification of labor that evolved in the settler colonies.

The colonization of labor accelerates after the 1834 abolition of slavery across the British Empire (Curthoys and Moore 1995). Yet, as Banivanua Mar explains in Chapter 4, in Queensland more than 63,000 Pacific Islanders from Vanuatu, the Solomons, and islands in the Torres Strait were indentured between 1868 and 1906. Banivanua Mar discusses how they were "technically not slaves . . . but the thriving trade in their bodies provided the cheap, bonded and expendable labor that kept colonial sugar industries in Queensland and the western Pacific competitive." *Colonized* labor so fundamentally "underpin[ned] the white economy," it was "seldom analyzed in its own right" and this erasure compounded the absence of these workers in labor history (Frances, Scates, and McGrath 1996: 191). While the term "slave" was frequently applied to describe Aboriginal or Indigenous laborers, *colonized* as workers, they were neither enslaved nor free and were treated as "inferior but useful" (Curthoys and Moore 1995: 4). Slavery also permeated definitions of labor in the United States where emancipation, or manumission, *ideally* afforded former slaves a new relationship to the marketplace; within this context citizenship or belonging, importantly, becomes defined by the *freedom* "to sell one's own labor" and with "self-sufficiency" (Kessler-Harris 2006: 13). And yet, in the United States, full citizenship, or the erasure of racial hierarchies, did not arrive with emancipation.

For the most part, the faith in the "male breadwinner" appointed principally white men as the most viable and deserving earners, with this status buttressed by unionism, wage policies, and other schemes that, without the insights of gender- or race-based analysis, appeared liberatory rather than exclusionary. Yet, the iconic worker was "historically male, his work and politics dependent on woman's absence, her location elsewhere, in the "private" sphere of personal service" (Lake 1994: 85). As Sangster notes, Canada's federal Indian Affairs similarly presumed the male bread winner as sole route for economic viability, as unquestioned for instance in a publication titled *A Survey of the Contemporary Indians of Canada: A Report on the Economic, Political, Educational Needs and Politics* (1966), colloquially known as the Hawthorn Report. Contemporary labor history in the Australian context embedded a preoccupation with *organized* male labor wherein the narrative of "violent class struggle" between capitalist owners and the propertyless working man consistently imagined labor's history as exclusively "a boys' story" (Lake 1994: 76). A failure to *see* women as workers prevailed.

Was Indigenous women's work so commonplace, or *colonized*, that their contributions entirely "evaporate" from economic and social accounting? In so many respects, settler colonial history like other forms of history retrospectively enacts an artful occlusion of female productive as well as reproductive labor; but by our new accounting women's work is the essential *infrastructure* upon which the non-Indigenous settler population depended, experienced elevated self worth, and economically thrived. Surely one cause of the erasure of women's contribution, and Indigenous women's contribution more specifically, is the recycling of the belief in the colonial "frontier" as an unadulterated product of masculine self-invention or self-sufficiency.

The web of colonial racisms, compounded by sexism, ensnared everyone. Unionists overlooked their participation or "complicity as colonizers" and by so doing fully harvested the benefits of imperialism; "they did not develop a consistent stance on Aboriginal labour, instead merely sharing the prevailing national mythologies, including those of primitivism and paternalism" (McGrath 1995: 43). In Australia's northern territory of the early twentieth century, racial dynamics fueled the purposeful exclusion of Aboriginal men from trade unions and the primary concerns of white unionists was "for their own conditions of labour. . . . [T]heir platform on aborigines was poorly formulated . . . few aboriginal workers belonged to unions and most unions made no effort to recruit them" (McGrath 1995: 40). Others openly rallied against the employment or importation of other nonwhite workers that "were employed so cheaply, they were characterized as 'a menace to the *white man*'" (emphasis added; McGrath 1995: 41, citing the *Northern Standard* June 1928). Prior to the 1960s, legislation stratified on the basis of race "supporting the idea that Aborigines not be paid but that 'half-castes' [those of mixed descent] receive wages" (McGrath 1995: 42). Thus, in Australia, a convoluted "half-caste apprenticeship scheme" was invented. Retrospectively the analysis of such schemes uncloak the self-interest and complicity of those who profited from racial hierarchies of settler colonialism.

If expunged from the published histories centering on white male "frontier" heroisms, Indigenous women's work was, in actuality, absolutely vital to settlement as many of the authors here and elsewhere demonstrate (McGrath 1978). Adapting to all shape of work relationships with the colonizers, and often in intimate proximity, women inhabited both sides of the colonial equation. Yet women were neither wholly victims nor "traitors" within this "frontier dynamic." Rather, they incorporated the labor they secured into their own "cultural framework," potentially working "for rather different reasons than European settlers might envisage" (McGrath 1995a: 370).

Nevertheless, the colonial regime conceived all women, irrespective of difference, as exploitable, compliant, or expendable, with employers believing that women should and did deserve less economic remuneration. In the case of white single women, their status in the workplace was commonly conceived as casual or temporary until marriage. If women secured the right to wage work the imbalance of legal and gender relations established by the legal terms of marriage tainted their "power to earn" (Kessler-Harris 2006: 14). Nonetheless, while the intimate relations of Indigenous women and men was intrusively monitored by the state, Indigenous women—married, common-law, or single—were not consistently regulated in the same manner as "respectable" white women. In territories where Indigenous populations outnumbered white, Indigenous women served as "sources of cheap and amenable labour" (McGrath 1978: 10). Performing pastoral and hard physical manual labor including the mustering, shepherding, and herding of livestock; clearing land; sinking wells; and building roads, dams, and fences (McGrath 1978; Huggins 1987; Frances, Scates, and McGrath 1996); therefore, prescriptions of femininity were judiciously "'relaxed'" when it came to "raced" labor. Plantation field labor, in the sugar industry of Queensland, was racially stratified while "seasonally engaged Aboriginal laborers did the nominally unskilled work," and "when women joined these workforces ... they did so under the same physical conditions as men" (Banivanua Mar, this volume; also Huggins 1987). A double standard trumped gender prescripts. As McGrath describes, "While the apportioning of occupations *did not* accord with European sex-roles, employers could accept the anomaly because the women—and the men too for that matter—were only 'niggers' (as they were popularly called in the Territory)" (1978: 8). In 1928, a union boycott of Darwin hotels with "black" employees rhetorically rationalized the displacement of these Indigenous laborers—women—from such waged service to argue that they were more appropriately relocated in the "privacy" of households to offset the "deprivations" of settler women who lacked dependable domestic help in remote settlements. In urban settings, Indigenous women similarly labored in casual or domestic situations. Isolated physically from other workers they were further disarticulated from "organizations, unions and strikes" (Lake 1994: 79).

Boundaries between private and public and between manual and domestic labor were decidedly permeable, particularly for racially marked—here meaning Indigenous—women workers. In Chapter 3, Lynette Russell discusses the assumption that resource maritime labor was exclusively performed by men. She argues that in southeastern Australia the success and wealth produced by the sealing industry up to 1815 and the subsequent economic stability of European men was wholly dependent on Tasmanian *pallawah* or Indigenous women's skills and expertise. For Susan Roy and Ruth Taylor, historical photographs uncover a lineage of women's involvement in hand logging in Squamish territory on the rugged northwest coast of British Columbia. As they note in Chapter 6, "The binary concepts of masculinized 'logging' and feminized 'basket making' grew largely from the colonial logic of gender normativity and separate spheres of activity. Colonial perspectives expected men to participate in industry, independently or as wage laborers; and women, in home-based cottage production." And in Chapter 5, Chris Friday shows Lummi women in northwest Washington state to be primary cultivators of potato agriculture and yet their roles in such production was effectively eclipsed as the heteronormative determinations of Indian agents characterized potato cultivation as exclusively masculine. Gender normativity held sway in the bureaucratic schemes wielded by the settler economy "making farmers [or manual laborers] of the men[.] ... [W]omen's contributions to the development of an agricultural economy were not ignored ... [but] reservation policies were developed to provide the biological and social reproduction of the Indian household ... [ultimately] affect[ing] women's primary or direct access to government issues, wage labor, and the use and control of tribal property" (Garrett Pool 1988: 159). Not unexpectedly, in Australia at least, missionary societies sanctioned the "protection" of Indigenous men and women with their attempt to remove women from pastoral "hard" manual labor or from sex-based labor and thereby reinforced heteronormative logic (McGrath 1995: 42–43).

If, in general, the unwaged reproductive labor of *all* women was undervalued, clearly Indigenous women of settler nations were significantly and differently burdened by punitive and moral expectations when it came to marriage and maternalism (Wanhalla 2008; Jacobs, this volume; Robert 2001). The widespread sterilization of Native American women without consent and the forced removal of Indigenous children from biological parents are two of the genocidal *applications* of such beliefs (Jacobs 2009; J. Lawrence 2000; Dillingham 1977; Torpy 2000; Child 1998). Indigenous women's abundant presence in social welfare records of the modern era arose from external determinations that they were incapable of caring or responsible parenting; as McGrath and Stevenson explain, removal "policies were premised on dominant representations of Aboriginal women as unfit mothers" (48). Little or no latitude allowed for the "progress" of Indigenous women as mothers; representational trends trapped them within the inflexible binary of "savages" or "sexual objects" or sometimes both (Hoskins 2000: 38). Domestic training and vocational programs for Indigenous girls and women adapted the rhetoric of feminine virtue to inculcate workers in "white cultural norms and middle class etiquette" and promised to *feminize* Indigenous women so they were "an asset to the State" rather than a "liability" (1914 correspondence cited by McGrath 1978: 12). In Chapter 11, Margaret Jacobs analyzes a domestic "outing" program in San Francisco between 1920 and 1940 wherein young Indian female workers were, on the one hand, dispatched to households to nurture the children of white women, and on the other, purposefully diverted from motherhood arising from the perception that they lacked competency to mother. The women themselves did not passively accept the contradictory characterization of themselves as able in service but maternally incompetent; they pen letters to political representatives, social workers, or employers expressing contrary ambitions against the assimilationist compulsions of Bureau of Indian Affairs administrators. But justice remains elusive. In New South Wales, for example, the Aborigines Protection Board listed some 850 white, mostly female, employers in Sydney's suburbs who "swapped and transferred successive servants between each other" (Haskins 2005: 148). Taken from birth families, young women were "outed" as servants in alignment with state mandates to remove Indigenous children for apprenticeship placement (148). Pay rates in these "outing" schemes were exceedingly low and paid by householders directly *to* the Protection Board who held, or withheld, wages; this action was justified on grounds "that 'the girls only waste the money'" (Haskins 2005: 149). Thus under the paternalistic ruse of "protection," or apprenticeship, domestic workers were obstructed from hard-earned wages and "the cycle of poverty and dependence" was ensured (150). Increasingly, child removal was legislated in the search to "place [children] under apprenticeship where, it was hoped, they would be increasingly absorbed by white society" (149). The right, or desire, to parent or to receive equitable treatment as workers was, in essence, actively deterred. The household or other domestic spheres remains one of the most unreconstructed and unregulated labor sectors for Indigenous and immigrant women. Moreover, in such circumstances the settler householder enabled or was complicit with state assimilationist mandates. These examples convince us of the urgency of a "reconceptualization of the public-private binary and a search for mechanisms of accommodations, resistance, and protest that emerge from private, even intimate, spaces, . . . household, cultural community (religion) tribe and nation, and consumption" (Kessler-Harris 2006: 18).

Conceived both as a basic civil right and as a social obligation, work "lies at the analytic intersection of gender, class, race and citizenship" but assumptions about work, like race, operate to "separate citizens from each other, first in terms of whether it is paid or unpaid, and second in terms of its particular relations to production" (Kessler-Harris 13) One's status as a worker is molded by other societal biases as well wherein "those who cannot, or will not [work]" are inevitably judged as lazy, dependent, or shirking social responsibility (13). A different history of labor awaits the telling precisely because of the multitude of ways Indigenous women—as *colonized* workers, as Indigenous, and as women—were disciplined and paternalistically presumed by the respective settler nations as *dependent or incompetent* rather than economically or socially sovereign. They were disenfranchised from the opportunity for economic self-sufficiency by virtue of their colonized subordination in the settlement's wage economy; disenfranchised geospatially from tribal communities and territorial land rights by virtue of colonial and gendered policies of assimilation and the occurrence of marriage to non-Indigenous men; and disenfranchised as women by virtue of overarching gender prescripts, by racism, and by relations imposed by Eurocentric sexual divisions of labor. Have Indigenous women circumvented the invasive "gazes" and "grips" that endeavored to constrain them legally, economically, and morally (McGrath 1995)? How have fictions about them as "racially marked" gendered dependents neither fully in nor outside the nation been contested? Unlike their aspirations for economic self-sufficiency that led to many creative adaptations of the market, the answer is not straightforward.

Nation, Indigeneity, and Gender

The United States, Australia, Canada, and Aotearoa/New Zealand, all colonized under British law, possess common attributes. The exercise of specious claims of authority including the application of *terra nullius* (the assumption that land was empty) or the *doctrine of discovery* resulted in the exercise of colonial sovereignty over preexisting Indigenous inhabitants who had long-established systems of rights, territory, and structures of self-governance. The *doctrine of conquest* presumed that Indigenous inhabitants lacked rudimentary conditions of social organization and that conquest was justified (Ivison, Patton, and Sanders 2000). Dispatches to the British Colonial Office from New Zealand's governor in 1859 blatantly exemplify self-interest: "The Europeans covet these lands and are determined to enter in and possess them . . . rightly if possible, if not, then by any means at all"(Macdonald 1990: 12). Moreover, as one comparative analyst of policies, legislation, and sovereignty initiatives in the United States and New Zealand determined, "after treaties were signed recognizing Indigenous peoples as sovereign powers, conservative legislation was quickly passed in both countries which sought to nullify treaty provisions and encourage assimilation" (Duffie 1998: 185). The psychological, spatial, cultural, class, and racial segregation of Indigenous peoples was exercised formally and informally with bureaucratic application tasked to individual "field agents" of civil society—missionaries, field matrons, educators, Indian agents.

Conventionally cast within history, education, law, and policy as "continentally cohesive" and constituted by European immigrants, settler nations invent pioneer "creation" myths. These narratives, as has already been noted, are not benign. For instance, "the [U.S.] conquest of islands including Puerto Rico, Guam, American Samoa, and the Hawaiian Islands" is diminished in U.S. history and slavery is consistently constituted as "the original racial sin of the nation" (Kahaleole Hall 2008: 273). Certainly critics do not deny the existence of slavery nor underestimate the systemic violence of black-white inequities in the United States; but these same critics suggest the reliance on the mythic "nation of immigrants" set alongside a "black-white 'race' dichotomy" generates amnesia about America's Indigenous origins (273). In the ongoing struggle for unresolved territorial and rights claims, Indigeneity was to "be documented and quantified to exist" with formal demonstrations of blood quantum (275). Blood quantum measures as applied to Indigenous Hawaiians exemplify how they were classified, divided, or partitioned as well as alienated from heritage and land. By 1949:

> being Hawaiian was a racial and cultural disadvantage rather than a national definition. The federal government had officially classified our people by blood quantum in 1921: those of us with less than 50% were not Native. "Fifty percenters," as they are known today, have claims to land; "less than fifties" do not have such rights (Trask 1996: 907).

Strategic Indigeneity as a contrary concept of identity stresses common bonds: tradition, roots in subsistence, an attachment to land, shared experiences of colonial conquest, and the loss of language and culture forced by another group (Lewallen 2003). Each settler nation is a diverse and unquantifiable synthesis of immigrant and variously defined Indigenous populations, jumbled by intimacy and intermarriage. Indigenous-identified populations are further diversified by other categories of identity yet possess unique historical relationships to communal practices, to the land, to water routes linking territories, and to experiences of urban relocation—coerced or policy-driven.

Political rights theorists, Indigenous activists, and traditional knowledge-holders of the four nations have long pursued rights claims and, in many instances, must resort to the international forum if standing grievances fall on "tin" ears at home.[4] After the 1872 land wars, for instance, chiefs from the Ngapuhi tribe of Aotearoa/New Zealand petitioned Queen Victoria against breaches in the Treaty of Waitangi[5] (Macdonald 1990) and then, in 1884, Wiremu Te Wheoro assembled a deputation to London "to lay our wrongs before her gracious majesty for we are weary of laying our grievance before the New Zealand government" (cited in Macdonald 1990: 14). In 1981 Sandra Lovelace, from Tobique in Canada's province of New Brunswick, successfully appealed against the Indian Act to the United Nations Human Rights Committee. Canada, it ruled, was in violation of the *International Covenant on Civil and Political Rights* "by denying Lovelace her rights to enjoy and participate in her Maliseet culture" (Perley-Dutcher and Dutcher 2010: 201).

Nonetheless, despite these highly publicized and potentially embarrassing political actions, the four settler nations stood among eleven to share the unenviable reputation of sustained opposition to *The United Nations Declaration on the Rights of Indigenous People* (at least until 2010 when Canada tentatively endorsed the declaration).[6] This intransigence reflects "the degree to which issues of Indigenous governance, sovereignty, and self-determination remain troubled and troubling sites of disruption of the nation state" (Byrd and Heyer 2008: 1–2). Sovereign Indigeneity is not easily accepted, as the refusal to ratify the U.N. declaration proves. Why such fierce hostility to *oppositional nationalisms*, manifestations of place and community that "combine[s] traditional practices related to ancestral territory or customs with the strategic willingness to accommodate introduced political circumstances" (Mohanram 1996: 57)? As one scholar explains, Indigenous sovereignty, a communal concept, is perceived as antithetical to capitalism "within a dominant society dedicated to the fetishization of individualism and deeply suspicious of group identities. In the United States, the contemporary conception of race is firmly anchored in civil rights ideologies, the idea of equality of *individuals* [emphasis mine] within one nation" (Kahaleole Hall 2008: 276).

Further, in state formations where unexamined applications of multiculturalism reign the Indigenous experience, whether tribal or individual, is conceptually and historically opaque (Ramirez 2007). State multiculturalism, however, is employed to "covertly signal racialized differences" (Gunew 1997: 24). Defined as a global discourse and a set of practices and values, associated with "the flow of migrants, refugees, diasporas," state multiculturalism masks "both a hidden norm from which minority groups diverge while failing to recognize prevailing power differentials" (Gunew 1997: 22–23). Indigenous responses to, and uses of, multiculturalism vary. In Australia, for instance, "Aborigines refuse to be included in multicultural discourse on the grounds that these refer only to cultures of migration, whereas in New Zealand 'biculturalism' is the preferred official term because multiculturalism is seen as a diversion from the Maori sovereignty movement" (Gunew 23–24). Canada's First Nations may incidentally be sheltered under multiculturalism's umbrella, notes Gunew, but remain "trapped between the two sides of the French-English divide" (24). And in the United States, Ramirez reports of the Native American "fight[ing] to assert their sovereign rights as tribal citizens within a colonial context rather than fighting for membership within the dominant nation-state" (2002: 66). These distinct relationships to the state rarely surface for popular consideration.

Overblown national and masculine narratives of settler "pioneerism" reinforce the notion of the heroic individual and to some degree arose from the erroneous beliefs that Indigenous people would not survive modernization. When one colonial authority reflected in 1856 that "our plain duty as good compassionate colonists is to smooth down their dying pillow" (Superintendent Dr. Isaac Featherstone cited in Macdonald 1990: 5), this is a clear disassembly of personal or political culpability; he had obviously witnessed some aspects of the Indigenous battle against the imposition of European thought and culture and the effects of introduced diseases. "The actual origins" of settlement, Bonita Lawrence writes, "began with displaced and marginal white men, whose success with trade, and often their very survival depended on their ability to insinuate themselves into Indigenous societies through intermarriage.... [S]ome form of negotiated alliances with local Indigenous communities [were] often cemented through marriage, and reliance on native women for survival" (2003: 8). Even the most junior textbook concedes that early settlers would not have survived if not for the labor and expertise afforded by Indigenous mediators, provisioners, or guides. In Chapter 9, Sherry Farrell Racette suggests that the "harsh reality" of northern plains and woodlands survival pushed traders into relationships with Indigenous women, perhaps initially as companions and helpmates but increasingly cognizant of women's seasoned proficiencies in harvest and provisioning as well as the tanning and preservation of hides. Without this expertise, the trading enterprise likely would have failed, Farrell Racette suggests. By the mid–nineteenth century, the reciprocity of Indigenous women is demographically confirmed, in "fifty-three distinct Métis communities in the Great Lakes area alone, whose inhabitations blended native and European ways of living in highly distinct ways" (V 1, section 6.2 150, The Royal Commission on Aboriginal Peoples cited by B. Lawrence 2003: 8).

Because identity and attachment to land were inextricably shaped by evolutions in external federal legislation, the constellation of personal identity, gender, land, and intimacy underpins any analysis of Indigenous women's wage and reproductive labor. During the final three decades of the nineteenth century, women were "live[ing] across the line"—or on and off the reserves. Native reserves, or reservations, were "carefully monitored by federal officials" and, like the fur trade, became "significant contact zones . . . gendered in their establishment and settlement" (Wanhalla 2008: 30). On Canadian reserves, agents apply "Euro-Canadian moral codes against women . . . through the use of financial control. . . . They could deny women their treaty and interest payments on the grounds of real or alleged sexual transgressions; they could take away their children; and they could grant or refuse relief in time of need. Indian agents' roles in controlling the people's money and dispensing social welfare greatly magnified their ability to discipline First Nations women" (Brownlie 2003: 142).

Women's economic sovereignty and "inner beings" were thus disciplined very decisively in Canada by "discriminatory legislation," where a federal Indian Act invented and authorized in law a category of identity known as the status "Indian" (McGrath and Stevenson 1996: 39). The result was the multigenerational economic and cultural disenfranchisement of women and their children from their cultural communities and territory. Unlike men who married "out,"[7] Indigenous women who married non-Indigenous men—or men not federally authorized as "Indian"—lost significant rights, including rights to property. The children of these unions did as well (Perley-Dutcher and Dutcher 2010). The Act's dissecting scope subjected individuals to a "regulatory regime" used to conceptually and materially "control every aspect of Indian life," and "in ways that are so familiar as to almost seem 'natural'" (B. Lawrence 2003: 3). Lawrence understands the Act, not "merely as a set of policies to be repealed, or even as a genocidal scheme" but as "a classificatory system produc[ing] ways of thinking—a grammar—that embeds itself in every attempt to change it" (2003: 4).

Women's relocation either on or off the reservation (or straddling economies of both town and reserve) was not a decision, therefore, entirely of their own making. Accordingly, a patchwork or an adaptive mixed economy approach emerges as a potentially defining characteristic of women's economic and laboring agency precisely because of the officially imposed relationship to territory or at least to reserves. Studied household economies distinguished between women who work off reservation and those who, often out of necessity, find it "economically impractical" to leave for wages (Conte 1982: 108). Navajo women, Conte observed, sustain traditionally derived, seasonal harvest and gathering labor of remote reservations while serving the cash-driven, often informal, economies of nearby urban centers. In Chapter 2, Alice Littlefield similarly records Michigan Anishinaabe women's long history of occupational mobility and creative adaptation against the impositions of federal policies from women's earliest involvement in the global fur trade of the seventeenth century to waged and entrepreneurial service in tourism of the Upper Peninsula. Enriched by interviews conducted in the early 1990s with women of the Saginaw Chippewa, Littlefield focuses on the postwar-era generations of women and their efforts to gain entry to postsecondary education and subsequently to white-collar and professional labor.

Littlefield shows how they secured opportunities unavailable to their mothers but only because foremothers were so resourceful and persevering. Using industrial survey reports, Melissa Rohde, in Chapter 8, shows how the entrepreneurial adaptation of Anishinaabe women at Lac Courte Oreilles and Lac du Flambeau in Wisconsin between 1900 and 1940 are vital to the economic transformation from a dependency on extractive logging resource industry to service-based tourism. Women's work within tourism, provisioning a diverse range of services and activities, usefully erodes formerly paternalistic or narrow conceptions of work and workplace. Rohde understands that tourism brought small freedoms offering "a new source of revenue without requiring Native women to conform to the government's program of stamping out what it considered the dangerous and backward aspects of American Indian culture." Heather Howard's interviews with Californian North Fork Mono women in Chapter 10 offers insights into seasonal grape and orchard labor in the San Joaquin Valley as workers recall an unregulated, yet profitable, agricultural sector. In her chapter, Howard writes of women who voice concerns about health and safety, accelerating employer demands, rates of pay, diminishing wages, and the competition with immigrant workers during the 1930s.

In the American southwest, Indigenous producers develop a viable commercial tourist market for so-called "traditional arts and crafts," but these goods, like women's contribution, are generally conceived as outside of both industrialism and global capitalism. Yet, by the century's turn, women market their hand-produced wares—ceramics, weaving, rugs, or baskets—in "public" urban doorsteps, train platforms, and street corners, new spaces of intercultural contact between consumers and producers (Raibmon 2006; M'Closkey 2002). With these entrepreneurial transactions—women's involvement in "casual" or doorstep economies—contact is sustained and assumptions about women's status as economic outsiders are refuted. In Chapter 7, Kathy M'Closkey records how rug "crafts" and spun wool produced by Navajo women were not only culturally meaningful but also were developed into major commodities in a competitive global market. In many ways, craft entrepreneurialism allowed women to strategically combat the economic deprivation of the reservation, build cultural capital, and nurture territorial and kin ties.

Despite proven entrepreneurial successes in the southwest, only 11 out of 156 U.S. federal work relief projects designated for Indian reservations during the Depression specifically targeted women. Those schemes, administered by home extension programmers, were, in essence, occupationally reductive and *domestic* in nature as Colleen O'Neill explains in her analysis of relief programs among Blackfeet women in Cut Bank, Montana, during the 1930s. Such programs, as she shows in Chapter 12, potentially shunt women, once again, to "the margins of the capitalist labor market in the 1930s." Even in the so-called enlightened modern era promised by the administrative renaissance of the U.S. Indian New Deal, economic policies were restrictively gendered in design and scope.

Structural racism impedes equity for Indigenous women in federal white-collar settings. Cathleen Cahill, in Chapter 13, retrieves a particularly poignant legal case that exposes the plight of a former BIA Indigenous worker whose status as a part-time laborer prevented receipt of her pension despite a sustained loyalty to the federal employer. Cahill describes circumstances when retirement benefits were withheld from Native employees and how those workers pointedly grieve workplace discrimination, daring to advocate for professional advancement within the bureaucratic culture of Indian Affairs.

Urban relocation from remote reservations produced a range of economic and cultural challenges while encouraging progressive alliances across tribal and re-gional diversity. In the United States, the federally mandated relocation programs of the 1950s stimulated the migration of 30,000 residents from reservations and three times that in the 1960s and 1970s (Burt 1986: 85–87). Another proposed solution to reservation poverty, relocation was opposed by some as a recycled attack on tribal sovereignty. Nonetheless, in Los Angeles, relocation generated "over a hundred different American Indian organizations ranging from beading and language classes to all-Indian bowling and sports leagues. Indians resisted the government's assimilative policies as much as possible and negotiated their own cultural identities to meet the demands of their new environment" (Blackhawk 1995: 24). For an earlier generation, urban mobility offered social opportunities, as Jacobs shows in Chapter 11: "despite the oppressive nature of domestic service, many Indian women gravitated to these jobs in urban areas where they formed a vibrant social network with other Indian youth and reveled in modern urban leisure pursuits." Women of postwar generations "support[ed] the structural development of native community organizations and promote[d] positive pride in Native cultural identity in the city" (Howard-Bobiwash 2003: 567). The 1960s urban migration to Thunder Bay, Ontario, for instance, afforded those from re-mote communities with employment and educational opportunities; and from the local Indian Friendship Centre, formed in 1964, emerges *Anishinabequek*, a women-specific political organization (Janovicek 2003). Contemporary women's grassroots activism in Aotearoa/New Zealand continued the historical legacy of Maori women's political leadership, including their participation in tribally based Maori women's committees; their presence in the Maori Parliament established in 1882; or social welfare activism in Maori women's institutes, in the Women's Health League, and—after World War II—in the Maori Women's Welfare League (Macdonald 1990; Else 1993; Harris and McCallum, this volume).

A new century of resurgent women's political leadership shatters the horizon. Aroha Harris and Mary Jane McCallum, in Chapter 14, comparatively determine how women's volunteer associations in New Zealand—the Maori Women's Welfare League—and in Canada—the Ontario Homemaker's Clubs—cleverly outwitted state imperatives for assimilation and feminine domestication. Leadership bent the mandates of such organizations to community political and cultural will rather than passively complying with the wishes of the social reform bureaucrats that supposedly managed them. In Chapter 15, Brenda Child mines the depth of women's urban community activism, drawing on an important set of interviews with Ojibwe women in Minneapolis. Child shows how for these activists "personal networks with other Indian people were essential to city survival, and their efforts were an expression of indigenous values, and cultural capital, that resulted in the emergence of distinctive urban Indian communities." Women's networks and their invention of unique community formations generated unanticipated opportunities leading to professionalization and higher education not only for themselves.

Collectively, therefore, these essays circumnavigate the victimizing effects of colonialism on women's labor productivity and working existence, favoring complex explanations of agency and economic sovereignty. Harris and McCallum, Child, and Locke document women's efforts toward the transformation of social milieu and as leaders of community consciousness-raising. The women are not complacent; they refuse to accommodate Eurocentric expectations of silence or subordination to men or family. Maori activists Ripeka Evans and Donna Awatere, as Cybèle Locke documents in Chapter 16, are outspoken and theoretically innovative critics of colonialism who pointedly denounce the racial exclusions enacted by contemporary settler feminism.

Conclusion

Indigenous Women and Work: From Labor to Activism acknowledges the disfigurement of colonial labor and the racism of the modern era but leaps far beyond victimizing narratives to chart women's emergence as workers or entrepreneurs, as educators, as professionals, and as community activists. The breadth of women's strategies of survival are reconstructed using an innovative combination of conventional and unconventional sources.

As laborers, women exhibit resiliency and decisive versatility. They adapt wage opportunities conventionally afforded or invent entrepreneurial and culturally innovative alternatives. The state's compulsion toward their cultural "disappearance" is strenuously resisted. The women portrayed do not react as much as *strategically engage* in the face of a limited, and yet ever-evolving, range of opportunities. Reviving the stories of strengths and determination, and highlighting aspirations for independence as well as significant efforts on behalf of family, kin, and community, these essays contest the homogeneity of male-dominated national narratives.

The reasons these laborers were consistently neglected or underestimated within historical recollection and commemoration initiated the preliminary motivation for *Indigenous Women and Work: From Labor to Activism*. Certainly colonial self-interest and other suspect motives allowed Indigenous workers to be unregulated, underwaged (or withheld from earnings), underenumerated, and judgmentally scrutinized. The presiding question is not so much *why* unjust and discriminatory treatment of Indigenous women occurred nor *whether* the parallel symptom of historical neglect within nation-building, Women's History, and Labor History resulted from fear, laziness, unconscious blindness, racism, or any combination therein. New approaches to labor history of Indigenous women, beyond history that is compensatory or contributory, are emerging because unique circumstances demand innovative questions. With theoretical roots in Marxism and thus centrally invested in narratives of conflict and class struggle, Labor History overlooked Indigenous women, as previously noted, because the forms of women's gender-specific activities—nurturing; food services; household maintenance; education, medical, and health services—escaped conventionally defined "production and relations of production" (Nye cited by Lake 1994: 77; McGrath 1995: 45); their manual labor was eclipsed because their racialized "otherness" tested the codes of femininity. Upholding the colonial legacy, and not always consciously, women settlers consistently failed to strike horizontal alliances across cultural, class, or racial divides. Women's History incorporated that failure, often blinded to the crucial factor of race and avoiding the biases of "whiteness."

Indigenous and postcolonial scholarship has radically transformed historical thinking about women's circumstances and the relationships between women, crafting new opportunities for a more honest and collegial enterprise. Debates around tradition, colonialism, historiography, and the narrative myths of national origins and exclusions have been animated; universal, or homogenous visions of Indigeneity, gender, and history are dismantled. In *Indigenous Women and Work: From Labor to Activism*, women's lives are embodied; their endeavors toward economic sovereignty are resolute and resourceful. The women recalled here, as Brant Castellano asserts in our Preface, are "the anchors of family and community through years much harsher than we have known." In retrospect, perhaps the basis for Indigenous women's absence from history writing is due to the "place" they were expected to compliantly assume: as a passive or unseen, *colonized* worker. But this volume is not about compliant, nor perhaps even heroic, women. Given colonialism's troubled landscape and the resurgent endeavor for tribal, political, cultural, and economic sovereignty, the reconceptualization of Indigenous labor is exceedingly overdue; particularly urgent, as these essays demonstrate, is the critical restoration of the trajectory and development of women's extraordinary laboring agency from within, and outside, women's and national histories.

Notes

1. Seeking a progressive nonracist, nonsexist, and non-Westerncentric theory of citizenship, Yuval-Davis conceives the state not as a top-down relationship with the individual but rather as multitiered inclusive of collectivities, ethnicity, origins, and urban or rural residences as well as situated within global and transnational contexts. Nira Yuval-Davis, "Women, Citizenship and Difference," *Feminist Review* 57 (Autumn 1997): 4–27.

2. In Aotearoa/New Zealand the white British or Europeans are known as *Pakeha*.

3. "An Ethical Framework in Aboriginal Context" is a required component of the Tri-Council Policy Statement: Ethical Conduct for Research Involving Humans issued by the Government of Canada to guide researchers. See Chapter 9, "Research Involving the First Nations, Inuit and Métis Peoples of Canada. www.pre.ethics.gc.ca (accessed January 2012).

4. Unable to comprehend the legal function of a song performed in the court by defendant Mary Johnson, a Gitxsan elder of the Tsimshian nation, Justice Allan McEachern in the land claim case *Delgamuuku v. British Columbia* declared, "It's not going to do any good to sing to me, I have a tin ear." His declaration is symptomatic of the irreconcilability of Indigenous and Eurocentric knowledge or literacy as played out in the spaces of the colonizer (Chamberlin 2003: 20, cited by E. B. Coleman and R. J. Coombe 2009). "A broken record: subjecting music to cultural rights." *Ethics of Cultural Appropriation.* Eds. J. C. Young and C. Brunck. London: Blackwell, 2009. 173–210. http://www.yorku.ca/rcoombe/publications/RCoombe_Broken_Record.pdf (accessed March 2012).

5. The Treaty recognizes Maori as Indigenous (*tangata whenua*), signifying the Crown's obligation and to guarantee the full rights of citizenship to Maori and "provides the starting point for the development of a living relationship between the crown, Maori, and other New Zealanders which encompasses mutual respect, equal rights and active promotion of Maori Culture" (CEDAW 1998: 6). The principals of bicultural partnership and the fiduciary obligation of the Crown to the Maori entrenched in the 1840 Treaty of Waitangi were granted greater legal force with the 1975 formation of *The Waitangi Tribunal*. The 1975 Tribunal was tasked to review the thefts of land and breaches of the treaty by settlers and settler government from the nineteenth to twentieth century; the Treaty via the contemporary Tribunal must be monitored and enforced. Accordingly, in 1985 New Zealand's Labour government "extend[ed] the tribunal's jurisdiction back to 1840 (Minority Report 1990: 4).

6. In a vote held in the United Nations General Assembly on September 13, 2007, 143 nations voted favorably and 11 abstained. Canada released "A Statement of Support on the United Nations Declaration on the Rights of Indigenous Peoples" on November 12, 2010. This statement may be found at http://www.ainc-inac.gv.ca/ap/ia/dcl/stmt-eng.asp (accessed January 2012).

7. Marrying out was not the only means by which women lost status rights; women whose mothers and paternal grandmothers lacked status also lost theirs. Additionally those who "enfranchised" as citizens of Canada had to voluntarily relinquish their "status" as Indians (Perley-Dutcher and Dutcher 2010: 198).

Works Cited

Barker, Joanne. "Gender, Sovereignty, and the Discourse of Rights in Native Women's Activism." *Meridians: Feminism, Race, Transnationalism* 7.1 (2006): 127–61.

Battiste, Marie. "Indigenous Knowledge: Foundations for First Nations." *WINHEC Journal* (2005). Poirua, New Zealand. http://www.win-hec.org (accessed January 2012).

Bennett, Judith. *History Matters: Patriarchy and the Challenge of Feminism.* Philadelphia: University of Pennsylvania, 2006.

Blackhawk, Ned. "I Can Carry On from Here: The Relocation of American Indians to Los Angeles." *Wicazo Sa Review* 11.2 (1995): 16–30.

Borrows, John. "Contemporary Traditional Equality: The Effect of the Charter on First Nations Politics." *UNB Law Journal* 43.19 (1994): 19–48.

Brant Castellano, Marlene. "Women in Huron and Ojibwa Societies." *Canadian Women's Studies: Introductory Reader.* Eds. Andrea Medovarski and Brenda Cranney. Toronto: Inanna Publications and Education Inc., 2006. 104–9.

Brownlie, Robin Jarvis. *A Fatherly Eye: Indian Agents, Government Power, and Aboriginal Resistance in Ontario, 1918–1939.* Don Mills, Ont.: Oxford University Press, 2003.

Burt, Larry. "Roots of the Native American Urban Experience: Relocation Policy in the 1950s." *American Indian Quarterly* 10.2 (1986): 85–99.

Byrd, Jodi A., and Katharina C. Heyer. "Introduction: International Discourses of Indigenous Rights and Responsibilities." *Alternatives* 33.1 (2008): 1–5.

CEDAW. (United Nations Convention on the Elimination of All Forms of Discrimination against Women). *Status of Women in New Zealand.* Wellington, New Zealand: Ministry of Women's Affairs, 1998.

Child, Brenda. *Boarding School Seasons: American Indian Families, 1900–1940.* Lincoln: University of Nebraska, 1998.

Coleman, Elizabeth Burns, Rosemary J. Coombe, and Fiona MacArailt. "A Broken Record: Subjecting 'Music' to Cultural Rights." *The Ethics of Cultural Appropriation.* Eds. James O. Young and Conrad G. Brunk. London: Blackwell, 2009. 173–210. Published online April 24, 2009.

Conte, Christine. "Ladies, Livestock, Land and Lucre: Women's Networks and Social Status on the Western Navajo Reservation." *American Indian Quarterly* 6.1–2 (1982): 105–24.

Curthoys, Ann, and Clive Moore. "Working for the White People: An Historiographical Essay on Aboriginal and Torres Strait Islander Labour." *Labour History* 69 (November 1995): 1–29.

Dillingham, Brint. "Indian Women and IHS Sterilization Practices." *American Indian Journal of the Institute for Development of Indian Law* 3.1 (1977): 27–28.

Duffie, Mary Kay. "Goals for Fourth World Peoples and Sovereignty Initiatives in the United States and New Zealand." *American Indian Culture and Research Journal* 22.1 (1998): 183–212.

Duncan, Kate. "Beadwork and Cultural Identity on the Plateau." *A Song to the Creator: Traditional Arts of Native American Women of the Plateau.* Ed. Lillian Ackerman. Norman: University of Oklahoma Press, 1996. 106–17.

Ellinghaus, Katherine. "Margins of Acceptability: Class, Education and Interracial Marriage in Australia and North America." *Frontiers: A Journal of Women's Studies* 23.3 (2002): 55–75.

Else, Anne, ed. *Women Together: A History of Women's Organizations in New Zealand Nga Ropu Wahine o te Motu.* Wellington, N.Z.: Historical Branch Department of Internal Affairs and Daphne Brasell Associates Press, 1993.

Frances, Raelene, Bruce Scates, and Ann McGrath. "Broken Silences? Labour History and Aboriginal Workers." *Challenges to Labour History.* Ed. Terry Irving. Sydney: University of New South Wales Press, 1996. 189–211.

Ganter, Regina. "Letters from Mapoon: Colonizing Aboriginal Gender." *Australian Historical Studies* 113 (1999): 267–85.

Garrett Pool, Carolyn. "Reservation Policy and the Economic Position of Wichita Women." *Great Plains Quarterly* 8.3 (1988): 158–71.

Gunew, Sneja. "Postcolonialism and Multiculturalism: Between Race and Ethnicity." *Yearbook of English Studies* 27 (1997): 22–39.

Haskins, Victoria. "'& So We Are "Slave-owners"!': Employers and the NSW Aborigines Protection Board Trust Funds." *Labour History* 88 (2005): 147–64.

Hoskins, Te Kawehau Clea. "In the Interests of Maori Women? Discourses of Reclama-
tion." *Bitter Sweet: Indigenous Women in the Pacific.* Eds. Alison Jones, Phyllis Herda,
and Tamasailau M. Suaalii. Dunedin, N.Z.: University of Otago Press, 2000. 33–48.

Howard-Bobiwash, Heather. "Women's Class Strategies As Activism in Native Community
Building in Toronto, 1950–1975." *American Indian Quarterly* 27.3–4 (2003): 566–82.

Huggins, Jackie. "'Firing on the Mind': Aboriginal Women Domestic Servants in the
Inter-War Years." *Hecate* 1.2 (1987): 5–23.

Ivison, Duncan, Paul Patton, and Will Sanders, eds. "Introduction." *Political Theory and
Rights of Indigenous Peoples.* Cambridge: Cambridge University Press, 2000. 1–21.

Jacobs, Margaret. "Working on the Domestic Frontier: American Indian Domestic Servants in White Women's Households in the San Francisco Bay Area, 1920–1940." *Frontiers: A Journal of Women Studies* 28 (2007): 165–99.

———. "Indian Boarding Schools in Comparative Perspective: The Removal of Indigenous
Children in the United States and Australia, 1880–1940." Digital Commons @ Univer-
sity of Nebraska-Lincoln. http://digitalcommons.unl.edu/historyfacpub/20 (accessed
January 2012).

Janovicek, Nancy. "'Assisting Our Own': Urban Migration, Self-Governance, and Native
Women's Organizing in Thunder Bay, Ontario, 1972–1989." *American Indian Quarterly*
27.3–4 (2003): 548–65.

Kahaleole Hall, Lisa. "Strategies of Erasure US Colonialism and Native Hawaiian Feminism." *American Studies Quarterly* 60.2 (2008): 273–80.

Kessler-Harris, Alice. "The Wages of Patriarchy." Eds. Eileen Boris, Joan Sangster, Mercedes
Steedman, Julie Greene, and Leon Fink. *Labor: Studies in Working-Class History of the
Americas* 2.3 (2006): 7–21.

Lake, Marilyn. "The Constitution of Political Subjectivity and the Writing of Labor History." *Challenges to Labour History.* Ed. Terry Irving. Sydney: University of New South
Wales Press, 1994. 75–87.

———. "Nationalist Historiography, Feminist Scholarship, and the Promise and Problems
of New Transnational Histories: The Australian Case." *Journal of Women's History* 19.1
(2007): 180–86.

Lawrence, Bonita. "Gender, Race, and the Regulation of Native Identity in Canada and
the United States: An Overview." *Hypatia* 18.2 (2003): 3–31.

Lawrence, Jane. "The Indian Health Service and the Sterilization of Native American
Women." *American Indian Quarterly* 24.3 (2000): 400–419.

Lewallen, Ann-Elise. "Strategic 'Indigeneity' and the Possibility of a Global Indigenous
Women's Movement." *Michigan Feminist Studies* 17 (2003): 105–39.

Macdonald, Robert. *A Minority Rights Group Report: The Maori of Aotearoa-New Zealand.*
London, U.K.: Minority Rights Group, 1990.

McGrath, Ann. "Aboriginal Women Workers in the Northern Territory, Australia, 1911–
1939." *Hecate* 4–5 (1978): 5–25.

———. "'Modern Stone-Age Slavery': Images of Aboriginal Labour and Sexuality." *Labour
History* 69 (1995a): 30–51.

———, ed. *Contested Grounds: Australian Aborigines under the British Crown.* St. Leonards,
U.K.: Allen and Unwin, 1995b.

McGrath, Ann, and Winona Stevenson. "Gender, Race, and Policy: Aboriginal Women
and the State in Canada and Australia." *Labour/Le travail* 38 (1996): 37–53.

McHalsie, Naxaxalhts'i Albert (Sonny). "We have to take care of everything that belongs to us." *Be of Good Mind: Essays on the Coast Salish*. Ed. Bruce Granville Miller. Vancouver: University of British Columbia Press, 2007).

M'Closkey, Kathy. *Swept Under the Rug: A Hidden History of Navajo Weaving*. Albuquerque: University of New Mexico Press, 2002.

Mohanram, Radhika. "The Construction of Place: Maori Feminism and Nationalism in Aotearoa/New Zealand." *NWSA Journal* 8.1 (1996): 50–69.

Monture-Angus, Patricia. *Thunder in My Soul: A Mohawk Woman Speaks*. Halifax: Fernwood Publishing, 1995.

Perley-Dutcher, Lisa, and Stephen Dutcher. "'A Home but Not At Peace': The Impact of Bill C-31 on Women and Children of the Tobique First Nation." *Making Up the State: Women in 20th Century Atlantic Canada*. Eds. Janet Guildford and Suzanne Morton. Fredericton, N.B.: Acadiensis Press, 2010. 197–216.

Raibmon, Paige. "The Practice of Everyday Colonialism: Indigenous Women at Work in the Hope Fields and Tourist Industry of Puget Sound." *Labor* 3.3 (2006): 23–56.

Ramirez, Renya. "Julia Sanchez's Story." *Frontiers: A Journal of Women Studies* 23.2 (2002): 65–83.

———. "Race, Tribal Nation, and Gender: A Native Feminist Approach to Belonging." *Meridians: Feminism, Race, Transnationalism* 7.2 (2007): 22–40.

Rasmussen, Birgit Brander. "Negotiating Peace, Negotiating Literacies: A French-Iroquois Encounter and the Making of Early American Literature." *American Literature* 77.3 (2007): 445–73.

Robert, Hannah. "Disciplining the Female Aboriginal Body: Interracial Sex and the Pretence of Separation." *Australian Feminist Studies* 16.34 (2001): 69–81.

Russell, Lynette. "'Dirty Domestics and Worse Cooks': Aboriginal Women's Agency and Domestic Frontiers, Southern Australia, 1800–1850." *Frontiers: A Journal of Women's Studies* 28.1–2 (2007): 18–45.

Sangster, Joan. "Making a Fur Coat: Women, the Laboring Body, and Working-Class History." *International Review of Social History* 52 (2007): 241–70.

Simpson, Audra. "From White into Red: Captivity Narratives As Alchemies of Race and Citizenship." *American Quarterly* 60.2 (2008): 251–57.

Sinha, Mrinalini. "Gender and Nation." *Women's History in Global Perspective, vol. 1*. Ed. Bonnie G. Smith. Champaign: University of Illinois Press, 2004. 229–74.

Smith, Shawn Michelle. *Photography on the Color Line: W. E. B. DuBois, Race, and Visual Culture*. Durham: Duke University Press, 2004.

Stasiulis, Daiva K. "Relational Positionalities of Nationalisms, Racisms, and Feminisms." *Between Woman and Nation: Nationalisms, Transnational Feminism, and the State*. Eds. Caren Kaplan, Norma Alarcon, and Minoo Moallem. Durham, N.C.: Duke University Press, 1999.182–218.

Torpy, Sally J. "Native American Women and Coerced Sterilization: On the Trail of Tears in the 1970s." *American Indian Culture and Research Journal* 24.2 (2000): 1–20.

Trask, Haunani-Kay. "Feminism and Indigenous Hawaiian Nationalism." *Signs* 21.4 (1996): 906–16.

Wanhalla, Angela. "Women 'Living across the Line': Intermarriage on the Canadian Prairies and in Southern New Zealand, 1870–1900." *Ethnohistory* 55.1 (2008): 29–49.

Williams, Lucy Fowler, William Wierzbowski, and Robert W. Preucel. *Objects of Everlasting Esteem: Native American Voices on Identity, Art, and Culture*. Philadelphia: University of Pennsylvania, Museum of Archaeology and Anthropology, 2005.

CHAPTER 1

Aboriginal Women and Work across the 49th Parallel

Historical Antecedents and New Challenges

Joan Sangster

Interpretations of Aboriginal women's work have shifted over time, but they have been absolutely central to First Nations women's experiences of colonialism. Yet, in both women's history and Aboriginal history, there has been a "mystification" of Indigenous women's labor, because it was often defined as nonproductive or marginal within capitalist economies; wage work was particularly neglected (Littlefield and Knack 1999: 4). Yet, by studying women's labor in its multiple forms (paid, unpaid, voluntary, ceremonial, commodity production), and in multiple contexts (bush, urban, reserve or reservation), we can gain immense insight into how colonialism was structured, experienced, negotiated, and resisted by women at the level of daily life. By perusing past academic writing on Aboriginal women and work, this paper explores some of the intellectual, political, and social influences that have shaped understandings of Aboriginal women's labor in Canada and the United States, asking what insights we have gained, what questions we need to answer, and what contradictions we still face in our research.[1] Arguably, we need a dialogue that crosses disciplines and theoretical approaches, with perspectives and traditions from Aboriginal history, feminist theory, and labor studies informing and challenging each other. There are transnational trends and shared perspectives in Aboriginal women's history that cross the 49th parallel; however, we also need to identify how and why national and regional histories and interpretations diverge. Still, one transnational commonality highlighted in this paper is the close connection between politics and research, between the present and the past: the questions posed by scholars have been stimulated and inspired by Aboriginal thought and organizing, and Aboriginal politics have benefited from scholarly research. Although *research* may still be difficult and contested terrain in Aboriginal–non-Aboriginal relations (Smith 1999; Biolsi and Zimmerman 1997), there is hope that scholarly dialogue might contribute productively to decolonization.

Perspectives on Aboriginal Work in the
Post–World War II Period, 1950–2000

In comparison to historians, anthropologists have a more extensive (if conten-
tious) history of studying Aboriginal economies, families, and gender relations:
when Ruth Landes's 1938 monograph, *Ojibway Woman* appeared, for instance,
there was nothing comparable in history. Even still, feminist anthropologists have
been intensely critical of the masculinist perspectives that shaped the discipline
of anthropology, the way in which male researchers filtered their interpretations
through their own ideas and experiences as well as through male informants,
paying less attention to women and gendered power relations within Aboriginal
nations (Fiske and Sleeper 1998). In the immediate post–World War II period,
anthropologists across Canada and the United States had substantial influence
as accepted experts on Native peoples and often acted as advisors to the state on
policy (Kulchyski 1993). The dominant paradigms of the time stressed culture,
cultural difference, and acculturation, with researchers primarily asking whether
and how Native peoples would integrate into the dominant norms of white society.
Anthropologist Harry Hawthorn's extensive study for the Canadian government,
for example, opened by rejecting the "assimilation" of "Indians" but his prognosis
for labor nonetheless saw integration into the industrial capitalist economy as the
best path for Aboriginal economic development. American studies of acculturation also assumed that Native Indians should be free to maintain their identity,
but that increasing economic integration was inevitable, save for the "conservative nuclei" of the population clinging to the past (Vogt 1957: 137). Many social
scientists nonetheless feared that Native culture was inherently inhospitable to
industrial work discipline and the acquisitive capitalist values of accumulation,
thus making acculturation to "modern" wage labor difficult, a view that mirrored
modernization theories of the time applied to the Third World.

Women's work was seldom analyzed seriously and critically, though unstated
assumptions about gender differences nonetheless pervaded the writing of many
social scientists. Hawthorn, for example, assumed a male breadwinner family as
the ideal for Native peoples, despite ample evidence that Aboriginal communities
were characterized by multioccupational, multiearner families. Even economists
who had insights about the colonial economies characterizing Native communities
tended to see women's work as ancillary rather than central to the family economy.
The impact of these gendered assumptions on policy development was significant.
In the 1950s, federal programs developed on both sides of the border to draw Native peoples away from "dying" reserves/reservations and into urban wage labor
promoted a rather rigid gender division of labor, with women trained for service,
or at best white-collar positions, while men were ideally to be miners and welders (McCallum 2008; MacKay 1987; Sangster 2007). Governments also acted on
these assumptions when they acted as labor contractors, "placing out" girls from
residential/boarding schools in domestic jobs, and boys in agricultural work.

The shifts that took place in academic thinking in the late 1960s and through the 1970s should not be underestimated: culture as a totalizing *explanation* for economic marginalization was supplanted by questions of global capitalism, colonialism, inequality, underdevelopment, and dependence. This "left turn" in scholarship was influenced by the emergence of global anticolonial movements, though new perspectives may also have been percolating below the surface within the research community in the postwar period (Ray 2003). By taking a structural view of colonial exploitation and dispossession, they hoped to negate the "blame the victim" approach (Loxley 1981: 154), rejecting cultural analyses that posited "Native values" as the impediment to the inevitable progress of capitalist development. This ideological shift was no doubt encouraged by Aboriginal political organizing, as Red Power and New Left activists increasingly described Native American lives in terms of conquest, destruction, and imperialism. Organizing on both sides of the 49th parallel assumed far more militant forms that also involved transnational protests, cooperation, and the provision of refuge for political activists. State policy reflected this turn to militancy, as governments nervously sought ways to incorporate Aboriginal youth into community-based development projects that were more benign than blockades and protests (Pineault 2011).

If these materialist, political economy explanations "overplayed the hand of capitalism as a force" on Aboriginal economies, notes Patricia Albers (2004), they at least avoided the "cumbersome dualisms of more culturally oriented theories." The limitation of Left political economy approaches was not so much their debt to historical materialism as it was their tendency to employ highly abstract models that lost sight of human beings' actual laboring activity and agency—including women's work. However, this scholarship did pose questions about the relationship between production and reproduction, household and the marketplace, that opened up new questions about women's labor. At precisely this time, feminists writing labor history were also arguing that women's labor could be studied only if one looked beyond the traditionally defined male workplace, taking in domestic and unpaid work as well (Kessler-Harris 1987), an admonition that was especially relevant for Aboriginal women's labor. The promise of an emerging feminist political economy was exemplified in Patricia Albers's scholarship, in which she struck a balance between a discussion of structural economic changes and state policies on the one hand, and the way in which these were experienced, translated, and negotiated by Dakota women on the other hand (Albers 1985). Similarly, Jo-Anne Fiske's analysis of Carrier women's role in the fishing industry indicated how state policies interacted dynamically with the existing gendered division of labor and cultural traditions, producing an unintended result: the increased financial importance of women's fishery work, and thus their enhanced role in both distributing economic resources and sustaining Native culture (1987).

This writing mirrored a transformation that was taking place across many disciplines as silences about women's lives were increasingly challenged by feminist writing. The same year that Rayna Green lamented the absence of historical writing on American Indian women's economic contributions, Sylvia Van Kirk's book *Many Tender Ties* appeared, making a new argument that women were central to fur-trade work and exploring the relationship between gender, class, and Métis identity (R. Green 1980; Van Kirk 1980). While anthropology had historically collaborated in the creation of a colonial gaze in which static or disappearing Indigenous cultures needed "salvaging" and "documenting" (Simpson 2007: 69) under the influence of new paradigms and self critique, the discipline interrogated its own "collusion" in colonialism and "representations of others" (Speed 2006: 66). Feminists turned to anthropology to understand the origins of gender inequality and western assaults on egalitarian Indigenous cultures, with an eye to critiquing and "overturning Western patriarchy" (Collier and Yanagisako, 27). An emerging feminist anthropology could build on the pathbreaking work of Beatrice Medicine who was already fashioning an "Indigenous anthropology" in which "Native women were seen through the lens of Native women" (Ross, 40; Medicine 2001). A new generation of Indigenous anthropologists, many asking feminist questions, would follow (for example, Guthrie-Valaskakis 2005; Ramirez 2007; Simpson 2007).

While an interest in Aboriginal women's work lives tended to be the preserve of feminists, historians in general were placing more emphasis on Aboriginal agency, cultural interchange, and—in Canada—on Métissage, indicating a conscious attempt to escape a straightjacket of victimhood in Aboriginal history.[2] Again, these new perspectives should not be interpreted only as shifts in academic writing; they were shaped in the context of new political ideas, movements, and activism. In North America, women were less prominent in the public reports of many Native American struggles, but this was a far cry from their actual work in radical organizations like AIM, in legal defense work, and in local campaigns for Native rights and social services (Hightower Langston 2003). Often located outside the dominant "media show," these women's foundational organizing may be fully recovered only if we pay particular attention to their life stories and testimony, published by themselves, or in conjunction with researchers (Castle 2003: 841; see also Anderson and Lawrence 2003; Culhane 2003). Aboriginal women were also building woman-centered campaigns, like the one against violence and forced sterilization in the United States (Torpy 2000; A. Smith 2005), or against the Indian Act's marrying-out clause in Canada (Silman 1987; Barker 2006), and new organizations like WARN (Women of All Red Nations) and the Native Women's Association of Canada (NWAC) were established. Their activism encouraged a concurrent scholarly dialogue about the interplay of individual, collective, tribal, human, and women's rights, as well as the discursive strategies employed in Aboriginal women's rights talk (Denetdale 2006; Fiske 1996; McIvor 1999; Nahanee 1993; Ramirez 2007).

By the 1980s, a feminist sensibility (rather than a specific feminist ideology) had sparked new investigations of how the church, the state, and white settlers had attempted to recast gendered work roles within Native cultures, often in their own patriarchal and middle-class image. Researchers, reflecting the strong emphasis of post-1960s feminist writing on the social, as opposed to the "natural" construction of gender roles, stressed how malleable definitions of work were across gender and cultural barriers; for example, while Native women in the American Great Lakes region were the iron ore miners, whites saw this as a job only suitable for men (Eldersveld Murphy 1998). Comparative research on a diverse range of tribal/national experiences of Aboriginal women also challenged a linear one-story-fits-all narrative of Native women's automatic fall from matriarchy or economic egalitarianism (Shoemaker 1995: 13–14). However important these feminist questions were, we should be wary of a Whig view of historical production, in which research achieves sophistication *only* when gender differences are explored. This theory of academic excellence assumes that one set of political priorities fits all contexts, when in fact class relations or imperialism may seem the more pressing historical problem for Indigenous women. Finding the right balance between posing a set of feminist questions about oppression and respecting colonized groups' desire to articulate their own political agendas is not always easy, though some Aboriginal women have fused feminist and anticolonialist ideas to create an Aboriginal feminism as a distinct political mode of thinking in its own right (J. Green 2007).

Although feminism was sometimes cast negatively in Indigenous writing as "untraditional, inauthentic, non-liberatory" (20), the recent appearance of special journal issues, books, and political forums on the topic reveals how feminism has been claimed, refigured, and recast by Aboriginal women.[3] Respecting and recovering women's experiences, "taking gender seriously as a social organizing process" (21) and critiquing the patriarchal legacies of colonialism are just a few of the themes explored; these are also essential to our understanding of women's labor as it changed in response to the resources available, family and community needs, state policies, and the inexorable engine of capitalist accumulation. Simplistic dichotomies equating feminism solely with liberal, white, middle-class women have been jettisoned in favor of historicized understandings of race, class, and the multiple feminisms in the women's movement, as Aboriginal women debate whether, and how, feminism might contribute to their critique of the masculinist and heteronormative underpinnings of colonialism (A. Smith 2011). While recognizing that social location shapes our experience and understanding (Moya 2000) in important ways, it does not completely determine our politics: for those of us who are non-Aboriginal, our project, like the workshop that spawned this book, is a political and scholarly commitment to an anticolonial critique.

Despite the extraordinary riches of writing on themes such as politics, representation, self determination and law (Barker 2006; Denetdale 2006; La Rocque 2010; Hernandez-Avila 2002; Sunseri 2000; Monture-Angus 1995), the history of labor has figured less prominently in scholarship, especially for the twentieth century. The same was true of urban Aboriginal women, though writing on the urban experience is now catching up with the large migrations of the post-1950s period (Peters 1998; Ramirez 2007; Lobo and Peters 2001; Krouse and Howard-Bobiwash 2003). Yet, even if labor is not the central question addressed, it may emerge as a key theme in other histories, for example of education, family, and domesticity. The labor-related educational aims of state and Church boarding and residential schools were analyzed as efforts to solidify appropriate gender roles and create "working-class Indians" (Littlefield 1999; Milloy 1999). Feminist writing also focused new attention on motherwork as work. State-run homemaker training offered on Canadian western reserves and through the U.S. field matron program were examples of "manifest domesticity," a fusion of imperialist expansionism and the belief that the superior practices of white domesticity should be imparted to Indigenous peoples (Emmerich 1997; Kaplan 1998). These programs were meant to "domesticate" Native women, removing them from outside agricultural work, and also to "uplift" and improve their domestic labor, deemed deficient according to the state's middle-class standards—though these programs failed to provide women with decent housing, and in Canada, and then blamed mothers for high levels of tuberculosis in their communities (White 1987). The parallels between the state regulation of motherwork in Canada, the United States, and Australia are striking, yet we need to look for differences as well as congruities in these national programs, explaining why and how women's labor changed over time. By moving beyond state-centered studies to take in Aboriginal women's voices, the story may also change: as Mary Jane McCallum argues in this volume, the IAB may have seen the Homemakers' Clubs as civilizing projects, but Native women used them as spaces to improve their communities, leading to their political activism. Thus, labor may be implicit, implied, and implicated in many thematics of Indigenous history. Recent scholarly attention to the racialized body, for instance, can advantageously connect representation and the creation of profit, the body and labor; as I have argued for the fur industry, the "gendered racialization" of Aboriginal women's bodies abetted a process in which they became "invisible" laboring bodies in the colonial context of capitalist accumulation (Sangster 2007: 255).

Our rethinking of Aboriginal women's work has been aided immeasurably by the academic labor of Aboriginal scholars. Like many feminists in academe, they often see teaching, research, advocacy, and education as mutually symbiotic, and their work has substantially altered our understanding of Aboriginal women's lives, whether this was accomplished through their own scholarly studies or their roles in creating Native American/Native Studies programs (Medicine 2001). To be sure, they are not an intellectually homogenous group; different political views are apparent, for example, in debates about the best legal strategies to address Native women's specific oppression (Eberts 2008). The retrieval of First Nations women's life histories, both in academic (Cruikshank 1990) and more popular forms, has also aided our reinterpretation of women's work. Autobiographies tell us much about the world of work; Maria Campbell's moving *Halfbreed* (1973) re-counts her difficult struggles to support herself and her children and also conveys a sensibility for Métis women's history. Campbell drew immense psychological strength from the stories her granny told her about Métis history: the history of women's work was not, therefore, completely 'lost' for Aboriginal women still enmeshed in these networks of kin and community, though it was in danger of being lost to Native children schooled, as many were, in cultural self-denigration and mainstream histories of Canadian nationhood.

Questioning Borders

Reacting against the confines of national history and influenced by new histories of empire as well as contemporary globalization talk, labor historians have pro-moted transnational history as a vital, new method of studying labor (Van der Linden 1999) ; it has also been employed productively in studies of Aboriginal political activism (Rivera-Salgado 1999). Not everything transnational is new; the concept, if not the word, as African American historians point out, has long underscored studies of the global movement of capital and labor, in exchanges and human diasporas that were characterized by imperialism and exploitation, as well as human agency and resistance (Kelley 1999). Definitions of transnational are widely, if not wildly, divergent: they range from a concern with the social, political, and economic relations across nation-states to attempts to "denaturalize" the nation, challenging what is taken as "self evidently national" by showing how the nation itself is ideologically "contested, interrupted, always shot through with contradictions" (Briggs, McCormick, and Way 2008: 627). Indigenous scholar Renya Ramirez (2007) has posited the urban "hub" as a transnational space where diaspora, home, and tribal/national identity all intersect, while Luana Ross sug-gests that the *transnational* offers the conceptual possibility of challenging the false "universalisms" of feminism with accounts of difference across multiply situated nations, thus encouraging "a more globally sensitive feminism" (Ross, 47).

Adopting a broad definition of the transnational as a process in which "people, events, and practices have been shaped by processes and relationships that have transcended the nation state" (Curthoys and Lake 2007),[4] I would argue that there are benefits to putting Aboriginal women's labor in a transnational context, though we should be wary of overidealizing such a method. At an abstract level, feminist critical race and anticolonial theorizing offers the possibility of compar-ing the "ideologies that locate women in particular exploitative circumstances" across borders so that we can better understand practices of gender domina-tion, and contemplate the common "interests" of these women workers—and thus possibilities of social change (Mohanty 1995). At a practical level, in North America, nation-state borders were imposed over existing cultural, trade, and kin connections between First Nations, and even after borders were established, the flow of ideas and peoples continued. Transnational history allows us to examine Aboriginal women's labor history based on shared cultures and also to suggest how different state policies or political movements affected women's economic options (or lack of them). Colonial practices of rule were discussed, imitated, or modified across borders (Curthoys and Lake 2007); settler societies like Canada, New Zealand, and Australia shared a British imperialist past and missionization efforts, and thus common ideas about race, gender, and class. Aboriginal ideas about resistance and decolonization also knew no borders, but took different forms within local contexts. Moreover, transnational studies, by highlighting differences in our political outlook and theoretical frameworks, may stimulate new critiques of our research assumptions and methods.

However, we also need to contemplate the problems associated with a more global perspective on women's labor. One possible danger, as Ann Curthoys points out, is "disconnection from local audiences and politics, the very connections that made Aboriginal histories so important in the first place." The "new" labor history, after all, recuperated the lives of more marginal workers by focusing on the rich tapestry of the local—parks, taverns, leisure, families, neighborhoods, immigrant and fraternal organizations—relating these topics to broader (and transnational) theoretical issues. Aboriginal histories have also excelled at in-depth studies in which knowledge of local language, culture, and landscapes are important. Will Aboriginal women's writing, centering on their immediate experiences, be neglected as too local and particular? Moreover, comparisons within nations are often rich in themselves: Peggy Pascoe's study (1990) of attempts to Americanize Native and Chinese women provides insight into how different groups of racialized women negotiated and resisted relations of power. International exchanges, as one European feminist noted, "should imply the willingness to actually listen to each other's local histories," understanding different "locales, historicity, and insights" (Bosch 1991: 143). In practice, this has not always happened, a warning we need to heed when thinking transnationally. Nor can we deny the importance of understanding the internal complexities of nation-state–based legal and political regimes, since these matter a great deal to women's economic and social status and opportunities.

We also need to ask questions about power relations in the construction of transnational history. Through whose eyes are we seeing this history? It has been pointed out that Native-Newcomer histories too often concentrate on the Newcomer. Will transnational histories necessarily help us change this? Scholars of colonialism in other contexts warn that transnational studies will not suddenly equalize the production, reception, and influence of history writing, erasing structural inequalities that exist in knowledge production (Cooper 2000). Some have suggested that more transnational understandings of metropole and colony, and attempts to de-center European colonialism have sometimes simply *reaffirmed* the cultural and historical centrality of the colonizer, and attempts to completely deconstruct the nation are less salient for Indigenous groups wishing to reclaim the sovereignty of nation that they have been denied by colonialism (Deloria 2003: 672). Moreover, writing which stresses fluidity, connections, border crossing and hybridity, without addressing global capitalism and imperialism is ultimately de-politicizing for the colonized (Zeleza 2006). Is there also a danger we will compare nation-states or policy at an abstract level, slighting the varied and distinct economic experiences of women in different First Nations, thus losing sight of women's actual laboring lives?

The overall contours of women's basic experiences of colonialism (dispossession), state policies (assimilation), and trauma (violence) appear similar across borders, not only in North America, but also in Australia and New Zealand. Yet the "regulatory regimes" (Lawrence 2003) that shaped women's work lives, including those defining who was an "Indian," and how one became a "citizen," through enfranchisement (Canada) or competency hearings (the United States), were distinct. The Canadian Indian Act's rules on women's identity were different from American blood quantum rules; the former, as Bonita Lawrence writes, "offered a (sexist) patriarchal system" with "covert" blood quantum, while the U.S. regime stressed a racial system of blood quantum and Native American "fragmentation" (20). Even small differences in policy could aid or retard women's economic independence; the Dawes Act at least allowed Native American women to own allotments of land; the Canadian Indian Act did not.

In the United States and Canada, education and employment policies were often intertwined, and were used as a means of proletarianization and acculturation, and to inculcate proper gender roles. Domestic training programs for girls were evident both in residential schools (Canada) and boarding schools (the United States), though these institutions were also not exact replicas of each other, and the Canadian system is perceived to have had an even more destructive impact over time on Aboriginal communities. The urban migration of women seeking work likely took on different forms across the border, in part because the infamous "marrying out" clause in Canada's Indian Act pushed women permanently out of reserves (Howard-Bobiwash 2003). Proportionately more Native American than Canadian Aboriginal women appear to have left their reservation homes during World War II to find war work, but did this have a long-lasting impact on patterns of wage labor? In the postwar period, both the U.S. BIA and the Canadian Indian Affairs Branch (IAB) developed labor programs designed to move Aboriginal women into "modern" wage labor, although a male breadwinner family model was often assumed as an ideal. Both programs were structured around a gendered division of labor, but the local contexts for these efforts mattered a great deal to their success (Lamphere in O'Neill 2005: 79). Native Americans in U.S. relocation and labor programs were also more likely to encounter competition from African American labor in urban areas; indeed, Native Americans in Chicago feared being "confused" with African Americans (Lagrand 2002: 120).

If the geography and political economy that framed women's work experiences were sometimes similar across borders, as with the Pacific Northwest hop or canning industries, they could also be quite different. The Navaho combination of pastoral sheep herding and mining, does not have a close Canadian approximation. Rather, the exalted beaver has a more dominant place in the economic history of Native peoples. These different economies in turn shaped what was seen *as significant* in history writing. Arguably, the longer reign of the staple of fur in Canadian economic history resulted in far more emphasis being put on the fur trade, and the resulting white-Aboriginal relations, including Aboriginal women's unpaid labor, their agency in making alliances with whites, and their Métis identity.

The nature of white settlement also varied across both national and regional borders, producing different historical interpretations of the moving Native-Newcomer encounter. White settler designs on land and Indigenous labor, shaped by distinct colonial economies and labor needs, were critical to ideologies about race and gender. The timing of colonial conquest mattered, as Adele Perry shows in her study of British Columbia, where demographic gender and race "imbalances" created white fears and strategies of social control long after these were deemed unnecessary in other areas of North America (Perry 2001). The presence of an immense expanse of Aboriginal territory in the Canadian North, which was never fully conquered or inhabited by whites and only became the focus of *intense* state designs after the 1940s, meant that discussions about Dene and Inuit land, work, economic development, and gender relations occurred in a very different historical context than nineteenth century constructions of the more southerly frontier. By the 1950s, nineteenth century theories of a vanishing race could no longer be entertained, and a new postwar human rights discourse combined with the anthropological stress on cultural relativism created a veneer of tolerance for Indigenous cultures. This is not to overidealize white views of the Inuit, which were also paternalistic and controlling, but the colonial project of conquering the land faced more obstacles in the later twentieth century Canadian North, and the politics of Aboriginal resistance led to the creation of a unique Aboriginal northern territory, Nunavut.

Whether we like it or not, much history writing has been associated with "the nation"; as a result, different national narratives about race and gender reverberate through historical writing, as past and contemporary historians endorse, explain, or counter the distinct forms of racialization and colonialism (or "internal colonialism") characterizing their nation. While a similar exportation of European discourses about race to white settler colonies and countries occurred in the nineteenth century, racial ideologies still assumed different national contours. Australian Aborigines, Katherine Ellinghaus (2002) argues, were placed "so far down the evolutionary ladder" that Australian policies on acculturation, education, and work were far more pessimistic than Canadian and American ones, even eschewing the cultural assimilation the latter countries favored. Historical writing has also produced different mythologies about the place of Aboriginal heritage in their national history (Francis 1992; Berkhofer Jr. 1978), but few comparative studies address where gender and work fit into these mythologies. Scholars are acutely aware of differences between Aboriginal and white ways of telling history (Lutz 2007), yet Canadian and American mythologies about the "mild" versus "wild" West also assumed different, and gendered, forms. Whiteness may have been assumed as superior by settlers on both sides of the border, but Canadians nonetheless portrayed themselves in political cartoons as innocent females and Americans as the rapacious, male imperialists (Carter 2003). How then, did Aboriginal women fit into these narratives? The impact of Hollywood's constructed wild West—which for decades justified racist violence in the name of protecting white womanhood—may have had a stronger cultural impact on the United States (Aleiss 2005; Marubbio 2006), yet in Hollywood movies depicting Canada it was the devious, violent Métis turncoat (even more than Native men) who symbolized danger to white women (Berton 1975). Other distinctions between our nation-states need more reflection: how did different views of immigrant integration in Canada and the United States shape understandings of Aboriginal women's labor? How were Native women's work lives shaped by the longer existence and impact of slavery in the United States, by the presence of other nonwhite races (or lack of them) and the way in which race history was then written in each national and regional context? Different histories of "external" imperialism, and how we are situated within them, may also shape our understanding of internal colonialism. Andrea Smith's astute critique of some American feminists' political analysis of the U.S. war on terror is a case in point. Their assumption that America recently experienced a "fall from (democratic) constitutional grace" into a new, aggressive use of state sovereignty, she argues, neglects a long history of violence in the name of state sovereignty, "based on the pillars of capitalism and colonialism," and waged against the bodies of Indigenous women (2008).

Recently, in Antipodian and North American writing, there has been less attention paid to the status of women in relation to work and gender roles and more focused on questions of representation, culture, and hybridity, reflecting postcolonial paradigms, an interest in identity, and likely also a desire of non-Indigenous scholars to engage with the exciting proliferation of Aboriginal culture production. Also, by the 1990s, Aboriginal politics and organizing put more stress on cultural renewal, including the embrace of traditional ways of knowing. The cultural turn in research was implied, for instance, in research on Aboriginal work in the tourist trade, which gave prominence to Native "performance" and its cultural meanings. Yet performance labor cannot be separated from the way it is appropriated and sold within the capitalist marketplace, and there is a danger that other forms of service labor, in the "back regions" of tourism might be overlooked (McCannell 1999: 94). This cultural turn in historical writing is associated with critiques of political economy and historical materialism, some of which tend to construe the latter as inherently alien to Indigenous thought, which, in contrast to a destructive European mindset of materialism, capitalism, and individualism, offers a more holistic, spiritual, and environmental perspective. (Churchill 1988; Bedford 1994).[5] Yet, the dialectical insights of historical materialism, and labor historians' writing on the work-culture dynamic might provide useful insights and comparisons: Herbert Gutman's explorations of immigrant workers' negotiation of changes in work—drawing on custom, rituals, and belief, as well as the solidaristic ties of kin and community—are a case in point (Gutman 1976). Similarly, in Vicki Ruiz's writing on Latina working women (1987), culture is a lived experience that is fluid and dynamic, but not abstracted from social and material relations. Latina working women—like Native Americans, seen as *in*, but not *of* the nation—negotiated multiple occupations and changing work roles by "borrowing, retaining, and creating" cultural forms that were "permeable, rooted in gender, class, region and generation."

The cultural turn has also led to new interest in exploring "alternative paths" (Hosmer and O'Neill 2005) taken by Aboriginal groups to economic development, as part of their commitment to their own cultural persistence. Unlike earlier underdevelopment theories, this approach acknowledges Aboriginal agency and rejects a linear view of permanent wage labor as the best and only economic model—though permanent, well-paying wage labor is becoming less of a possibility and reality for everyone now. U.S. collections have put particular stress on how Aboriginal peoples accommodated themselves to the marketplace while trying to protect their cultural autonomy. Does a stress on successful *adaptation*, however, not imply a less critical view of the structures of the marketplace (just as earlier cultural writing of the 1950s did), and is it really possible to talk about preserving cultural values "'outside" capitalism (Champagne 2005) when work cannot be separated from the wider political economy? Resignation to the idea that adaptation to the capitalist market is the only option may be a depressing sign of the suffusion of neoliberal ideology into academic as well as political life.

Drawing on traditions of Left political economy, which has had some resilience in Canada, even in recent times, Frank Tough has critiqued this overprivileging of culture and the stress on agency as a good in itself: after all, "exercising one's agency to secure . . . cultural survival may *still* place Native peoples in a relationship of increased dependence or poverty," surely not something to be celebrated. An inordinate stress on cultural persistence may simply "render capitalism," (and its handmaiden, colonialism) "invisible" (Tough 1996: 299). This critique bears directly on questions of how and why women made decisions about wage labor. Robin Brownlie suggests that historians' inordinate emphasis on cultural preservation as the impetus behind Aboriginal wage labor reflects contemporary concerns "more than the motivations of Aboriginal peoples in the past." The Aboriginal wage-earning women she studied were primarily concerned with economic survival and livelihood and took it for granted that family and cultural survival was bound up in this—as did many immigrant working-class women of the time period.[6]

Methodological questions are also usefully reexamined across borders, not the least because national historiographies can become too consensus-driven.[7] Generalizations about Native women's work can be tested out with oral histories and participatory research, yet these methods are not without controversy. Life histories are an old anthropological method, but they are now undertaken with more attention to gender analysis and to how different cultural groups classify, explain, and understand their histories.[8] The argument that oral histories are better done by Aboriginal researchers has merit, yet if non-Aboriginal historians only analyze policy, representation, and the white gaze—however critically—will this reinforce an (unfortunately) detached view of Aboriginal women?[9] In a discussion of Native "scabs" from the Six Nations reserve during an industrial strike, Julie Guard (2004) uses very limited sources to argue that white, ethnic, working-class women condescendingly portrayed Native women strike breakers as "inauthentic workers." Unfortunately, what the First Nations women themselves worked at, why they crossed the picket line, how they understood their work, is inaccessible with these sources, leaving them again historically silenced and marginalized.[10]

The Politics of History

The writing of Aboriginal, women's, and labor history has always been shaped by social, political, and ideological questions and events of the times. The increasing entanglement of labor and Aboriginal history was built on scholarly antecedents such as fur trade studies, yet it was also shaped by Left political economy critiques of capitalism and colonialism, calls for justice and redress for First Nations, and later, by new investment in cultural renewal and identity. Feminist historians initially perceived important links between women's and Aboriginal history, as both groups were on the margins of national histories, though over time, feminists have acknowledged the potential tensions in this pairing: after all, a white woman's "agency" might be an Aboriginal woman's oppression. Far fewer non-Aboriginal scholars would now claim they wish to retrieve Native women's "experience" or probe their consciousness: to do so would seem to be epistemologically arrogant. There is a realization that attempts to write about Aboriginal women in the past led to practices of "intellectual colonialism," and a history in which Aboriginal peoples were "misread and misrepresented" (Carlson 2007: 46). Perhaps, however, we should not confuse the goal of understanding and empathy—surely a positive aim—with past research methods and theories that were culturally superior and un–self-reflective. To assume all research exploring experience and subjectivity is inevitably contaminated by colonialism may leave us in a politically paralyzing cul-de-sac.

At no point in time have the contradictions between academic writing and Aboriginal politics been more complex. As Arif Dirlik points out, it is a "matter of faith" for some postcolonial writers "that nations are invented, cultures are constructed, subjectivities are slippery." Yet the "burden of the past haunts contemporary politics in a reassertion of cultural identities and subjectivities, particularly by a Fourth World of marginalized Aboriginal peoples" who wish to lay claim to their history, their land, and their rights based on what they see as an authentic Aboriginal identity or ideologies (1999). Perhaps the questions to focus on are not how all pasts are constructed and contingent, but rather, what are the economic, social, and cultural relations of power that frame these historical issues, and how are issues of gender linked to questions of sheer survival for Aboriginal groups—these questions may also bring us back to questions of labor. Labor was at the core of Aboriginal women's lives in the colonial context: it was a necessary means of survival, a source of pride, a contested realm of discrimination, and an exemplar of their exploitation by capitalist colonialism. Although labor, in all these manifestations, may have been a theme underemphasized in past scholarly writing, shifts in feminist theory, labor history, and Aboriginal studies all indicate the tide is shifting.

Notes

1. Due to the limitations of length, I have used examples of writing, rather than definitive lists. There may be strong representation of Canadian writing, which is unusual in comparative pieces dealing with North America.

2. Some scholars have asked whether this emphasis on Aboriginal agency obscured racism and implicitly "absolved" colonialism. Robin Brownlie and Mary Ellen Kelm, "Desperately Seeking Absolution: Native Agency As Colonialist Alibi?" *Canadian Historical Review* 75.4 (1994): 543–56.

3. A few examples are: Joyce Green, *Making Space for Indigenous Feminism*; special issues of *Wicazo Sa Review* 24.2 (Fall 2009); forum "Native Feminisms Engage American Studies," *American Quarterly* 60.2 (June 2008); *Hypatia* 18.2 (2003); *American Indian Quarterly* 27.3 (Summer and Fall 2003) .

4. Curthoys and Lake 2007: 5. Some definitions of transnationalism are inclusive of comparative history, some are not. I have used an expansive definition. See Carter 2003: 565.

5. For a different view, see John Bellamy Foster, *Marx's Ecology: Materialism and Nature*, New York: Monthly Review Press, 2000.

6. Brownlie 2008: 41–68.

7. This is a particularly Canadian problem: see Coates 2000: 99–114.

8. Carlson 2007: 46–68. Comparisons with working-class life histories may reveal some similarities in terms of how family and community histories were understood.

9. McGrath argues this should not be a "whites only" space of research: Ann McGrath 1995: 30–51.

10. Guard 2004. Two interviews and information from strike bulletin and pamphlet are used as indications of how the scabs were viewed. The only voice of a Native woman

is the published recollection of one Mohawk woman who lived at the time but was never involved in the strike.

Works Cited

Albers, Patricia. "Autonomy and Dependency in the Lives of Dakota Women: A Study in Historical Change" *Review of Radical Political Economics* 17 (1985): 109–34.

———. "Labor and Exchange in American Indian History." *A Companion to American Indian History*. Eds. Philip Deloria and Neal Salisbury. Oxford: Blackwell, 2004. 269–86.

Aleiss, Angela. *Making the White Man's Indian: North America and Hollywood*. Westport, Conn.: Praeger Publishers, 2005.

Anderson, Kim, and Bonita Lawrence. *Strong Women Stories: Native Vision and Community Survival*. Toronto: Sumach Press, 2003.

Barker, Joanne. "Gender, Sovereignty, and the Discourse of Rights in Native Women's Activism," *Meridians: Feminism, Race, Transnationalism* 7.1 (2006): 127–61.

Bedford, David. "Marxism and the Aboriginal Question: The Tragedy of Progress." *Canadian Journal of Native Studies* 14.1 (1994): 102–17.

Berkhofer, Robert, Jr. *The White Man's Indian*. New York: Alfred Knopf, 1978.

Berton, Pierre. *Hollywood's Canada: The Americanization of Our National Image*. Toronto: McClelland and Stewart, Ltd., 1975.

Biolsi, Thomas, and Larry Zimmerman, eds. *Indians and Anthropologists: Vine Deloria Jr., and the Critique of Anthropology*. Tucson: University of Arizona Press, 1997.

Bosch, Mineka. "Internationalism and Theory in Women's History." *Gender and History*. 3.2 (1991): 137–46.

Briggs, Laura, Gladys McCormick, and J. T. Way. "Transnationalism: A Category of Analysis" *American Quarterly*, 60.3 (September 2008): 625–48.

Brownlie, Robin. "'Living the Same as White People': Mohawk and Anishinaabe Women's Labor in Southern Ontario, 1920–40" *Labour/Le Travail* 61 (Spring 2008): 41–68.

Campbell, Marie. *Halfbreed*. Toronto: Seal Books, 1973.

Carlson, Keith Thor. "Reflections on Aboriginal History and Memory." *Myth and Memory: Stories of Indigenous European Contact*. Ed. John Lutz. Vancouver: University of British Columbia Press, 2007.

Carter, Sarah. "Transnational Perspectives on the History of Great Plains Women: Gender, Race, Nations, and the Forty-Ninth Parallel." *American Review of Canadian Studies* 33.4 (Winter 2003): 565.

Castle, Elizabeth. "Keeping One Foot in the Community" *American Indian Quarterly* 27.3–4 (Summer-Fall 2003): 840–61.

Champagne, Duane. "Tribal Capitalism and Native Capitalists: Multiple Pathways of Native Economy." *Native Pathways: American Indian Culture and Economic Development in the Twentieth Century*. Eds. Brian Hosmer and Colleen O'Neill. Boulder: University of Colorado Press, 2005: 308–30.

Churchill, Ward, ed. *Marxism and Native Americans*. Boston: South End Press, 1988.

Coates, Ken. "Writing First Nations into Canadian History: A Review of Recent Scholarly Works." *Canadian Historical Review* [CHR] 81.1 (March 2000): 99–114.

Collier, Jane, and Y. and Sylvia Yanagisako, "Theory in Anthropology since Feminist Practice," *Critique of Anthropology* 9.2 (1989): 27–37.

Cooper, Frederick. "Africa's Pasts and Africa's Historians." *Canadian Journal of African History* 34.2 (2000): 300.

Cruikshank, Julie. *Life Lived like a Story: Life Stories of Three Yukon Native Elders*. Vancouver: University of British Columbia Press, 1990.

Culhane, Dara. "Their Spirits Live within Us: Aboriginal Women in Downtown Eastside Vancouver Emerging into Visibility." *American Indian Quarterly* 27.3–4 (Summer -Fall 2003): 593–606.

Curthoys, Ann, and Marilyn Lake, eds. *Connected Worlds: History in Transnational Perspective*. Sydney: University of New South Wales, 2007.

Deloria, Philip J. "American Indians, American Studies and the ASA." *American Quarterly* 55.4 (2003): 669–80.

Denetdale, Jennifer Nez. "Chairman, Presidents, and Princesses: The Navajo Nation, Gender, and the Politics of Tradition." *Wicazo Sa Review* (Spring 2006): 9–28.

Dirlik, Arif. "The Past As Legacy and Project: Postcolonial Criticism in the Perspective of Aboriginal Historicism." *Contemporary North American Political Issues*. Ed. Troy Johnson. Walnut Creek, Calif.: Altamira Press, 1999. 73–98.

Eberts, Mary, Sharon McIvor, and Teressa Nahanee. "The Women's Court Decision in the Appeal of NWAC v. Canada." *Canadian Journal of Women and the Law* 18.1 (January 2008): 67–119.

Eldersveld Murphy, Lucy. "To Live among Us: Accommodation, Gender and Conflict in the Western Great Lakes Region, 1760–1832." *Contact Points: American Frontiers from the Mohawk Valley to the Mississippi, 1750–1830*. Eds. Andrew Robert Lee Cayton and Fredrika J. Teute. Chapel Hill: University of North Carolina Press, 1998. 368–414.

Ellinghaus, Katherine. "Margins of Acceptability: Class, Education and Interracial Marriage in Australia and North America." *Frontiers* 23.2 (2002): 55–75.

Emmerich, Lisa E. "'Save the Babies!' American Indian Women, Assimilation Policy, and Scientific Motherhood, 1912–1918." *Writing the Range: Race, Class, and Culture in the Women's West*. Eds. Elizabeth Jameson and Susan Armitage. Norman: University of Oklahoma Press, 1997. 393–409.

Fiske, Jo-Anne. "Fishing Is Women's Business: Changing Economic Role of Carrier Women." *Native Peoples, Native Lands: Canadian Indian, Inuit and Métis*. Ed. Bruce Cox. Ottawa: Carleton University Press, 1987 186–98.

Fiske, Joanne. "The Womb Is to the Nation as the Heart Is to the Body: Ethnopolitical Discourses of the Canadian Indigenous Women's Movement." *Studies in Political Economy* 51 (Autumn 1996): 65–96.

Fiske, Joanne, and Susan Sleeper, eds. *New Faces of the Fur Trade: Selected Papers of the North American Fur Trade Conference*. Lansing: Michigan State University, 1998.

Francis, Douglas. *The Imaginary Indian: The Image of the Indian in Canadian Culture*. Vancouver: Arsenal Press, 1992.

Green, Joyce. *Making Space for Aboriginal Feminism*. Black Point, N.S.: Fernwood Books/ Zed Books, 2007.

Green, Rayna. "Native American Women." *Signs* 6.2 (1980): 248–68.

Guard, Julie. "Authenticity on the Line: Women Workers, Native 'Scabs,' and the Multi-Ethnic Politics of Identity in a Left-led Strike in Cold War Canada." *Journal of Women's History* 15.4 (Winter 2004): 117–38.

Guthrie-Valaskakis, Gail. *Indian Country: Essays on Contemporary Native Culture*. Waterloo, Ont.: Wilfrid Laurier University Press, 2005.

Gutman, Herbert. *Work, Culture and Society in Industrializing America*. New York: Alfred Knopf, 1976.

Hawthorn, Harry Bertram. *A Survey of the Contemporary Indians of Canada: A Report on Economic, Political, Educational Needs and Policies.* Ottawa: Indian Affairs Branch, 1966.

Hernandez-Avila, Ines. "It Is What Keeps Us Sisters: Indigenous Women and the Power of Story." *Frontiers: A Journal of Women's Studies* 23.2 (2002): ix–xviii.

Hightower Langston, Donna. "American Indian Women's Activism in the 1960s and 1970s." *Hypatia* 18.2 (Spring 2003): 114–32.

Hosmer, Brian, and Colleen O'Neill, eds. *Native Pathways: American Indian Culture and Economic Development in the Twentieth Century.* Boulder: University of Colorado Press, 2005.

Howard-Bobiwash, Heather. "Women's Class Strategies As Activism in Native Community Building in Toronto, 1950–75." *American Indian Quarterly* 27.3–4 (2003): 566–82.

Kaplan, Amy. "Manifest Domesticity." *American Literature* 70.3 (1998): 581–606.

Kelley, Robin D. G. "'But a Local Phase of a World Problem': Black History's Global Vision, 1883–1950." *Journal of American History* 86.3 (December 1999): 1045–77.

Kessler-Harris, Alice. "A New Agenda for American Labor History." *Perspectives on American Labor History: Towards a New Synthesis.* Eds. Carroll Moody and Alice Kessler-Harris. DeKalb: Northern Illinois University Press, 1987.

Krouse, Susan Appelgate, and Heather Howard-Bobiwash. "Preface: Keeping the Camp-fires Going: Urban American Indian Women's Community Work and Activism." *American Indian Quarterly* 27.3–4. *Special Issue: Urban American Indian Women's Activism* (Summer Autumn 2003): 489–90.

Kulchyski, Peter. "Anthropology in the Service of the State: Diamond Jenness and Canadian Indian Policy." *Journal of Canadian Studies* 28 (Summer 1993): 21–40.

Lagrand, James. *Indian Metropolis: Native Americans in Chicago, 1945–75.* Champaign: University of Illinois Press, 2002.

La Rocque, Emma. *When the Other Is Me: Native Resistance Discourse, 1850–1990.* Winnipeg: University of Manitoba Press, 2010.

Lawrence, Bonita. "Gender, Race, and the Regulation of Native Identity in Canada and the United States: An Overview." *Hypatia* 18.2 (Spring 2003): 3–31.

Littlefield, Alice. "Indian Education and the World of Work in Michigan, 1893–1933." *Native Americans and Wage Labor: Ethnohistorical Perspectives.* Eds. Alice Littlefield and Martha Knack. Norman: University of Oklahoma Press, 1999. 100–121.

Littlefield, Alice, and Martha Knack, eds. *Native Americans and Wage Labor: Ethnohistorical Perspectives.* Norman: University of Oklahoma Press, 1999.

Lobo, Susan, and Kurt Peters, eds. *American Indians and the Urban Experience.* Walnut Creek, Calif.: Altimira Press, 2001.

Loxley, John. "The Great Northern Plan." *Studies in Political Economy* 6 (Autumn 1981): 151–82.

Lutz, John, ed. *Myth and Memory: Stories of Indigenous European Contact.* Vancouver: University of British Columbia Press, 2007.

MacKay, Kathryn. "Warriors into Welders: A History of Federal Employment Programs for American Indians, 1898–1972." PhD dissertation, University of Utah, 1987.

Marubbio, Elise M. *Killing the Indian Maiden: Image of Native American Women in Film.* Lexington: University of Kentucky Press, 2006.

McCallum, Mary Jane. "Labour, Modernity and the Canadian State: A History of Aboriginal Women and Work in the Mid-Twentieth Century." PhD dissertation, University of Manitoba, 2008.

McCannell, Dean. *The Tourist: A New Theory of the Leisure Class*. Berkeley: University of California Press, 1999.

McGrath, Ann. "Modern Stone-Age Slavery: Images of Aboriginal Labour and Sexuality." *Labour History* 69 (1995): 30–51.

McIvor, Sharon Donna. "Self Government and Aboriginal Women." *Scratching the Surface: Canadian Anti-racist, Feminist Thought*. Eds. Enakshi Dua and Angela Robertson. Toronto: Women's Press, 1999, 167–86.

Medicine, Beatrice. *Learning to Be an Anthropologist and Remaining 'Native': Selected Writings*. Champaign: University of Illinois Press, 2001.

Milloy, John. *A National Crime: The Canadian Government and the Residential School System, 1879–1986*. Winnipeg: University of Manitoba Press, 1999.

Mohanty, Chandra. "Third World Women and the Politics of Feminism." *Third World Women and the Politics of Feminism*. Eds. Chandra Mohanty, Ann Russo, and Lourdes Torres. Bloomington: Indiana University Press, 1991. 1–50.

———. "Women Workers and Capitalist Scripts: Ideologies of Domination, Common Interests and the Politics of Solidarity." *Feminist Genealogies, Colonial Legacies, Democratic Futures*. Eds. M. Jacqui Alexander and Chandra Talpade Mohanty. New York: Routledge, 1995. 7–11.

Monture-Angus, Patricia. *Thunder in My Soul: A Mohawk Woman Speaks*. Halifax: Fernwood, 1995.

Moya, Paula. "Postmodernism, Realism and the Politics of Identity." *Reclaiming Identity: Realist Theory and the Predicament of Postmodernism*. Eds. Paula Moya and Michael Hames-Garcia. Berkeley: University of California Press, 2000.

Nahanee, Teresa. "Dancing with A Gorilla: Aboriginal Women, Justice and the Charter." *Aboriginal Peoples and the Justice System Report of the National Round Table on Aboriginal Justice*. Ottawa: Canada, Royal Commission on Aboriginal Peoples, 1993. 359–82.

O'Neill, Colleen. *Working the Navajo Way: Labor and Culture in the Twentieth Century*. Lawrence: University Press of Kansas, 2005.

Pascoe, Peggy. *The Search for Female Authority in the American West, 1874–1939*. New York: Oxford University Press, 1990.

Perry, Adele. *On the Edge of Empire: Gender, Race, and the Making of British Columbia, 1849–1871*. Toronto: University of Toronto Press, 2001.

Peters, E. J. "Subversive Spaces: First Nations Women and the City in Canada." *Society and Space* 16.6 (1998): 665–86.

Pineault, Kelly. "Shifting the Balance: Indigenous and Non-Indigenous Activism in the Company of Young Canadian." MA thesis, Trent University, 2011.

Ramirez, Renya. "Race Tribal Nation, and Gender." *Meridians: Feminism, Race, Transnationalism* 7.2 (2007): 22–40.

———. *Native Hubs: Culture, Community and Belonging in Silicon Valley and Beyond*. Durham: Duke University Press, 2007.

Ray, Arthur. "Aboriginal Title and Treaty Rights Research: A Comparative Look at Australia, Canada, New Zealand and the United States." *New Zealand Journal of History* 37.1 (2003): 5–17.

Rivera-Salgado, Gaspar. "Mixtec Activism in Oaxacalifornia." *American Behavioral Science* 42.9 (June 1999): 1439–58.

Ross, Luana. "From the 'F' Word to Indigenous/Feminisms." *Wicazo Sa Review* 24.2 (Fall 2009): 30–52.

Ruiz, Vicki. *Cannery Women, Cannery Lives: Mexican Women, Unionization, and the California Food Processing Industry, 1930–1950.* Albuquerque: University of New Mexico Press, 1987.

Sangster, Joan. "Making a Fur Coat: Women, the Labouring Body, and Working-Class History." *International Review of Social History* 52 (2007): 241–70.

———. "Colonialism As Work: Labour Placement Programs for Aboriginal Women in Postwar Canada." *Aboriginal History: A Reader.* Eds. Kristin Burnett and Geoff Read. Toronto: Oxford University Press, 2012.

Shoemaker, Nancy, ed. *Negotiators of Change: Historical Perspectives on Native American Women.* New York: Routledge, 1995.

Silman, Janet. *Enough Is Enough: Aboriginal Women Speak Out.* Toronto: The Women's Press, 1987.

Simpson, Audra. "On Ethnographic Refusal: Indigeneity, 'Voice' and Colonial Citizenship." *Junctures* 9 (2007): 67–80.

Smith, Andrea. *Conquest: Sexual Violence and American Indian Genocide.* Cambridge: South End Press, 2005.

———. "American Studies without America; Native Feminisms and the Nation-State." *American Quarterly* 60.2 (June 2008): 309–15.

———. "Queer Theory and Native Studies: The Heteronormativity of Settler Colonialism." *Queer Indigenous Studies: Critical Interventions in Theory, Politics, and Literature.* Eds. Qwo-li Driskill, Chris Finley, Brian Joseph Gilley, and Scott Lauria Morgensen. Tucson: The University of Arizona Press, 2011. 43–65.

Smith, Linda Tuhiwai. *Decolonizing Methodologies: Research and Indigenous Peoples.* New York: Zed Books, 1999.

Speed, Shannon. "At the Crossroads of Human Rights and Anthropology: Toward a Critically Engaged Activist Research." *American Anthropologist* 108.1 (March 2006): 66–76.

Sunseri, Lina. "Moving Beyond the Feminism versus the Nationalism Dichotomy: An Anti-Colonialist Feminist Perspective on Aboriginal Liberation Struggles." *Canadian Women's Studies* 20.2 (2000): 143–48.

Torpy, Sally. "Native American Women and Coerced Sterilization on the Trail of Tears in the 1970s." *American Indian Culture Research Journal* 24.2 (2000): 1–22.

Tough, Frank. *As Their Natural Resources Fail: Native Peoples and the Economic History of Northern Manitoba, 1870–1930.* Vancouver: University of British Columbia Press, 1996.

Van der Linden, Marcel. "Transnationalizing American Labor History, *Journal of American History* 86.3 (December 1999): 1078–92.

Van Kirk, Sylvia. *Many Tender Ties: Women in Fur Trade Society in Western Canada, 1670–1870.* Winnipeg: Watson Dwyer, 1980.

Vogt, Evan. "The Acculturation of American Indians." *Annals of the American Academy of Political and Social Sciences* 311 (1957): 137–46.

White, Pamela. "Restructuring the Domestic Sphere—Prairie Indian Women on Reserves: Image, Ideology and State Policy, 1880–1930." PhD dissertation, McGill University, 1987.

Zeleza, Paul Tiyambe. "The Troubled Encounter between Postcolonialism and African History." Online *Journal of the Canadian Historical Association* 17.2 (2006): 89–129.

CHAPTER 2

Making a Living

Anishinaabe Women in Michigan's Changing Economy

Alice Littlefield

Increasing scholarly focus on issues of gender in recent decades has served to highlight the many silences about women's lives in the earlier anthropological and historical literature. One result has been a florescence of ethnographic and ethnohistorical research on women in Indigenous North American cultures, and a more richly nuanced understanding of gender roles in many of these cultures and of the gendered consequences of colonization. Scholars have also given increased attention to women's work lives in the contemporary global economy, resulting in an expanding corpus of research and theory examining ethnic and gender aspects of the ongoing global restructuring of capital. Some of this literature also emphasizes the historical and ongoing importance of national policies in shaping the kinds of opportunities open to women.

These trends led me to ask questions about the work experiences of Indigenous women in Michigan, questions I found largely unanswered by the existing literature twenty years ago. Anthropological scholars of the Great Lakes region in the early part of the last century were largely interested in archaeology or the supposedly pristine cultures of the early contact period. Historians likewise largely missed the opportunity to record the ongoing changes in work lives of Indigenous men and women occurring before their eyes. Nonetheless, glimpses of these changing work lives can be gleaned from various sources.

In my own work, I have sought to expand our information on the subject through oral history. In addition to published sources, the information drawn together here comes from: (1) interviews conducted in the 1980s with former students of a residential school for Anishinaabe children; (2) interviews on work history conducted in the early 1990s with several women of the Saginaw Chippewa Tribe; (3) federal recognition research carried out in the 1990s for the Nottawaseppi Huron Band of Potawatomis, and in the early 2000s for the Burt Lake Band of Ottawas and Chippewas. I have also drawn to some extent on information gathered in less formal ways, such as conversations with Anishinaabe friends and acquaintances.

In this paper I attempt to survey the changes in Indigenous women's economic lives in Michigan in the context of both the changing regional economy and the ever-shifting policies of government. I hope to show that changing U.S. federal policies have played a key role in the process. At this point, a brief summary of these policies may be in order.

The U.S. Policy Environment

From the Treaty Era (early 1800s in Michigan) to the present, significant changes in U.S. federal policy have shaped the contours of opportunities open and closed to Indigenous people. The emphasis on assimilation in the nineteenth century involved two major programs designed to achieve this—the privatization of Indigenous landholdings and the establishment of schools to teach English and Euro-American culture to Native American children. A system of residential schools was the keystone of the educational program. By the 1920s, critics began to challenge the wisdom of these policies, pointing to widespread poverty among the supposed beneficiaries, and arguing that the residential schools did little to prepare students to earn an adequate living in the evolving economy (e.g., Meriam 1928).

The 1930s brought the Great Depression and government attempts to promote recovery. Among these attempts was the "Indian New Deal," including a systematic reform in federal-tribal relations. The most enduring legacy of this period is the Indian Reorganization Act of 1934, which sought to restore limited sovereignty and recognition to the tribal governments that the United States had tried so hard to destroy in the previous era. Although the 1930s reforms had limited immediate impact, they had a significant effect on developments that were to take place later (Littlefield 1993a).

The years after World War II brought a renewed emphasis on assimilation. In the 1950s some tribal governments were terminated and the urban relocation program was launched as the solution to Indigenous poverty. This trend was actively resisted by Indigenous people and was relatively short-lived. By the 1960s and 1970s tribal governments were beginning to tap into federal social programs (especially the "War on Poverty" programs of the Johnson administration) that expanded their ability to deliver health, education, and economic services to their members. President Richard Nixon (1968–73), not otherwise known for his love of people of color, declared the termination policy a dead letter and supported several pieces of legislation that enhanced tribal sovereignty (Nagel 1996).

During the 1980s and 1990s, several Michigan tribes bypassed for recognition in the 1930s were able to reaffirm their status as federally recognized tribes, either through administrative rulings by the Bureau of Indian Affairs or through

Congressional legislation. The number of federally recognized tribes in Michigan grew from four to twelve in the twenty years between 1980 and 2000.

This expansion coincided with the growth of casino gaming by recognized tribes across the country. Under U.S. law, a large part of tribal lands fall under federal rather than state jurisdiction; hence tribally operated gaming is not subject to state regulation of gaming or state taxation. In Michigan, most of the recognized tribes have established casinos. These provide jobs to members and, in some cases, per capita profit-sharing for tribal members.

Michigan's Anishinaabeg

By the late eighteenth century, the predominant groups inhabiting the area of the western Great Lakes that is now Michigan were the Ojibwas/Chippewas, Ottawas/Odawas, and Potawatomis/Bodawatomis, with a smaller number of Hurons/Wyandots in the Detroit area. Here I will focus on the first three of these groups. They speak closely related languages, refer to themselves as Anishinaabeg and as the People of the Three Fires. All of the historically American Indian communities and federally recognized tribes in Michigan today are Anishinaabeg. Although each of the three groups dominated particular geographic areas, areas that were formally delimited during the treaty era—Ojibwas in the Upper Peninsula and eastern Lower Peninsula, Ottawas in the western Lower Peninsula, and Potawatomis in southern Michigan and nearby parts of Indiana and Illinois—their hunting territories overlapped, interdigitated, and shifted over time in such a way as to preclude clearly fixed boundaries. Marriages and trade among members of the three groups were also common, serving to establish and maintain close ties.

During the nineteenth century, treaties were signed, reservations established, and census rolls created in such a way as to impose fixed geographic locations and more enduring political identities on local groupings that had been more fluid in the past. Individuals could collect annual treaty payments only by remaining in or returning to their communities of origin.

During the same period, missionaries and government officials exerted strong pressures on Michigan Anishinaabeg to adopt Christianity, the English language, and Euro-American culture, including Euro-American agricultural practices.

Anishinaabeg in the Expanding Global Economy

Tribes of the western Great Lakes entered into the fur trade with the French in the middle of the seventeenth century. Their involvement in the fur trade continued to be important into the early nineteenth century. Although the trade brought with it significant changes in many aspects of life, the subsistence economy—based on hunting, fishing, gathering, and gardening, and involving seasonal movements among varied resource territories—remained important well into the nineteenth century.

Women's labor was an integral part of subsistence activities and also important to the fur trade. Although most furs were trapped and traded by men, women did much of the preparation of furs for the trade. Scattered data also indicate that some women traded on their own account in provisioning fur traders with items such as maple sugar, berries, birch-bark containers, and other items, all products of women's traditional productive activities. Items they acquired from traders included cloth, needles, scissors, kettles, beads, and other goods. Anishinaabe women also played an important role in mediating between the two societies. It was common for traders to marry Anishinaabe women, and their wives and daughters often had considerable influence in their communities (White 1991).

Increasing Euro-American settlement in southern Michigan in the early 1800s brought pressure on the tribes to sign treaties ceding land to the United States. In the short period between 1807 and 1836 the Anishinaabeg ceded nearly all the land in the Lower Peninsula and half of the Upper Peninsula. The removal policies of the 1830s forced many Potawatomis out of the state. Other tribes were also threatened with removal, but ultimately most were able to remain, albeit as marginal participants in the emerging economy with tenuous control over their small landholdings.

Those who stayed in Michigan survived through a wide variety of economic strategies—by continued subsistence activities where possible; by commodifying fish, maple sugar, wild berries, harvested crops, baskets, and other craft products; and, increasingly, by participating in wage labor as lumberjacks, farmworkers, and domestic servants. In the late nineteenth century, Anishinaabe women also worked as harvest laborers for Euro-American farmers, cooked and did laundry for men in lumber camps, and worked as servants in settler households and in tourist hotels (Littlefield 1996; McClurken 1996).

Federal policies of the period emphasized the assimilation of Indigenous people into Euro-American society by dividing tribal lands into individual farms and establishing schools for their children. In Michigan, as elsewhere, the creation of a regime of private-property ownership led to the rapid decline in Native-owned lands. By the 1890s, most of their allotments had been sold or lost through debt or fraud (Rubenstein 1974). The majority of Anishinaabeg were left with few alternatives but to seek wages where they could find them. Without productive resources, they often lived in small rural communities near settler towns, dependent on seasonal work and occasional odd jobs.

James McClurken's research on Michigan Ottawas (1991, 1996) provides some details about this process. By 1900, he found, fewer than 10 percent of the Ottawas living along the Manistee River remained on their original land parcels. Their participation in wage labor began in the 1870s with the introduction of commercial fruit farming by the settlers. During the summer and fall, Ottawas harvested cherries, peaches, pears, and apples, an activity in which women's labor was especially important. In winter, many men turned to work in lumber camps, where they were sometimes accompanied by wives and children. In the camps, Anishinaabe women cooked and laundered for Euro-American lumberjacks as well as their own families (McClurken 1996: 78).

Farther north, the Ottawas along Little Traverse Bay adopted much of the settler culture; became successful farmers and fishermen; and built their own town on Lake Michigan at Harbor Springs, with two stores, a hotel, a school, and a church. As settlers began to push into the region in the 1870s, Ottawa control over the land and the local economy was eroded. With the arrival of the railroad in 1873, lumbering became the predominant economic activity and many Ottawas entered into the pattern already described for those living on the Manistee River (McClurken 1996: 91–94).

These developments were to be repeated over and over as the lumber industry moved rapidly northward through the state, drawing the Ojibwas of the Upper Peninsula into the lumber camps. By 1920, almost all the forests in Michigan had been cut.

At Harbor Springs, another source of employment for the Ottawas developed: the tourist industry. Resort hotels sprang up as soon as rail connections with major cities opened. Men were employed in construction, maintenance, and groundskeepng; women cooked, cleaned, and laundered for the tourist hotels. The tourist industry also provided a ready market for fish caught by men and for women's crafts, such as baskets and fine porcupine-quill work (McClurken 1996: 94–95).

In 1893, the federal government established a residential vocational school for Anishinaabe children at Mt. Pleasant, Michigan, with eight (later nine) years of instruction. Over a forty-year period, the school trained large numbers of Anishinaabe boys and girls in the skills of Euro-American rural living: agriculture, and carpentry for boys; cooking, cleaning, sewing, and laundry for girls. Ironically, only a minority of these children became farm operators or farm wives, because Michigan Anishinaabeg no longer had much land. Rather, the training provided at Mt. Pleasant served, for the most part, to channel children into menial employment in agriculture and construction for men, and in domestic service for women (Littlefield 1989: 1993a).

In the 1980s I conducted interviews with thirty-five former students, including twenty women, who had attended the Mt. Pleasant Indian School in the 1920s and 1930s. These interviews, supplemented by school records, provide some insight into the economic roles of Michigan Anishinaabeg during the early years of the twentieth century. In the school's annual report for 1912, for example, the school superintendent described the Indigenous economy in these terms:

> There are about 10,000 Indians in this state. . . . Some are . . . marine captains and engineers, firemen, railroad men, lumbermen, farmers, and fishermen. . . .

But still another class of our Michigan Indians are the poorer ones, who are found in the Indian villages or settlements adjoining some lumber camp, town, or summer resort. . . . They are a nomadic people like their forefathers, and are continually moving from place to place . . . where ever [*sic*] they can find work and make a living. During the winter a great many are employed in the lumber camps and take their families with them to those forsaken out of the way places (U.S. Bureau of Indian Affairs 1912: 4–5).

Other occupations mentioned in reports from this period include commercial fishing and agricultural labor in sugar beet fields and fruit orchards.

Although the Bureau of Indian Affairs reports reveal little detail about women's work, the interviews with former students were more informative. They were asked about both their own occupational histories and the kinds of work their mothers did. In what follows, I refer to these two groups of women as mothers and daughters.

About half of the former students I interviewed reported that their mothers earned cash through restaurant or hotel work, private domestic service, basketry, sewing, beadwork, berry-picking, and/or seasonal work in fruit canneries. Often, women combined several of these activities, shifting as seasonal opportunities and family responsibilities permitted.

The life of Josephine B. provides an example of this pattern. Born in the late nineteenth century in the Petoskey–Harbor Springs area on Lake Michigan, she attended the Mt. Pleasant Indian School, where she became an expert seamstress. After finishing the eighth grade, she worked for the school briefly as an assistant sewing instructor. She then married a young man who had taken tailoring classes at Mt. Pleasant. He found steady work in a tailor shop in Petoskey, where they settled and raised five children. During the summers she did laundry for vacationers at the nearby Bay View resort community and sometimes worked as a chambermaid. She also helped her husband with tailoring and alterations, made cakes to order, and did beadwork for sale.

For other women of Josephine's generation, the most common work undertaken for pay was domestic labor, either in private homes or tourist resorts, and making baskets or quill boxes for sale.

By the 1920s, Michigan's economy began to shift away from reliance on agriculture and the extraction of raw materials. The lumber industry, which had provided fortunes for lumber barons and jobs for lumberjacks for fifty years, largely met its demise with the cutting of the last old-growth forests. The same years brought hard times in agriculture, with diminishing opportunities for farm labor. Manufacturing and urban employment took up some of the slack. For Nottawaseppi Potawatomi women, fruit harvesting, basketry, and subsistence gardening continued to be important during these years (Littlefield 1993b).

In 1925, the school superintendent reported that of the male graduates "the majority have gone to the city and have secured good jobs with the various automobile companies" (U.S. Bureau of Indian Affairs 1925). For young women, however, available opportunities in these years were not much better than for their mothers. Most of the daughters who attended the school in the 1920s reported that their first jobs after leaving school were as live-in domestic servants. This was true even for the two women who completed secondary secretarial courses at the Haskell Indian Institute in Kansas. In contrast with an earlier period, however, many of these jobs as domestics were in large cities rather than small towns.

The 1930s brought even worse economic conditions as the Great Depression set in. When the Mt. Pleasant Indian School closed in 1933, the head matron and the school social worker arranged for some of the girls to live with families in the Detroit area or other cities, doing housework or child care in return for room and board, while attending public high schools. These arrangements did not always work out well, but at least some girls got additional schooling this way.

The effects of the Depression were especially harsh in rural areas, with the end of lumbering and a scarcity of agricultural work. Although some Anishinaabeg received small amounts of public relief during this period (e.g., a bag of flour for a day's work on the roads in Muskegon County), subsistence gardening, hunting, and fishing were important in helping people survive (Cheney 1933). Various sources also mention basketry as a common activity during this period, for both women and men. A Nottawaseppi Band woman born in 1926 reported making baskets with her grandmother and hitchhiking with her to a nearby city to deliver large quantities of baskets to merchants in exchange for dry goods and food (interview by Littlefield May 21, 1992). A social worker employed by the Bureau of Indian Affairs regularly bought birch-bark boxes decorated with porcupine quills from Ottawa women at Grand Traverse Bay during the mid-1930s, paying $3.00 to $5.00 for each one (interviews with former students, Mt. Pleasant Indian School).

World War II had a significant impact on the lives of Michigan Anishinaabeg, drawing many of them into kinds of employment from which they had previously been excluded. Although there was a small concentration of Indigenous people living and working in Detroit as early as the 1920s (Meriam 1928), the city's Anishinaabeg population jumped significantly during the 1940s. Both men and women found work in factories, though some women were still working as domestic servants (Danziger 1991). It was during the war years also that many Anishinaabeg migrated to other Michigan cities, especially Grand Rapids and Lansing, both industrial cities. Among the Ottawas of the Little River band, most young men joined the armed forces, while the young women took jobs in factories in Grand Rapids (McClurken 1996). Women from the Nottawaseppi Band of Potawatomis worked in factories and food processing plants in Battle Creek during these years (Littlefield 1993b).

During the postwar period several women of the daughters' generation worked in restaurants and in institutions such as hospitals and nursing homes, jobs in which the domestic skills taught at the Mt. Pleasant school were useful. Four daughters found jobs as clerical workers. Two worked in sewing factories. One woman, a single mother who lived in a small town, supported her family by cleaning houses throughout her adult life.

Unlike most of those in the daughters' generation, Emily G., who studied bookkeeping at Haskell, postponed marriage for a dozen years after leaving school. She worked briefly as a maid in Kansas City and then went home to northern Michigan to care for younger siblings when her mother died. It was the height of the Depression, and there were few opportunities for clerical jobs, especially in a rural area where Indians faced considerable discrimination. Eventually, she secured an office job with the Economic Recovery Administration, a Depression-era federal agency, where she earned $65.00 a month. Later, she worked as a waitress in Mackinac City (a resort town) and Lansing before securing a bookkeeping job in an automobile agency in the 1940s. After a number of years she was able to qualify for a civil service job with the State of Michigan and to retire with a state pension (interview by Littlefield July 21, 1986).

Another exceptional case is that of Mary S. She attended beauty school while working in an automobile factory in Lansing during World War II. After several years as a beautician, she opened her own salon. Before retiring, she owned three salons and also sold real estate (interview by Littlefield August 4, 1984).

Other occupations pursued by these women were quite varied: one sold insurance; another ran a boat livery with her husband. Two secured jobs in Native American–related programs late in their careers, one running a tribal lunch program for elders, the other as Indian Education coordinator for a public school system.

As the story of Emily G. suggests, the 1940s brought some breach in the wall of discrimination, allowing her finally to secure the clerical work for which she was trained. For women with less education, however, the work opportunities were more likely to involve factory work or service jobs.

Migration to urban areas in the postwar period was influenced by high labor demand in the industrial sector. By contrast, the demand for rural labor continued to decline as agriculture increasingly mechanized. During the 1950s, the federal Indian relocation program also played a role in encouraging migration to urban areas, but in Michigan it merely added impetus to trends that were already well underway.

By the 1960s, Michigan's Anishinaabe population was largely an urban one. Even in rural areas, the subsistence sector had been largely replaced by primary reliance on wage labor. In Mt. Pleasant, several women from the Saginaw Chippewa Tribe worked for a state institution for the developmentally disabled. This institution, ironically, was located on the site of the old Mt. Pleasant Indian School. One woman worked for several years in a county nursing home. Older women continued to supplement family incomes with basket-making. Local employment in agriculture had largely disappeared from the picture by this time, but some families from the Saginaw Chippewa reservation still traveled to the northern Lower Peninsula each summer to pick fruit for farmers with whom they had longstanding ties (interviews with Saginaw Chippewa women by Littlefield 1993).

Michigan Anishinaabeg in the Contracting Industrial Economy

Given the trends of the postwar years, one might easily have predicted the continued decline of rural Anishinaabe communities and their rapid assimilation into the urban labor force. By the 1970s, however, the global economy was undergoing major changes. Among Anishinaabe women born in the postwar period, one finds a significantly different set of occupational experiences than among their mothers. These women reached maturity at a time when Michigan's industrial economy was entering into long-term crisis, much of it a result of global restructuring in the automobile industry. In spite of achieving higher levels of education than their parents, neither they nor their male partners were able to count on jobs in the urban industrial sector. At the same time, expansion of federal and tribal programs created a demand for people to work in a variety of new capacities.

In the 1990s I interviewed several Saginaw Chippewa women in this age group and found that many of them had worked mostly for tribally operated programs. Unlike their mothers and grandmothers, these women seldom report working as private domestic workers.

Sarah M. was born in Mt. Pleasant in 1954, the youngest of ten children. With support from her mother, her girlfriends, and an Indian teacher, she graduated from Mt. Pleasant High School in 1973 with training in secretarial skills and attended college for one semester. With the exception of two years as a clerical employee at Central Michigan University, she has worked for the Saginaw Chippewa Tribe all of her adult life. Her positions have included housing rehabilitation administrator, legal secretary, economic development planner, court clerk, magistrate, and executive secretary to several tribal chiefs. In addition, she served on the tribal council for many years (interview by Littlefield 1993).

Diane K. was born in 1957. Her parents were among those who migrated to the region's cities in the 1940s, her mother employed as a trained practical nurse and her father as a truck driver. He later became a state employee in a small town in northern Michigan. In the high school Diane attended, she and her siblings were the only Native American students. As a college student, she worked part-time at the tribe's youth center. After three years of university, she took a full-time job with the tribe as a community health representative and later became the tribal housing director. With no previous training in management or accounting, she was able to turn around a floundering housing program far in arrears on federal loans. She subsequently became manager of the tribe's then-new slot machine facility, eventually finished her college degree, and took a managerial position with another Michigan tribe (interview by Littlefield 1993).

The career of Loretta C., a Nottawaseppi Band member born in 1950, shows some similarities to those of the two Saginaw Chippewa women. After working briefly in a factory, she took a secretarial position with the Grand Rapids Inter-tribal Council, attended community college, and worked in an Indian education program (known as Title IV) in the Grand Rapids schools. In the late 1970s she started working for the Nottawaseppi Band, which was then in the process of seeking federal recognition. After a brief stint as executive director for the Band, she took a position with Michigan Indian Employment and Training Services, where she worked for ten years. During these years, she also completed a social work degree (interview by Littlefield 1992).

Although exceptional lives in some respects, these careers exemplify the importance for the postwar generation of employment in tribal programs or federally funded agencies serving Native American populations. They also exemplify a tendency for tribal members to be given responsibilities that, in the nontribal economy, would be available only to those with significantly more training and experience.

The most numerous jobs available to Anishinaabe women in recent decades are in the casinos launched since the 1980s by several of the state's tribes. The tribes are now the largest employers in several of the localities where they have gaming operations (e.g., the Saginaw Chippewa Tribe in Isabella County, the Little River Band of Ottawas in Manistee, and the Sault Ste. Marie Tribe in Sault Ste. Marie). The jobs available to women through the growth of casinos are diverse, ranging from dishwashing to middle- and upper-management positions. These tribes also have large numbers of non-Indigenous employees working for Anishinaabe supervisors, reversing the status positions historically prevalent in the region.

Income from gaming has also supplemented federal funding, allowing tribes to expand a wide range of services to their members, including police and fire protection, tribal courts, medical services, education programs, housing, and cultural programs. As these programs have grown, so have tribal bureaucracies, creating employment opportunities for many Anishinaabe women.

It may be that women face less gender discrimination in tribal organizations in Michigan than in the larger economy, a by-product of tribal hiring policies that favor members over nonmembers. Although much tribal hiring reflects the occupational patterns of the larger society—e.g., women in teaching, nursing, and social work—Anishinaabe women also hold many of the management positions in these same fields as well as in the casino and hotel enterprises.

Conclusions

The scattered evidence brought together in this paper suggests that Anishinaabe women's involvement in the Michigan economy has responded to changes in federal policy, to local variations in economic opportunities, and to periodic restructuring in the regional and global economies (see also Littlefield 1993a).

In the nineteenth and early twentieth centuries, the federal policies of land division and education were instrumental in helping to channel Michigan Anishinaabeg into the wage labor force, primarily in rural areas until the 1920s and then increasingly in urban areas. At a later time, other federal policies had profound effects in restructuring economic opportunities. The relocation programs of the 1950s reinforced the trend toward urban migration, a trend that has been reversed more recently by federal policies encouraging the growth of tribal enterprises, including gaming, and of tribal services, especially health and housing programs.

Federal decisions to provide official recognition to some tribes and not others have also been extremely important in their effects: most of the twelve recognized tribes in Michigan are able to provide employment, health care, education, housing, and infrastructure for thriving communities. By contrast, members of unrecognized bands (e.g., the Burt Lake Band of Ottawas and Chippewas) have largely scattered to the major cities, with only remnant populations remaining in the traditional home areas.

Local economic conditions have also had a major influence on the productive roles of Anishinaabe women and men. Agricultural wage labor was historically more important in the Lower Peninsula than in the Upper Peninsula, especially in the fruit-growing areas along Lake Michigan. After the harvesting of other crops was mechanized, Anishinaabeg continued to participate in seasonal fruit harvesting into the 1960s. In the Upper Peninsula, the lumbering economy lasted longer than in the Lower Peninsula, but there were fewer opportunities for agricultural or factory employment.

Some communities were favorably situated for involvement in the tourist industry. The Charlevoix–Petoskey–Harbor Springs area along Lake Michigan, an area made famous by the stories of Ernest Hemingway, has been a summer vacation area for wealthy people from Chicago and other major cities for 130 years. Anishinaabe women in that area were drawn into service jobs in the tourist sector in the late nineteenth century, and continue to participate in such employment today. They also found a ready market for craft products, and some of them performed in Indian pageants and powwows staged for the benefit of tourists. Until the advent of casino gaming in the 1980s and 1990s, most other Anishinaabe communities in Michigan had far less involvement in tourism.

The effects of periodic restructuring of the regional economy are evident in the rise and subsequent decline of the lumber industry and in the early growth of tourism as a response to the interests of wealthy people from Chicago, Detroit, and other cities in the region. Other far-reaching effects of economic restructuring include the shift to urban industrial employment, which began during World War I and accelerated during and after World War II. As a consequence of this shift, the majority of Michigan's Anishinaabe population lives in urban areas today. More recently, the decline of smokestack industries and the growth of tribal enterprises and tribal social programs have encouraged reverse migration from the cities back to traditional homelands. Among the returning migrants are retirees, many of whom have spent their entire working lives away from the communities of their birth.

The appearance of Indian casinos as a growth niche in an otherwise stagnant economy represents a creative form of adaptation for tribes, but one which brings with it new kinds of contradictions. A new process of class differentiation between tribal bosses and tribal workers is unfolding in the heart of communities that were once more homogeneous, in terms of class position and income. Casino revenues allow for the funding of projects of cultural renewal, such as language classes, art and dance programs, museums, and the like. At the same time, prosperity brings increasing consumption of all that the dominant society has to offer and a decline in traditional but low-paying activities such as basketry. Much of the basketry found in casino gift shops in Michigan originates in Ontario.

The picture I have sketched in this paper is based on data gathered from a variety of sources, and subsequent research may foster its modification. At this point, however, I wish to turn to a larger question: What can we learn about the interconnections of work, gender, and ethnicity through a lens that focuses on the historically specific experiences of Michigan Anishinaabeg?

One lesson has to do with the continuing role of government policies in structuring and restructuring economic opportunities in ways that differentially affect gender-stratified and ethnically stratified segments of the labor force. The importance of federal policy in structuring differentiated labor markets is not a new point (see e.g., Littlefield 1993a), but it may be especially salient in the case of Indigenous people in the United States, people whose lives have been closely managed and regulated by the federal government for over 150 years. The decline of domestic work and rise of public sector employment for women are trends that can also be observed for other women in the United States as social service programs expanded during the twentieth century. Additional research on women's work in public bureaucracies, bureaucracies that are often involved in managing other women's lives, should be fruitful in developing our understanding of the intersection of policy, gender, and ethnicity.

Another lesson involves the assumption that integration of Indigenous peoples into the labor force is accompanied by assimilation into the dominant society. The extent to which Anishinaabeg have maintained distinct cultural identities, in spite of significant integration into the urban labor force and heavy pressures to assimilate, is impressive. The growth of tribal enterprises, including gaming, suggests a new, complex process, one that may reinforce Indigenous identity while at the same time altering the content of that identity in both profound and subtle ways. These developments among Indigenous Americans suggest a need for comparative analyses of processes of ethnic maintenance and change as these relate to the political economy.

A third implication of this research relates to the intersection of work, gender, and ethnicity and the way these have been theorized. A number of researchers have looked at situations in North America in which a labor force comprised largely of women of color has been employed in enterprises owned or managed by Euro-American males. These studies have provided interesting analyses of the coping strategies and modes of resistance utilized by such workers. In the new tribal enterprises, however, the contradictions between Indigenous bosses and Indigenous workers are muted by appeals framed in terms of a common cultural identity and a common historical struggle against the larger society. This situation points to the need for more fine-grained studies of work and gender relations in these enterprises to understand more general processes of accommodation, resistance, and class division within tribal communities.

Works Cited

Cheney, Lela. Report of School Social Worker, U.S. Indian School, Mt. Pleasant, June 30, 1933. Typescript. RG 75, National Archives. Entry 723, Office File of W. Carson Ryan, Box 3.

Danziger, Edmund Jefferson, Jr. *Survival and Regeneration: Detroit's American Indian Community.* Detroit, Wayne State University Press, 1991.

Littlefield, Alice. "The B.I.A. Boarding School: Theories of Resistance and Social Reproduction." *Humanity and Society* 13.4 1989: 428–41.

———. "Learning to Labor: Native American Education in the United States, 1880–1930." *The Political Economy of North American Indians.* Ed. John Moore. Norman: University of Oklahoma Press, 1993. 43–59.

———. "Response to Bureau of Acknowledgment Research, Nottawaseppi-Huron Potawatomi Band." Unpublished ms., 1993.

———. "Indian Education and the World of Work in Michigan, 1893–1993." *Native Americans and Wage Labor: Ethnohistorical Perspectives.* Eds. Alice Littlefield and Martha C. Knack. Norman: University of Oklahoma Press, 1996. 100–121.

McClurken, James M. *Gah-Baeh-Jhagwah-Buk: The Way It Happened.* East Lansing: Michigan State University Museum, 1991.

———. "Wage Labor in Two Michigan Ottawa Communities." *Native Americans and Wage Labor: Ethnohistorical Perspectives.* Eds. Alice Littlefield and Martha C. Knack. Norman: University of Oklahoma Press, 1996. 66–99.

Meriam, Lewis, et al. *The Problem of Indian Administration.* Baltimore: John Hopkins University Press, 1928.

Nagel, Joane. *American Indian Ethnic Renewal: Red Power and the Resurgence of Identity and Culture.* New York: Oxford University Press, 1996.

Rubenstein, Bruce Alan. *Justice Denied: An Analysis of American Indian–White Relations in Michigan, 1855–1889*. PhD dissertation, Michigan State University, 1974.

United States Bureau of Indian Affairs. "Annual Report of the Superintendent, Mt. Pleasant School." In National Archives Microfilm Publication M1011, *Superintendents' Annual Narrative and Statistical Reports from the Field Jurisdictions of the BIS, 1907–1938*, Reel 89. Washington, D.C.: National Archives, 1912, 1925.

White, Richard. *The Middle Ground: Indians, Empires, and Republics in the Great Lakes Region, 1650–1815*. New York: Cambridge University Press, 1991.

CHAPTER 3

Procuring Passage

Southern Australian Aboriginal Women and the Early Maritime Industry of Sealing

Lynette Russell

Prelude

I have both an intellectual and personal engagement with the history of sealing in southern Australia. A number of years ago, at a family funeral, after having completed a doctorate in historical studies, I engaged in conversation with an elderly distant cousin. He acknowledged his descent from both Aboriginal and European ancestors, as I did. He was explaining to me that his great-great-grandparents had been sealers, she a Tasmanian Aboriginal woman and he a British immigrant seaman. I confidently asserted that such women experienced terrible hardship and were often virtual slaves, pressed into involuntary labor. I had reached this understanding after extensive reading of conventional academic historical work in the area, especially revisionist feminist histories written in the 1970s and 1980s. My cousin, however, untrained and without formal education, stunned me when he suggested that this characterization vilified his grandfather and, much worse, reduced his grandmother to status of victim, removing any agency from her actions. He emphasized that his family's oral history described both of them as sealers and not as I had previously regarded them a sealer and his "woman" or common law "wife." My rendering of this history, informed by academic histories, in his opinion failed to take account of her labor as well as her agency, though he used neither of these terms. This relatively simple exchange was epiphanous and it sent me on the journey to understand in a more nuanced and sympathetic manner the complexity of what was the southern Australian sealing industry.[1]

Introduction and Background

Australia was colonized by Europeans in 1788 when Captain Arthur Philip, on behalf of the British government, established the penal colony of Port Jackson,

Sydney. The Colonial Office in London intended that this tiny struggling settlement, which battled food shortages and economic disasters, should ostensibly govern all of the country, then known as New Holland. In reality Port Jackson was unable to exert control beyond its immediate geographic boundaries. This meant that, in the 1790s, when the plentiful sealing grounds of southeastern Australia were identified, they could be exploited with scant regard for the colonial authorities. Although the colonial officials desired to control all trade, production, imports, and exports into and out of the fledgling colony, the immense distance between the sealing grounds and Sydney ensured that this control was virtually impossible.

The development of a maritime industry was vitally important for the struggling colony. The colonists had found few exploitable resources; the "tyranny of distance" made trade difficult and preservation was a serious problem (F. Watson 1997). On a world scale sealskins and seal and whale oil were vitally important for creating export opportunities with Europe and Asia, most notably with China. Whalers, especially those who whaled in the areas where the seal breeding grounds were located, supplemented their catches by hunting seals for their skins and their oil. Seal oil, which burned slowly, provided a bright light and, most importantly, was essentially smokeless. Whaling in the southern oceans took vessels close to the massive Antarctic seal grounds where the opportunity to increase the trade was seized. Consequently the seal industry was always connected to, and a subsidiary of, pelagic whaling. Vessels out of North America, notably New Bedford, also pursued sealing in both Antarctic and Arctic waters when, after the Revolutionary War, large numbers of their vessels were fitted out to secure cargoes of fur sealskins to carry to the Chinese market (A. Watson 1931: 476). China was the main trade partner for sealskins from both the Pacific and Atlantic oceans.

By the early 1800s the southern coastal region of Australia and its offshore islands were occupied by hundreds of men: British, European, American, Maori, and others (Little 1969: 109–27; Stuart 1997: 47–58; Taylor 1996, 2002[a, b]; Townrow 1991). Although there is evidence that at least one or two of these Newcomers brought wives with them, the overwhelming majority were unattached men who maintained semipermanent bases on small peninsulas and offshore islands (figure 3.1).

Exchange Relations between Aboriginal Men and Groups

In what was perhaps a simplistic description of the situation, Robert McNab, writing from New Zealand, observed that at first the sealers captured, traded, and bartered with the women for sex but later found them to be essential companions, as they "could hunt wallabies, seals and collect all manner of other foods" (McNab 1907: 45). Many previous authors have, I believe, overemphasized the

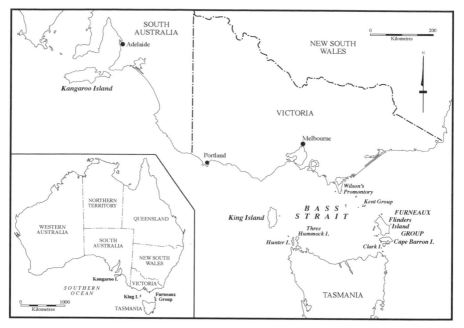

Figure 3.1. Map of Southeastern Australia Sealing Grounds. Reproduced with permission of Lynette Russell.

sexual nature of these relationships. Although interracial sexual relationships were important, the actual industry and the subsequent economic survival of the European men was absolutely dependent on the presence of Aboriginal women, their labor and their knowledge (45). The women brought well-honed skills to the industry, passed down and perfected in their traditional economies. In traditional precontact Tasmanian society women hunted and butchered seals. There is no historic, ethnographic, or archaeological evidence, however, that they treated or prepared skins, which was almost certainly a new skill and one that they must have learned from the European men.

Traditionally, Tasmanian Aboriginal people in the precontact era consumed significant quantities of seal meat. George Augustus Robinson, government-appointed missionary, conciliator, and protector, described them as "remarkably fond" of it (N. Plomley 1966: 117). Woorrady, an Aboriginal woman who had lived with European sealers for many years, amused Robinson and others with tales of Aboriginal men unsuccessfully hunting seals. In Woorrady's stories the men were often the figure of fun, less competent than the women and prone to movements that startled the seals and forced them to attack, rearing up and, in one case, grabbling a man by the cheek and holding him underwater (554). Despite the sparse firsthand evidence, Woorrady seems to imply that it was usually Aboriginal women who hunted seals.

There is only one detailed extant description of the process of hunting seals. This comes from Captain James Kelly (1815) who asked that a group of women demonstrate the hunting process. From this description it is clear that the women were very competent hunters.

> We gave the women each a club . . . to kill the seals with. They went to the water's edge and wet themselves all over their heads and bodies, which operation they said would keep the seals from smelling them as they walked along the rocks. They were very cautious not to go to windward of them, as they said "a seal would sooner believe his nose than his eyes when a man or woman came near him." The women all walked into the water in couples, and swam to three rocks about fifty yeards [*sic*] from the shore. There were about nine or ten seals upon each rock lying apparently asleep. Two women went to each rock with their clubs alongside. Some of the seals lifted their heads up to inspect their new visitors and smell them. The seals scratched themselves and lay down again.
>
> The women went through the same motions as the seal, holding up their left elbow and scratching themselves with their left hand. The seals seemed very cautious, now and then lifting up their heads and looking round scratching themselves as before and lying down again; the women still imitating every movement as nearly as possible. After they had lain upon the rocks for nearly an hour, the sea occasionally washing over them (as they were quite naked, we could not tell the meaning of their remaining so long) all of a sudden the women rose up in their seats, their clubs lifted up at arms length, each struck the seals on the nose and killed him; in an instant they all jumped up as if by magic and killed one more each. After giving the seals several blows on the head, and securing them, they commenced laughing out loud and began dancing. They each dragged the seal into the water, and swam with it to the rock upon which we were standing, and then went back and brought another each, making twelve seals, the skins of which were worth one pound each in Hobart Town (Bowden 1964: 40–41).

For me, these women seem also to be in control of the process itself, and I imagine them enjoying the opportunity to make the men wait as they lay in the warm sun on the rocks.

The key ingredient in the success of the industry was the hunting and processing labor of Aboriginal women. Although there are estimates that there were as many as 200 Newcomer men involved in the industry, it was usual for each man to have between three and five Aboriginal women working with him. In some years the islands yielded between ten and twenty thousand sealskins. The processing of each of these skins required tremendous energy expenditure. As Captain Kelly observed, each hunting episode required the women to club the seal and drag it to the beach, where they would begin the butchering process. The pelt would have been removed using a sharp knife with great care to remove the entire skin without damaging it. The pelt would then have been pegged out in a shallow pit covered and with salt, which was the essential ingredient in the process.

The women, whose names were rarely recorded, also developed useful skills in boat handling and other associated aspects of the industry. Like so much of colonial history and the history of colonized peoples, there are competing versions of the narratives. Some contemporary Tasmanian Aborigines have told me shocking stories passed down to them from their elders. These are histories where women were left stranded on islands when the men moved on, and others were drowned or murdered once the European men had no further need of them. Yet there are others with fond "memories" of their male sealing ancestors.

By 1810, the sealing industry was all but over and organized crews of sealers were replaced by island-dwelling settlers (Skira 1993: 50). The short-lived intensive industry was followed by a second phase in which newly formed and semisettled communities developed. This led to the long-term occupation of the islands by the men, Aboriginal women, their children, and extended family, who remained long after the seals were virtually extinct. Like the early phase, trade and exchange during this period was dependent on Aboriginal labor, and, in particular, on the labor of women. The complex society that emerged out of the interactions between Aboriginal women and Newcomers provided the basis for the contemporary Tasmanian Aboriginal community.[2] The Tasmanian Aboriginal scholar Ian Anderson has observed a great paradox in the relationships that developed in this region between the Aboriginal women and the Newcomer men. In many ways the men were responsible for the near-genocide of the Tasmanian Aboriginal people; yet by intermarrying and having families with the Newcomer men the women ensured the descendant community that survives today. I am not suggesting that this was a conscious strategy, but rather that their simple act of surviving ensured the community's continuity. As Native title and other legal cases have shown, today the descendants of the sealing women constitute the majority of the Tasmanian Aboriginal community.

Newcomer men and Aboriginal women established families, farms and settlements, and small businesses. Based on the Bass Strait Islands, these families provided all manner of provisions to ships passing from Hobart and Port Dalrymple (in northern Tasmania). They traded wallaby, possum, and sealskins and seal oil for slops, clothing, spirits, and other trade items (Little 1969: 112; Shillingshaw 1879: 48). Despite the decimated seal population there remained sufficient seal numbers "for independent sealers to remain and make their homes on the islands in eastern Bass Strait," as Ryan has noted (1996: 67). Over the subsequent decade (from 1810 onward) these communities, made up of little more than independent domestic economies, expanded and settled. Importantly, the incorporation of these women into these particular "settlements" was not complete; it did not mean they lost their culture. Aboriginal people, and especially the sealing women, resisted, adapted, negotiated, and survived in these and other settlements in varied ways. Even when ostensibly accommodating a new set of social circumstances they exercised subtle but effective resistance to colonialism.

One of the most obvious and enduring facets of this resistance can be seen in the ongoing use of Aboriginal language in these settlements. Language was a key way that survival was facilitated. Many observers arriving in these island communities described the men and the children using a lingua franca consisting of traditional Aboriginal language as well as English. Even the trade system whereby boats would call into the island to secure fresh water and provisions was conducted using this fused language.

In the late 1820s and early 1830s the colonial government, concerned with a growing community of "half-castes," as well as increasing violence on mainland Tasmania, decided to establish a government station to incarcerate all Tasmanian Aborigines. Despite their relative economic independence the government deemed that, via Robinson, the women were to be removed from the "sealers" and placed in the mission-station at Wybalenna on Flinders Island. This location ensured that they were distant to the mainland of Tasmania where the majority of European colonizers had settled.

For an agent of the colonial project like Robinson, the economic independence and actions of resistance of these Aboriginal women sealers undermined his paternalistic attempts to "protect" and "civilize." Many of the sealing women simply refused to join Robinson, who frequented his journal with comments saying that the women who remained on the islands with their families and partners were the source of innumerable problems. He had unsuccessfully attempted on many occasions to entice them to leave the islands and join the Aboriginal mission at Wybalenna.[3] Only fourteen of the dozens of the sealing women consented. Yet, perhaps ironically, although these departures were seen as the hallmark of his success, these women in fact caused him the most difficulty at the mission. He endeavored to convert these women to God-fearing Christians:

> [T]heir better health, familiarity with European customs, and readiness to dispense with some of the more "distasteful" traditional ceremonial dances had led him to believe that they could form the vanguard of his new society (Ryan 1996: 191).

Once housed at Wybalenna, Robinson was frustrated, and his journal is liberally notated with his disappointment. Far from being accommodating and prepared to abandon their ceremonies and dances, Robinson discovered that the women enthusiastically performed the new distasteful dances they had developed in cohabitation with the sealers. They were sufficiently proficient in English, which was "liberally strewn with epithets, and [. . .] the lingua franca they introduced to the establishment was a powerful weapon of ridicule" (Ryan 1996: 191).

These women did not easily abandon their culture. Exposure to the sealers, their relative economic independence forged through their engagement in the colonial labor system, and the process of accommodating and negotiating the boundaries of a new lifestyle on the islands had enabled them to develop new strategies, new ceremonies, and even a powerful new language (Skira 1993: 52). This newly emerging identity permitted these women to engage and negotiate with colonial society as independent agents defining their own terms. Sometimes these negotiations and engagements saw them travel vast distances away from families and all that was familiar. The life of one Aboriginal woman from Tasmania, Renanghi, also known as Sarah Dutton, illustrates precisely the ways in which this agency was developed and deployed.

The Story of William Dutton and Renanghi

In 1828 an Australian-born Englishman William Pelham Dutton ventured into the Bass Strait and Kangaroo Island region, eight years before its official settlement.[4] Dutton had a sealing party that worked the area and collected skins for trade with London and China via Hobart. During this time he lived semipermanently on the coast, building a house and planting a garden of vegetables for himself and for trading. He lived in this manner for five years. After the seal population was reduced, and aware that migrating whales were plentiful in the region, Dutton built a whaling station. By 1833 he was captaining the *Henry*, a small ship owned by Griffiths and Company. According to various ship captains' journals, an Aboriginal woman accompanied him. This woman, whom he called Sarah, had the tribal name Renanghi. She was from Tasmania, but when she joined Dutton it was from Kangaroo Island where she had been living with another sealer. A passing ship's captain gave Renanghi to Dutton after the captain had possibly rescued her from Kangaroo Island. Over time, together they built a whaling station:

> [S]helters would be built on shore; huts for the men, a cookhouse, a cooperage and storerooms; tryworks would be built for boiling down blubber and a ramp for hauling up the slabs of blubber from the beach; and a watchtower or other good lookout post. . . . The establishment of a whaling station was quite involved. A station carried equipment worth thousands of pounds and needed tradesmen of many skills to do the work: blacksmiths, carpenters, shipwrights, bricklayers, coopers, factory hands and the whalers themselves (Broughton 1980).

Renanghi and Dutton lived in a small hut and they had an infant daughter, Sophie. While Dutton was out whaling, usually away for weeks or months, Renanghi managed the whale station. She probably dealt with passing ships and traded with them for provisions in exchange for vegetables from her garden. When the whales were towed into shore, Renanghi was there to assist and work alongside the other whalers. Renanghi was removed from Kangaroo Island by a ship's captain who feared for her life, such was the violence of the man she lived with. After her years as a sealer on Kangaroo Island the work with Dutton, though strenuous, was probably a significant improvement (Mollinson 1976).

In the mid-1830s other white settlers moved into the region. These were re-cently immigrated English people who viewed themselves as "respectable" and were deeply offended by the relationship between Dutton and the Native woman he called his wife. On January 5, 1836, these new settlers forcibly removed Sarah Dutton from her home and sent her to join other Aboriginal people at the gov-ernment mission station while Dutton was away whaling. Dutton never saw her again, though there is evidence that he managed to find his daughter, Sophie; he returned with her and raised her with the help of his recently arrived sister.

In many ways this simple—spare—story of this relationship, both domestic and economic, might be merely an interesting anecdote were it not for one very significant postscript: the story of Renanghi and Dutton is virtually unknown in Australian history. Even Dutton's role as the first white permanent settler in the area known today as Victoria has been virtually erased. Like much of Australia's history, there has been a conscious, perhaps even deliberate, whitewash of this interracial past. However, through fragmentary historical records we glimpse the important presence of Aboriginal women who traveled and worked in the sealing and whaling industries. Here, key roles played by Aboriginal women such as Renanghi disrupt the masculinist history so often written.

The Travels and Adventures of Aboriginal Women

In the 1820s a small number of Aboriginal women traveled from their home in Tasmania by ship, first to Sydney and then on to Western Australia, Mauritius and the sub-Antarctic islands of the southern Indian Ocean. Here the women were contracted to deliver sealskins to the ship's captain on his return in a year or so. Although the captain failed to return to collect them, the women negotiated with another ship's captain and the French colonial government of Mauritius and secured their return home. There is a commonly held impression in Australia that most Aboriginal people in this period were dispossessed onto missions and other reserves and generally did not engage with the colonial system beyond that of being victims of its power. However, as the work of Bain Attwood and Ann McGrath, among others, has shown, many Aboriginal people actively sought the "laboring" opportunities that this new society offered (Attwood 1989, 1999; McGrath, Saunders, and Huggins 1995; McGrath 1987). Aboriginal women's labor in the pastoral industry as cooks and "drover's boys," for example, was crucially important to Australia's economic development.[5] The sealing women of southern Australia demonstrate these interactions with the colonial economy dating back to the very earliest phase of the Australian colony.

In 1832 Quaker missionaries James Backhouse and George Washington Walker were surprised to encounter Aboriginal women who spoke French (Backhouse 1843; N. Plomley 1966: 685; B. Plomley and Henley 1990). These women were among the five who had traveled from Tasmania, along with children and dogs, to Mauritius, Rodriguez, Amsterdam, and St. Paul Islands in the southern Indian Ocean. The decision to travel to the Indian Ocean in pursuit of seals can be understood as an example of Aboriginal women exercising agency and engaging with Newcomers on their own terms. Yet the women's agency was attenuated; they had diminished choices and were restricted in much of what they could do. Furthermore this agency was negotiated and controlled though their labor, meaning they literally negotiated it bodily. The Tasmanian women supplied European colonizers with desirable goods through their physical actions—their sealing labor and expertise. Although the archives reveal only a fragment of these circumstances and their decisions, there is enough there to create a slightly more nuanced picture. Unfortunately though, we do not hear the women's own words or voices in any of the official colonial documentation. Instead, we know about their actions almost entirely through the words of government officials.

At Kings Island in Bass Strait on August 3, 1825, a contract was negotiated between three male sealers and the captain of the sealing vessel *Hunter*. Not unsurprisingly the agreement, although relating to the labor provided by the sealing women, was not signed by them but rather by three male sealers. The men were known as Jack Tyack, Thomas Taylor, and John Seweler, a Tahitian Native. There was an agreement that the women, children, and their dogs would sail to Isle de France and be free to choose where they wished to stay, and this included the option of returning to their homeland. It appears that the women had sexual and possibly domestic relationships with some if not all of these men. The agreement read:

> This is to certify that Thos Taylor, John Seweler and five women natives of Van Diemen's Land are left on Rodriguez Island to remain until the vessel returns from the Isle of France to convey them to the Island of St Pauls [*sic*] and Van Diemen's Land.
> Signed GW Robinson, lodged with John Finniss [the Acting Chief of Court Police, based in St Louis] in Mauritius.

Archival materials suggest that Tyack did not remain on Rodriguez Island for long. Instead, he moved on to Mauritius where he found employment, possibly to help support his family and the remainder of the group. The group remained on Rodriguez Island and nearly a year later the Mauritian authorities believed that they had been abandoned. The colonial authorities were concerned about the situation and continued the documentation with a statement from the sailors. It is not clear whether the Aboriginal women were present when the statement was made or if the women made statements of their own. The official wrote that the group:

> declared that they were shipped at Kings Island, under an *agreement* [my emphasis] to work for the Schooner *Hunter*, with five women and a child who

joined the vessel with them, on the purpose to take charge of their things and assist them at St Paul's Island to process seal skins, to remain on the Island if they chose for their own account, and if they do not choose to remain there or on any other Island.

Apparently en route to Mauritius the group had been placed on various island groups where they had been employed to harvest sealskins. The trip took more than a year. Once they reached Rodriguez Island south of Mauritius they were given provisions for seven weeks, after which time the captain was to return. Over the course of the next twelve months the women harvested seals and preserved the skins, negotiating with passing ships for provisions. However, when French vessel *Les Deux Charles* arrived they were told that their captain had shipped out of Mauritius twice since leaving them on the island and the group assumed that he had abandoned them again, so they secured passage on the *Les Deux Charles*.

From December 1826 for nearly five months the archive is silent. The women were somewhere in Mauritius, presumably within the township of Port Louis. On March 3, 1827, the colonial authority observed that a single child, a boy, was to remain in Mauritius with his father [Tyack] provided "his mother voluntarily allowed him to stay." The official witnessed this in his own office and permitted the boy to remain with his father. Tyack subsequently secured employment in the Office of the Registry of the Admiralty. The Mauritian Colonial Office arranged for the group to be transported to Sydney. On May 12, 1827, Alex McLeay of the Colonial Secretary's Office in Sydney noted they had arrived "on board the *Orpheus* at the NSW government's expense the women, their two children and several dogs." The group was thereafter transported on the *Admiral Cockburn* to Van Diemen's Land for the sum of five pounds.

Unlike Renanghi, whose name has been recorded for history, the Tasmanian Aboriginal women described in the Mauritian and colonial office documents remain mostly anonymous. On March 3, 1827, the government official recorded that "One woman died." Unfortunately he entered no name in his journal; however, on the death certificate he put her name as Wateripitau. In death at least she had a name. Although the descendants of these women recall their names the historical archive has rendered them both mute and anonymous. Despite their labor being crucial to the export industry of sealing, their identities, or personhood, was not. These women, who traveled across the Indian Ocean and returned home, engaged with colonial society at both an economic and a personal level. They made choices and exercised an attenuated agency within the confines and impositions of the Empire. Nonetheless, as Aboriginal women, they were restricted in what they could and could not do. However, they also sought freedoms that, as these examples demonstrate, they sometimes achieved. Perhaps the greatest tragedy is that most of the women, despite their autonomy, eventually spent their days in the government mission station on Flinders Island.

I have shown in this chapter that Aboriginal women's labor was integral to the economic success of the early colonial maritime industries of southeastern Australia. The significance of this labor and expertise held by certain women was that it enabled them to negotiate independent lives for themselves and their children while minimizing government intrusions. Once the need for this labor was removed, as the sealing industry became unsustainable or exhausted through overharvesting, many of the women found themselves unable to maintain their autonomy and were removed to the government mission stations. The tragedy of these missions was that disease was rife and by 1869 there remained only three Aboriginal women (and no men) alive within them. By 1878 the Tasmanian Aboriginal people had been reduced to the descendants of the sealing communities living on the islands, when the last (in the parlance of the day) "full blood" died. The islanders who traced their ancestry from the sealers and the Aboriginal women are today the ancestors of the modern Tasmanian Aboriginal community.

Acknowledgments

I would like to thank the participants at our Trent University workshop for their engagement with my work. I would also like to acknowledge members of the Tasmanian Aboriginal community. I have spoken to many people over the course of this research, and in particular I thank Greg Lehman, Ian Anderson, and Kerrie and Kristel Keheler. Thanks also to Julie Gough. Finally, this paper has benefited from the careful and considered reading, writing, and editorial skills of Dr. Sarah Pinto.

Notes

1. This chapter is a distillation of work I conducted for my book, *Roving Mariners: Australian Aboriginal Whalers and Sealers in the Southern Oceans, 1790–1870*, Albany: SUNY, 2012. The material has been reworked in and reconsidered in terms of women's labor history.

2. Probably the definitive reference to the historical circumstances and development of the contemporary Tasmanian Aboriginal communities can be found in Lyndall Ryan's work. To this day the contemporary Tasmanian Aboriginal Community is the most underrecognized in the country. Sections of the media, and particularly conservative commentators, frequently refer to the "pale skin" of Tasmanian Aborigines, as if this is a measure of their authenticity (Ryan 1977: 27–51). See also her revised and updated *Aboriginal Tasmanians* (1996).

3. See numerous references in Ryan's *Aboriginal Tasmanians* (1996) and Plomley's *Friendly Mission* (1966).

4. The story of Dutton has been deduced from Wiltshire's amateur historical research and a close reading of the Henty Papers, Box SLV119/3, State Library of Victoria, Mel-

bourne. The playwright David Mence has also drawn my attention to collections of material housed at the State Library of Victoria. J. G. Wiltshire, *Captain William Pelham Dutton, First Settler at Portland Bay, Victoria: A History of the Whaling and Sealing Industries in Bass Strait 1828–1868*, revised and reprinted, Portland: Wiltshire Publications, 1994.

5. A "drover's boy" was often a young Aboriginal girl or woman who worked alongside the men during the day and was the object of their sexual attention at night.

Works Cited

Attwood, Bain. *The Making of the Aborigines*. Sydney: Allen and Unwin, 1989.

———. *"My Country": A History of the Djadja Wurrung 1837–1864*. Melbourne: Monash Publications in History, Department of History, Monash University, 1999.

Backhouse, James. *A Narrative of a Visit to the Australian Colonies*. London: Hamilton, Adams and Co., 1843.

Bowden, K. M. *Captain James Kelly of Hobart Town*. Melbourne: Melbourne University Press, 1964.

Broughton, Alan. *The Mills Brothers of Port Fairy*. Melbourne: A. Broughton, 1980.

Little, Barbara. "The Sealing and Whaling Industry in Australia before 1850." *Australian Economic History Review* 45 (1969): 109–27.

McGrath, Ann. *Born in the Cattle: Aborigines in Cattle Country*. Sydney: Allen and Unwin, 1987.

McGrath, Ann, Kay Saunders, and Jackie Huggins, eds. *Aboriginal Workers*. Sydney: Australian Society for the Study of Labour History, 1995.

McNab, Robert. *Murihiku and the Southern Islands: A History of the West Coast Sounds, Foveaux Strait, Stewart Island, the Snares, Bounty, Antipodes, Auckland, Campbell and Macquarie Islands, from 1770 to 1829*. Invercargill: William Smith Printer, 1907.

Mollinson, Bill. *Chronology of Events Affecting Tasmanian Aboriginal People since Contact by Whites (1772–1976)*. Occasional Paper, Psychology Department, University of Tasmania, Hobart, 1976.

Plomley, Brian, and Katherine Henley. "The Sealers of Bass Strait and the Cape Barren Island Community." *Papers and Proceedings of the Tasmanian Historical Research Association* 37.2–3 (1990): 37–127.

Plomley, Norman James Brian, ed. *Friendly Mission: The Tasmanian Journals and Papers of George Augustus Robinson, 1829–1834*. Hobart: Tasmanian Historical Research Association, 1966.

Ryan, Lyndall. "The Struggle for Recognition: Part Aborigines in Bass Strait in the Nineteenth Century." *Aboriginal History* 1–2 (1977): 27–51.

———. *The Aboriginal Tasmanians*. St Lucia: University of Queensland Press, 1996.

Shillingshaw, John J., ed. *Historical Records of Port Phillip: The First Annals of the Colony of Victoria*. Melbourne: Government Printer, 1879.

Skira, Irynej Joseph. "Tasmanian Aborigines and Mutton Birding: A Historical Examination." PhD dissertation, University of Tasmania, 1993.

Stuart, Iain. "Sea Rats, Bandits and Roistering Buccaneers: What Were the Bass Strait Sealers Really Like?" *Journal of the Royal Australian Historical Studies* 83.1 (1997): 47–58.

Taylor, Rebe. "Sticking to the Land: A History of Exclusion on Kangaroo Island, 1827–1996." Masters thesis, University of Melbourne, 1996.

———. "Savages and Saviours: The Australian Sealers and Aboriginal Survival." *Journal of Australian Studies* 66 (2002[a]): 73–84.

———. *Unearthed: the Aboriginal Tasmanians of Kangaroo Island*. Adelaide: Wakefield Press, 2002[b].

Townrow, Karen. *An Archaeological Survey of Sealing and Whaling Sites in Victoria*. Melbourne: Report to the Department of Conservation and Environment, 1991.

Watson, A. A. "A Voyage on the Sealer *Emmeline* and the Journal from Washington Fosdick's Manuscript Preserved in the Museum of the Old Dartmouth Historical Society at New Bedford." *Zoologica* 9.14 (1931): 476.

Watson, Frederick, ed. *Historical Records of Australia*. Series I, Volume IV. Sydney: Government Printer, 1997. 173.

CHAPTER 4

The Contours of Agency

Women's Work, Race, and Queensland's Indentured Labor Trade

Tracey Banivanua Mar

Introduction

She stands in a freshly furrowed field at the end of a row of cane sets ready for planting. She is slightly bent over with a young baby at her feet, and in the background, out of focus and on the periphery of the viewer's vision stands a figure in a horse and cart (figure 4.1). This image would be uninteresting and bleak if not for eye-catching detail. An invisible breeze has picked up and plays with

Figure 4.1. Kanakas–Bundaberg District, circa 1897. Photographer unknown. Image #142325. With permission from John Oxley Collection, State Library of Queensland.

her heavy, mud-laden skirts, creating a dynamic blur as she looks into the lens of a cumbersome nineteenth-century camera before her. The result is a candid image from which her smile radiates toward the viewer in a rare gaze in the history of colonial photography, where women of her color were more often gazed upon and rarely photographed looking back. The image is one of hundreds of photographs deposited in the anachronistically titled "kanaka" box held in the John Oxley Collection at the State Library of Queensland.[1] Numbered 142325, it carries simply a functional and descriptive title, "Kanakas—Bundaberg District, ca: 1897," and like the vast majority of images in the box, little to nothing is known of its origins, the photographer who produced it, or the anonymous figure in the image. Amid hundreds of these images it is this, number 142325, that may be said to have distilled the experiences and contributions of Pacific Island women in Queensland. Moreover, perhaps it is the romantic composition of the image with its passing similarity to the distant but ideologically connected tradition of peasant painters; or perhaps it is the rarity of the smile; or the movement that is captured, but the image also distills the delicacy with which we need to interpret the agency of women working in colonial situations where agency was shaped by contexts of colonization that reached deep into their lives.

The anonymity of the woman in image 142325 reflects the discarded and largely forgotten history of South Sea Islanders, and particularly Islander women, whose predominant experience of colonization was molded by their work as bonded laborers in Queensland throughout the latter half of the nineteenth century. Between 1868 and 1906, over 63,000 Pacific Islanders were taken from, or left, their homes in the western Pacific Islands to labor in the British settler colony of Queensland. Mostly they came from Vanuatu, the Solomons Islands, and the islands around the Torres Strait, and all came under varying conditions of coercion as laborers indentured for three years to white sugar growers. They were technically not slaves in the British Empire's postabolition world. But the thriving trade in their bodies provided the cheap, bonded, and expendable labor that kept colonial sugar industries in Queensland and the western Pacific competitive in a transnational colonial market where slave labor continued to keep sugar production costs low.[2] Outside of slavery, only the bonds of indenture could enable planters to forcefully extract labor the way they did, under physical conditions that produced consistently high rates of illness and fatality among Islander laborers. Throughout this period, Islanders' mortality rates never dropped below five times the rate of white settlers in Queensland, and rose as high as fifteen times in the early 1880s (Banivanua Mar 2007: 131).

For many of the descendants of both those who went to Queensland and those who were left behind in the islands, this working history has been remembered as one amounting to slavery irrespective of the token remuneration workers received, or the extent to which individuals acted with agency. To this extent the memory of the trade as a history of slavery captures the imbalance of power that defined it. This imbalance in turn is reflected in the relative memories of Queensland's settler society, which actively forgot Islanders when the majority was deported from Queensland after 1906 and the Island communities that have remembered. In both the popular historical consciousness of settler Australia, as well as in much work that has theorized and explored settler-colonial histories, the indentured labor trade has been largely ignored. Subject to a double dose of forgetting, Islander women were for a long time subsumed by memories of a largely masculine history. According to Queensland's Pacific Islander labor laws introduced in 1868, only boys and men over the age of sixteen and women who were the partners of recruited men could be indentured. In reality, people of all ages, male and female, partnered or otherwise, came. Only a handful of historians have focused on, and debated the histories of, this trade (Munro 1995; Banivanua Mar 2007: 1–19), and fewer still have considered the experiences and treatment of women, or explored the gendered nature of their work (Saunders 1980). Theirs is a story that can be painstaking to access in the archives, for if Islanders were a subaltern group written out of colonial memory, Islander women were doubly so.

In a contrast that points to the deeply gendered nature of race relations in settler colonial histories, while Indigenous Australian women in Queensland were the specific target of scrutiny from the colonial state so that their lives appear in the archives in invasive detail, Islander women were studiously ignored (McGrath and Stevenson 1996). It was Islander men who were the objects of often inarticulate settler fears of miscegenation that haunted Queensland's colonial history (Anderson 2006). The colonial archive therefore registers few qualitative traces of the thousands of Islander women who labored in Queensland. Historians in the 1970s managed to record invaluable oral histories of the men and women that built the foundations of what is today the Australian South Sea Island community, and from this we have learned something of the physical and emotional hardship of working on and around the plantations (Mercer and Moore 1976; Moore 1979). But still our historical analysis is mostly limited to observing that women were there, too. The ways in which they experienced and adjusted to the impact of a gendered colonization has yet to be explored in available sources.

As other chapters in this collection have explored, and as the images that appear in this chapter further illustrate, colonial photography can be a critical means of filling archival silences. But how do we unpack the images we have? In particular how do we use images that remain anonymous in ways that do not reproduce the effacing and objectifying effect of photography laden with colonial signifiers? With particular focus on image 142325, I reflect in this chapter on how we may read this photography in layers, both as a candid snapshot of the physical world of the past, as well as a more subtle register of that world's ideological composition (Lydon 2010). This is significant in the context of colonial histories in the western Pacific and Australia where Indigenous and colonized women's labor, and their contribution to colonial and colonized societies, has been subjected to the violence of a structural amnesia (Huggins 1995; Curthoys and Moore 1995). For as this chapter argues, and as the particular character of image 142325 illustrates, photography offers not only visual evidence of a barely told history of Pacific Islander women's labor as told through the agency of their physical presentation. In addition, the medium itself, the photograph and its visual language, points in interesting ways to the discursive contours that shaped Indigenous and colonized women's agency. In reflecting on these we gain a deeper understanding of the vertical pressures that structured their lives.

Visualizing Women's Work

> In each furrow [Islanders] remove any tree roots and stones, and after these were carted away the land would be harrowed . . . a two horse team . . . operated by a white laborer, would open up drills five feet apart. Bags filled with cane plants . . . were carted and placed in heaps at the end of the drills, from here the plants were collected in armfuls and dropped in the furrow about one foot apart, the Kanaka walking in the drills pressing each plant in the loose soil with his foot
> —Herbert Turner, in *Rural Life in Sunny Queensland*

While image 142325 has a poetic resonance about it, other images that appear in this chapter are representative of the kinds of candid and posed shots of the working lives of Islander women with which we may now visualize that past. Figures 4.2 and 4.3 show scenes of planting and harvesting, respectively; Figure 4.4

Figure 4.2. South Sea Islander women planting sugarcane by hand at Bingera, Queensland, circa 1897. Photographer unknown. Album APO-32, Image #171280. With permission from John Oxley Collection, State Library of Queensland.

Figure 4.3. Kanaka Women working in the sugarcane. No date. Photographer unknown. Image #12941. With permission from John Oxley Collection, State Library of Queensland.

Figure 4.4. Group of South Sea Island workers on a property in Cairns, circa 1890. Photographer unknown. Album ABO-25, Image #12941. With permission from John Oxley Collection, State Library of Queensland.

shows a mounted white overseer and a group of female laborers. What these and hundreds of images in the public archive offer, is the visual evidence of the profound reliance of Queensland's colonial industries on the labor of Indigenous and colonized peoples from throughout Queensland and the Torres Strait, from other Australian colonies, and from areas of British influence throughout the western Pacific. Through archival and oral sources, historians such as those cited in this chapter have recovered from silence this historical dependence of Queensland's settler societies on labor as a colonizing force while also examining the racialized and gendered ways it was experienced. At a fundamental level, these images bring to these histories a most humble historical fact: that women were there, too. Indigenous and colonized women in Queensland were not only present in the colonial workforce, they labored in a diverse range of occupations, the range of which ran contrary to long-held assumptions that when Indigenous or Islander women worked, they did so predominantly as domestic laborers and were "nearly always given house work and cooking" (Turner 1955: 62). In the case of Islanders, it is true that they were given domestic work, and this is reflected in the textual, visual, and oral records of the period. But their work was also physically diverse and critical to the survival in Queensland of today's South Sea Islander communities. Acknowledging this as a central element of this history is critical to building gender into the histories of Indigenous and colonized peoples' adaptations and resistance to colonization. For the diversity of work, paid and otherwise, that these Islander women did shaped the communities that emerged.

The history of women's work has a limited presence in written archives. Pacific Islander women's labor, more than men's, was more likely to have been undocumented, and not only because for many women, like children, their arrival in Queensland was legally tenuous. In addition from the 1870s, it became more difficult for Islanders already in Queensland to obtain legal employment. Increasingly restrictive laws constrained Islanders' economic and physical mobility in Queensland. By the 1890s, they could not legally seek employment more than thirty miles from the coast, and even then could only be employed in unskilled labor in the sugar industry. Also by the 1890s, Islanders could be employed only under periods of indenture, could not be employed as free labor, and could be deported if they remained out of contract for too long (Banivanua Mar 2007: 75–90). Just because it was illegal, of course, does not mean that Islanders did not actively seek opportunities as diversely employed free labor. But they did so in ways that were necessarily outside the law and therefore less accessible in government archives. This was despite the fact that throughout the nineteenth century, the Islander community was under constant surveillance from a colonial government increasingly nervous about the imagined threats they posed to the whiteness of the colony and Queensland's closely controlled racial boundaries (Saunders 1988; Anderson 2006). While this surveillance recorded valuable demographic detail regarding the size, employment, location, and health of the

Islander community, it also tended to present a laboring history that Islanders, and employers, presented to government inspectors as legal, sanitized, or generic. In 1891, for example, three-quarters of Islander women in Queensland were recorded as being employed under the generic category of "Sugar Growers' Labourer" (587), and a handful were officially employed as domestic labor. Of those who were employed off the plantations in 1891, and who were not "children at home" or "wives" (76 and 31, respectively), the great majority were employed as nondescript "agricultural laborers," "general servants," and "cooks" (4) (*Queensland Votes and Proceedings* 1892: 825).

Although written archives therefore allow some access to the world of work that women entered into when they arrived in Queensland, photos allow us to see and begin to appreciate the physicality of what the majority of women did as "sugar growers laborers" and to begin to gauge its potential impact on peoples' ability to adjust to the impact of colonialism. For this reason it is worth taking the time to observe the physical extent of an average sugar laborer's working day.

Plantation labor, such as that depicted in the images of this chapter, was hot, heavy, labor-intensive and evidently back-bending work—whether it was domestic or field labor (see figure 4.2). Particularly in the early decades of the sugar industry plantation, workforces were large and driven in gangs to clear and prepare sometimes vast areas of land. Plantation sizes varied enormously from 640 acres at Narbrook, to 4,242 acres at Pioneer, or 13,000 at Homebush. With workforces of up to two hundred, plantations were multiracial microcosms of colonial society, often adopting a physical layout of racial segregation and stratification (Mullins and Gistitin 2006; Hayes 2001). This physicality reflected a social makeup on the plantations where European laborers worked in the skilled, free, and higher-paid jobs or as overseers; and indentured Pacific Islanders, small numbers of Malaysian or Chinese, and seasonally engaged Aboriginal laborers did the nominally unskilled work (Wrathall 1884: 409–11; *Queensland Votes and Proceedings* 1889: 150, 174, 194). When women joined these workforces, we know from the occasional written and oral records, and increasingly from visual records, that they did so under the same physical conditions as men.

Field labor in the sugar industry, particularly in the first twenty years of the trade, was on a massive and intensive scale that revolved around a seasonal cycle, and was organized into an average daily routine of "6 A.M. to 6 P.M. and a full hour off at midday and from 6 to 4 o'clock on Saturdays" (Turner 1955: 62–66). The labor that was performed on the plantations is epitomized by the tools Islanders worked with: the "hoe, mattock, axe, digging bar, shovel, fork, stone hammer and of course the cane knife." Islanders were socially and later legally barred from using the less back-breaking machinery amid a convenient attitude that as a race, they "would be no good with machinery. They're too careless" (Turner 1955: 62–66; Lawson [n.d.]: 64). Their tools, in other words, were those of the menial heavy work of clearing, planting, weeding, cutting, and loading. The felling, burning, and clearing of scrub and bush; the uprooting and burning of tree stumps; and the drilling and blasting of rocky and stony ground for cultivation were an ongoing element of plantation labor as new crops were constantly established on land only recently taken from Indigenous owners. During the cooler winter months, which offered respite from the stifling heat and humidity of summer work "consisted chiefly of 'trashing' that is to say, stripping off the dry and superabundant leaves by hand to admit the light and air freely to the lower part of the canes" as well as "banking up the roots, and keeping down the weeds" (Eden 1872: 327). Throughout the seasons, workers' routines consisted in large part of pest control, where pests such as the cane grub of the 1890s were removed individually and by hand from the ground (Turner 1955: 62–66). The most spectacular and frenetic phase of plantation labor, and that which attracted the most literary flourishes at the time, was harvest; the cutting, loading, and carting of cane was done by hand over punishingly long hours for most of the nineteenth century. As Flora Lugard wrote for the *Times*:

> While one row of blue-shirted Kanakas is busy under the waving plume of green, which gradually fell before the advancing knives, another row is engaged in picking the cut cane from the thick litter of leaves amongst which it lies . . . the work is heavy . . . and the bearers sink sometimes knee deep in the trash that lies upon the ground (Lugard 1893: 12).

The photographs discussed in this chapter allow us to visualize the physicality of the labor that Islander women performed in the sugar fields as "sugar growers laborers." Moreover they offer something of a counterpoint to the few written descriptions of laboring Islander women offered by contemporary observers such as Percy Clarke, who wrote in 1886 of the jarring sight of women in the canefields. In language inflected with the racial context he spoke within, he wrote of seeing "big strapping women . . . laughing, shrieking Amazons" and "in picturesque colours [feeding] . . . three great rollers" (Clarke 1886: 295).

While most women who were indentured worked with men in field gangs, younger children and some women were also given domestic work in either the kitchens, or cleaning and nannying for planters' families. In a trend captured photographically by numerous family portraits of white planter families being served by anonymous Islander and Aboriginal nannies and domestic staff, women experienced the power relations of plantations in different ways in the closer confines of domestic service. In important ways, women in domestic service could experience a vulnerability not faced in the fields and enhanced by their isolation and social distance from those engaged in field labor. Those who recalled the experiences of their grandparents and parents in the 1970s were careful to make the point, for example, that while working in canefields was exhausting, its gang nature potentially eased the loneliness and alienation of displacement in Queensland. Working in groups offered some level of protection, support, and experience, particularly for those newly arrived in the predominantly male plantation world and often buffered newly arrived recruits from the potentially more savage discipline of planters and overseers (BOHC 1977: 17).[3] At the same time, however, the closer proximity of a domestic setting, compared to the relative anonymity of working in field gangs, could render ambiguous established colonial divisions while bringing the violence that stalked the canefields intimately into the working days of domestic staff (Russell 2007; Huggins 1995). Reflected in common attitudes that having a "Mary" clean your floors was a guarantee that they would end up dirtier (Clarke 1886: 293–94) the potential for casual violence structured women's working lives in domestic service. As one interviewee recalled of her grandmother's split earlobe:

> The mistress hooked her finger in the lobe and pulled her over to what she wanted her to do (she couldn't understand what the mistress was talking about) and she broke it . . . when we were kids, we saw Grandmother's ear like that. She said that they would get flogged and the little girls were very badly treated too—they were very, very badly treated . . . they were whipped or flogged and made to do what the woman told them (Moore 1979: 33).

While violence was by no means an everyday occurrence on the plantations, it nevertheless overshadowed all work performed by indentured laborers in Queensland—whether domestic or otherwise. The trade itself was a legally and socially sanctioned structure that relied upon the potential for violence as a means of maintaining the viability of the sugar industry at large. In visual ways we can catch glimpses of this in the captured plantation hierarchies of workers and their mounted overseers and planters (see figure 4.3). It is to a reflection on how, with the limited visual record we have, we might gauge the pressures—violent and otherwise—that shaped women's work in the colonial context. For to a significant extent, it is only through this that we can properly appreciate the work Islander women did.

The Shaping of Agency

For much of the life of Queensland's indentured labor trade, its supporters argued that Islander labor was essential because tropical plantation labor would be fatal for white workers. In reality, planters simply would not pay free white laborers enough to do the work consistently and voluntarily. Coercion in other words was an economic imperative. But in one sense the argument was true. The labor did impact on mortality—but not because of the enigma of race. Rather, high rates of mortality and illness plagued Pacific Islanders in Queensland throughout the nineteenth century. Although in the physical prime of their lives, Islanders' mortality remained at 6 percent, with wild fluctuations and peaks, such as during the mid-1880s, when as many as two out of every ten recruits died in Queensland in

their first three years in the colony (Banivanua Mar 2007: 131). Various inquiries
and a Royal Commission concluded that unspecified pulmonary illness and com-
municable diseases such as tuberculosis and dysentery were the most common
cause of illness (*Queensland Votes and Proceedings* 1884; *Queensland Legislative
Council Journals* 1885; Shlomowitz 1987). In other words, while exposure to new
germ environments might partially account for initially high death rates, the conditions that killed were ones that thrived in exhausted bodies. The high mortality
rates did not escape the attention of the colonial state either. Indeed, through the
efforts of organizations like the Anti Slavery Society and the Aborigines Protection Society, various governments in Queensland remained acutely aware of the
physical toll that Islanders paid. Some governments even attempted to address
the problems by legislatively requiring the building of Pacific Islander hospitals
and mandating the recording of all Islander deaths (Banivanua Mar 2007: 121–47).
Yet the mortality rate was never an imperative to close down the trade, but was
rather a latent violence naturalized by the ideological matrix that produced it.
We may detect this in the resonances of images of the period.

Colonial photographs were discursive in their representation of the colonial
world. In the nineteenth century, photographs were structured reflections of an
image created as much by the photographer as by the photographed. As such
they may also be read as mirrors in which we can see both photographer and
viewer reflected in the visual language of the image. In image 142325, the lone
figure planting cane sets in a freshly ploughed and sequestered landscape, bears a
striking resemblance to nineteenth-century visual traditions of romantic artists.
Its composition (intentionally or not) mirrored the iconic figure of European
romanticism's nostalgia for the dignity of labor, *The Sower*. Made famous by
Jean-Francis Millet and Vincent Van Gogh in the nineteenth century, the figure
of the sower was emblematic of contemporary critiques of the social impacts of
the passing of the preindustrial age. First exhibited by the peasant painter Jean-
Francis Millet in 1850–51, *The Sower* along with a host of images of stooped, mostly
male potato harvesters and gleaners, were part of a wider romantic tradition in
western Europe that celebrated the dignity of labor, condemned poverty, and
romanticized landed and seasonal work in a rapidly industrializing world (Van
Tilborg 1989: 9–22). As a critique of Europe's agrarian and industrial reforms,
such romantic scenes of cultivation and harvest—of the dignity of labor—were a
commentary on the ideological traditions or discursive archive on progress and
industry that were readily exported to the colonies. In the British colonies, this
archive underpinned, or naturalized, the so-called civilizing mission and positioned the colonization of land and labor as improvement and progress (Horn
1976; Casey and Rhodes 1977). The composition of image 142325, in other words,
was framed by a wider discursive universe.

Although passing stylistic similarities are a point of interest, the color and
gender shift that inverts—or mirrors—the romantic traditions of peasant painters

offers the greatest opportunity to reflect on the ideological composition of Islander women's world. The Queensland sower encapsulates visually the kind of gendered racialization of Islanders that occurred throughout the nineteenth century, and particularly the taxonomies and rankings that would often arbitrarily rank races in relation to European classes. Michael Davitt, an Irish republican who traveled in Queensland in the 1890s, for example, typifies the social uptake of circulating scientific theories of race and racial difference when he likened Islander women in the canefields to "a Connemara peasant woman digging turf" and added that:

> The Kanakas are very intelligent-looking, both men and women. The men, as a rule, are of moderate stature, averaging five feet six or seven, but well proportioned and strong. The faces are in no way repulsive. They suggest potential passions, however, of a bad kind if provoked into activity. The heads are well formed, and are not like negro heads except in colour. The forehead does not slope inwards. It forms a favorable intellectual comparison with the heads of land laborers among European races. Kanakas are fond of melody, and like to play accordions and other of the simple instruments of music (Davitt 1898: 274).

The practice of reflecting on racial taxonomies based on the singular features of encountered strangers, was a practice frequently engaged in with passing interest by travelers, observers, government agents, planters, and amateur ethnologists alike, and was as unscientific and wildly inconsistent as Davitt's own speculations. But it was rarely arbitrary, and more often it tapped a deeper archive. Throughout the nineteenth century's frequent debates about colonial activity in Australia and the Pacific, it was widely agreed that if labor was dignifying in Europe, it could civilize in the colonies—provided it remained below that which could keep the white working classes alive and employed. As the first planter to introduce indentured laborers to Queensland from the Pacific in 1863, Robert Towns, put it, the introduction of savage but pliable men and women from the islands "would save us from the *inhumanity* of driving to the exposed labor of field work, the less tropically hardy European women and children" at the same time as it would convert headhunting, cannibalistic Islanders to "an industrious, tractable, and inoffensive race" (Towns 1864: 3). His argument was echoed across the political spectrum for the life of the indentured labor trade.

The striking composition of image 142325 and its (quite likely accidental) echoing of a now famous artistic tradition of the nineteenth century draws attention to the ideological composition of the colonial project. The discipline of labor in the Queensland colonial project was notoriously framed as a civilizing force and a means of converting savages into colonial subjects. Hence, while the visage of white women and children laboring in the hot sun was horrifying to colonial sensibilities fearful of an imagined racial degeneration in 1863—so much so that Towns hoped to shock his opponents into agreement at the thought of it—the image of Native and Black women working in the hot sun was an edifying sign of the triumph of colonialism's moral project; particularly when set amid scenes of agriculture that showcased the transformation of Indigenous wilderness into productive settled lands. Image 142325 and the other images that have appeared in this chapter were part of a wider visual and textual conversation that emanated from Queensland in the 1890s and celebrated the triumphant occupation of Queensland and the progressive impact on colonized people of their own colonization. As such, these photos joined the busy production, in the late nineteenth century and beyond, of photographic postcards pitching the desirability of Queensland and other colonial sites as places where land was conquered and available; where bores, wells, machinery, and industry replaced trees; and where "Natives" could be seen either disappearing or being coaxed through progressive states of civilization (Banivanua Mar 2010).

By reflecting on the wider discursive context of image 142325 we are able to read the photograph historically in an enhanced way. By viewing it as a construction deliberately chosen by the photographer at various stages of production, we can contemplate the visual resonances with which the photographer presented, and viewers later understood, the image. Its visual language is historically inflected with its racialized and colonial context. In the case of this image it was a complex of moral, economic, and social imperatives enabling the legal coercion of individuals to work in a regime of labor that extracted an excessively high physical toll. This was the framework in which Islanders exercised their own choices and adjusted, survived, or resisted the pressures of an increasingly aggressive settler state whose growing number of restrictions and levels of surveillance reflected an ever-hardening resolve to create and police a White Australia (Lake and Reynolds 2008; Anderson 2006). This emergent white nationalism of the Australian colonies near the turn of the nineteenth century was the critical context in which we can begin to fully appreciate the nature, limits, and extent of the choices and experiences of Islander women's work.

Conclusion

The physical toll of Islander women's work as sugar laborers during the nineteenth century is well demonstrated by photographs of the period. Alongside the archival glimpses, we can reconstruct that experience to some extent. But these photos also offer passing glances of working women whose experiences were both racialized and gendered—partly because the work they did differed to that of men, as in the case of domestic service, and partly because it did not. Each of the images presented in this chapter so far, and particularly the first, offers telling visual evidence of the way doing the same work as men in the field produced a gendered form of hidden work. In each image of working women in this chapter, the workers were accompanied by children and babies. This was noted occasionally by contemporary observers. In 1898, Davitt, wrote nostalgically of seeing Islander women working in the cane "like a man if not nursing a child" (272–73). Moreover, the children and grandchildren of Islander women have told of, or remembered, their mothers and grandmothers doing field labor beside the men while pregnant or nursing, strapping their babies on their backs while cutting cane, or leaving them in the care of older children while working in the cane fields (BOHC 1974: 10, 17; Fatnowna 1989: 112–13; Bandler 1977: 35).

It was this added dimension of the work women did that proved critical to the way Islanders in Queensland resisted the imposed structures of the indenture system and wider settler-colonial context. Far from playing their part in colonial society as temporary and expendable units of labor, Islanders resisted categorization and containment as merely "Kanaka" laborers. They stayed in Queensland, although they were not permanently welcome, and made lives there. To the growing disapproval, anxiety, and intense scrutiny of settler society, they built homes, planted gardens, led lives, and literally gave birth to communities of permanence. A visual record of this is captured in photos of Islander men, women, and children in studio shots before backdrops of neoclassical Victorian finery, or in their Sunday best, wedding regalia, or outside their huts and homes on the plantations. Their descendants recalled in the 1970s how important portrait shots were as a symbol of autonomy within the colony among this original generation (BOHC 1974). Forming a subtle subversion of a powerful form of colonial surveillance, the images that have been left to us collectively paint a world outside the all-consuming laboring life and offer a suggestion of the autonomous lives Islanders built.

Indenture was legally structured to make work all-consuming in its transformation of individuals, albeit temporarily, into units of labor. Life was fitted in around the punishing time-disciplined requirements of the plantations in ways that it never had been in the islands. As women, female recruits confronted distinct forms of exploitation on sugar plantations, and as mothers they performed work for both employers and their new community. While photographs pay tribute to the strength and autonomy of these women, for each image we must also pay attention to the colonial background to more completely understand their stories. For it is here that the wider social relations and hierarchies of the plantations are captured. These remind us of the violence that was legally sanctioned and embedded in the economic logic of the sugar industry and the predominant ideological context of the colony. As such, these images offer us evidence of the complexity of working women's lives, the agency they exercised, and the discursive atmosphere that shaped them.

Notes

1. *Kanaka* was a generic and usually racially derogatory term used in Queensland and parts of the Pacific to refer to Islanders.

2. The issue of whether the indentured labor trade may rightly be compared to slavery has been a central point of historiographical debate since the 1970s. For an overview, see Munro 1995; Shineberg 1999.

3. Requirements of access to the Black Oral History Collection include maintaining the anonymity of interviewees. For this reason, only tape numbers and no names are referenced.

Works Cited

Anderson, Warwick. The Cultivation of Whiteness: Science, Health, and Racial Destiny in Australia. Durham: Duke University Press, 2006.

Bandler, Faith. *Wacvie*. Adelaide: Rigby, 1977.

Banivanua Mar, Tracey. Violence and Colonial Dialogue: the Australian-Pacific Indentured Labor Trade. Honolulu: University of Hawai'i Press, 2007.

———. "Carving Wilderness: National Parks and the Unsettling of Emptied Lands." Eds. T. Banivanua Mar and P. Edmonds. *Making Settler Space: Perspectives on Race, Place and Identity*. London: Palgrave, 2010.

Casey, Daniel, and Robert Rhodes. *Views of the Irish Peasantry, 1800–1916*. Hamden, Conn.: Archon Books, 1977.

Clarke, Percy. *The "New Chum" in Australia*. London: J. S. Virtue and Co., 1886.

Curthoys, Ann, and Clive Moore. "Working for the White People: An Historiographic Essay on Aboriginal and Torrs Strait Islander Labour." *Labour History* 69 (1995): 1–29.

Davitt, Michael. *Life and Progress in Australasia*. London: Methuen, 1898.

Eden, Charles. *My Wife and I in Queensland*. London: Longmans, Green and Co., 1872.

Fatnowna, Noel. *Fragments of a Lost Heritage, 1929–59*. North Ryde, N.S.W.: Angus and Robertson Publishers, 1989.

Hayes, Lincoln. On Plantation Creek: A Community History of the Australian South Sea Islanders in the Burdekin Shire,. Burdekin, Qld.: Burdekin Shire Council, 2001.

Horn, Pamela. *Labouring Life in the Victorian Countryside*. Dublin: Gill and Macmillan, 1976.

Huggins, Jackie. "White Aprons, Black Hands: Aboriginal Women Domestic Servants in Queensland." *Labour History* 69 (1995): 188–95.

Lake, Marily, and Henry Reynolds. Drawing the Global Colour Line: White Men's Countries and the Question of Racial Equality. Cambridge: Cambridge University Press, 2008.

Lawson, Will. *So Freedom Came*. Sydney: Frank Johnson, n.d.

Lugard, Lady Flora. Letters from Queensland by the Times Special Correspondent. London: Macmillan, 1893.

Lydon, Jane. "'Behold the Tears': Photography As Colonial Witness." *History of Photography* 34.3 (2010): 234–50.

McGrath, Ann, and Winner Stevenson. "Gender, Race, and Policy: Aboriginal Women and the State in Canada and Australia." *Labour/Le Travail* 38 (1996): 37–53.

Mercer, Patricia, and Clive Moore. "Melanesians in North Queensland: The Retention of Indigenous and Magical Practices." *Journal of Pacific History* 11.1 (1976): 66–88.

Moore, C., ed. The Forgotten People: A History of the Australian South Sea Island Community. Sydney: The Australian Broadcasting Commission, 1979.

Moore, Clive. *Kanaka: A History of Melanesian Mackay*. Port Moresby: University of Papua New Guinea, 1985.

Mullins, Steve, and Carol Gistitin. "'Mere Colloquial Things': South Sea Islanders and the Memory of Place." *Community, Environment and History: Keeper Bay Case Studies.* Eds. Steve Mullins et al. Rockhampton: Central Queensland University Press, 2006: 173–92.

Munro, D. "Revisionism and Its Enemies: Debating the Queensland Labour Trade." *Journal of Pacific History* 30.2 (1995): 240–49.

Russell, Lynette. "Dirty Domestics and Worse Cooks." *Frontier* 28.1/2 (2007): 18–46.

Saunders, K. "'The Black Scourge': Racial Responses towards Melanesians in Colonial Queensland." *Race Relations in Colonial Queensland: A History of Exclusion, Exploitation and Extermination.* Eds. Ray Evans, Kay Saunders, and Kathryn Cronin. St. Lucia: University of Queensland Press, 1988, 147–234.

Saunders, Kay. "Melanesian Women in Queensland 1863–1907: Some Methodological Problems Involving the Relationship between Racism and Sexism." *Pacific Studies* 4.1 (1980): 26–44.

Shineberg, Dorothy. *The People Trade: Pacific Island Laborers and New Caledonia, 1865–1930.* Honolulu: University of Hawaii Press, 1999.

Shlomowitz, Ralph. "Mortality and the Pacific Labour Trade." *Journal of Pacific History* 22.1 (1987): 34–55.

Towns, Robert. *South Sea Island Immigration for Cotton Cultivation: A Letter to the Hon. The Colonial Secretary of Queensland.* Sydney: Reading and Wellbanck, 1864.

Turner, Herbert. *Rural Life in Sunny Queensland.* Bundaberg: Glovers Printing Works, 1955.

Van Tilborg, Louis, ed. *Van Gogh and Millet.* Trans. Martin Cleaver. Zwolle, The Netherlands: Waanders, 1989.

Wrathall Bull, John. *Early Experiences of Life in South Australia and an Extended Colonial History.* London: Sampson Low, Marston, Searle and Rivington, 1884.

GOVERNMENT PUBLICATIONS

"Death Rate of Pacific Islanders in 1884–5," *Queensland Votes and Proceedings*, 1884.

"Report . . . Royal Commission Appointed to Inquire into Circumstances in Which Labourers Have Been Introduced," *Queensland Legislative Council Journals*, 1885.

"Report of the Royal Commission into the Sugar Industry." *Queensland Votes and Proceedings*, 1889.

"Occupation of Polynesians. . . . Census of 1891." *Queensland Votes and Proceedings*, 1892.

ORAL HISTORY INTERVIEWS

James Cook University Oral History Collection, Black Oral History Collection, Clive Moore and Patricia Mercer: Tape 7B, Side B, 1974.

James Cook University Oral History Collection, Black Oral History Collection, Matt Peacock interviews: Reel to Reel tape 10, 1977; Reel to Reel tape 17, 1977.

CHAPTER 5

From "Superabundance" to Dependency

Women Agriculturalists and the Negotiation of Colonialism and Capitalism for Reservation-era Lummi

Chris Friday

In 1857, the first agent on the Lummi Reservation in Northwest Washington, Edmund C. Fitzhugh, observed: "their women are industrious, and do most of the work and procure the principle part of their sustenance; they cultivate potatoes, and generally have a superabundance, so that they dispose of a great many to whites. . . . [They] raise a goodly number of potatoes" (*ARCIA 1857*: 326, 329). Such efforts were not part of a federal push to create agriculturalists out of fishers.[1] Instead, agricultural cultivation (including potatoes) was an integral cultural and economic feature of Indian[2] peoples' lives in the greater Puget Sound. Exactly when potatoes became deeply embedded in these cultivation practices is unclear, but by the late 1820s they were common fare throughout the region (Suttles 1951, 1954; Deur 2002; Williams 1996). With the onset of the inland fur trade in the 1820s and the establishment of a European American settler society (circa 1850s), potato production expanded.

Most scholars recognize women as the primary cultivators prior to the reservations, but what happened to the importance of their roles in production after that is seldom addressed. At first glance, it appears that a "masculinization" of agriculture reached fruition by the late 1910s under federal modernization and assimilation programs and cultural imperatives of late-nineteenth- and early-twentieth-century capitalism. By then, federal agents promoted a "Boys Potato Club" in which the boys planted and tended different potatoes varieties until the fall when they exhibited them at the annual Lummi Agricultural Fair. In contrast, agents sponsored, a "Girls Canning Club" to encourage home economics competitions at the same fair (RG 75 Box 205 [*Tulalip Bulletin*] May 1917, July 1917,). Such divisions mirrored middle-class American gender divisions of labor and "civilizing" reforms idealized by federal officials (Deloria 1999: 95–127).

Potato production among the Lummi in the reservation era, however, offers a means to assess Indian approaches to agricultural production, their responses to federal programs, and influences on gender roles. Scholars do not agree upon the role that agriculture played on reservations, but generally recent research highlights the creative negotiation of changes wrought by imperialism and capitalism while recognizing that the policies created a framework for dependency (Leavelle 1998: 433–34; Meyer 1990; Osburn 1985). In terms of the impact of agricultural production on gender roles among Native Americans, the scholarly record is virtually silent, and comparative studies of the issue in developing countries is divided. Some authors find that commercialized agriculture diminishes women's contributions while others hold it allows women to maintain central social and economic roles (Ankarloo 1979; Lewis 2000; McMurry 1992; Wright 1983; Safilios-Rothschild 1985; de Leal and Deere 1979). The case of how Lummi engaged agriculture, with special attention to the gendered implications of potato farming, suggests the negotiation of outside influences through the social and environmental conditions of place (Andrews 1998; Perry 2001; Sahlins 2000; Vlasich 2001).

Lummi and other Coast Salish Aboriginal subsistence patterns were robust, but most scholarship has focused on male-centered salmon fisheries (Boxberger 2000). Salmon were important to Lummi, but a singular focus obscures agricultural production. If as much as 40–60 percent of the caloric intake came from gathering and cultivating activities, the contribution was no small matter (Deur 2002: 20–24, 29; Doolittle 1992; Vibert 1997).

Ethnographic and historical evidence of agricultural production among Coast Salish clarifies women's contributions. Stern (1934) noted that about "twenty-five varieties of berries and sixteen varieties of roots are gathered by . . . [Lummi] women" (51).[3] His description of spring camas harvests demonstrates that women intensively cleared, cultivated, and maintained gathering grounds (42–43). In an early account Gibbs (1877) noted "Inclosures [*sic*] for garden-patches were sometimes made by banking up around them with refuse thrown out in cleaning the ground, which, after a long while, came to resemble a low wall" (186). There were two types of root and tuber cultivation areas. Some were near significant "permanent" village averaging 4 to 5 acres and "owned" by a given clan or village but subdivided into individually inheritable plots (like those Gibbs described) among the village's most influential women who tended and guarded them from incursions. Others were in more distant clearings near seasonally occupied sites and were typically not exclusively claimed (Mike 1927; Collins 1980; Deur 2002: 20–24; Judson 1966: 13–15, 55; Louis et al. 1973; Suttles 1951: 281–82, 1974). These long-standing patterns of intensive cultivation meant Coast Salish women were the primary agents in the incorporation of newly introduced crops—especially potatoes—that came with the sustained presence of European Americans in the late eighteenth and early nineteenth centuries.

Europeans introduced potatoes to the area between 1790 and 1820 and cultivation spread rapidly (Suttles 1951: 272–88, 1987:138–40; Williams 1996: 20–23). By
1840, there were numerous and widespread reports of potato patches among Coast
Salish. Harvests at such plots as well as gathering activities elsewhere were socially
significant for women: Friends interacted and daughters returned regularly to
their mothers' plots to reconnect and to labor for a family economy (Collins
1980; Suttles 1951, 1954). Yields on intensely cultivated plots were significant. One
clearing might produce 12 or more tons of potatoes annually and because of that,
potatoes came to equal wealth and status. Upriver from the Lummi, people would
recall that those with potatoes and flour were "rich" families (Bosler 1973; Charles
1973; Louis et al. 1973; Solomon 1973). Evidence of "first crop" rituals that welded
subsistence (and trade) practices to "religion" illustrate that other foods beyond
salmon were significant (Lambert 1926: 969; Waheneka 2005). Furthermore, at
the 1855 Point Elliott Treaty Council, Lummi headman Chowitsut noted: "I work
on the ground (raise potatoes) and build houses" (Gibbs 1855). House building
was a major sign of one's status and claim to a locale and the link to planting
further suggests that rights to a place rested upon the cultivation of potatoes.

Americans at the treaty council recognized the importance of the crop to Indians. Governor Stevens emphasized: "I want you . . . to be fed and clothed, and
made comfortable and happy. . . . We want to place you in homes where you can
cultivate the soil, raising potatoes and other articles of food, and where you may
. . . catch fish, and . . . get roots and berries" (Gibbs 1855: 4, 7). Stevens may only
have had the barest sense of what potatoes meant to the area's original inhabitants,
but the evidence before him upheld the centrality of the tuber (Harmon 1998: 74;
Williams 2005: 462–67).

On the new reservations federal officials pushed for agricultural development
led by men, but Lummi women continued prior cultivation practices (*ARCIA
1854*: 247–48; *ARCIA 1857*: 326, 329; Suttles 1987: 145). At first, the areas under
cultivation were relatively small. An 1859 survey of reservation boundaries reveals
several potato patches on the survey lines. The largest was 132 by 198 feet (.6 of an
acre) with a likely yield of 2.5 tons (Di Domenico 1982: 3, 8, 23). That same year,
the reservation agent noted that Lummi were asking for additional seed potatoes
and he fretted they "used nothing but *common hoes*, so the mode of cultivating
has been the same as the Indians have always employed." Lummi farmers were,
"very anxious to get a team and plows, so they can go to work on a large scale"
to expand potato production (*ARCIA 1859*: 393, 399). More than conforming
to assimilation pressures, Lummi wanted to open up more lands and generate
greater surpluses.

Throughout the 1860s, farmer-in-charge C. C. Finkbonner regularly reported
potato cultivation. His 1867 report suggests a greater scope and scale of production than in earlier accounts with as much as "150 acres in potatoes and
other vegetables" (*ARCIA 1867*: 59). Subsistence and commercial activities often

involved entire families. Significant cooperative efforts were led by women for farm clearing and maintenance tasks, as well as for seasonal harvests (Hillaire n.d.; Solomon 1973; Wilson n.d.). These were not individual efforts, but those of a community accustomed to group participation in generating surplus for the entire community.

Indian agricultural production was also vital for non-Indian settlers who were "almost entirely" dependent on that source during their first several years in the area and in any lean year (Carhart 1926: 91; Edson 1968: 6, 18, 47, 137, 192). Non-Indian men who migrated to the area hoping to find marketable timber or coal often gained access to prime agricultural lands through intermarriages with Indian women. Such was the case for several of the first prominent men to settle along the Nooksack River to the north of the Lummi Reservation. Marriages not only gave them locally recognized rights to land (distinct from the legal filing for title under the provisions of the Oregon Donation Land Claim Act) but also access to seasonal labor through their wife's extended family. In turn, men marketed the goods produced by their wives and families for export through the local trading post to distant markets in San Francisco (Edson 1968: 137; McDonough 1874–1884, 1874–1913).

Prior to the 1880s and the emergence of the hop industry, potatoes were *the* major agricultural crop in greater Puget Sound. Between the 1850s and 1870s, thousands of bushels (and even tons) of potatoes found their way aboard ships principally bound for San Francisco, where they sold at rates as much as four and five times higher than in the Puget Sound (BBIC March 15, 1874, April 10, 1874, April 18, 1874; Edson 1968: 18, 31, 36, 192; Williams 1996: 22). Accordingly, Lummi expanded agricultural production and sought outside markets. In 1871, they sold over 98 tons of potatoes to the "San Francisco market" via coal ships running south from the nearby coal mine (RG 75, Microfilm Roll 2 [Finkbonner] February 28, 1871; March 31, 1871). That spring, "encouraged by finding ready sale for their potatoes . . . at good prices," Finkbonner noted that many planned "to expand the acres of their crops this spring" (April 30, 1871). That August he reported "most of the Indians . . . [have] scattered off, some in search of game and berries, and others in marketing some of their potatoes in New Westminster, B.C., where they are in good demand at remunerative prices" (August 29, 1871). Potatoes provided cash *and* a way to escape the Indian agent's scrutiny.

By the 1870s, potatoes had become part of the primary subsistence and commercial activities of the Lummi, but their involvement was out of their own volition, not federal pressure to become agriculturalists. Many expressed a desire for assistance from the federal government in order to be more productive (*ARCIA 1863*: 461; RG 75, Microfilm Roll 907 [Finkbonner] April 12, 1866). In 1870 the superintendent at Tulalip reported that the Lummi "want their annuities in future in tools and farming implements" (*ARCIA 1870*: 43). Tribal member Al Charles explained retrospectively that he wanted to return to the days when the local agent was helpful in agricultural pursuits and his disappointment over the cancellation of assistance programs. Suttles and more recently Deur (2002: 20–24, 27–29) argue that scholars have either "ignored cultivation" among Indians or attributed it to "White influence" rather than to long-standing agricultural patterns. That the generation of substantial agricultural surpluses came "without wholesale change" warrants remembering (Suttles 1987: 148).

Lummi translated agricultural production into material rewards through an increase in cultivated lands but in turn grew increasingly dependent on agriculture to generate cash. The masculinization of agriculture attended that shift. Heads of families, by which agents meant men, had become the owners of the lands and its yield rather than women, as had been the case prior to the establishment of the reservation (*ARCIA 1867*: 59). Federal officials and other "friends of the Indian" were explicit. In 1871, Chairman of the Board of Indian Commissioners Affairs[4] Felix R. Brunot held a special council on the Lummi Reservation hoping to consolidate several reservations. Brunot paternalistically likened Indians in general and the Lummi more specifically to "a little child among the white people." Nonetheless, he outlined how that "child" should progress into manhood:

> When it grows to be a man he gets a piece of land and works on it; builds a house, plows one field, after awhile another field; buys a cow and pigs, and they grow while he sleeps; after awhile he becomes a great chief (*ARCIA 1871*: 140).

He claimed that the only way Lummi could hope to keep their lands from whites and grow to "great men" would be to engage in farming and other "civilized pursuits" (*ARCIA 1871*: 140–41). At least in the public forum, Lummi men claimed agriculture. Even though women were present, only two Lummi men spoke on record (both the sons of Chowitsut). David Crocket pointedly told Brunot: "all I want is my land secured to my children, and the implements necessary to cultivate it, that my children may cultivate it when I am dead" (*ARCIA 1871*: 142). By the early 1870s discourse was thoroughly masculinized.

In the 1870s and 1880s agents and Lummi linked agricultural production to self-sufficiency. All spoke enthusiastically of Lummi success as agriculturalists, and of the "natural" productivity of the reservation (Ficken 2005: 499, 454). In the early 1870s, vegetable and potato production accounted for approximately 27 percent of the income generated. The $3,500 earned for those goods sent to market equaled what Indian men earned in a day in wage labor activities (at a nearby coal mine), outstripped income from "canoe service," and dwarfed the mere $300 per year generated by fishing, which would not become significant commercially until *after* 1880 (Buswell 1870). Agents regularly groused about the lack of Lummi commitments to farming, but production grew steadily. In 1887 on nearly 1,100 acres of land Lummi produced 10,000 bushels of potatoes (273 tons) and 3,500 bushels of "other vegetables." They also harvested 18,500 bushels of other grains and some 350 tons of "wild grass" hay, which they used to help feed 643 cattle, 230 horses, 314 sheep, 262 hogs, and 516 chickens (*ARCIA 1887*: 217, 378, 390). For some 300 year-round residents this was impressive and the agent noted, "Many [Indians] depend solely upon their farms for support and take as much pride in their stock and crops as white farmers" (*ARCIA 1889*: 288) (figure 5.1).

Potato harvests peaked in the late 1880s immediately following the allotment of reservation land, largely because of strong local and regional agricultural markets. However, potatoes never really became a "crop" (the lands never exceeded more than about 6 percent of the total cultivated area) under the push for intensified agriculture. Instead, Lummi and the Indian agents consistently associated potatoes with the women's gardens, not men's farms. Potatoes continued to be an important mainstay, but Lummi increasingly looked to sales of other agricultural products for income.

Complicating matters, between 1890 and 1910 Lummi agriculturalists found it difficult to compete in local and regional markets. Lummi called for better machinery and tools from the federal government but when they tried to

Figure 5.1. Thomas Jefferson and Family at Lummi Indian Reservation home place. Photograph #1784, Howard E. Buswell Papers and Photographs Collection. Courtesy of the Center for Pacific Northwest Studies, Western Washington University, Bellingham, Wash. Some Lummi families had substantial homes, gardens, orchards, and farms by 1900.

purchase larger harvesting machines through the Tulalip Agency, the super-intendent balked, leaving Lummi dependent on communal activities such as "work bees" in which multiple families assisted in major projects and harvests (RG 75, Box 98 [Bristow] September 1901, and Box 242 [McCluskey] November 1920). Despite limitations, annual reports demonstrate an overall upward trend in land cultivated with potatoes always in the mix (RG 75, Boxes 311–15). Ulti-mately, however, the lack of capital that restricted the purchase of machinery necessary to compete as commercial agriculturists (*ARCIA: 1903*: 339; Solomon 1973) (figure 5.2).

While cultivated lands and select crops increased, evidence regarding women's roles in agricultural production is contradictory. In 1914 Emma Garrison and her husband cleared, fenced, and plowed an allotment. Initially they cleared 35 acres and had "about three acres in truck garden . . ., [which] took an awful lot of work" (RG 75, Folder 4–7T, Box 190, April 26, 1915). The following winter they cleared nearly 60 acres "patiently by hand with an axe and a brush hook" (December 30, 1914). Emma proudly told the agent, "I want a home perma-nently and something . . . that will be a help to my children" (December, 1914, Folder 5–7G, Box 183). Garrison's letters reveal her ownership and care of the

Figure 5.2. George Boone and three women working Boone's farm at Neptune Beach. Photograph #1, Howard E. Buswell Papers and Photographs Collection. Courtesy of the Center for Pacific Northwest Studies, Western Washington University, Bellingham, Wash. Most Lummi women cultivated small plots with limited technology and the help of family labor. George Boone's well-dressed appearance for the photo suggests a claim being made on women's cultivation.

lands but never once explicitly mentioned her role in agricultural production (November 9, 1914).

A 1909 case reveals expectations. Elias Hoskins requested the early release of his eldest son from the Tulalip Boarding School to help the family. Suffering horribly from stomach cancer (RG 75, Folder 2, Box 99, May 31, 1909), he explained, "I am not able to do the garden work nor any other kind of work to support my family and my wife has a baby to tend to . . . so she can do very little with the garden work [and] my potatoes need cultivating. . . . I want my oldest son to come home as he could help me" (June 11, 1909). His plea reveals that his wife provided unpaid labor necessary to run the small farm and tend the "garden" in normal times, but he claimed the potatoes as his. Likewise, in 1919 Mrs. Richard Ballew petitioned for her son's return from boarding school to help her husband with "plowing and putting in of crops as they are entirely without help at present" (RG 75, Box 242, May 12, 1919). A 1914 Lummi Agricultural Fair photograph shows a row of six seated women readied for a "spud peeling" contest and symbolizes women's embodiment of domestic, reproductive labor while failing to recognize their productive cultivation (figure 5.3). Although the women had not forsaken patterns established by ancestors a century earlier, they were no longer in the

Figure 5.3. Solomon Balch and August Martin behind a group of women at a Lummi Fair spud-peeling contest. Photograph #47, Howard E. Buswell Papers and Photographs Collection. Courtesy of the Center for Pacific Northwest Studies, Western Washington University, Bellingham, Wash. The spud peeling contest reinforced women's domesticity, even as their roles in family economies were substantial.

central position that their grandmothers and mothers had occupied in agricultural production. The appeals and the photograph reveal the "subjugation" to gendered notions of agricultural production and domestic reproduction (Biolsi 1995; Devins 1992; Emmerich 1991; Jacobs 1996; White 1988).

The tenuous position women held in agriculture would erode as the century progressed. Lummi agricultural producers—men and women alike—found themselves without the resources necessary for commercial success because early-twentieth-century farmers needed increasing capital investments to stay afloat (Pisani 1984; Watkins 1996). In Washington State, white farmers in 1910 invested an average $301 in agricultural equipment, but by 1920 the average investment was $831—a 276 percent increase. While comparable data for Indian farms is unavailable, the records reveal that in 1930 and 1940, Indian farms respectively averaged a mere $355 and $390 in farm equipment, barely half of what white-owned farmers invested in those same years and only slightly better than those for white farmers in 1910, suggesting that Indians were not keeping abreast in capital investments (U.S. Bureau of the Census 1942b).

Access to capital was difficult for farmers, Indian or not, but the Lummi Reservation dike project compounded problems. The project had been designed to open up new lands for cultivation but the fees within the district for dike building and maintenance disadvantaged Lummi landholders. As early as the 1930s, Lummi tribal members testified before a U.S. Senate Subcommittee on Indian Affairs (1934): "All this land is now charged with heavy liens for the next 20 years" (17197, 17221). By the mid-1950s, such debts contributed to the loss of reservation lands and the diminution of Lummi agriculture.[5]

In the first three decades of the twentieth century, new transportation systems (roads, highways, and bridges) put Lummi farmers in competition with agriculturalists from increasingly greater distances. Growing capitalization requirements for commercial activities also forced them out of other key enterprises such as commercial salmon fisheries (Boxberger 2000: 125–26). Increased competition did not eliminate Lummi commercial agriculture or fisheries, but only better capitalized enterprises succeeded, leaving Lummi as a whole economically marginalized.

While the slide into dependency was occurring for Lummi agriculturalists, the Depression posed new difficulties, and subsistence agriculture went through a temporary resurgence. In 1933 and 1934, the U.S. Office of Indian Affairs surveyed reservation households revealing that 73 of 114 Lummi households grew potatoes but 67 tons harvested was considerably lower than previous yields (RG 75 [Tulalip Agency] n.d.). Most households harvested 200 to 1,000 pounds and only a few families produced substantially more. These figures reveal the prominence of "kitchen garden" production and household participation in a "family economy" illustrated by patches like that of the Brown family in which members played complementary roles (U.S. Bureau of the Census 1932: 447; U.S. Bureau of the Census 1942: 605; Messer 2000; Thomas 2010) (figure 5.4).

Figure 5.4. Brown family of five posing for picture outside their home at Gooseberry Point. Photograph #237, Howard E. Buswell Papers and Photographs Collection. Courtesy of the Center for Pacific Northwest Studies, Western Washington University, Bellingham, Wash. In the 1930s, Lummi women continued to make vital contributions to their households through cultivation.

Depression-era Lummi potato cultivation clustered around three models. The most common was a nuclear family household—a husband and wife, often with children—representing nearly 80 percent of reservation households. Peter and Winifred Victor, aged fifty-four and forty-eight, respectively, had no others living with them at the time of the survey. From their kitchen garden they stored 300 pounds of carrots, 50 pounds of dried beans and almost 3.25 tons of potatoes from less than an acre of their 22-acre holding (12 "cultivated" acres were in hay and grains). They stored all but 1 ton of potatoes for personal consumption and because no sale was recorded, they likely traded the balance or distributed it to other family members. The pattern of shared labor among women in the same extended family supports this supposition. With the milk cows, other livestock, and poultry, the Victors managed to earn about half their cash for the year from the farm. Winifred supplemented the family income selling arts and crafts, while Peter earned the other half of the family income from wage work.

Likewise, Eugene and Elizabeth Paul, ages forty-two and thirty-eight, and their five children, ages two to twenty-one, owned dairy cows and grew potatoes, corn, cabbage, carrots, and beans. They gathered 2,000 pounds of potatoes from their "excellent" garden and stored half selling the remainder for $15. Like Winifred Victor, Elizabeth contributed substantially, not only through the kitchen garden but also by canning of 200 quarts of fruit, presumably from the family's two pear and two apple trees. Eugene found wage work for 244 days of the previous year while their eldest son worked half the year for wages suggesting they left the daily maintenance of the 67-acre farm to Elizabeth and the children. By leasing 10 acres for $120 and earning $447 from the sale of dairy products and oats, the family did comparatively well.

Records indicate that women headed 13.2 percent of reservation households and fell into two categories: an elder woman dependent on others for land management; or larger, multigenerational extended families of women with children (and sometimes younger couples) residing with an older woman. Representative of the former, seventy-five-year-old Susan Sam planted a garden. While "weeds took it," she harvested 600 pounds of potatoes and stored other vegetables. She kept thirty chickens and earned $25 from knitting "arts and crafts" with wool from ten sheep. Yet Sam relied on her two sons to keep 35 of the 40 acres in her allotment in cultivation. Comparatively younger than Sam, fifty-seven-year-old Amelia Cush oversaw 15 acres of uncultivated grazing land. She harvested 2,800 pounds of potatoes and canned 200 quarts of fruit. Cush stored 800 pounds of the potatoes and sold 400 pounds for a small amount of cash. The remaining 1600 pounds went unaccounted for. Perhaps she gave it to nearby relatives Dan and Justina Cush, ages forty-one and forty-two, to help support their family of ten who harvested only 1,500 pounds of potatoes from their garden.

At fifty-six, Elizabeth Tom represented those women who oversaw large, apparently women-headed, extended-family households. Living with her in the nine-room house were eight others: Eva Edwards (twenty-one); Margaret Johnson (thirty-eight) and her three children (five, thirteen, and fifteen); and Isadore and Laura Tom (twenty-eight and seventeen) and their infant daughter. Elizabeth oversaw a kitchen garden from which she harvested and stored only 220 pounds of potatoes, a small part of the modest $20 of garden produce she consumed. Eva Edwards worked about half the year earning 50 cents a day. Margaret Johnson earned $1.96 a day when employed, but listed none for 1933. Her teenage son showed no earnings. Isadore Tom brought in the most cash—$250 from wage work—while Laura Tom canned 150 quarts of fruit. Elizabeth owned livestock and harnesses, the survey showed no cultivation other than that for the garden. Nonetheless, the household banded together out of need and expectations of reciprocity.

Women's long-standing patterns of agricultural production provided a ready framework during the Depression. Although potato crops did not generate significant cash, they were critical to subsistence, much like the prereservation era (Bosler 1973; Solomon 1973). As had been the case for nearly a century, women working in teams and with their extended families remained vital up to midcentury. Families came together to put up fences, thresh oats and barley, put up hay, and dig potatoes. Aurelia Celestine later recalled: "When they had a . . . bee . . . well they all go and help" (Solomon). Women combined these practices and relied on their own ingenuity to provide significant resources for household economies.

In the three decades following the Depression, the ready availability of cheap staple goods at chain stores and the rising reliance on wage labor (rather than subsistence gathering and cultivating) meant that previous modes of collaborative, woman-centered agricultural production dissolved into occasional and highly individualized practices. Collins (1980) reported on her first 1942 visit to the nearby Upper Skagit people that "traditional" practices in gathering and cultivating were abundantly apparent. By her last visit in 1969, few continued subsistence gathering and cultivation and the attendant sharing of labor (239–41).

In the second half of the twentieth century, Indian women found new areas in which they could assert economic, social, and political influence in jobs created by the Bureau of Indian Affairs and other federal agencies (Iverson 1998; St. Pierre 1991). Yet the history potato production among Lummi suggests tremendous loss. Up to the mid–twentieth century women maintained their roles as subsistence agriculturalists for family, clan, and community economies despite federal emphases on agriculture for men and domesticity and service-sector jobs for women. A host of factors contributed to the "subjugation" of Lummi women to the American political economy (Biolsi 1995, 1998),[6] including changes in American agriculture (Pisani 1984), the privileging of salmon in treaty rights (unmarked as male) over women's gathering rights and agricultural production, and new economic and political opportunities for women. In the end, though, Lummi women lost twice—once with the dramatic assertion of men as the primary agriculturalists in the first century of the reservation (though women did hold some ground as contributors to subsistence), and again with the loss of agriculture itself. This was the path from "superabundance" to "dependency."

Notes

1. The 1855 Treaty of Point Elliott included Lummi, and the U.S. Senate ratified it in 1859 (Kappler 669–73).

2. "Indian," "Native American," "American Indian," and "Aboriginal" are all used within this essay with the same general meaning.

3. When considering subsistence patterns Stern (1934) provides only two paragraphs on women's gathering and cultivation (41–53).

4. President Ulysses S. Grant established the Board of Indian Commissioners as a continuation of an earlier body of Christian reformers who had advised the President on Indian affairs (Prucha 506–7).

5. Construction charges could be $1,000, and operation and maintenance fees could be up to $457 (RG 75, Box 34, Western Washington Agency: 18–21).

6. Biolsi sees subjugation of the individual to class constraints as more critical than gender or race though he holds that each has its own logic (1995: 44–45, n. 3).

Works Cited

Andrews, Tracy J. "Crops, Cattle, and Capital: Agrarian Political Ecology in Canyons de Chelly and del Muerto." *American Indian Culture and Research Journal* 22.3 (1998): 31–78.

Ankarloo, Bengt. "Agriculture and Women's Work: Directions of Change in the West, 1700–1900." *Journal of Family History* 4.2 (1979): 111–21.

ARCIA. U.S. Office of Indian Affairs. *Annual Report of the Commissioner of Indian Affairs.* Washington: GPO.

BBIC. Letterbook, 1873–81. File 1, Box 1. Bellingham Bay Improvement Company Records. Center for Pacific Northwest Studies. Western Washington University. Bellingham, Wash.

Biolsi, Thomas. "The Birth of the Reservation: Making the Modern Individual among the Lakota." *American Ethnologist* 22.1 (1995): 28–53.

———. *Organizing the Lakota: The Political Economy of the New Deal on the Pine Ridge and Rosebud Reservations.* Tucson: University of Arizona Press, 1998.

Bosler, Christie, James McKay, and Rosemary Placid. Interview Transcript 1. June 1, 1973. Tape 42. File 16, Box 3. Northwest Tribal Oral History Interviews. Center for Pacific Northwest Studies. Western Washington University. Bellingham, Wash.

Boxberger, Daniel L. "The Omaha Treaty of 1854 As a Model for the Stevens Treaties." Omaha/Stevens Treaties Folder, Box 34. Northwest Ethnohistory Collection. Center for Pacific Northwest Studies. Western Washington University. Bellingham, Wash., n.d.

———. *To Fish in Common: The Ethnohistory of Lummi Indian Salmon Fishing.* Seattle: University of Washington Press, 2000.

Buswell, Howard E. "Notes on Lummi Indians, 1870 cont." Folder 1, Box 7. Howard E. Buswell Papers and Photographs. Center for Pacific Northwest Studies. Western Washington University. Bellingham, Wash.

———. *George Boone and Three Women Working Boone's Farm at Neptune Beach.* Photograph 1. Howard E. Buswell Papers and Photographs. Center for Pacific Northwest Studies. Western Washington University. Bellingham, Wash.

———. Native American Family ("Brown Family") of Five Posing for Picture Outside Their Home at Gooseberry Point." Photograph no. 237. Howard E. Buswell Papers and Photographs. Center for Pacific Northwest Studies, Western Washington University, Bellingham, Wash.

———. *Solomon Balch and August Martin behind a Group of Women at a Lummi Fair Spud Peeling Contest.* Photograph 47. Howard E. Buswell Papers and Photographs. Center for Pacific Northwest Studies. Western Washington University. Bellingham, Wash.

Carhart, Edith Beebee. *A History of Bellingham, Washington: Compiled from Newspaper Articles, Directories and Books of Local History.* Bellingham, Wash: Argonaut Press, 1926.

Charles, Al. Interview Transcript. April 26, 1973. Tape 23. Folder 5, Box 3. Northwest Tribal Oral History Interviews. Center for Pacific Northwest Studies. Western Washington University. Bellingham, Wash.

Collins, June M. *The Valley of the Spirits: The Upper Skagit Indians of Western Washington.* Seattle: University of Washington Press, 1980.

de Leal, Magdelena Leon, and Carmen Diana Deere. "Rural Women and the Development of Capitalism of Columbian Agriculture." *Signs* 5.1 (1979): 60–77.

Deloria, Philip J. *Playing Indian.* New Haven: Yale University Press, 1999.

Deur, Douglas. "Plant Cultivation on the Northwest Coast: A Reconsideration." *Journal of Cultural Geography* 19.2 (2002): 9–35.

Devins, Carol. "'If We Get the Girls, We Get the Race': Missionary Education of Native American Girls." *Journal of World History* 3.2 (1992): 219–37.

Di Domenico, Thomas. Transcribed from Microfilm. *Original Surveyor's Notes for Townships 38 and 39N, Range 1, 2, 3E, and Township 40N, Range 2E, 1859–1873.* 1982. File 8, Box 11. Center for Pacific Northwest Studies Pamphlet Collection. Center for Pacific Northwest Studies. Western Washington University. Bellingham, Wash.

Doolittle, William E. "Agriculture in North America on the Eve of Contact: A Reassessment." *Annals of the Association of American Geographers* 82.3 (1992): 386–401.

Edson, Lelah Jackson. *The Fourth Corner: Highlights from the Early Northwest.* Bellingham, Wash: Whatcom Museum of History and Art, 1968.

Emmerich, Lisa E. "'Right in the Midst of My Own People': Native American Women and the Field Matron Program." *American Indian Quarterly* 15 (Spring 1991): 201–16.

Ficken, Robert E. "After the Treaties: Administering Pacific Northwest Indian Reservations." *Oregon Historical Quarterly* 106.3 (2005): 442–61.

Gibbs, George. "Gibbs Journal, Tuesday, January 16, 1855." File 17, Box 17. Northwest Ethnohistory Collection. Center for Pacific Northwest Studies. Western Washington University. Bellingham, Wash.

———. *Tribes of Western Washington and Northwestern Oregon.* Washington: Government Printing Office, 1877.

Gibson, James R. *Feeding the Russian Fur Trade: Provisionment of the Okhotsk Seaboard and the Kamchatka Peninsula, 1639–1856.* Madison: University of Wisconsin Press, 1969.

Harmon, Alexandra. *Indians in the Making: Ethnic Relations and Indian Identities around Puget Sound.* Berkeley: University of California Press, 1998.

Hillaire, Frank. Witness for the Plaintiff. United States. Court of Claims. *Duwamish et al.* File 6, Box 46. Northwest Ethnohistory Collection. Center for Pacific Northwest Studies. Bellingham, Wash., n.d.

Iverson, Peter. *We Are Still Here: American Indians in the Twentieth Century.* Wheeling, Ill.: Harlan Davidson, 1998.

Jacobs, Margaret D. "Making Savages of Us All: White Women, Pueblo Indians, and the Controversy over Indian Dances in the 1920s." *Frontiers: A Journal of Women's Studies* 17.3 (1996): 178–209.

Judson, Phoebe Goodell. *A Pioneer's Search for an Ideal Home: A Book of Personal Memoirs.* Tacoma: Washington State Historical Society, 1966.

Kappler, Charles. J. "Treaty with the Dwamish, Squamish, 1855, January 22, 1855, 12 Stat. 927, Ratified March 8, 1859, Proclaimed April 11, 1859." *Indian Affairs: Laws and Treaties, Vol. II: Treaties.* Comp. and ed. Charles J. Kappler. Washington: GPO, 1904. 669–73.

Lambert, Eva Charroin. "The Nuh-Lummis Indians." *History of Whatcom County: Volume II.* Lottie Roeder Roth. Chicago: Pioneer Historical Publishing Company, 1926. 963–78.

Leavelle, Tracy Neal. "'We Will Make It Our Own Place': Agriculture and Adaptation at the Grande Ronde Reservation, 1856–1887." *American Indian Quarterly* 22.4 (1998): 433–56.

Lewis, Kathleen Phillips. "Women in the Trinidad Cocoa Industry, 1870–1945." *Journal of Caribbean History* 34.1–2 (2000): 20–45.

Louis, Joe, and Nooksack Women. Interview Transcript, Part II. May 1, 1973. Tape 36. Folder 13, Box 3. Northwest Tribal Oral History Interviews. Center for Pacific Northwest Studies. Western Washington University. Bellingham, Wash.

McDonough, Bernard N. Business Records, 1874–1913. Howard E. Buswell Papers and Photographs. Center for Pacific Northwest Studies. Western Washington University. Bellingham, Wash. "Notes on the McDonough Business Records." File 5, Box 8.
———. "Account Books." 1874–1884. Boxes 15 and 16.
McMurry, Sally. "Women's Work in Agriculture: Divergent Trends in England and America, 1800 to 1930." *Comparative Studies in Society and History* 34.2 (1992): 248–70.
Messer, Ellen. "II.B.3.—Potatoes (White)." *The Cambridge World History of Food*. Eds. Kenneth F. Kiple and Kreimhild Conee Ornelas. New York: Cambridge University Press, 2000. February 2010. http://www.cambridge.org/us/books/kiple/potatoes.htm (accessed January 2012).
Meyer, Melissa. "Signatures and Thumbprints: Ethnicity among the White Earth Anishinaabeg, 1889–1920." *Social Science History* 14.3 (Fall 1990): 305–45.
Mike, Louis. Witness for the Plaintiff. United States. Court of Claims. *Duwamish et al.* File 6, Box 46. Northwest Ethnohistory Collection. Center for Pacific Northwest Studies. Bellingham, Wash., 1927.
Moodie, D. Wayne, and Barry Kaye. "Indian Agriculture in the Fur Trade Northwest." *Prairie Forum* 11.2 (1986): 171–83.
Osburn, Katherine M. B. "The Navajo at Bosque Redondo: Cooperation, Resistance, and Initiative, 1864–1868." *New Mexico Historical Review* 60.4 (1985): 399–413.
Perry, Adele. *On the Edge of Empire: Gender, Race, and the Making of British Columbia, 1849–1871*. Toronto: University of Toronto Press, 2001.
Pisani, Donald J. *From the Family Farm to Agribusiness: The Irrigation Crusade in California and the West, 1850–1931*. Berkeley: University of California Press, 1984.
Prucha, Francis Paul. *The Great Father: The United States Government and the American Indians, vol. I*. Lincoln: University of Nebraska Press, 1984.
Raibmon, Paige. *Authentic Indians: Episodes of Encounter from the Late-Nineteenth-Century Northwest Coast*. Durham: Duke University Press, 2005.
RG 75. Records of the Bureau of Indian Affairs. Record Group 75. National Archives and Records Administration. Seattle, Wash. Puget Sound Agency: Microfilm Roll 2.
———. Tulalip Agency: Folder 1, Box 98; Folder 2, Box 99; Folder 5–7G, Box 183; Folder 4–7T, Box 190; Folder 6b, Box 205; Folder 11–12b, Box 210; Folder 5–11f, Box 236; Folder 1-C, Box 242; "Annual Reports," Boxes 311–15.
———. Washington Superintendency: Microfilm Roll 907.
———. Western Washington Agency: Box 34.
Roth, Lottie Roeder. *A History of Whatcom County. vol. II*. Chicago, Ill.: Pioneer Historical Publishing Co., 1926.
Safilios-Rothschild, Constantina. "The Persistence of Women's Invisibility in Agriculture: Theoretical and Policy Lessons from Lesotho and Sierra Leone." *Economic Development and Cultural Change* 33.2 (1985): 299–318.
Sahlins, Marshall. "Cosmologies of Capitalism: The Trans-Pacific Sector of 'The World System.'" *Culture in Practice: Selected Essays*. Ed. Marshall Sahlins. New York: Zone Books, 2000. 415–70.
Solomon, Felix, Dora Solomon, Angeline Alexander, and Aurelia Celestine. Interview Transcript 1. April 13, 1973. Tape 25. Folder 6, Box 3. Northwest Tribal Oral History Interviews. Center for Pacific Northwest Studies. Western Washington University. Bellingham, Wash.

Stern, Bernard J. *The Lummi Indians of Northwest Washington*. New York: Columbia University Press, 1934.

St. Pierre, Mark. *Madonna Swan: A Lakota Woman's Story—As Told through Mark St. Pierre*. Norman: University of Oklahoma Press, 1991.

Suttles, Wayne. "The Early Diffusion of the Potato among the Coast Salish." *Southwestern Journal of Anthropology* 7.3 (1951): 272–88.

———. "Post-Contact Culture Changes among the Lummi Indians." *British Columbia Historical Quarterly* 18.1–2 (1954): 29–102.

———. *Coast Salish and Western Washington Indians: The Economic Life of the Coast Salish of Haro and Rosario Straits*. New York: Garland, 1974.

———. *Coast Salish Essays*. Seattle: University of Washington Press, 1987.

Thomas, G. "Hidden Treasure: Potato World." *International Year of the Potato. 2008*. Trans. M-T. Brun, J. Gong, Y. el-Jaber, and R. Nuñez. U.N. Office in Belarus, February 1, 2010. http://www.potato2008.org/en/world/index.html (accessed January 2012).

United States. Bureau of the Census. "County Table V." *Fifteenth Census of the United States: 1930, Agriculture, Volume II, Part 3*. Washington: GPO, 1932.

———. "County Table XV." *Sixteenth Census of the United States: 1940, Agriculture, Volume 1, Part 6*. Washington: GPO, 1942.

———. "State Table 12." *Sixteenth Census of the United States: 1940, Agriculture, Volume 1, Part6*. Washington: GPO, 1942.

United States. Cong. Senate. Subcommittee of Committee on Indian Affairs. *Survey of Conditions of the Indians in the United States: Part 32, Idaho and Washington*. 1934. 72nd cong. 1st sess. Washington: GPO, 1934.

Vibert, Elizabeth. *Traders' Tales: Narratives of Cultural Encounters in the Columbia Plateau, 1807–1846*. Norman: University of Oklahoma Press, 1997.

Vlasich, James A. "Postwar Pueblo Indian Agriculture: Modernization versus Tradition in the Era of Agribusiness." *New Mexico Historical Review* 76.4 (2001): 353–81.

Waheneka, Et-twaii-lish Marjorie. "Indian Perspectives on Food and Culture." *Oregon Historical Quarterly* 106.3 (2005): 468–74.

Watkins, Marilyn P. *Rural Democracy: Family Farmers and Politics in Western Washington, 1890–1925*. Ithaca: Cornell University Press, 1996.

White, Richard. *The Roots of Dependency: Subsistence, Environment, and Social Change among the Choctaws, Pawnees, and Navajos*. Lincoln: University of Nebraska Press, 1988.

Williams, Jacqueline B. "Potatoes: A Washington Tradition." *Columbia* 10.3 (1996): 20–23.

———. "Picturing Food and Power at the Treaty Councils." *Oregon Historical Quarterly* 106.3 (2005): 462–67.

Wilson, John Andrew. Witness for the Plaintiff. United States. Court of Claims. *Duwamish et al.* File 6, Box 46. Northwest Ethnohistory Collection. Center for Pacific Northwest Studies. Bellingham, Wash., n.d.

Wright, Marcia. "Technology, Marriage, and Women's Work in the History of Maize-Growers in Mazabuka, Zambia: A Reconnaissance." *Journal of Southern African Studies* 10.1 (1983): 71–85.

CHAPTER 6

"We Were Real Skookum Women"

The shíshálh Economy and the Logging Industry
on the Pacific Northwest Coast

Susan Roy
Ruth Taylor

> *The name Sechelt comes from chat-lich or "going over logs."*
> —shíshálh elder Gilbert Joe, in tems swiya Museum display,
> Sechelt First Nation

On prominent display in the Sechelt First Nation's tems swiya Museum is a large photograph depicting a group of shíshálh women—Mary Joe, Violet Jeffries, Mary Anne Jeffries, Carrie Joe, and Madeline Joe—rolling cedar logs down the mountainside in the early 1940s (figure 6.1). The women hold sticks designed for the task, and Mary Anne Jeffries, who stands in the center, displays the large handsaw used to cut the tree into more manageable sections. Carrie Joe provides the explanation for the image: "We used to make our own wood in them days. We even cut the tree down, hand logged, sawed it by handsaw. We took all of the blocks down with these things rolling them." She adds, reflecting on the power and strength of a previous generation of women and on her own youth, "We were real skookum women. Today I couldn't do it" (tems swiya Museum).[1] The image is part of a series of community-produced photographs that capture shíshálh people working in various capacities in British Columbia's forestry and fishing industries during the twentieth century. Throughout shíshálh traditional territory, on what is now known as British Columbia's Sunshine Coast, the shíshálh participated in the logging industry, first as hand loggers and wage earners of small logging enterprises that operated along the coast, and later as employees in much larger industrial logging operations. "The Sechelt nation were hand loggers for many years because timber was so plentiful right from the edge of the water up," explained Gilbert Joe. "The Sechelt Band members have production second to none in their modern high-lead logging industry. We've got records that have never been beaten" (tems swiya Museum). The shíshálh's ongoing use

Figure 6.1. Mary Joe, Violet Jeffries, Mary Anne Jeffries, Carrie Joe, and Madeline Joe rolling large cedar sections at Sechelt, 1939. tems swiya Museum Photography Collection. #10.016. Reproduced with permission of the Sechelt First Nation.

of the coastal forest and contributions to the logging industry is a major theme of the community's museum display.

But for many non-Aboriginal museum spectators, the image of women engaged in forestry presents an *unexpected* history, to use Philip Deloria's term (2004), and challenges the Western association of Indigenous peoples with a "traditional" economy in a pristine forest. Museum visitors are surprised to see women—especially ones who in other respects seem to comply with the mores of their time—out in the woods hauling logs. The photograph disrupts the Western dichotomy that separates economy from culture, workplace from domestic sphere, manly from feminine, and—importantly—forest from home. Instead, the photograph suggests a more complex relationship to the coastal rain forest and to the range of women's economic and cultural activity. It is evidence of the persistence of a shíshálh economy organized by the specific relationships that connected shíshálh families to the territory.[2]

A second photograph, also from the tems swiya Museum, depicts an intergenerational group of women—Ellen Paul, Christine Julian, Janet Louie, and Mary Ann Jeffries—sitting on the grass in front of the Paul home, engaged in basket making, conversation, and child minding (figure 6.2). shíshálh women became well known in the Pacific Northwest as expert and sought-after cedar-root basket weavers, also a dominant theme of shíshálh self-representation in their museum. The scene suggests that basketry and other "handicraft" production fit easily and neatly into women's daily, and largely domestic, lives. Such home-based production could be readily picked up while women were engaged with other "reproductive" work, such as caring for children. A viewer might see the image as clearly gendered female: "light" work perceived as supplementary to the family economy and, unlike logging, negligible to the provincial economy.

But was this really the case? As these photographs suggest, the labor of women—and men, for that matter—and their role in the economic and cultural strategies of the shíshálh was much more complex than the above interpretation allows. Indian Agent Earl Anfield reported, for example, that in 1944 Sechelt and Cowichan women made a substantial income from the production of hand-knit Cowichan sweaters—more in a week than during an entire season working at

Figure 6.2. Ellen Paul, Christine Julian, Janet Louie, and Mary Anne Jeffries, with the young boy Val August, making cedar-root baskets in front of the Paul home, 1940. tems swiya Museum Photography Collection. #2.008. Reproduced with permission of the Sechelt First Nation.

the Rivers Inlet canneries in northern British Columbia (Anfield 1944). As many scholars have pointed out, the wage-labor, subsistence, and cultural-production work of Coast Salish women was integral to family and community survival. They produced goods for extended family and community use and brought in hard cash, enabling both survival and the persistence of Indigenous economies (Sparrow 1976; Williams 2005; Raibmon 2005; Lutz 2006, 2008).

The concepts of masculinized "logging" and feminized "basket making" grew largely from the colonial logic of gender normativity and separate spheres of activity. In the colonial view, men were expected to participate in industry, independently or as wage laborers, and women, in home-based cottage production—both strategies, in the minds of non-Natives, by which Aboriginal peoples could enter the modern economy and become self-sufficient, individualized wage earners in the capitalist market. This division brought with it a series of gender-inflected dualities: strong/delicate, dangerous/safe, forestry/gathering, commercial/subsistence, active/passive, production/reproduction, public/domestic, and so forth.

From the shíshálh point of view, however, there is not a rigid conceptual distinction between the labor required for logging and that required for basket production, nor is there the conventional Western notions of industry that distinguish between the harvest (trees and plants) and the product (baskets, shingles, logs, and firewood, for example). While men and women certainly performed different roles within the family, their spheres overlapped and were complementary. Just as shíshálh women contributed to forestry, men participated in the cultural production of baskets. They dug roots and drove boats to the city, where the baskets were sold. This paper argues that these two activities—logging and basket making—as well as other forest-based production, should be considered together, as related activities that are central to the shíshálh culture and economy. The element that unites them is the coastal forest, and within that, the cedar tree. Seen in this light, an industrial practice such as logging is also the extension of a long-standing relationship to the coastal forest. In the context of restrictive legislation limiting Indigenous peoples' participation in the industrial economy of the twentieth century, long-standing relationships to territory, established and maintained through Indigenous legal frameworks, continued to inform community and family economic strategies (Menzies and Butler 2000, 2008). Forest production was a family venture, and women's role in it not only contributed significantly to the shíshálh economy but also helped maintain women's larger connections to kin networks, cultural and ceremonial practices, land- and water-based resources, and shíshálh territory.

Much shíshálh oral history describes the shíshálh women of earlier generations as ambitious, smart, strong, powerful, or *skookum*, a Chinook word meaning all of those things. "The women worked hard. They are the ones that kept the family together at Deserted Bay, Salmon Arm, and all these places," concurs Benny Joe (tems swiya Museum). These expressions were a kind of shorthand for the range of contributions made by shíshálh women, who resisted, adapted, and survived the challenges and constant shifts of colonialism, a system that outlawed traditional ceremony, sent children to residential schools to transform them into Christian citizens, restricted residency to small Indian reserves, placed women under the gender discrimination of the *Indian Act*, alienated traditional lands and resources, and pressed women—through education, incentives, and prohibitions—to pursue those economic activities deemed appropriate to their race and gender. In spite of this rupture and displacement, shíshálh women and their families, like other Indigenous peoples on the Pacific Northwest Coast, developed mixed-economy strategies and incorporated a wide variety of economic and cultural activities into their work.

This paper is inspired by the photographs and oral histories describing shíshálh labor—the work of women and their families, including men—described above. The Sechelt First Nation has a well-established research program in support of land and resource management, cultural and language revitalization, education, and the tems swiya Museum, which presents shíshálh history and culture for tourists visiting the coastal community, emphasizing the shíshálh's enduring relationship with cedar and ties to the territory. Such public displays, which are also performances of unified community identity and history, are linked to internal initiatives aimed at securing state and public recognition of Aboriginal title and rights, increased control over the management of natural resources, and restitution of traditional lands. In British Columbia, unlike other areas of Canada where treaties were negotiated with First Nations, the state followed a policy of setting apart small Indian reserves at a reduced number of locations where Aboriginal people resided and/or fished. Aboriginal communities look at their history in terms of the assertion of rights, the continuity of the kin-based structures that organize rights and privileges of access to land and resources, and the minutia of colonial processes and dislocations as played out on the ground. Labor, widely conceived, is a central structure in the expression of these rights, but it is also an expression of colonial dislocations. Logging or any other industrial activity by non-Natives is typically framed as "infringement" of title or "alienation" of lands. And since Western legal interpretive frameworks demand evidence of ongoing Indigenous use and occupancy of territories, usually through "laboring" the land, the diversity and breadth (both geographical and sectoral: resource extraction, manufacture, commerce) of both women's and men's work is a focus of inquiry.

This does not mean that community-based researchers are impervious to the risk of imposing Western theoretical frameworks on their subjects (for example, by confining research to expectations surrounding women's cultural and economic activity, or by distinguishing "subsistence" from "commercial" activity) that limit greater understanding of the mixed-economy and resource-management strategies of Aboriginal women and the wider community. But the Sechelt "archive"—its oral histories, visual records, and historical documents—allows a vision of historical transformation and continuity from the perspective of a localized Indigenous community and prioritizes community-based research and concerns.

The Sechelt First Nation

shíshálh people today are the descendents of a number of interrelated peoples associated with different places—including xénichen, ts'únay, téwánkw, and sxixus—who spoke sháshishálem and occupied the lands in southern coastal British Columbia in what is today called Jervis Inlet.

shíshálh peoples knew (and know) this territory as an integrated physical, temporal, and spiritual landscape full of natural and supernatural beings and marked with significant places and sacred sites (figure 6.3). People lived in a spiritually animated and sometimes dangerous world: oral histories speak of logging camps, gardens, and food caches being invaded by foul-smelling *smaylah*, or sasquatches, and other mysterious creatures. shíshálh people participated in a large regional network of relations and alliances that reached throughout and beyond the territory. They moved through this land- and waterscape on seasonal journeys to exploit resource sites, visit relatives, and participate in ceremonial and political culture. The region's waterways and rain forest provided numerous marine and land resources, and, importantly, timber—the focus of this study— used to make large plank houses, monumental carvings, baskets, firewood, and

Figure 6.3. Map of shíshálh territory within British Columbia, 2009. Reproduced with permission of the Sechelt First Nation.

canoes. shíshálh hunters, gatherers, and fishers needed the ritual and cultural knowledge to locate and obtain these resources, as well as the appropriate kin connections to access resource sites and trading networks (Sechelt First Nation 2007; Kennedy and Bouchard 1990). Such knowledge, including songs, chants, prayers, affiliations with spiritual nonhuman beings, and oral traditions, are not aspects of most Western economic models.

In Coast Salish society the rights to status, names, and other hereditary prerogatives were organized through bilateral descent. People with shared ancestors were members of a kin-based group, or "family," that comprised the primary corporate group and structured access to resources and land (Miller 2007: 19). Colonialism brought intense challenges to kin-based society—and to women's standing within it. *Indian Act* policies that prioritized male heads of households as leaders, denied legal Indian status to women who married non-Natives, and discriminated in numerous other ways against women were particularly challenging to the maintenance of bilateral patterns of descent, status, and privilege, and generally destabilized shíshálh women's authority and power. As Theresa Jeffries explains (1992: 93), "These actions of government served to create divisions not only in the community but within and between families." In this context, shíshálh people, like other Aboriginal peoples in Canada, engaged in legitimizing and relegitimizing their familial identities, sometimes in ways that reaffirmed women's status and power and sometimes in ways that proved devastating and violent (Fiske 1991; Lawrence 2004; Kelm and Townsend 2006).

Despite the impositions of the *Indian Act*, access to resources and lands, including reserve lands, were still organized around family connections to the territory, if in a transformed state. For example, in 1927, Tel-es-cl-wet, a shíshálh woman, described the significance of a pictograph at Agamemnon Channel: "Each family of note," she said, "had its totem or family mark. . . . These totems were always marked within certain well defined districts, which were regarded as preserves for the families." She added, "These preserves were regarded as sources of food supplies to the families, who were known to have hunting and fishing right[s] therein, and anyone caught trespassing was dealt with according to the chief's wishes" (Smith 1927). Even harvested timber was identified as the property of an individual family. Madeline Joe described the practice in the 1930s (Joe and Joe interview 1997): "And they [women] tie up their cedar shakes, they make them long like as high as the house going to be, eight feet, tie a bundle, big bundle like this, tie it together and each family's got their own colour of tie so they know who's who, who owns it." Such markers and colored flags can be viewed as a manifestation of family property rights and the association of groups with the lands and resources of specific areas of the territory. Women were a primary force in defending and preserving these ties to territory and were often recognized as such within their communities. In Benny Joe's words, cited above, "Women kept the family together at these places." Despite colonialism's attempts to shatter Indigenous cultures, legal frameworks, and economies, Indigenous principles and systems persisted (Borrows 2002).

shíshálh Hand Logging and the Colonial Regime

In the 1860s, the establishment of sawmills in Burrard Inlet, a short distance south of shíshálh territory, led to the intense logging of Jervis Inlet and to the eventual depletion of forestry resources. Early on, however, the shíshálh took advantage of emerging economic opportunities that accompanied European settlement. In 1852, for example, the shíshálh attempted to sell split-cedar shingles to the Hudson's Bay Company coal mining operations in Nanaimo on the adjacent Vancouver Island coast at prices the Bay men found extravagant (McKay 1852). shíshálh families supplied timber to the sawmills, as Gilbert Joe explained (interview September 1979), prioritizing male labor, "A lot of the timber that our forefathers hand logged were used to build up Vancouver." Logging was a significant activity, as suggested by the wide range of sháshishálem words describing its processes. According to Chris Julian (interview 1979), *xi'xixits-nach*, hand logging, involved felling a tree and shaving the bark off one side, a technique called *lhekw'iwesáls*, or log barking, so that it would skid or slide down the hill into the water, where it was gathered together in a *schek '* (log boom).

When the shíshálh found that non-Aboriginal interest in forestry resources challenged their sovereignty, they took more dramatic measures to ensure control of the territory. In 1874, a group of shíshálh men armed with muskets drove several white hand loggers from Jervis Inlet. Registrar General A. T. Bushby, who investigated the incident, reported (1874) that "Chief Sheel" opposed the granting of preemptions and timber leases in the Inlet and that the shíshálh "became alarmed lest the Whites should monopolize what they considered to be their own by right." As the demand for logs grew, the shíshálh competed with white loggers for timber leases and control of their resources. From 1876 to 1877, shíshálh representatives repeatedly petitioned the Indian reserve commission for two timber reserves. The commission recommended, without success, that the shíshálh be ensured timber reserves where they would have "the right, exclusively to themselves, of cutting timber" (Anderson, McKinlay, and Sproat 1876).

By the late 1880s, most, if not all, shíshálh men were involved in logging—either working with the support of their families as independent hand loggers or employed in non–Native-owned logging operations within the traditional territory. Well into the twentieth century, Indian Agents reported that visiting the shíshálh to conduct business proved impractical before June, because they were "all away logging in different places" (McDonald 1904; Ball 1933). The shíshálh, like other Aboriginal and non-Aboriginal hand loggers, obtained provincial licenses to cut timber on specific tracts of land (Clarence Joe Sr. 1980). Income from hand logging paid for and provided the timber for major building projects on the reserve, such as the construction of the residential school in 1903[3] and a new church in 1909, as well as providing the timber required for rebuilding numerous homes destroyed by fire. In 1911, the income from logging was so substantial that the Indian Agent used it as a pretext to deny shíshálh extra fishing "privileges" (Byrne 1911).

The hand logging tide was turning, however. By 1910 revisions to the *British Columbia Forestry Act* prioritized capital-intensive, large-scale production and increasingly alienated the shíshálh and other Aboriginal hand loggers in the province from the industry (Knight 1996: 237–39). Most tenures within shíshálh territory went to non-Native operations. As Chief Julius told the McKenna-McBride commission in 1915, "A few years ago we used to make our living by logging; that is hand logging, but we had to buy a license to do so but now in these late years we cannot do that" (Lutz 2008: 245–47). According to Indian Agent R. C. McDonald (1907; 1908), the timber available for hand logging, located alongside waterways to facilitate transportation of the logs, had already been cut or was in the hands of speculators. He advised the shíshálh either to seek the less profitable employment available with the mills or arrange to log on their own reserve lands. Thus, the shíshálh turned to applying, through departmental processes, for permits to log themselves or to sell the timber on their reserves, with the proceeds to be distributed among community members. The department granted permission, in many cases, only on the condition that the shíshálh bring land under cultivation and not "go all over the reserve picking out and logging good pieces of timber" (Byrne 1912). The colonial obsession with turning the shíshálh and other Aboriginal peoples into small-scale farmers was accompanied by efforts to steer them away from independent industry and toward wage earning. Cultivation restricted mobility and kept people close to their reserves. In this way, the administration of on-reserve logging was a form of bureaucratic and disciplinary power: "good management" of the forest was intertwined with the management of the reserve population though Indian Act processes such as maintaining Band membership and distribution lists (Schreiber 2010).

Assumptions about the gender of labor, combined with the fact that officials, in keeping with the *Indian Act*, negotiated the management of Band affairs with newly government-appointed male "chiefs," who may or may not have been leaders in customary legal systems, and with the adult male membership alone, have effectively deleted women's forestry work from much of the written record described above. With rare exceptions, the numerous petitions from shíshálh requesting permission to log their reserve lands or sell mercantile timber do not make explicit the extent of women's involvement in resource management. However, in February 1924, members of the shíshálh's Pender Harbour reserves asked the department to release for sale all the timber on Tsawcombe Reserve No. 1. Women accounted for over half the signatures on the petition (Billy et al. 1924). Such a large representation suggests the importance of women's involvement in community decision-making despite the gender discrimination of the Indian Act under which women did not formally vote on such matters.

The shíshálh Economy and the Coastal Forest

Among the shíshálh, forestry was a family affair, incorporated into the seasonal cycles of fishing, travel, and wage labor at the Fraser and Skeena River canneries. Men usually felled the trees and women provided numerous contingent tasks, as Clarence Joe Sr. describes (1980):

> In the days of my dad, when they were building the school and the church, they put in some labor towing logs to the booming grounds. When the logs hit the water, the women were there with their canoes. They were the one[s] that towed it into the booming grounds—tie it up in the booming ground. Then the tree came down from up on top—skidded down into the water, it would be a lot of walking from up on top for a man to come down, get the canoe, tow in the boom; and then come back and climb again to fall another tree. So it was the women's job at that time. I'm going back in the hand logging days again . . . The women played a big role in the hand logging days—they towed the logs to the boom and tied it.

For the shíshálh, "logging" went beyond the felling of a cedar and included activities such as tying the log booms; transporting the family in gas-powered canoes throughout the territory; cultivating extensive gardens and fruit trees; and supplying vegetables, fish, and game to the logging camps. The tasks of men and women in this integrated labor system echo an account by Andy Johnson Sr. about mountain goat hunting in his grandparents' time. He explained (interview 1987) that while the men followed the trail round the mountain and hunted, the women took the canoes round to pick up the game and transport it down to Sechelt. In logging, women and men performed different but complementary tasks; their labors formed part of a larger, integrated, and flexible strategy of combining a wide variety of economic and cultural activities in support of the extended family. Even Gilbert Joe (interview August 1979) handed over his first earnings from hand logging, made in the mid-1940s as a twelve-year-old, to his mother.

Also during this period, shíshálh women produced decorative and utilitarian baskets to meet the non-Native demand for Indian "curios." Basket weaving was time consuming. It had taken Mrs. Dan Paul "over two months to dig up the roots, dry, splice and dye them, and make the basket" that she had planned to sell to a white woman in Vancouver for $100.00 (Ball January 1937). Extensive knowledge was required to collect suitable cedar roots for basket production, as Madeline Joe explains (Joe and Joe interview 1986): "You got to start from anywhere. You find a little root and follow it and it branches out. . . . You know it's cedar root. You know how the cedar root looks like. You just follow it. There may be three, four trees in front of you but you follow that one root." Benny Joe, like many shíshálh boys, learned to dig for red cedar roots and gather the wood and saplings from expeditions with his mother and grandparents (interview 1987): "I know a lot to dig what kind of roots and cedar, for certain kind of cedar for framing for certain kinds of baskets. We were taught how to follow that and what part to take out." Joe's grandmother taught him to choose roots that were "firm and straight" and about five or six feet long. Root digging was not a simple task and required great cultural knowledge and physical strength to trace, dig out, and pull buried roots—"to know" what to do. According to Theresa Jeffries (1992: 91–92), these activities were also occasions "for affirmation of the family and our traditions," for learning about family, history, and responsibilities.

Despite numerous obstacles to hand logging, according to shíshálh accounts, the practice continued well into the 1950s. However, as the forestry industry became a magnet for big capital and developing technology and was conducted on an ever-larger scale, Aboriginal loggers working in all sectors of the industry were marginalized (Clarence Joe interview August 1979). Some shíshálh men continued to work for wages, but shíshálh women, despite a long and multifaceted relationship with forestry, were almost entirely excluded. Reflecting on the history of discrimination in a 1963 conference with the Department of Indian Affairs, Clarence Joe noted that "in earlier days Indians of the lower coast had been very industrious and quite successful in the fishing and logging industries," but today "it is difficult for Indians to finance fishing operations or to obtain timber rights for small family logging operations" (Report of Conference 1963).

Since the 1970s, First Nations in Canada strove to record information showing intense, ongoing use and occupancy of land in support of assertions of Aboriginal title and rights. Researchers directed their questions to Elders with the aim of pinpointing on a map the locations of traditional use: Where did you hunt mountain goat? Where did you collect gooseberries? (Korsmo 1999: 120). Western law rather than Indigenous concepts of territory dictated the line of questioning, prioritizing the site-specific model of occupation and the linking of laboring the land with ownership. In this view, only sites of physical "input"—villages, fishing stations, hunting and berry-picking grounds, and other delimited places that can be marked on a map—constitute association to land. In other words, Western law conceives of Aboriginal lands and waterways as property instead of sovereign territory, which, for any other nation-state, would include "unlabored" and even unknown or unexplored lands. This approach downplays the role of kinship lines and considerations other than labor in the organization of territory (Roy 2010: 26–27).

In the case of Indigenous peoples' relationship to their territories, this has important implications. Much of women's labor has been described as "gathering" or food-related and depicted as gentler and less invasive (images of women berry picking and collecting medicinal herbs may come to mind) than the labor of men. The forest industry, by and large, was first "masculinized" and then "racialized"; it was presumed to be the rugged dominion of men, and by the 1950s, of a working class of white men, alone. Historically, the gendering of Aboriginal women's labor, its location as something less than work and somewhere short of industry, helped, we suggest, justify the dispossession of Aboriginal lands.

Western dichotomies that distinguish women's labor from men's, subsistence from commercial, and traditional from modern contribute to the redefinition of the Indigenous coastal forest as sites of non-Native male industry, technology, and capital—in short, as land and resources available for industrial exploitation. The colonial processes of territorial dispossession in this sense have been inherently gendered and racialized—the supposedly passive labor of Indigenous women discounted and the commercial activity of men, whether it occurred in the forest or at concentrated sites of industry, conceived of as a shift from traditional Indigenous practice and, therefore, as less authentic or legitimate. These distinctions have implications in the current struggles to have Aboriginal title and rights recognized by the Canadian state. The logging activity of Aboriginal women, which represents both continuation of the traditional economy and adjustment to the industrial economy, is rarely considered evidence of ongoing use and occupation. The distinction between traditional plant gathering practices of women and industrial and commercial activity has construed Indigenous participation in the logging industry as a break from tradition rather than as ongoing use of the coastal forest.

A final photograph (figure 6.4) for consideration depicts the shíshálh high rigger Johnny Joe Dixon in the 1940s, the days of "high-lead" logging, when individual hand-felled trees were dragged out to a landing by a cable attached to the top of a spar tree. He is perched high in the tree, arms extended in a gesture of confidence. Its composition and subject matter (a man logging) are typical of the photographs that adorn the covers of books on resource history. But this image now suggests something more complex—more than an individual at work in the resource-extraction industries. If we return to the photograph of the shíshálh women demonstrating basket making (see figure 6.2), we'll see a large pile of cedar root sections in the foreground and the house in the background, sided with milled cedar shakes. This picture reveals that women's use of the coastal forest is not so distinct from the activities that are commonly masculinized as forestry. The women are, after all, extracting parts of the tree for industry. And indeed, the cedar tree is a reflection, though incomplete, of the shíshálh economy:

> The cedar tree is a very important wood to the coastal Indians, a very, very important tree. The people, when they come to a cedar tree, they talk to the cedar tree, the cedar is a tree . . . cutting it down, this is a tree they hew for canoes. The cedar bark, shakes, is what they use for their longhouse. Cedar tree is used for totem pole, carving totem poles. The cedar branch is what they use for their herring spawn, herring roe. The cedar roots is what they use for baskets, like the

one hanging on the wall there, the cedar, the wood that is around that basket is the cedar sapling, the sap of a cedar. A cedar is only . . . about twelve, fourteen inches in diameter. They cut that down and they take the sap of it. That's what the women use for weaving baskets. So the cedar wood is a very, very important tree as far as the coastal Indians are concerned (Clarence Joe interview June 1979).

While this observation emphasizes "traditional" uses of cedar, throughout the twentieth century the tree, in its broadest manifestation, provided for a wide range of cultural, political, and economic activities, including ceremony, manufacturing, infrastructure, and sale for cash. Conceived in this way, the tree—its roots, bark,

Figure 6.4. Johnny Joe Dixon felling a tree, 1940. tems swiya Museum Photography Collection #10.008. Reproduced with permission of the Sechelt First Nation.

sap, and wood—is not separated into distinct economic categories of subsistence, traditional, or industrial labor. The mixed economy of the shíshálh—bridging extraction, manufacture, and commerce as well as cultural production and reproduction—began before contact and continued, with modifications, afterward, alongside the development of modern industry. The roots on the ground next to shíshálh basket weavers Ellen Paul, Christine Julian, Janet Louie, and Mary Ann Jeffries, and the tree sections that Mary Joe, Violet Jeffries, Mary Anne Jeffries, Carrie Joe, and Madeline Joe roll down the hill remind us and are evidence of a larger history of women's labor, shíshálh resource management, and mobility throughout shíshálh territory.

Notes

1. We thank Chief Gary Feschuk and Council for permission to conduct research into shíshálh history; Robert Joe, Ashley Joe, Jasmine Paul, Heidi Brown, and Peter Merchant, of Sechelt's Aboriginal Rights and Title Department, for their generous support and guidance. Thanks also to Beth Piatote and Carol Williams, who provided insightful comments on drafts of this paper. Jessica Casey, curator of the tems swiya Museum, and Amir Gavriely kindly assisted with the photographs.

2. A noteworthy exception to the lack of research on Aboriginal women's participation in the B.C. logging industry is Menzies and Butler (2000).

3. shíshálh labor and timber contributed to the construction of the St. Augustine Residential School. Parents expected the school to provide children with the education necessary to succeed. However, soon afterward, they made numerous complaints of deplorable conditions, poor food, improper care, and abusive tactics. See Ball (February 1937).

Works Cited

Anderson, Alex C., Archibald McKinlay, and G. M. Sproat, to the Chief Commissioner of Lands and Works. December 7, 1876. B.C. Ministry of Lands, 3138/76.

Anfield, F. Earl, Indian Agent, to Major D. M. McKay. August 26, 1944. RG 10, vol. 7553, File 41,152-2. Library and Archives of Canada (LAC).

Ball, F. J. C., Indian Agent, to R. A. Hoey. January 20, 1937. RG 10, vol. 7553, File 41,167–2. LAC.

Ball, F. J. C., Indian Agent, to Secretary, Indian Affairs. February 4, 1937. RG 10, vol. 6461, File 887-23, pt. 1. LAC.

Ball, F. J. C., Indian Agent, to H. W. McGill. September 1, 1933. RG 10, vol. 10905, File 167/1922–1941. LAC.

Billy, Moses, et al. to Charles C. Perry, Indian Agent. February 18, 1924. RG 10, vol. 7082, File 987/20—7-5—1. LAC.

Borrows, John. *Recovering Canada: The Resurgence of Indigenous Law*. Toronto: University of Toronto Press, 2002.

Bushby, A. T., to Dr. Powell, Indian Commissioner. December 18, 1874. RG 10, vol. 3614, File 4213. LAC.

Byrne, Peter, Indian Agent, to Chief Julius. July 9, 1912. RG 10, vol. 1476. LAC.

Byrne, Peter, Indian Agent, to A. J. McKenna. November 2, 1911. RG 10, vol. 1450. LAC.

Deloria, Philip Joseph. *Indians in Unexpected Places*. Lawrence: University Press of Kansas, 2004.

Fiske, Jo-Anne. "Colonization and the Decline of Women's Status: The Tsimshian." *Feminist Studies* 17 (Fall 1991): 309–33.

Jeffries, Theresa M. "Sechelt Women and Self-Government." *British Columbia Reconsidered: Essays on Women*. Eds. Gillian Creese and Veronica Strong-Boag. Vancouver: Press Gang Publishers, 1992.

Joe, Benny. Interview by Del Paul, May 5, 1987. Sechelt First Nation (SFN).

Joe, Carrie, and Madeline Joe. Interview, May 2, 1986. SFN.

Joe, Clarence. Interview, June 15, 1979. SFN.

———. Interview, August 25, 1979. SFN.

Joe, Clarence, Sr. "In My Father's Time, In My Grandfather's Time." August 1980. Frank Fuller Papers, File 10, Box 2,. Special Collections. University of British Columbia.

Joe, Gilbert. Interview by Frank Fuller, August 13, 1979. SFN.

———. Interview by Frank Fuller, September 4, 1979. SFN.

Joe, Madeline, and Margaret Joe. Interview chaired by Andrew Peacock, January 22, 1997. SFN.

Johnson, Andy, Sr. Interview by Del Paul, July 9, 1987. SFN.

Julian, Chris. Transcript of interview by Frank Fuller, August 15, 1979, with "List of Sechelt Logging Terms." SFN.

Kelm, Mary Ellen, and Lorna Townsend, eds. *In the Days of Our Grandmothers: A Reader in Aboriginal Women's History in Canada*. Toronto: University of Toronto Press, 2006.

Kennedy, Dorothy I. D., and Randall T. Bouchard. "Northern Coast Salish." In *Handbook of North American Indians, vol. 7, Northwest Coast*. Ed. Wayne Suttles. Washington: Smithsonian Institution, 1990: 435–75.

Knight, Rolf. *Indians at Work: An Informal History of Native Labour in British Columbia 1858–1930*. Vancouver: New Star Books, 1996.

Korsmo, Fae L. "Claiming Memory in British Columbia: Aboriginal Rights and the State." *Contemporary Native American Political Issues*. Ed. Troy R. Johnson. Walnut Creek, Calif.: Altamira, 1999: 119–34.

Lawrence, Bonita. *"Real" Indians and Others: Mixed-Blood Urban Native Peoples and Indigenous Nationhood*. Lincoln: University of Nebraska Press, 2004.

Lutz, John Sutton. "Gender and Work in Lekwammen Families, 1843–1970." Kelm and Townsend, *In the Days of Our Grandmothers*.

———. *Makúk: A New History of Aboriginal-White Relations*. Vancouver: University of British Columbia Press, 2008.

McDonald, R. C., Indian Agent, to A. W. Vowell. May 10, 1904. RG 10, vol. 1466. LAC.

———. March 31, 1907. RG 10, vol. 1466. LAC.

———. January 28, 1908. RG 10, vol. 1467. LAC.

McKay, Joseph William, to James Douglas. September 16, 1852. A/C 20.1/N15, File 8. British Columbia Archives.

Menzies, Charles R., and Caroline F. Butler. "Out of the Woods: Tsimshian Women and Forestry Work." *Anthropology of Work Review* 21.2 (June 2000): 12–17.

———. "The Indigenous Foundation of the Resource Economy of B.C.'s North Coast." *Labour/Le Travail* 61 (Spring 2008): 131–49.

Miller, Bruce Granville, ed. *Be of Good Mind: Essays on the Coast Salish*. Vancouver: University of British Columbia Press, 2007.

Raibmon, Paige. *Authentic Indians: Episodes of Encounter from the Late-Nineteenth-Century Northwest Coast*. Durham: Duke University Press, 2005.

Report of Conference between Indians from British Columbia and Indian Affairs Branch Headquarters Staff. November 22, 1963. RG 10, vol. 7141, File 1/3–7, pt. 1. LAC.

Roy, Susan. *These Mysterious People: Shaping History and Archaeology in a Northwest Coast Community*. Montreal: McGill-Queen's University Press, 2010.

Schreiber, Dorothee. "Making Civilized Space: On-Reserve Logging at Cape Mudge, 1910–1920." Unpublished paper, 2010.

Sechelt First Nation. "Lil xemit tem swiya nelh mes stutula: A Strategic Land Use Plan for the shíshálh Nation." Unpublished Report, August 2007. SFN.

Smith, Harlan I. "Information from an Old Indian" January 16, 1927. Harlan I. Smith Collection, Box 9, File 2. Canadian Museum of Civilization Archives.

Sparrow, Leona M. "Work Histories of a Coast Salish Couple." MA thesis, University of British Columbia, 1976.

Williams, Carol. "Between Doorstep Barter Economy and Industrial Wages: Mobility and Adaptability of Coast Salish Female Laborers in Coastal British Columbia, 1858–1890." *Native Being, Being Native: Identity and Difference: Proceedings of the Fifth Native American Symposium*. Eds. Mark B. Spencer and Lucretia Scoufos. Durant: Southeastern Oklahoma State University, 2005. 16–27.

CHAPTER 7

Unraveling the Narratives of Nostalgia

Navajo Weavers and Globalization

Kathy M'Closkey

Introduction

For decades, researchers have investigated the impact of market economies on Indigenous peoples' lifeways and natural resources. My chapter reveals how incorporation of Navajo pastoralists into the American wool and livestock markets via the trading-post system initiated a turning point in Diné history. The passage of the Dawes Act in 1887, during Grover Cleveland's first administration, triggered the loss of over 80 million acres of tribal lands and ultimately impoverished thousands of Native Americans. That same year, revisions proposed to the wool tariff initiated a change in federal policy that ultimately held profound consequences for Navajo woolgrowers and weavers. Although their reservation was periodically enlarged to accommodate the need for increased grazing lands (Bailey and Bailey 1986: 80), Navajos' livelihood was significantly compromised. Wool was an internationally traded commodity for centuries, yet no critical analysis exists that positions Navajo growers and weavers within a global context or scrutinizes the economic consequences of the emergent differences between breeds of sheep raised by Navajo and off-reservation stock owners. Thus, as livestock owners *and* weavers, Navajo women were doubly disadvantaged by changes in the domestic wool tariff coupled with patriarchal assumptions that obliterated their contributions to subsidizing the reservation economy from 1880 to World War II.

Navajo oral histories confirm the centrality of weaving in sustaining Navajo lifeways and livelihood (M'Closkey 2002; Willink and Zolbrod 1996) (figure 7.1). During interviews, weavers relate aspects central to Navajo culture that revolve around the concept of *k'e*, kinship and reciprocity (McCloskey 2007; Weisiger 2009). The centrality of this concept may provide the key to understanding the escalation of textile production sustained by thousands of women despite difficult circumstances (M'Closkey 2002). Although ethnographer Gladys Reichard (1934) paints an enduring portrait of several weavers who patiently tutored her

Figure 7.1. Weaver
Grace Joe, Red Valley,
Arizona. October 1992.
Photographer Kathy
M'Closkey.

in the craft, she neglects the significance of their productivity to the regional economy. Instead, Reichard frames weavers' feelings about their work within an art historical context, noting that a certain percentage of weavers were artists "who would experiment with colors for hours." Perceived as "cultural performers" rather than "workers," this conceptual separation of weavers from the politicoeconomic sphere falsifies their experiences in crucial ways: "Treated in legendary terms as part of a timeless . . . tradition and ancient lore, the so-called authentic work . . . is situated in a popular play of mythic images rather than in a progression of actual historic events" (Albers 1996: 248). Such historic silencing perpetuates a false idealism that misrepresents the conditions under which Navajo weavers labored and detaches their work from the world capitalist system.

Historical Context

Over 200,000 Navajo or Diné occupy an 8000-hectare reservation in the south-west United States. By 1800, the Navajo wearing blanket had become the most valuable trade item in an extensive intertribal network comprised of Pueblos, Havasupai, Apache, Utes, and groups further north and east (Hill 1948). As pastoralists for centuries, weaving, wool production, livestock, and horticulture provided their subsistence until the Depression. Van Valkenburgh and McPhee (1974: 42) acknowledged the blanket as "the mother from which all external Navajo trade developed."

In 1863, the federal government initiated a costly and destructive four-year campaign of incarceration at Hwééldi (Bosque Redondo), in an attempt to subdue the largest "wild tribe" (Denetdale 2008; Iverson 2002; Roessel 1973). By 1868, with the post–Civil War economy in shambles, the government set aside a 3.5-million acre reservation, a portion of Navajos' previous homeland, and issued sheep to ensure self-support. Wool clipped from Navajo flocks increased over 200 percent between 1890 and 1910, yet textile production escalated more than 800 percent. Government-licensed traders, nearly all of whom were Anglo men, wholesaled Navajo textiles as a more lucrative means to market the nonstandardized wool clip subject to intense competition from low-priced imports. Annual agency reports to the Commissioner of Indian Affairs often tabulated the quantity and value of weaving: incorporating such information in the livestock and wool production figures demonstrates the bureaucratic perception of weaving as an extension of the livestock industry (U.S. Government SANSR). Between 1900 and 1940, the number of reservation trading posts increased from 79 to 170 (Weiss 1984: 151), and the value of textiles shipped from the reservation rose fortyfold, from $24,000 in 1890 to $1 million by 1930.

This "alternative means to market wool" (Bailey and Bailey 1986: 152) resulted in the survival of the nascent trading-post system during the 1890s, a period when 30 percent of wool growers nationally went bankrupt (NWGA 1927: 38). This is particularly striking since Navajo wools sold for less than the fine wools produced by Anglo-owned flocks.

Weavers and Traders

Don Lorenzo Hubbell, the "czar" of Navajo trade and the "father" of the Navajo rug, and his family actively influenced the growth and development of reservation commerce from 1883–1950 (McNitt 1962).[1] Because the Hubbells controlled a significant portion of Navajo trade for decades, their papers provide a barometer of the regional economy. The ledger books reveal that textiles, skins, and wool were the "currency" by which the Hubbells paid creditors, and for decades their annual profits in blanket sales averaged twelve times their wool profits. After 1900, the Hubbells typically shipped more pounds of weaving annually than sheep pelts and goatskins combined. Hubbell ledgers show over 400,000 pounds of handspun, handwoven blankets and rugs shipped from their trading posts between 1891 and 1909 (M'Closkey 2002: 97). How is it possible that such productivity could result in sustained impoverishment for Navajos? By World War I, 85 percent of the population was "poor, average or destitute" (Weiss 1984: 83). The clues to this paradox emerged from my analysis in other words, "the more they wove, the poorer they became."

Thus business records reveal how Navajos' livelihood was undermined in a manner not readily apparent from the government documents (Bailey and Bailey 1986; Iverson 2002; White 1983). The Hubbells' business records and correspondence reveal that textiles were treated like a renewable resource acquired from weavers by *weight* until the mid-1960s (Hubbell Papers). Trader interference not only caused weavers to lose control of the marketing of their textiles; they also lost access due to commercial manufacturers such as Pendleton Woolen Mills who capitalized on Navajos' unawareness of copyright protection. Trade blanket manufacturers appropriated the form, materials, and Navajo designs, and through traders, sold scores of mechanically woven blankets to many consumers formerly provisioned by Navajo weavers (M'Closkey 2002: 87–93) (figure 7.2). Whereas other scholars contend that the Arts and Crafts movement alongside an increase in tourism drove rising production of Navajo weaving (Weigle and Babcock 1996), I argue that the enormous influx of cheap carpet wools propelled production while generating widespread impoverishment.

Figure 7.2. "Pound" handspun and aniline-dyed wool rug produced circa 1905. Photographer Kathy M'Closkey (1988).

While traders' financial success was linked to their coopting the marketing of Navajo textiles, concrete macro-level evidence concerning the effect of fluctuating values of wool internationally was needed. The Hubbells' business records exposed the fingerprints of free trade.[2] The lack of information in extant literature was frustrating. In U.S. Congressional Records and Tariff regulations, I discovered that wool had been one of the most volatile internationally traded commodities for centuries (Bensel 2000; Cole 1926; North 1895; Smith 1926; Taussig 1920; Wright 1910). Discrepancies between the proceeds that traders were receiving for Navajo wool, and that of the annual average price per pound as reported in national records (Bailey and Bailey 1986 Appendix B) offered the first inkling that something was amiss. Navajo wools typically sold for 50–70 percent less than clothing wools. In order to understand why Navajo wools were devalued compared to finer wools it is necessary to understand important distinctions between different breeds of *sheep*.

Sheep Woes

The livestock issued to Diné after Bosque Redondo (1868–69) were *churros* (Baxter 1983*)*. The hardy *churro*, well adapted to the Navajo range, was a lightweight in both meat and fleece yet produced excellent coarse wool for rug weaving (although only .003 percent of U.S. population, Navajos owned 2 percent of the sheep) (Aberle 1983). A growing number of government-licensed traders acquired the Navajos' annual clip and sold it to regional wholesalers who then shipped it to wool brokers located in Boston and Philadelphia (Gross-Kelly Company Papers; Hubbell Papers). By 1890, Diné growers, many of whom were women, continued to raise churros.

Although Indian agents had periodically introduced fine-wooled sheep into Navajo flocks, upbreeding yielded mixed results. The nonstandardized nature of Navajo herds produced a less desirable product for the national market and decreased the value of their wools in competition with foreign wools. After 1900, weavers processed 30 percent of the annual clip into saddle blankets and rugs; the upbreeding had altered its positive characteristics for rug weaving and threatened traders' profit margins because wool marketed in rug form brought three to six times more revenue to traders. Reichard reiterates the differences between Navajo flocks and those sheep owned by off-reservation growers; she admits that not only were rugs sold by weight, *their values change with fluctuations in the wool market* (1936: 192). Although Diné wools reached record values during World War I due to constrictions in the availability of foreign wools, the situation was reversed by World War II when, in 1943, federal guidelines mandating quality and types of wool to clothe and blanket the military classified Navajo wools as "substandard" and rejected them for military purposes (NAWM 1943). Having thousands of women weave fleece into textiles provided a more secure means of diversification for traders faced with continual price oscillations in the international wool markets.

Global Wool Markets—The "Missing Link"

Wool was England's first great industry, and it brought wealth and power to the country for 700 years. During the Middle Ages, wool was the staple of England's export trade and every European country relied on England for it. As demand for wool grew, other European countries vied for the lucrative market. By the mid–nineteenth century, Australia became another key producer. As a Commonwealth country, her production contributed to the 70 percent of the global market controlled by England (Bensel 2000; GBEMB 1932; North 1895). For much of the nineteenth century, wool and cotton production for textile manufacturing was the third most important U.S. industry, following agriculture and steel (U.S. Census 1975). Next to Great Britain, the U.S. was the next greatest consumer of wool in the world, and although domestic wool growers clipped 300 million pounds annually after the Civil War, manufacturers required over .5 billion pounds (the United States produced 10 percent of the world's wool but consumed 25 percent). Increasingly unwilling to risk dependence on foreign sources, Congress legislated high duties to protect domestic growers referring to the wool tariff "as the keystone of the arch of protection" (Smith 1926; Wright 1910).

Although characteristics greatly vary, wools were classified into three types: Classes I and II were clothing and combing wools (worsteds) and Class III was comprised of coarser carpet wools. By 1890, non-Navajo growers had upbred their flocks to clothing-quality wool (Class I and II). Fine wools were subject to much higher duties and ad valorem. Because domestic growers were unable to adequately supply U.S. textile manufacturers, the latter imported clothing wools primarily from Australia, New Zealand, and British South Africa, whereas carpet manufacturers imported coarser wools from three dozen countries including China. Prior to 1900, 75 percent of the wool imported into the United States was carpet-quality. Sheep bearing Class III carpet wools were inexpensively raised in China, Argentina, Russia, Turkey, India, and Asia and imported as raw material (NAWM; North 1895; Wright 1910).Technological advances in shipping vastly accelerated the movement of goods, including wool, across and between continents and advances in communications such as the telegraph allowed close monitoring of supplies, demand, and price fluctuations of key global commodities. The power looms invented by Erastus Bigelow during the 1850s revolutionized carpet manufacturing, and the United States shifted from importing carpets to becoming the largest carpet manufacturer in the world (Ewing and Norton 1955). The only wool grown within the United States that was classified Class III coarse carpet-grade was produced by *churros*. However, Diné growers produced less than 3 percent of the more than 100 million pounds necessary to service the carpet industry annually. As a result, by 1890 manufacturers had successfully lobbied Congress to allow Class III wools into the country duty-free, or with a small ad valorem (Cole 1926; Smith 1926; Wright 1910). In 1894, President Grover Cleveland placed all classes of wool on the duty-free list. For four years, 1 billion pounds of wool were imported into the country under free trade, of which 50 percent was Class III carpet wool. Given the increasing state emphasis on the import of Class III wools, *it is no coincidence that the Navajo blanket was transformed into a rug during that decade and weavers' productivity increased fourfold*. Although the cost of living quadrupled for Navajos between 1900 and the Depression, the value of their textiles stalled at 1902 levels, indicating that *the wholesale price of weaving was pegged to the price of imported carpet wool*. Textiles, skins, and wool (in season) were weighed, baled, and shipped weekly to regional wholesalers to pay down traders' debits (Hubbell Papers). Thousands of "dark-skinned housewives" effectively subsidized the reservation trading-post system for decades, because Navajo wools were in competition with duty-free carpet wools to accommodate the U. S. carpet manufacture (M'Closkey forthcoming).

The "Domestication" of Navajo Weavers

My research also incorporates a *gender* perspective probing how prevalent images of female domesticity complemented patriarchal values and shaped the perceptions of government authorities (Albers 1996; Etienne and Leacock 1980; Kehoe 1983; Littlefield and Knack 1996; Weisiger 2009). Witherspoon (1987) conservatively estimates that 100,000 women have woven *1 million textiles* over the past two centuries. Extant analyses of the Navajo economy have failed to adequately take account of weavers' productivity because women wove at home and not in factories. Marxist economist Larry Weiss cited Amsden's (1934: 235) classic text:

> With weaving, these [favorable] circumstances are spare time and cheap wool. [T]he Navajo woman weaves when she has nothing better to do, or when the family wool crop cannot be sold to better advantage in the raw. . . . [W]ool in rug form brings a little more money.

The above-mentioned evidence challenges the romanticist stereotyping of Navajo weavers and traders reproduced in this statement by Weiss, and demonstrates the multiple ways in which Navajo women's production has been marginalized by various authorities and scholars. Weavers' abilities, the quality of their work and their industriousness were frequently remarked upon and celebrated by missionaries, anthropologists, traders, and government personnel. Yet these authorities failed to substantively acknowledge the importance of weaving to the southwest economy because it would have counteracted the prevailing Western attitudes about what constituted "appropriate behavior" and the proper sphere for women in general (Kehoe 1983; Shoemaker 1995). Although large accounts were drawn against weavers' creations, assuring a continuing supply of textiles while diminishing women's bargaining position, agency reports confirmed that textile production by Navajos was "the most profitable of the native industries . . . and is done by women in their spare time" (Sells 1913: 36). Navajo women were categorized as weavers, and their extensive production of handspun, dyed, and woven textiles was referred to as an industry (U.S. Government ARCIA). Yet their industriousness was minimized. For example, many argued that women continued to weave because it was their "favorite past-time" (Luomala 1938; Reichard 1934, 1936; Williams 1989), or "for their beloved pin-money" (Maxwell 1963). By 1930, however, the products of this "leisure-time" activity were valued at 1 million dollars annually, comprising one-third of the Navajo economy and outstripping waged labor between 1890 and the Depression. For many observers, only non-subsistence labor performed outside the home counted as *work*:

> Weaving a rug can be a lot of work . . . we hear reports that a Navajo weaver is poorly paid. . . . Unfortunately there is much truth to this, but . . . but rug weaving is a spare-time avocation. . . . Which brings up a very important point. Although weaving is an essential part of the reservation economy it is not exercised as a full-time occupation. . . . A Navajo woman will do most of her weaving in her spare time, as some of our non-Indian ladies will knit a wool dress in their spare time (trader Gilbert Maxwell 1963: 19–20).

Like Maxwell, Reichard (1936: 186, 192) also acknowledges the importance of weaving, yet underestimates its value, commenting that interruptions were so numerous, and the work so erratic that "time must be left out of the calculation . . . it is a mistake to estimate the weaving on this basis . . . handcraftsmanship must be reckoned not only in dollars and cents, but also in satisfaction." Although thousands of Navajo women and girls were weavers at this time, participation in the seemingly "informal" economy translated into invisibility. Maxwell's and Reichard's comments confirm the rationalization for ignoring the significance of women's labor, while simultaneously demonstrating the role that its productivity played in subsidizing the formal market sector and its vital role in capital accumulation (Kuokkanen 2007: 11).

The Southwest Wool and Textile Trade

The consequences of free trade for Navajo woolgrowers and weavers are calibrated in the business records and correspondence among eastern wool brokers, southwest regional wholesalers, and reservation traders (M'Closkey forthcoming). During the early 1880s, the wool buying firm Eisemann Brothers of Albuquerque, New Mexico Territory, encountered difficulties selling Navajo wools. There was no market at all for black wool from 1888 to 1890, which comprised 25 percent of the annual clip (Hubbell Papers Boxes 26, 64, 66, 91, 92). By the mid-1880s, reservation trader Clinton Cotton was doing a brisk business shipping bed and saddle blankets from Ganado and buying commercially produced trade blankets for his clientele. By September 1890, Cotton encountered difficulty disposing of blankets because regional wholesalers were overstocked. From 1894 through mid-1897, all classes of wool imported into the country were exempt from duty under the Wilson-Gorman tariff. During February 1895, Cotton wrote Arizona Lumber and Timber offering to trade large stockpiles of handwoven blankets for one or two *carloads* of lumber to build his warehouse in Gallup, New Mexico. The Flagstaff, Arizona, company declined the exchange as they, too, held an abundance of blankets (AL&T 2/2/1895). Cotton then transferred the Ganado trading post to Lorenzo Hubbell and by 1898, over 90 percent of nearly 200 business accounts were for weaving, thereby demonstrating how crucial textile production was to Hubbell's financial success during the free-trade era. By 1903, Hubbell acquired blankets from 300 women weaving in the Ganado area alone, and he owned five other posts.[3] Although Hubbell preferred to wholesale textiles in large quantities, he encountered limited success due to intense competition and remoteness of his post's location: the closest telegraph station was sixty miles away. Even so, he sold $40,000 of weaving that year. Correspondence between Hubbell family members and off-reservation wholesalers including Gross-Kelly and Company, whose relevance is explained below, reveals their concerns as well as strategies to cope with the volatile market fluctuations, including selling wool in the form of rugs (M'Closkey forthcoming).

Gross-Kelly and Company (Gross-Blackwell prior to 1900) were regional wholesalers headquartered in Las Vegas, New Mexico (M'Closkey 2002: 35). The company used Private Telegraph Code books dating from 1888, containing over eighty pages of words used as ciphers to encrypt information related to buying, selling, wool qualities, and so forth. The use of code books for decades demonstrates how fiercely competitive the wool market was, necessitating secretive correspondence between traders, regional buyers, and eastern brokers in daily contact with foreign buyers in order to purchase wools at optimum prices.

In 1913, all classes of wool were again placed on the duty-free list. As the price of weaving was pegged to the price of wool, rug values plummeted (HP Box 99). However, by 1915, World War I triggered an escalation in wool and livestock values; they peaked in 1918 and rapidly declined in 1920. Although Congress passed an emergency tariff in 1922 to salvage a failing economy, carpet wools remained on the duty-free list, placing additional pressures on weavers to increase their output to provision their households.

Although Navajo flocks sheared over 4 million pounds of wool annually after World War I, or 75 percent of the 6 million pounds clipped by other Arizona growers, there were no reservationwide organizations formed to collectively market their clips. Indian traders were highly individualistic and purportedly quite competitive (Blue 2000). The Federal government preferred competition as a means to prevent monopolies and ostensibly maintain lower prices internally. As small businesses often far from the railroad, many posts were inefficient by prevailing standards since individual marketing brought higher processing and freight costs. In contrast, by the mid-1920s, woolgrowers from many western states had formed cooperative marketing groups (AWGA and NMAWMC). Woolgrowers' associations were formed not only for marketing purposes, but also to address the status of the tariff, which was frequently the first "order of business" in their bulletins and newsletters. The Woolgrowers' Associations of Arizona and New Mexico were unsympathetic to Navajos: they expressed resentment at Indians living at taxpayers' expense, deplored the enlargement of the reservation, and accused Navajo sheep of harboring scabies, a highly infectious disease. Although Navajo men and women comprised the largest group of flock owners in the state, they were seldom mentioned in the associations' monthly newsletters.

For nearly a century weavers' productivity served as a crucial source of revenue for reservation traders, yet according to the United Indian Traders' Association (UITA 1998) "pawn was considered the cornerstone of trade." This claim is soundly refuted by traders' business records. For example, in 1908, there were 1500 transactions registered in the Ganado pawn ledgers totaling nearly $3500 (M'Closkey 2002: 129). In 1909, Don Lorenzo sold $60,000 of Navajo weaving and netted a $27,000 profit (M'Closkey 2002: 97). A spreadsheet analysis of the business records of traders E. S. Crumm and C. N. Cotton, partners at a little-known post located at Round Rock, Arizona (July 1915 through December 1916), confirms that women's productivity guaranteed the post's financial success. Of the three top categories, the value of textiles ($8076) outperformed livestock ($7025) and wool sales ($7358), respectively, and 80 percent of these textiles were "I.I.F." or half-fancy rugs, woven of handspun wool and colored with aniline dyes. Surprisingly, the extant history of Navajo weaving continues to recycle a dual-strand explanation of the genesis and escalation of rug production: the growth of tourism coupled with antimodernism's preference for the handmade over commercially produced goods as embraced by the Arts and Crafts Movement (Bsumek 2008; Weigle and Babcock 1996; Wilkins 2008). Despite the compelling statistical and archival evidence that confirms how weavers' productivity subsidized the regional economy; the romantic narratives explaining the impetus for increased production persist.

Modernity and "Progress"

O'Neill (2005: 146) comments on how American Indian policy was shaped by modernization theory anchored by concepts of linear progress. Incorporation of Navajos into the U.S. market was theorized by policy makers as the solution to growing impoverishment; they proposed that Indian adherence to "tradition" was reactionary. This supposition, conceived by those unfamiliar with local circumstances, may partially explain why weavers were never integrated into development planning: perceived as outdated, Indigenous home-based, and female-dominated, textile production would only perpetuate "tradition" to impede Native modernization. According to government policy, economic self-sufficiency was best achieved through male-dominated, extraction of nonrenewable resources (Aberle 1983; Ruffing 1979; Weiss 1984). Placing Navajo men in waged-labor positions affirmed their status as heads of households and conformed to Euro-American gender values. However, such large-scale "development" has had unintended detrimental environmental and health consequences, generating over 1100 uranium dumps, acres of strip-mined land, polluted aquifers, and increased cancer rates in Navajoland.

Additional evidence suggests that there were reasons other than overgrazing that triggered the infamous stock reduction during the Depression, in which nearly 50 percent of Navajos' livestock was destroyed (Roessel 1974; Weisiger 2009). In a recent conversation with the "sheepman" at Utah State responsible for the recent reintroduction of churros, Dr. Lyle McNeal confirms that government authorities had singled out churros for destruction. Dr. McNeal's findings corroborate what this essay reveals, that churro wool was too nonstandardized for domestic carpet manufacturers; thus only wholesale slaughter would "solve the problem." During an interview, ninety-year-old weaver Martha Benally recalled Commissioner John Collier's comment: "the blood of your sheep is no good."

Weavers' Voices of Today

When women speak about weaving during interviews, they frequently reference plants, animals, the land, their kin, and the importance of provisioning (Denetdale 2007; Mitchell 2001; M'Closkey 2002). These references reveal sets of relationships overlooked in current publications that simplistically reduce their analysis of Navajo production to the "aesthetics" embedded in gallery-displayed textiles (Hedlund 2003; Wheat 1996; Whitaker 2002). Human reciprocity (k'e) may occur only within the context of human/nonhuman reciprocation (McNeley 1987; Willink and Zolbrod 1996). The technical aspects of weaving are embedded in such cultural processes. It appears that the empirically based ecological understandings of the Navajo are intimately tied to their social structures. Weavers' interviews and perspectives emerging from traditional ecological knowledge reveal how the patterns of relations that brought Navajo rugs into existence are fractured when cultural pattern is split from commodity. Weavers' feeling for *hózhó* (beauty/harmony/local order) encompasses far more than the Western concept of aesthetics that locates "beauty" in the isomorphic object. Only by reformulating outmoded concepts of aesthetics can readers surmise the threat posed by the antiquities market to Diné lifeways (and economic self sufficiency).

Conclusion

Situating reservation traders and regional wholesalers within the economic history of the southwest and the larger international wool market, illuminates a more nuanced understanding of Navajo history, in particular the significance of Navajo women's nonwaged labor to the regional economy. My analysis challenges the following common assumptions: (1) traders seemingly saved Navajo weaving by developing off-reservation markets; (2) traders were primarily responsible for design changes; (3) acquiring blankets by weight among traders was a short-lived phenomenon; (4) rug weaving decreased when wool prices were high and increased when wool prices dropped; (5) traders' greatest profits lay in wool; (6) weavers benefited financially by exchanging their own handwoven textiles for machine-made trade blankets (M'Closkey 2002). Museologists emphasize how the incorporation of commercial yarns and dyes compromised the quality of postreservation textiles, yet neglect to note that the primary ingredient of a Navajo rug is comprised of wool from their sheep. Without the "wool story," it remains impossible to comprehend the enormous contributions made by thousands of Navajo women weaving under difficult circumstances. Massive shipments impoverished weavers and their families, and pauperization continues today as the historic "pound blankets" are recycled in the antiquities markets, depressing the demand for contemporary rugs. Historic Navajo textiles are valuable investments sought by wealthy collectors—an estimated $100 million have sold through international auctions or private transactions since 1970, undermining the market for contemporary creations woven by an estimated 20,000 weavers (M'Closkey 2002).

Currently domestic growers clip 44 million pounds of wool annually—less wool than the United States imported from China alone in 1910! This essay highlights the remarkable parallels between the "hidden" history of Navajo weavers and woolgrowers and the dilemmas challenging Indigenous producers worldwide in their struggles to cope with free trade and globalization. These interrelated factors, linking local events to national and international processes, are crucial to historicizing the unacknowledged economic contributions of thousands of anonymous Navajo weavers and wool growers within a transnational context.

Acknowledgments

I wish to thank workshop organizers Drs. Joan Sangster and Carol Williams, and staff members at the following libraries: the National Archives, Washington, D.C.; the Newberry, Chicago; Special Collections, University of Arizona, Tucson; the Cline at Northern Arizona University; the Center for Southwest Research, University of New Mexico, Albuquerque; and the Baker Business Library, Harvard University. Dr. Rahim Akbarzadeh assisted with archival research at the Cline.

David Brugge kindly translated weavers' names from the Hubbell Papers. The Newberry Library provided support under the auspices of a National Endowment for the Humanities fellowship in 1998–99, and the Social Science and Humanities Research Council of Canada provided operating grants from 1997 to the present. The Social Justice and Globalization Data Archive at the University of Windsor have offered invaluable assistance by providing office space and technical support. I am indebted to Director Suzan Ilcan and data archivist Stephen Richter. I greatly appreciate the constructive editing suggested by Dr. Carol Williams and graduate students Kelly Pineault and Lynnette Schick.

Notes

1. The original trading post located in Ganado, Arizona is now a national historic site operated by the U.S. Park Service and visited by thousands of tourists annually. Available for study since 1977, the Hubbell archives have been woefully underutilized in substantively assessing the importance of textile production to traders' financial success (M'Closkey 2002, 2004, and forthcoming).

2. Remarkably, the terms *wool tariff* and *free trade* remain absent from the vast literature on Diné (Bahr 1999; Bailey and Bailey 1986; Iverson 2002; White 1983).

3. In the ledger books, weavers are usually identified by their relationship to male kin. For example: (HP Box 344 Weavers' Accounts 1904): Béégashi Hólóni Ba'áád No 1 translates as "Wife of (Man) Who Has Cows No 1." *Dooyattj'* translates as "Silent Man's Son's No 2 Wife." See O'Neill (2005: 77–80) for further discussion of this topic.

Works Cited

Aberle, David F. "Navajo Economic Development." *Southwest* 10 (1983): 641–58. Ed. Alfonso Ortiz. Washington, D.C.: Smithsonian Institution.

Albers, Patricia. "From Legend to Land to Labor: Changing Perspectives on Native American Work." *Native Americans and Wage Labor: Ethnohistorical Perspectives.* Eds. Alice Littlefield and Martha Knack. Norman: University of Oklahoma Press, 1996. 245–73.

Amsden, C. A. *Navajo Weaving, Its Technique and History.* Salt Lake City: Peregrine Smith, Inc., 1975 [1934].

Arizona Lumber and Timber. Mss 266. Cline Library Special Collections, Northern Arizona University, Flagstaff.

Arizona Woolgrowers Association 1886–1950. Mss 233. Cline Library Special Collections. Northern Arizona University, Flagstaff.

Bahr, Howard. *Diné Bibliography to the 1990s: A Companion to the Navajo Bibliography of 1969.* Lanham, Md.: Scarecrow Press, 1999.

Bailey, Garrick, and Roberta Bailey. *A History of the Navajo: The Reservation Years.* Santa Fe, N.Mex.: School of American Research Press, 1986.

Baxter, John. "Restocking the Navajo Reservation after Bosque Redondo." *New Mexico Historical Review* 58.4 (1983): 325–45.

Bensel, Richard F. *The Political Economy of American Industrialization, 1877–1900.* Cambridge, U.K.: Cambridge University Press, 2000.

Blue, Martha. *Indian Trader: The Life and Times of J. L. Hubbell*. Walnut, Calif.: Kiva Press, 2000.

Bsumek, Erika. *Indian-Made: Navajo Culture in the Marketplace, 1868–1948*. Lawrence: University Press of Kansas, 2008.

Cole, Arthur. *The American Wool Manufacturer*. Cambridge: Harvard University Press, 1926.

Crumm, E. S., and Cotton Trading Post ledger book. Round Rock, Ariz., 1915–16. George Babbitt Collection. Mss 44. Box 2, Series IV, Miscellaneous 1915–25. Special Collections, Cline Library, Northern Arizona University, Flagstaff.

Denetdale, Jennifer Nez. *Reclaiming Diné History: The Legacies of Navajo Chief Manuelito and Juanita*. Tucson: University of Arizona Press, 2007.

———. *The Long Walk: The Forced Navajo Exile*. New York: Chelsea House Publishers, 2008.

Etienne, Mona, and E. Leacock, eds. *Women and Colonization*. New York: Praeger, 1980.

Ewing, John S., and Nancy Norton. *Broadlooms and Businessmen: A History of the Bigelow-Sanford Carpet Company*. Cambridge: Harvard University Press, 1955.

Great Britain Empire Marketing Board. *Wool Survey: A Summary of Production and Trade in the Empire and Foreign Countries*. London: His Majesty's Stationary Office, 1932.

Gross-Kelly and Company Collection 1863–1955. Mss 96. Center for Southwest Research, University of New Mexico, Albuquerque.

Hedlund, Ann Lane, ed. *Blanket Weaving in the Southwest*. Tucson: University of Arizona Press, 2003.

Hill, W. W. "Navajo Trading and Trading Ritual: A Study of Cultural Dynamics." *Southwestern Journal of Anthropology* 4.4 (1948): 371–96.

Iverson, Peter. *Diné: A History of the Navajos*. Albuquerque: University of New Mexico Press, 2002.

Kehoe, Alice. "The Shackles of Tradition." *The Hidden Half*. Eds. Patricia Albers and Bea Medicine 53–76. Lanham, Md.: University Press of America, 1983.

Kuokkanen, Rauna. "The Politics of Form and Alternative Autonomies: Indigenous Women, Subsistence Economies and the Gift Paradigm." Working Paper Series 07/2, Institute on Globalization and the Human Condition, McMaster University, Hamilton, Ontario, 2007.

Littlefield, Alice, and Martha Knack, eds. *Native Americans and Wage Labor: Ethnohistorical Perspectives*. Norman: University of Oklahoma Press, 1996.

The Lorenzo Hubbell Papers. 1865–1965. Ariz. 375. Special Collections Library, University of Arizona, Tucson.

Luomala, Katherine. *Navajo Life of Yesterday and Today*. U.S. Department of the Interior, National Park Service. Berkeley, California, 1938.

Maxwell, Gilbert. *Navajo Rugs: Past, Present, Future*. Palm Desert, Calif: Best-West Pub., 1963.

McCloskey, Joanne. *Living Through the Generations. Continuity and Change in Navajo Women's Lives*. Tucson: University of Arizona Press, 2007.

M'Closkey, Kathy. *Swept Under the Rug: A Hidden History of Navajo Weaving*. Albuquerque: University of New Mexico Press, 2002; reprinted 2008.

———. "The Devil's in the Details: Tracing the Fingerprints of Free Trade and Its Effects on Navajo Weavers." *Native Pathways: Economic Development and American Indian*

Culture in the Twentieth Century. Eds. Brian Hosmer and Colleen O'Neill. Boulder: University Press of Colorado, 2004. 112–30.

———. *Why the Navajo Blanket Became a Rug: Excavating the Lost Heritage of Globalization.* Albuquerque: University of New Mexico Press, forthcoming.

McNeley, Grace. "Home: A Family of Land and People." *Dine Be'iina': A Journal of Navajo Life* 1.1 (1987): 161–64.

McNitt, Frank. *The Indian Traders.* Norman: University of Oklahoma Press, 1962.

Mitchell, Rose. *Tall Woman: The Life Story of Rose Mitchell, a Navajo Woman, 1874–1977.* Ed. Charlotte Johnson Frisbie. Albuquerque: University of New Mexico Press, 2001.

National Association of Wool Manufacturers' Bulletins 1865–1926. Newberry Library, Chicago, IL, and 1927–45, Baker Business Library, Harvard University, Cambridge, Mass.

National Wool Growers Association. "The Wool Outlook." 2:38. Salt Lake City, Utah, 1927.

New Mexico–Arizona Wool Marketing Corporation, 1929–61. Mss 288. Center for Southwest Research, University of New Mexico, Albuquerque.

North, S. N. D. "A Century of American Wool Manufacture." *National Association of Wool Manufacturers Bulletin* 25 (1895): 40–70.

O'Neill, Colleen. *Working the Navajo Way: Labor and Culture in the Twentieth Century.* Lawrence: University Press of Kansas, 2005.

Reichard, Gladys. *Navajo Shepherd and Weaver.* New Mexico: Rio Grande Press, 1968 [1936].

———. *Spider Woman.* New York: Macmillan, 1974 [1934].

Roessel, Ruth. *Navajo Stories of the Long Walk Period.* Tsaile, Ariz.: Navajo Community College Press, 1973.

———. *Navajo Livestock Reduction: A National Disgrace.* Tsaile, Ariz.: Navajo Community College Press, 1974.

Ruffing, Lorraine Turner. "Dependence and Underdevelopment." *Economic Development in American Indian Reservations.* Ed. Roxanne D. Ortiz. 91–113, Native American Studies, I. Albuquerque: University of New Mexico Press, 1979.

Sells, Cato. Annual Report of the Commissioner of Indian Affairs. Washington, D.C.: GPO, 1913.

Shoemaker, Nancy, ed. *Negotiators of Change: Historical Perspectives on Native America Women.* New York: Routledge, 1995.

Smith, Mark. *The Tariff on Wool.* New York: Macmillan, 1926.

Taussig, Frank. *Free Trade, the Tariff and Reciprocity.* New York: Macmillan, 1920.

United Indian Traders' Association. 1998. Cline Library, Northern Arizona University. www://nau.edu/library/speccoll/exhibits (accessed January 2012).

United States Bureau of the Census. *Historical Statistics of the United States: Colonial Times to 1970.* Washington: GPO, 1975.

United States Government. Annual Reports of the Commissioner of Indian Affairs (RCIA). National Archives, Washington, D.C.

———. Superintendents' Annual Narrative and Statistical Reports. [Eight Navajo Agencies], 1910–35. Record Group 75. National Archives, Washington, D.C.

van Valkenburgh, Richard, and J. McPhee. *A Short History of the Navajo People.* New York: Garland, 1974.

Weigle, Marta, and Barbara Babcock, eds. *The Great Southwest of the Fred Harvey Company and the Santa Fe Railway.* Tucson: University of Arizona Press, 1996.

Weisiger, Marsha. *Dreaming of Sheep in Navajo Country*. Seattle: University of Washington Press, 2009.

Weiss, Lawrence. *The Development of Capitalism in the Navajo Nation: A Political Economy History*. MEP Publications #15, Studies in Marxism, Minneapolis, 1984.

Wheat, Joe Ben. "Navajo Blankets." *Woven by the Grandmothers*. Ed. E. Bonar. Washington, D.C.: Smithsonian Institution, 1996. 69–86.

Whitaker, Kathleen. *Southwest Textiles: Weavings of the Pueblo and Navajo*. Seattle: University of Washington Press, 2002.

White, Richard. *The Roots of Dependency: Subsistence, Environment, and Social Change among the Choctaws, Pawnees, and Navajos*. Lincoln: University of Nebraska Press, 1983.

Wilkins, Teresa. *Patterns of Exchange: Navajo Weavers and Traders*. Norman: University of Oklahoma Press, 2008.

Williams, Lester. *C. N. Cotton and His Navajo Blankets*. Albuquerque: Avanyu Press, 1989.

Willink, Roseanne, and Paul Zolbrod. *Weaving a World: Textiles and the Navajo Way of Seeing*. Santa Fe: Museum of New Mexico Press, 1996.

Witherspoon, Gary. "Navajo Weaving: Art in Its Cultural Context." Flagstaff: Museum of Northern Arizona #37, 1987.

Wright, Chester. *Wool Growing and the Tariff: A Study in the Economic History of the United States*. Cambridge: Harvard Economic Studies, 1910.

CHAPTER 8

Labor and Leisure in the "Enchanted Summer Land"

Anishinaabe Women's Work and the Growth of Wisconsin Tourism, 1900–1940

Melissa Rohde

In 1922 the federal Indian service conducted a series of industrial surveys on reservations aimed at determining the success of its effort to educate and assimilate the nation's Native people. Officials at the Lac du Flambeau and Lac Courte Oreilles Ojibwe reservations in northern Wisconsin began visiting homes in the spring. Trudging from home to home, officials collected data on employment and family relations and recorded their impressions of the industriousness of the people they examined. Although local officials evaluated women primarily on the basis of their ability to "keep house," their reports nevertheless revealed that female members of the tribe carried out a variety of tasks inside and outside the home. Even though compliments came in gendered terms—Lac du Flambeau's Mrs. Margaret Brown was said to "work like a man"—these surveys provide a window onto a diverse world of labor and entrepreneurial adaptation. Agents reported Ojibwe women combined wage labor with gardening, gathering, and commodity production and were key to the survival and success of their households (Reports of Industrial Surveys, Lac du Flambeau).

The work undertaken by Ojibwe women in 1922 was all the more important because of dramatic shifts underway in the economies of the reservation and the surrounding community of non-Indian towns and farms. As the lumber industry exhausted available timber and moved on from northern Wisconsin, communities struggled to reinvent themselves and find new ways to make a living. Anishinaabe women at Lac Courte Oreilles and Lac du Flambeau were key actors in this economic transformation, because they played a central role in the region's shift to a service economy based on tourism. Within Anishinaabe communities tourism work provided an avenue where women could respond to changes in the political, economic, and natural environments of their reservations. As local tribes lost control of their forests and lakes, Indians had no choice but to adapt to the arrival of tourists from industrial cities like Milwaukee and Chicago. In addition, the advent of tourism work also enabled Ojibwe women to retain control over their households and their annual cultural and subsistence routines. Tourism-related work offered a new source of revenue without requiring Native women to conform to the government's program of stamping out what it considered the dangerous and backward aspects of American Indian culture.

In northern Wisconsin, Anishinaabe communities were able to use tourism work and tourists to counter Office of Indian Affairs (OIA) programs that sought to destroy their cultures and curb their autonomy. Through their innovation and adoption of aspects of tourism work, Ojibwe women continued a gendered system of labor that was key to the culture of work in their communities. Considering women's work in these two communities reveals the ways in which American Indians were able to hold onto and adapt fundamental structures of labor in communities and also the critical role that women played in this process.

Tourism work upset not only the U.S. federal government's narrow, paternalist model of labor but it also challenges a perspective that has limited scholars' ability to incorporate American Indian women's labor into their histories of work. Tourism labor is valuable in this regard because it requires a broad conception of work and workplace. It includes many activities in which women played a vital role, such as commodity production, domestic labor, farming, gathering, and performance, and that contributed to the maintenance of Native American households and communities. Yet such activities have been largely overlooked at times by scholars who operate with a narrow definition of work as primarily waged labor (Kessler-Harris 1993). It brings together types of work that have been separated by binary constructions of labor according to gender or to their supposed reflection of "traditional" or "modern" economic systems (O'Neill 2004). In doing so, tourism work challenges divisions within labor history and highlights women's contributions to reservation economies and their role in maintaining and adapting cultural systems of labor division.

The range of activities that came to be associated with tourist work also suggests how diverse and complex Native subsistence strategies had become by the 1920s. People like the residents of Lac Courte Oreilles and Lac du Flambeau followed a yearly, opportunistic circuit that exploited the rich and varied resources of the local environment. Rooted in ancient lifeways, this circuit had not disappeared with the advent of non-Indian settlement. If anything, it had become more complex. Ojibwe households worked, in season, in the sugar bush–producing maple sugar and syrup in the early spring. Then, in the summer, Anishinaabeg worked at fishing grounds, in gardens, and in berry patches. From there, they migrated to camps at wild rice beds in the late summer or early fall. Finally, in the late fall and early winter, households traveled to their hunting grounds (Danzinger 1979: 10–13). In the winter, households spent most of their time in dome-shaped wigwams, which held up to eight persons. In summer, communities converged at more permanent summer villages (9–10). In each of these locations, men and women engaged in gendered work that contributed to the survival of households, the clan, and community.

In the nineteenth century, Ojibwe men added wage labor in the lumber industry, railroads, and other industries to their circuit. As seasonal work, these occupations were well-suited to the old pattern and they provided substitutes for resources that had been lost (through the decline in the fur trade and the disappearance of some game) (Shifferd 1976: 16, 36). Adding to the complexity of the new subsistence cycle, wage labor typically gendered male required yet another economic adaptation in which women were key—a service economy of providing food and goods, housing, and services for the men involved (Jensen 2006: 51–54). Activities including wage labor were folded into seasonal patterns of work as one more strand within highly diversified economic strategies that drew on men's and women's work.

Finding means, such as through wage labor, to supplement economic strategies centered around natural resources became increasingly important in the twentieth century because of the combined factors of the environmental impact of the timber industry and the increasing regulation of hunting and fishing by the State of Wisconsin. By the early twentieth century, the timber industry that had been very profitable in the region was beginning to dry up and could no longer serve as a reliable source of cash for Anishinaabe communities. These changes in the lumber industry were compounded by the increasing regulation of Ojibwe access to natural resources by the State of Wisconsin. The first official land cessions of the Anishinaabeg of northern Wisconsin came with the treaties of 1837 and 1842, in which Ojibwe ceded lands to the U.S. federal government. In both treaties, however, Wisconsin Ojibwe reserved the right to access and harvest fish, wildlife, and plants from the ceded area. This was also the case in the Treaty of 1854, in which Wisconsin Anishinaabeg averted relocation but were confined to four reservations, Lac du Flambeau, Red Cliff, Bad River, and Lac Courte Oreilles (Silvern 2000: 132). The Wisconsin Supreme Court, however, reversed this policy in 1908 in *State v. Morrin*, ruling that Ojibwe off-reservation harvesting rights, established in the treaties of 1837 and 1842, were abrogated when Wisconsin became a state in 1848 (Satz 1991: 85). After 1887, the state of Wisconsin also employed conservation wardens to regulate fish and game and enforce state laws (Valliere 2004: 47–48). As with the decreased opportunity for employment in lumber camps, the increased regulation of natural resources and denial of Ojibwe treaty rights put pressure on reservation economies. The strain placed on hunting and fishing—both male tasks—and wage labor in the lumber industry made women's labor all the more important to communities in this period. This pressure also caused both men and women in Ojibwe communities to seek new areas of employment and labor including tourism work.

By the early twentieth century, then, Anishinaabe men and women had already incorporated a variety of opportunities from the non-Indian economy into their economic lives. They had also initiated various activities that can be thought of as tourism work, including "export" commodity production, performance, and guide and service work. These activities were united by their focus on an influx of outsiders as their audiences and consumers. As with other activities that were part of the seasonal round and Anishinaabe economies, tourism work could be combined with other forms of labor to contribute to household economies.

In the early years of the tourism economy in northern Wisconsin, fishing became a primary factor attracting tourists to Ojibwe reservations. It eventually spawned other forms of tourism labor, including women's work. This fit well with Wisconsin tourism promoters' attempts to sell the state as a site of outdoor recreation and adventure (Shapiro 2005: 63, 87–89, 211–21; Bawden 2001: 64–69). Chicago and North Western Railway promotions focused on the boating, fishing, sporting, and other activities a vacationer could enjoy in northern Wisconsin, which it called the "Enchanted Summer Land" (*My Rambles* 1882). Anishinaabe men were able to capitalize on tourists' interest in fishing through their work as guides. Guide work comprised one of the earliest and most reliable forms of tourism work for Anishinaabeg in northern Wisconsin and served as a foundation upon which other forms of labor were built.

Ojibwe women also engaged in work related to tourism's growth and contributed to households' and communities' economic survival, as shown in the 1922 industrial surveys. The surveys record the continuation of mixed economic strategies and gendered labor systems. Of 135 households surveyed at Lac du Flambeau, the surveyor indicated some kind of labor for 123 women. The most common kinds of labor listed were bead work (68 women); making moccasins (65 women); making maple sugar and syrup (59 women); gathering, selling, and/ or canning berries (42 women); making birch-bark items (33 women); making reed mats (33 women); making rag rugs (34 women); tanning hides (19 women); and harvesting wild rice (20 women). Twenty women indicated some kind of wage work, with eleven women working at resorts and four others engaged in work, such as doing laundry and cooking for tourists, which was clearly linked to vacationing. The latter work would not have been altogether different from that performed in connection with the lumber industry. Another five were involved in some kind of business including a hotel and a pop shop (Reports of Industrial Surveys. Lac du Flambeau). Like men's wage labor, women's tourism work was integrated into a diversified economy; it was an important part, but not the exclusive means by which people sustained themselves and earned cash. In the case of Lac Courte Oreilles, 138 household surveys were conducted. Although these provide less detail than those conducted at Lac du Flambeau, they mark women's contributions in the realms of gardening, stock raising, and wage labor (Reports of Industrial Surveys. Hayward Indian School).

If the industrial surveys show the commonality of some of these activities, the industrial sections of Office of Indian Affairs superintendents' annual reports show their economic contributions. Beadwork, the most common activity listed for Lac du Flambeau women, engaged 200 people at Lac du Flambeau in 1911, bringing in $2,000 (1911 Statistical Report. Lac du Flambeau). A decade later, beadwork and articles manufactured from buckskin brought in $3,000 in each of two consecutive years. In those same years, basket-making and birch-bark work brought in $2500 each year (1922 Statistical Report and 1923 Statistical Report. Lac du Flambeau). At Lac Courte Oreilles, women found a ready market for beadwork in tourists and sold from $800 to $1000 in beadwork in a year, making this a key source of revenue for those on the reservation (McQuigg 1916). Women's role in this industry and the profit derived from the work was reflected in 1920 when Superintendent Balmer brought up women's craft sales as well as men's guide work as a reason the fish hatchery at Lac du Flambeau should be rebuilt to help attract tourist dollars (Balmer 1920). In years with good berry crops, women also sold berries to tourists (Balmer 1922). Even as fishing may have been a foundation for Wisconsin tourism, women's work and sales came to be a critical part of tourism's potential to bring cash to communities.

The growth of tourism in Wisconsin came with economic costs as well as gains for communities, however. Tourism created a series of political and economic problems. As the natural environment became an increasingly valued commodity to Wisconsin's tourism industry, the state took issue with American Indian populations' hunting, gathering, and fishing outside of reservation boundaries (Nesper 2002: 49). Thus, tourism was an industry with the potential to both insulate Anishinaabeg economically from strains on natural resources but also to feed into State of Wisconsin policies that rejected and ignored Ojibwe treaty rights.

Tourism work also contributed to a loss of land for Ojibwe communities. In the 1910s at reservations such as Lac du Flambeau, certain government officials encouraged the selling of prime lakefront property as a means of bringing in cash to the reservation and also attracting future tourists (1914 Narrative Report. Lac du Flambeau). While not explicitly stated, the push for land sales rather than encouraging Anishinaabeg to develop hotels and other tourism infrastructure reflected the paternalist mindset of the Office of Indian Affairs toward American Indian communities in the period, which held that they were in need of guidance and reeducation. Superintendent Sickels wrote in 1911, "The Flambeau Indians compare quite favorably with others as to industry and ability to support themselves up to a certain standard—but like most members of the Red race they are lacking in thrift and perseverance. They are but as children—most of them—reckoned from the white man's standard, and it is hard to inculcate in their minds the value of their money, any ideas of economy, business management, future welfare, effects of alcoholism, or anything else" (1911 Narrative Report. Lac du Flambeau). Thus, in the case of valuable lakefront property, tourists arrived to expedite a process of dispossession that was connected to the assimilationist policies and paternalist mindset of the era.

While the overall economic benefits of tourism are questionable at best, this arena of labor buttressed the Native communities' ability to counter the government's ongoing campaign to undermine and eradicate their community traditions. Ojibwe women took part in a series of undertakings that helped influence the cultural meaning of tourism work by altering the meanings of federal government programs and contesting their definitions of work. Along with communal land ownership and education, government programs aimed at cultural assimilation took an interest in labor. Wage and especially agricultural labor were seen as critical pathways to self-sufficiency (Hoxie 1984). The meanings of these programs were often changed, though, between the time of their inception and their implementation in communities. In the case of Ojibwe communities in Wisconsin, women played a key role in this transformation.

Through their participation in fairs, Anishinaabe women fostered a market for crafts and aided the expansion of a culturally centered tourism. Although the agricultural fairs promoted agricultural achievements and showcased the production of communities beginning in the 1910s, exhibitors and visitors also derived their own meanings from the exchanges that took place (Jensen 2006: 81). Lac du Flambeau women aided the expansion of markets for their own goods through their participation in annual agricultural fairs after 1915 (1915 Narrative Report. Lac du Flambeau). A 1919 report illustrated the excitement that accompanied the fair: "The opening day was attended by practically all reservation Indians and several hundred visitors and tourists in that region of Wisconsin. Over 100 automobiles were parked in the fair grounds or on the premises, and the Indian productions were sought with wonderful avidity by the visitors. Practically everything in Indian Handicraft, such as beadwork, moccasins or buckskin bags, rugs, quilts or other fabrics, and such curios and articles as were made by these Indians—all were sought and fancy prices paid for every product" (1919 Narrative Report. Lac du Flambeau). By Lac du Flambeau's fifth annual agricultural fair, OIA Superintendent James Balmer reported that tourists would have purchased all craft items on the first day of the fair if officials had not prevented it (1920 Narrative Report. Lac du Flambeau). Ojibwe women took advantage of a space in which their work could be showcased, one in which it was not necessarily intended to be the main focus. Only 25 percent of the prize money at the 1915 Lac du Flambeau fair, for example, went to nonagricultural items such as women's crafts (List of 1915 Fair Prizes. Lac du Flambeau). Yet, as reports show, women's work generated a great deal of interest for the fairs and altered their overall meaning for those displaying their goods and those purchasing crafts.

In utilizing fairs in this way, Ojibwe women also helped reshape Wisconsin tourism. Increasingly American Indian communities including Lac du Flambeau and Lac Courte Oreilles became a visible presence in advertisements for Wisconsin tourism (Bawden 2001: 69, 93–96). Tourism promotional material drew travelers to the region by tapping into these desires to escape from the city and witness something unique in Wisconsin, part of a larger trend of antimodernism in America (Lears 1981; Deloria 1998). In the case of Wisconsin, urban vacationers from Milwaukee and particularly Chicago were a vital source for travelers to the region (Shapiro 2005: 65, 213; Bawden 2001: 7). After indicating that Lac du Flambeau offered a good location for fishing muskies, black bass, and pike, the Chicago and North Western Railway's pamphlet "Lakes and Resorts of the Northwest" continued, "The Indian village and their modes of living, as seen on the reservation, is well worth the trip itself" ("Lakes and Resorts" 1916: 20). The Indian Village or Old Village had developed as an enclave at Lac du Flambeau that consciously resisted the influence of Euro-American society in residential decisions, personal contacts, recognition of leadership, and work patterns (Valliere 2004: 32). By making an antiassimilationist enclave the focus of tourism material, advertisements responded to a popular desire of urban populations in the early twentieth century to reconnect with nature through both activities and the observation of "exoticized" populations (Deloria 1998).

Ojibwe women incorporated these trends into their work patterns. They took advantage of such advertisements and sold goods directly from their homes at Lac du Flambeau, hanging bracelets and other goods from a string across their window so that tourists could see what they were making and stop to buy goods (Tornes 2004: 89). The 1926 pamphlet "Summer Outings: Wisconsin, Michigan," featured an image of a performance by Native Americans with a large crowd of onlookers, and stated, "The Indians, with their tribal dances, are a great attraction in this Great North Woods Country" (9). Here, American Indians came to be more than facilitators of the Wisconsin vacation that centered on fishing and outdoor recreation; they served as a tourist spectacle in and of themselves. Women played a critical role in this transition in tourism by participating in performances and offering goods for sale, which allowed visitors to consume a part of the culture that attracted them.

In taking part in this transition in tourism, Ojibwe women also contributed to a contestation over definitions of work. While the federal government offered a vision of specific kinds of labor being the most culturally and morally advantageous for American Indian communities, these ideas often were at odds with the material realities of the areas in which American Indian communities resided. Such was the case in northern Wisconsin where all of the government's advocating of farming could not transform the soil that made farming for all in the region difficult at best (Gough 1997: 4–5).

When the government's vision conflicted with the material reality of circumstances, community members countered it in their labor, as was the case in northern Wisconsin. The issue of proper work and behavior became the most heated around the matter of dance. In the 1910s and 1920s, particularly following Commissioner of Indian Affairs Charles Burke's famous Circular 1665 (1921) in which he denounced dances, efforts were undertaken around the United States to record instances of and to regulate American Indian dances (Ellis 2003: 65). Commissioner Burke wrote to Lac Courte Oreilles expressing his concern about the potential influence of tourism: "In an inspection report relative to your reservation, it is stated that there has been a great influx of tourists to that part of the country who encourage Indians to engage in their old-time pow wows, dances, etc., with the result that they neglect their homes and make little preparation for winter. This condition, of course, is undesirable, and every effort should be made to remedy it so far as practicable" (Burke 1925). At Lac du Flambeau, the OIA agency had fought a nagging but largely unsuccessful battle against various phenomena that they identified as hindrances to assimilation on the reservation during the 1910s. Key among their concerns was dancing, which a 1916 report identified as "a very important factor in the slow progress which has been made by these Indians" (1916 Narrative Report. Lac du Flambeau; Ellis 2003: 55–77; Jacobs 1999).

While superintendents embraced the potential of certain parts of tourism labor, dancing for tourists remained a point of contention. In the 1925 report Lac du Flambeau's superintendent reflected on an increasing commercialization of dances and on their new role as a revenue-producing activity on the reservation, viewing it as coming at a great cost to cultural reform on the reservation (1925 Narrative Report. Lac du Flambeau). The popularity of these dances came to be seen as a threat to agency authority at Lac du Flambeau in the 1920s. Superintendent Hammitt proclaimed his helplessness to prevent them because the public and tourists expected dances at the reservation. He wrote in 1927, "To endeavor to stop [Indian tribal dances] by drastic measure will inflame the 'Dear public' and cause endless trouble." At the same time he also observed how the exchange between Anishinaabe performers and tourists had deflected OIA policy. He lamented, "Were it not for this same public and the tourist, [the dances] would have probably been dead by this time" (1927 Narrative Report. Lac du Flambeau). This suggests that in responding to the demands of the consumer, Anishinaabe men and women were able to insulate themselves against the power of the Lac du Flambeau agency in its efforts to control dancing on the reservation as part of its agenda of cultural assimilation (see also Raibmon 2005: 48–49). In countering this vision, dancers exerted their own views of acceptable work and behavior for their communities.

The debates over dances reveal how definitions of tourism labor and work more generally were politically charged in Wisconsin in the early twentieth century. In attempting to assert authority at Lac du Flambeau, Superintendent Hammitt refused to include them within his own definition of work. He readily acknowledged that money could be made through dances, but he remained unwilling to see dances as a form of legitimate labor, on par with farming. Expressing his frustration with Flambeau residing in the Old Village he wrote, "[T]he dance gives them a little ready cash. The answer is, therefore, plain, 'Why work!'" (1926 Narrative Report. Lac du Flambeau). Tourist dollars complicated ideological debates about which forms of work could be considered proper and constructive among local communities and the Office of Indian Affairs, and economic evidence at times challenged the theoretical ideas of government officials about work and uplift (Ellis 2003; Moses 1996).

However, if this revenue was not convincing for Superintendent Hammitt, it seems performers were more flexible in their definitions. In 1929, Lac du Flambeau saw $1000 in gate receipts for dances (1929 Narrative Report. Lac du Flambeau Agency). Lac Courte Oreilles Ojibwe also charged fifty cents per person to on-lookers at dances held on summer Sundays in Reserve and experienced "good patronage" (Ryder 1925). Funds from public performances were divided among the men and women dancing ("The Industrial Situation" 1931). Wanda Brown Hunt later recalled of such events "[T]here were a lot of tourists . . . So I think it was a moneymaking thing too" (Tornes 2004: 232). In these cases, the men and women who participated in tourism labor defended the ability of communities to chart their own course in the realm of work and culture.

Along with monetary concerns, many of these events had an important social function for communities. Hunt highlighted community as well as economic importance in her descriptions, stating, "It was for both [the community and tourists]. . . . Those were big powwows, all kinds of activities out there, not just dancing. Races and things like that, games" (232). Annual fairs also included social events and contests including a "ladies race" (Program for 1917 Indian Fair Lac du Flambeau). Community and socializing was likely a key motivation for the Lac Courte Oreilles Ojibwe who participated in the Apostle Islands Indian Pageant in the mid-1920s. Despite having earned only about 8 dollars for their participation in the three-week pageant during the 1924 event, about 225 Lac Courte Oreilles Ojibwe returned the next year, where they earned about the same amount (Everest 1925). The opportunity to engage in sports and visit with friends and relatives be-tween performances may have been more attractive than the meager pay (Everest 1924). Thus, tourism events could provide important social venues for workers as well as tourists. Such labor also continued an important aspect of Ojibwe work culture where during activities such as picking berries and harvesting wild rice, community togetherness and labor were intertwined (Norrgard 2009: 37, 43, 52). In furthering Wisconsin tourism that focused on the consuming of American Indian cultures, Ojibwe women continued this culture of labor.

Tourism proved an important form of work during the difficult economic times of the 1930s. Agnes Archdale, who worked in the kitchen and waiting tables at Ben C. Gauthier's resort, later recalled of the period, "[Resorts] and guiding, that's the only jobs there were." (Tornes 2004: 89). The importance of tourism at Lac du Flambeau was reaffirmed by its centrality in New Deal reforms and programs on the reservation. In the fall of 1936, the Lac du Flambeau tribal council decided to allocate money for advertising in an attempt to attract tourists to the region ("Chippewa Tribe to Advertise" 1935: E7). In 1938, the Lac du Flambeau reserva-tion borrowed money from the Indian Reorganization Act's revolving loan funds to develop summer cottages on Fence Lake in the reservation ("Lac du Flambeau

Chippewas" 1938: 30). Such production was further encouraged between 1939 and 1941, when a unit of the Indian Weaving Program operated at Lac du Flambeau producing, among other things, items to sell to tourists (Boardman 1994). These efforts suggest how initiatives of the 1930s focused on tourism as a key part of the economic future of northern Wisconsin Ojibwe communities.

In their incorporation and adaptation of tourism work, Anishinaabe women at Lac du Flambeau and Lac Courte Oreilles engaged in forms of economic and cultural innovation critical to communities. Tourism development certainly impacted communities in negative ways such as the role it played in Wisconsin's failure to uphold Anishinaabe treaty rights in 1908 and in land sales to tourists and developers, which expedited the dispossession of communities' land bases in the twentieth century. However, exploring the activities in Anishinaabe communities in the context of the tourism industry reveals tourism was more than a story of exploitation. Native Wisconsin communities invested meaning in this labor. In catering to the ever-changing demands of tourists and promoting culturally centered tourism, Ojibwe women maintained a gendered and balanced labor system in their communities. They also contested the power of outsiders to define proper work for them and found ways to incorporate social aspects with labor in ways that supported traditional meanings of work. The case of Anishinaabe women's tourism work in northern Wisconsin reveals the creative ways American Indian communities met changes in the market and contributed toward economic and ideological visions for their communities in their labor.

Works Cited

1911 Narrative Report. *Annual Reports, 1909–1916*, Lac du Flambeau Agency.

1911 Statistical Report. *Annual Reports, 1909–1916*, Lac du Flambeau Agency.

1914 Narrative Report. *Annual Reports, 1909–1916*, Lac du Flambeau Agency.

1915 Narrative Report. Lac du Flambeau. *Superintendents' Annual Reports.*

1916 Narrative Report. Lac du Flambeau. *Superintendents' Annual Reports.*

1919 Narrative Report. Lac du Flambeau. 88855-19-Lac du Flambeau-910, Box 108, Lac du Flambeau School and Agency. *Central Classified Files.*

1920 Narrative Report. Lac du Flambeau. *Superintendents' Annual Reports.*

1922 Statistical Report. Lac du Flambeau. *Superintendents' Annual Reports.*

1923 Statistical Report. Lac du Flambeau. *Superintendents' Annual Reports.*

1925 Narrative Report. Lac du Flambeau. *Superintendents' Annual Reports.*

1926 Narrative Report. Lac du Flambeau. *Superintendents' Annual Reports.*

1927 Narrative Report. Lac du Flambeau. *Superintendents' Annual Reports.*

1929 Narrative Report. Lac du Flambeau. *Superintendents' Annual Reports.*

Annual Reports, 1909–1916. Lac du Flambeau Agency. Record Group 75. National Archives, Great Lakes Branch, Chicago, Ill.

Balmer, James W., Superintendent Lac du Flambeau. Letter to the Commissioner of Indian Affairs. September 23, 1920. 79867-20-Lac du Flambeau-338, Box 55, Lac du Flambeau Agency. *Central Classified Files.*

————. Letter to the Commissioner of Indian Affairs. June 26, 1922. *Reports of Industrial Surveys*, Lac du Flambeau.

Bawden, Timothy. "Reinventing the Frontier: Tourism, Nature, and Environmental Change in Northern Wisconsin, 1880–1930. PhD dissertation, University of Wisconsin-Madison, 2001.

Boardman, Michelle. "Ojibwa Weavers and Works Progress Administration Work Relief: A Study of the Indian Weaving Unit, Lac du Flambeau, Wisconsin, 1939–1941." MS thesis, University of Wisconsin-Madison, 1994.

Burke, Charles H., Commissioner of Indian Affairs. Letter to James Ryder, Superintendent Hayward Indian School. November 28, 1925. Reservation—1925, Box 7, 1924–26. *General Correspondence of the Superintendent, 1914–31*, Hayward Indian School.

Central Classified Files (#121). Record Group 75. National Archives, Washington, D.C.

"Chippewa Tribe to Advertise." *New York Times* (September 13, 1935): E7.

Danzinger, Edmund Jefferson, Jr. *The Chippewas of Lake Superior*. Norman: University of Oklahoma Press, 1979.

Deloria, Philip J. *Playing Indian*. New Haven: Yale University Press, 1998.

Ellis, Clyde. *A Dancing People: Powwow Culture on the Southern Plains*. Lawrence: University Press of Kansas, 2003.

Everest, P.S., Superintendent La Pointe Indian Agency. Letter to the Commissioner of Indian Affairs. September 10, 1924. 1363-La Pointe 1924-047, Box 2, La Pointe Agency. *Central Classified Files*.

————. August 19, 1925. 1363-La Pointe 1924-047, Box 2, La Pointe Agency. *Central Classified Files*.

General Correspondence of the Superintendent, 1914–31. Hayward Indian School. Record Group 75. National Archives, Great Lakes Branch, Chicago, Ill.

Gough, Robert. *Farming the Cutover: A Social History of Northern Wisconsin, 1900–1940*. Lawrence: University Press of Kansas, 1997.

Historical Pamphlet Collection. Wisconsin Historical Society, Madison, Wis.

Hoxie, Frederick. *A Final Promise: The Campaign to Assimilate the Indians, 1880–1920*. Lincoln: University of Nebraska Press, 1984.

"The Industrial Situation." Received January 19, 1931. 3340-H1930-916, Box 109, Hayward Indian School. *Central Classified Files*.

Jacobs, Margaret. *Engendered Encounters: Feminism and Pueblo Cultures, 1879–1934*. Lincoln: University of Nebraska Press, 1999.

Jensen, Joan. *Calling This Place Home: Women on the Wisconsin Frontier, 1850–1925*. Minneapolis: Minnesota Historical Society Press, 2006.

Kessler-Harris, Alice. "Treating the Male as 'Other': Redefining the Parameters of Labor History." *Labor History* 34.2–3 (1993): 190–204.

"Lac du Flambeau Chippewas Build Summer Colony." *Indians at Work* 5:13 (August 1938): 30.

"Lakes and Resorts of the Northwest." *Historical Pamphlet Collection*. Chicago: Chicago and North Western Railway Passenger Department, 1916.

Lears, T. J. Jackson. *No Place of Grace: Antimodernism and the Transformation of American Culture, 1880–1920*. New York: Pantheon Books, 1981.

List of 1915 Fair Prizes. 83106-15-Lac du Flambeau-047, Box 2, Lac du Flambeau Agency. *Central Classified Files*.

McQuigg, H. J., Superintendent Hayward Indian School. June 6, 1916. Letter to the Commissioner of Indian Affairs. Circulars—Replies to 1914–16, Box 1, 1914–16. *General Correspondence of the Superintendent, 1914–1931*. Hayward Indian School.

Moses, L. G. *Wild West Shows and the Images of American Indians, 1883–1933*. Albuquerque: University of New Mexico Press, 1996.

My Rambles in the Enchanted Summer Land of the Great Northwest, during the Tourist Season of 1881. Chicago: Rand McNally Co., 1882.

Nesper, Larry. *The Walleye War: The Struggle for Ojibwe Spearfishing and Treaty Rights*. Lincoln: University of Nebraska Press, 2002.

Norrgard, Chantal. "From Berries to Orchards: Tracing the History of Berrying and Economic Transformation among Lake Superior Ojibwe." *American Indian Quarterly* 33.1 (2009): 33–61.

O'Neill, Colleen. "Rethinking Modernity and the Discourse of Development in American Indian History, an Introduction." *Native Pathways: American Indian Culture and Economic Development in the Twentieth Century*. Eds. Brian Hosmer and Colleen O'Neill. Boulder: University of Colorado Press, 2004: 1–24.

Program for 1917 Indian Fair. 4617-1918-Lac du Flambeau-047, Box 2, Lac du Flambeau Agency. *Central Classified Files*.

Raibmon, Paige. *Authentic Indians: Episodes of Encounter from the Late-Nineteenth-Century Northwest Coast*. Durham: Duke University Press, 2005.

Reports of Industrial Surveys (#762). Hayward Indian School. Record Group 75. National Archives, Washington, D.C.

———— Lac du Flambeau. Record Group 75. National Archives, Washington, D.C.

Ryder, James P., Superintendent. Hayward Indian School. Letter to the Commissioner of Indian Affairs. December 9, 1925. Reservation—1925–26, Box 7, 1924–26. *General Correspondence of the Superintendent*, 1914–31. Hayward Indian School.

Satz, Ronald N. *Chippewa Treaty Rights: The Reserved Rights of Wisconsin's Chippewa Indians in Historical Perspective*. Eu Claire, Wis.: The Wisconsin Academy of Sciences, Arts, and Letters, 1991.

Shapiro, Alex. "'One Crop Worth Cultivating': Tourism in the Upper Great Lakes, 1910–1965." PhD dissertation, The University of Chicago, 2005.

Shifferd, Patricia A. "A Study in Economic Change: The Chippewa of Northern Wisconsin, 1854–1900." *Western Canadian Journal of Anthropology* 6.4 (1976): 16–41.

Silvern, Steven E. "Reclaiming the Reservation: The Geopolitics of Wisconsin Anishinaabe Resource Rights." *American Indian Culture and Research Journal* 24.3 (2000): 131–53.

"Summer Outings: Wisconsin, Michigan." *Historical Pamphlet Collection*. Chicago: Chicago and North Western Line, 1926.

Superintendents' Annual Reports, National Archives Microfilm Publications M1011.

Tornes, Elizabeth, ed. *Memories of the Lac du Flambeau Elders*. Madison, Wis.: Center for the Study of Upper Midwestern Cultures, 2004.

———. "Interview with Agnes Archdale and Liza Brown." Conducted by Verlaine Farmilant. *Memories of the Lac du Flambeau Elders* 76–90.

———. "Interview with Wanda Brown Hunt." Conducted by Verlaine Farmilant. *Memories of the Lac du Flambeau Elders*, 225–38.

Valliere, Leon, Jr. "A Brief History of the Waaswaaganing Ojibweg Lac du Flambeau Chippewa Indians Gaa-izhiwebak ishkweyaang." Tornes, *Memories of the Lac du Flambeau Elders* 2004: 9–75.

CHAPTER 9

Nimble Fingers and Strong Backs

First Nations and Métis Women in Fur Trade
and Rural Economies

Sherry Farrell Racette

Nurse Tracy, from Wally Dion's *Red Worker Series* (2005–6) is the Saulteaux
artist's visual response to those who suggest that the demographic shift toward
an Aboriginal majority in the province of Saskatchewan will lead to economic
collapse (figure 9.1). Dion's *Red Workers*, with their obvious references to the
heroic workers of Soviet Socialist Realism and the propaganda art of the Chinese
Cultural Revolution challenge the prevalent and persistent construction of

Figure 9.1. Wally Dion,
"Nurse Tracy," 2005.
Acrylic on wood panel,
48 × 38¾ inches.
Collection of the Canada
Council Art Bank, Ottawa,
Ontario. Reproduced with
permission of the artist.

Aboriginal people (both male and female) as nonproductive and nonworking. The large portrait of *Nurse Tracy* sets a strong young woman gazing into the future, her shoulders squared, against a stormy prairie sky. The subtle grid that cuts the painted surface into squares suggests the categories and attitudes that confine and restrict her. Among these confining and restricting paradigms, are the two principal, and contradictory, constructions projected onto the female Indigenous body: the lazy squaw and the squaw drudge. In that paradigm, women are both lazy (unwilling to work) AND engaged in drudgery (hard, boring work). Aboriginal women are constructed as nonproductive and peripheral, yet in many regions of Canada, from the fur trade to the twentieth century, aspects of Euro-Canadian economies have been dependent on a pool of female Aboriginal laborers.

This relationship between women and European economies began during the fur trade, although hard work has always been part of women's lives. Survival in the northern forests and plains required constant activity and strategic thinking. It was that harsh reality that pushed European men and their enterprises toward the skills of women. The necessity of having First Nations women as companions and helpmates was an accepted aspect of life during the fur trade unacknowledged in Canadian historiography until Jennifer Brown's *Strangers in Blood* (1980) and Sylvia Van Kirk's *Many Tender Ties* (1980). These seminal works emphasized women's roles in the network of fur trade families and communities, recognizing the importance of their knowledge of the country, their work as mothers, guides, negotiators, and interpreters. Other aspects of their lives as workers are less known.

They Are Virtually Your Honor's Servants

While female skills and women's power were essential to connect European men into social and economic networks necessary for physical survival and business success, the two major fur trade enterprises, the Hudson's Bay Company (est. 1670) and the North West Company (est. 1779) were ambivalent about the reciprocity that developed between men and women. By 1683, the Hudson's Bay Company's London Committee saw women as an alarming and expensive distraction, writing a directive stating

> we have been much prejudiced by the entertaineing [*sic*] of Indian women in our Forts & factories for thereby our serveants [*sic*] have not only been debauched but our goods and provisions have been extravagantly spent wherfor [*sic*] in the next place we doe [*sic*] absolutely prohibit you to permitt [*sic*] any such familiaritys [*sic*] as formerly have   been and . . . suffer no women to be entertained or admitted into our Forts or houses under penallty [*sic*] of the forfeiture of their wages (Rich 1948: 75).

The London Committee's position was difficult to enforce, as Andrew Graham observed after his retirement in 1775: "The Company permits no European women to be brought within their territories, and forbid [sic] any natives to be harboured in the settlements. This latter has never been obeyed" (Calloway 2008: 157).

The North West Company's strategy was to take the trade inland, increasing reliance on Indigenous networks and knowledge, but they also were concerned with the growing populations at fur trade posts. Alexander Henry the Younger, a North West Company clerk and later partner, frequently enumerated men and their families in his journals (1799–1814). The journals documented his movement from 1799 to 1814 from one North West Company post to another in present-day Manitoba, Minnesota, North Dakota, Saskatchewan, and Alberta. In 1800 Henry's Red River outfit consisted of twenty-one men, four women, and four children (Gough 1988: 23–24). By 1809, he was in charge of Fort Vermillion, home to thirty-seven men, twenty-seven women, and sixty-seven children (448–49). Henry's Report of the North West Population, 1805 revealed that the combined total of women and children at individual fur trade posts often outnumbered the men (Gough 1988: 188). His report may have been preparatory to a motion passed by the partners of the North West Company at their 1805 annual meeting at Kaministiqua, which described the "heavy burden" of provisioning growing communities "maintained at the expense of the Concern." The resulting motion proposed stiff fines and penalties for any man, "either Partner, Clerk or Engagé" taking "under any pretense [sic] whatsoever, any woman or maid from any of the tribes of Indians now known or hereafter become known in this Country to live with him in the fashion of the North West" (Wallace 1934: 211). Supervising officers were to be fined 100£ for failing to control the actions of men under their jurisdiction. Ironically, the signing partners had been partially responsible for creating "the fashion of the North West" as each had at least one family of their own, which no doubt provided the rationale for including an important appendum: "It is however understood that taking a daughter of a White man, after the fashion of the Country should be considered no violation of this Resolve" (211) In this way, the partners simultaneously provided for the development of sexually self-sufficient communities, a means to integrate their own daughters into the social and economic life of the fur trade post.

Between 1802 and 1803, the London Committee of the Hudson's Bay Company negotiated the role of women with their respective employees at York Factory, Eastmain, and Moose Factory, acknowledging both their presence and the value of their work. The men of York Factory wrote a spirited defense in 1802, reminding the committee of women's critical roles in the operations of the post and the business of trade:

> [T]he women are deserving of some encouragement and indulgence from your honors, they clean and put into a state of preservation all beaver and otter skins brought by the Indians undried and in bad condition—they prepare line for snowshoes and knit them also without which your honor's servants could not give efficient opposition to the Canadian traders. They make leather shoes for

the men who are obliged to travel about in search of Indians and furs and are useful in a variety of other instances—in short they are virtually your honors servants and as such we hope you will consider them (Ballenden et al. 1802: 41).

The London Committee appears to have been beleaguered by an advocacy campaign, possibly in response to punitive policies. Officers at Eastmain informed the committee that their "wives are in general out hunting in winter" and traded their furs for "cloathing [*sic*] for their children and themselves" countering any opinion that women were nonproductive and dependent (Governor and Committee 1803: 1d). Their use of the term "wives" advocated respect. Payment in trade goods was also the subject of the committee's correspondence with the men of Moose Factory in 1802, "we do not object to the women being paid for their services in trapping martens etc. it [*sic*] is the omissions in the account books of 'articles' expended we dislike—it conveys to us that our property in many instances is distributed at random" (269). While the quibbling indicates managerial tensions around women, the exchanges affirm that women were essential to the trade, were valued by their husbands, and received both recognition and remuneration for their work.

As previously noted, Henry's journals are a window into the contradictory characterizations of women's work at fur trade posts wherein women were simultaneously viewed as integral to daily economic life, and as a burden on company provisions, much of which their own labor provided. It becomes apparent when reading Henry and other diarists that fur trade economies adopt the seasonal harvesting cycles of Indigenous communities, with that work performed by the women at the post. In March 1801 at Pembina, Henry described "the Indian women making sugar" (Gough 1988: 112). On April 1, he noted the women were "having excellent sport" when an entire herd of buffalo broke through the ice of the Park River, their bodies trapped and preserved by the ice (113). The women harvested the buffalo for the entire month of April, processing meat, tongues, and tallow until the weather warmed and the flesh was too decomposed to be useful. In spring and fall the women gathered and processed spruce gum, storing it in kegs for later use waterproofing canoes and roofs. At Fort Vermillion and Terre Blanche in late July and August women gathered and preserved gallons of saskatoons, raspberries, strawberries, blueberries, gooseberries, and cranberries as each came into season. In 1808 Henry noted with satisfaction, "Our people now feast daily upon Poires, Straw Berries, Rasp Berries and the small Red Cherries" (459). Women also tilled the gardens, planting and harvesting potatoes, corn, and squash.

While most of these activities were, by necessity, synchronized with natural cycles, the fur trade also imposed demands on resources that pushed women's harvesting practices beyond traditional cycles. *Wattap*, or spruce root used for stitching birch bark, was generally gathered in the early spring when the ground was moist and the sap ran. When the roots were moist and close to the surface, they could be pulled, cleaned, and split with relative ease, and processing was easier. Henry kept a sharp eye on wattap harvest and supplies because spruce root was essential for canoe construction and repair. During the period of intense competition prior to the merger of the two companies in 1821 each company moved aggressively, traveling during inclement weather, risking lives and cargo. Each canoe in every "brigade" was supplied with gum, bark, and wattap for repairs en route (Rich 1938: 166). This demand placed pressure on both supplies and suppliers.

As Henry's entry for July 19, 1810, noted, "Women raising Wattap, each eight bundles, Thirty-three women," a total harvest of 264 bundles of spruce root collected in a single day. In preparation for a move in the early spring of 1811, Henry pushed his workforce to build canoes and gather supplies. The ice was still on the river, and snow, sleet, rain, and hail were mentioned in his journal entries. During this time, women collected and processed five and a half kegs of spruce gum for caulking and Michel Langlois's wife "received an abortion while raising Wattap," no doubt her condition triggered by the strain of pulling spruce roots from the frozen ground and the treacherous walking conditions (Gough 1988: 605–6).

In addition to these activities, each family was required to produce a "Quart de Lodge," with the men securing buffalo and the women tanning the hides and preserving the meat (418). This was usually done in the winter, when some of the meat could be roughly butchered, and frozen for later use and processing.

> I sent Parrenteau to Tents in the plains to hunt Buffalo on the South side, and Crevier and Perrin to haul the meat in, and put it on the stage. This is called making their *Quart de Lodge*, and each man is obliged to put twenty Animals upon the stage, and haul nearly the same number in to the Fort. . . . Each man must also raise Buffalo hides sufficient to make 20 Pemmican Bags, for which purpose their woman generally go with them to make their *Quart de Lodge*, where they have the advantage of getting the Tallow and other offals of the Buffalo, which are of great service to them in their ménage (418).

In procuring their *Quarts de Lodges*, families worked as an economic unit, with women transforming raw materials provided by men. Between 1809 and 1810, Henry described women processing and preserving meat, preparing pemmican, tanning and smoking hides, sewing pemmican bags, sewing moccasins, and netting snowshoes. All these activities were essential not only to the operation of the post, but the survival of its occupants. However, Henry had no difficulty cutting families off the post food supply during a food shortage in July 1810, issuing pemmican only to working men, assuming that women had "dried Provisions of their own" (449). It was not an unusual strategy to either cut women off from post supplies or send families away from the post to fend for themselves. In July 1820 William Brown at Fort Wedderburn ordered James Isbister not to supply

Captain John Franklin's men, and also to withhold "fish to the women of this place, but let them fish for themselves." To Franklin, Brown explained "I have been obliged to send all the women & children from the Fort" (Houston 1994: 335). Ultimately, women were responsible for themselves and their own families.

From Domestic Partner to Contracted Laborer

While fur traders occasionally paid local women outside their community for food or furs, for much of the fur trade working women were also wives and mothers. However, women associated with men in higher positions sometimes enjoyed greater privilege (and did less work). In 1779, Philip Turnor described the luxuries, offered by the North West Company to lure Hudson's Bay Company men and their female partners, into their employ:

> [T]hey should make your honors Servants great offers which is constantly the case, when they give Men . . . One Hundred Pounds Pr Annum, his Feather Bed carried in the Canoe, His tent which is exceeding good, pitched for him his Bed made and he and his girl carried in and out of the Canoe, and when in the Canoe never touches a Paddle unless for his own pleasure (Tyrrell 1931: 252).

The luxuries granted the Nor'wester were extended to "his girl," but according to Turnor the lot of a Hudson's Bay Company man and his domestic partner afforded no such pleasures. However, as fur trade posts developed into permanent settlements and food supplies began to stabilize, women's work increasingly signified social order and status. The wives of Hudson's Bay Company officers focused on their own domestic arrangements, while the wives of laborers, interpreters, and tradesmen did more menial and physical tasks often fulfilling the role of domestic servant in the homes of Chief Factors and Chief Traders or contracting their services as "laundry women" to single men. By the closing decades of the century, women were also contracted for hard manual labor.

The Qu'Appelle post journal for 1872–73, supplemented by the memoirs of Isaac Cowie, the assistant clerk, reconstructs the varying domains of women's work at a small fur trade post in present-day southeastern Saskatchewan. The working women described included "Indian" women contracted as itinerant laborers. Cowie, listed the "people of the fort": Archibald McDonald, Clerk-in-Charge until his promotion to Chief Trader in 1873; ten engaged "servants"; four Scottish laborers; and five "monthly employees" (Cowie 1993: 214–15). Most were "Half Breeds," Métis, or Cree. Eleven families received rations as part of their contractual relationship with the company. All of the women were Native, including Ellen McDonald, wife of the man in charge. She was the daughter of Red River merchant, John Inkster, and Mary Sinclair, and the granddaughter of Chief Factor William Sinclair and his Cree wife Nahovay (McDonald 1879).

The McDonalds occupied the best accommodations of the post and employed a nursemaid to care for their two sons. The company's notion of duty required the other women of the post to earn their rations and accommodation by "scrubbing" their own homes and "the big house"—serving as de facto domestic servants to the McDonalds. They were also required to keep "the square clean," make "a certain number of tracking shoes for the voyageurs," and plant and harvest the potatoes (Cowie 213). Keeping the large square clean involved sweeping and removing debris, cleaning up after the dozens of sled dogs that wandered loose, and shoveling snow in the winter. Cowie recalled, "After a snowfall it was pleasant to see them all in bright colors, with cheerful faces and active limbs, enjoying themselves, assisted by their children, sweeping up the snow in piles" (214). Clearing snow in subzero temperatures is hardly the enjoyable play Cowie suggests; yet his nostalgic descriptions provide an uncritical reconstruction of stratification, where "happy" workers take their place in a hierarchy of labor and status.

In addition to the employees and their wives, others were contracted for short terms and specific tasks. Contract labor, as defined by the Northern Council in 1868 included "Indian labor" and "voyaging," paid and supplied from the resources of each individual post. As a result, unlike the massive Hudson's Bay Company Servant accounts tabulating employees contracted for periods of two to three years, records for short-term contract laborers are only found in notations in the post journals or the few surviving "blotter books." The notations in the Qu'Appelle post journal document female contract workers and the nature of their work.

In addition to the buildings and public spaces inside the walled perimeter of the fort, a very large garden, five acres of potatoes, and a large hay field were considered the domain of female laborers. Although planting and harvesting potatoes was expected of "post" women, contracted "Indian" women supplied additional labor, as indicated by references scattered throughout the 1872–73 notations:

May 25   3 Indian women grubbing.
May 28   Four squaws grubbing new ground.
May 31   Indian women still grubbing.
June 14   Indian women employed mudding the new shop.
July 1   Indian women grubbing and cleaning potatoes.
July 6   Indian women employed as yesterday.
July 9   The Indian women at odd jobs.
July 23   Also some Indian women went down to work at the hay.
Sept. 4   The Pisqua women cleaning out the Grease Bin & rendering
           the Grease.
May 23   Indian women weeding the garden.

Grubbing or digging—both for potatoes or to break prairie sod—was the bulk of the work, although haying, weeding, and other jobs are also noted. In some entries women appeared to be working with, or possibly for, other contracted workers. In October, Horsefall, a man contracted to plough the potato fields, was assisted by "a gang of Indian women gathering up the Potatoes." The following week, White Crow, a contracted "Indian" laborer, was "mixing mud" and "Pisqua's women" mudded house walls, assisting a post employee on house construction and repair. While First Nations and Métis men were generally noted by name, contracted female laborers were not. However, the women noted as "Pisqua's women" or "the Pisqua women" are perhaps assumed to be members of the nearby Chief Pasqua's Saulteaux.

The wives and daughters of post families primarily worked inside the fortified walls. Neighboring Métis women were occasionally contracted to work inside the post, while First Nations women from outside the community were employed for more physically demanding tasks including those beyond its walls. This system might be visualized as concentric circles ordered by varying degrees of First Nations ancestry: fairer women married to company officers working for their own families, possibly with servants of their own; Métis, and occasionally First Nations women, married to company servants working for both their own family and the company; and finally, "Indian" women working with the men in the field.

Working Women on the Labrador Coast

> The few Englishmen each took a wife of the sort and they never sorry
> that they took them for they was great workers.
> —Lynne D. Fitzhugh citing Lydia Campbell

With these words, Lydia Campbell (née Brook), the daughter of an English trapper and his Inuit wife, described her mother and other women of her unique regional community. Living conditions along the Labrador coast were often grim, and outsiders typically described the local people as impoverished and desperate. However, many of those who diminished these communities came to rely upon them. A rare cluster of women's contracts at Hudson's Bay Company posts along the Labrador coast (1877–1908) reveal both shifts in the domestic arrangements of fur trade posts and an ongoing reliance on the country knowledge and skills of "the great workers." Most of the eight women hired to work as cooks and housekeepers at the Cartwright and Rigolet posts of Davis Inlet were the descendants of fishermen, trappers, or tradesmen who married local women. Known as Labradorians, Livyeres, and more recently as Labrador Métis, Edward Feild, the Bishop of Newfoundland described them, in 1848, as "a brown-skinned race of Indian or Eskimo extraction on the maternal side. These are the Liveyeres,[1] as they are called to distinguish them from the Newfoundland fishermen and the Indian" (Feild 1849: 17). Feild identified the people at Sandwich Bay as "Anglo-Esquimaux," and those at Battle Harbour as "half Indian" (18–19). Living in scattered interconnected communities, by the mid–nineteenth century they formed the majority of the population along the coast. They were essential companions on any regional expedition or enterprise. The men worked as guides, interpreters, and hunters, while the women provisioned food and clothing suited to the climate.

In 1894, two medical missionaries visiting Rigolet Post remarked enthusiastically on the skills of eighty-two-year-old Hannah Michelin (née Brook). Eliot
Curwen photographed her with her long double-barrel rifle and observed

> [S]he is a half-breed Esquimaux & is a fine specimen doing the work of two or
> three others; last winter she shot a great number of partridges walking 20 miles
> in a day and would herself dig a hole through 3 or 4 feet of ice to fish for trout
> with a hook & a piece of meat for bait she used to hunt & trap animals & drive
> the comatic [komatic] or sledge . . . she continues to drive a dog team, though
> now, of course, three or four dogs are all she could manage (Rompkey 1996: 89).

His companion, Wilfred Grenfell affirmed, "the most marvelous old lady I ever
saw, as besides being a good seamstress and a tidy housewife, she is a good
bootmaker and an excellent carpenter" (94). Lydia Campbell spoke of her sister
Hannah as a model of female courage and industry:

> I have known her fighting with a wolverine, a strong animal of the size of a
> good sized dog. She had neither gun nor axe but a little trout stick, yet she
> killed it after a long battle. I wish there were more Hannahs in the world for
> braveness. She brought up her first family of little children when their father
> died, teached them all to read and write in the long winter nights and hunt with
> them in the day. She would take the little ones on the sled, haul them on over
> snow and ice to a large river, chop ice about three feet thick, catch about two
> or three hundred trout and haul them and the children home, perhaps in the
> night (Campbell 2000: 7–8).

Previous generations of Hudson's Bay Company men might have married such
women, but late-nineteenth-century senior company officers commonly arrived
with wives and children in tow, seeking domestic help. The job of "mess cook" also
suggests that Labrador posts hired single men who ate together around a common table. Women like Hannah Michelin were increasingly viewed as domestics.

The first woman to secure a Hudson's Bay Company contract in the region was
Mary Jane Learning, whose father William Learning was employed as a laborer
at Rigolet Post (Learning 2000).). Hired in 1877 as a cook for the Esquimaux Bay
district, she held that position for twelve years. She was subsequently contracted
as a cook for the Ungava district in 1892 and 1894 and as a "domestic servant"
in 1894 (Learning 1877–1894). In 1906, Learning was enumerated as "Freemen,
Labrador," implying that she may have engaged in independent trade.

Elizabeth Deer, another local woman, signed a handwritten contract on June
18, 1881, at Cartwright, agreeing to the following terms:

> I Elizabeth Deer do hereby acknowledge to have agreed with the Hudson's Bay
> company to serve them or their agents or assigns as an able Cook or in any
> other capacity whatever as I may be directed from the date herof [sic] until 31st
> day October 1881 and having performed such duties and without any neglect
> or hindrance I am to receive as wages The sum of Ten Pounds Cy. The balance

of my wages to be settled at the expiration of my service after deducting what may have been advanced me and paid for my Account (Deer 1881).

A note on the file "Summer 10 £" and a subsequent contract for the same period in 1882 as "Able Housekeeper" indicates summer or part-time contracts for four months' work by Deer. Between 1904 and 1908, an additional six women were hired (Table 9.1).

Mess cooks Elizabeth Adams and Sarah Jane Webb were Inuit who had married into the local community, and the other women were third- and fourth-generation Labradorians (Fitzhugh 1999: 258). A photograph of the Ladies Sewing Guild taken at Cartwright in 1910 reveals the community work groups from which company laborers were potentially recruited. Four of the women in the missionary-sponsored Sewing Guild had been contracted to the post: Jemima (Martin /Perry) Williams, Betsy (Deer) Painter, Mary (Bird) Learning, and Isabella (Pottle) Saunders.

Elders recall women sewing sealskin boots late into the night, often after full days working on fishing stages, cooking, or hunt-related labor. Hannah Michelin was not a contract employee at the company post at Rigolet, but her sister Lydia recalled that she was hired "to make a lot of things pants, shirts, flannel slips, draws, sealskin boots, deerskin shoes for the winter, socks, leggings, mitts made of duffel and deer-skins, coats, caps, as well as washing, starching, ironing and what not" (Campbell 2000: 9).

A sealskin coat and boots made by Clara Lane for Sir William MacGregor, the governor of Newfoundland and Labrador (1904–9), exemplify Labradorian clothing production.[2] Lane and her husband Julius assisted missionaries, naturalists, government officials, and the newly minted Royal Canadian Mounted Police who used their home at Port Burwell on Killinek Island as a rest stop and supply depot. Remembered as "Good Mrs. Lane" by Moravian missionaries, she sewed MacGregor's fine sealskin coat and embroidered sealskin boots during his 1907 tour of Labrador (Foreign Mission 1899: 415–16).[3] The confident tailoring, precise sewing, creative combination of materials, floral embroidery, and carved ivory and bone toggles are an embodied synthesis of women's knowledge and skill (figures 9.2, 9.3).

Table 9.1. Women's contracts at Hudson's Bay Company Posts in Labrador, 1904–8 (Servant Contracts A32/20-58)

Date	Name	Post	Position
1904	Isabella Saunders	Cartwright	Men's kitchen cook
1906	Elizabeth Adams	Davis Inlet	Mess cook
1906	Jemima Perry		Cook
1907	Sarah Jane Webb		Mess cook
1908	Lizzie (Elizabeth) Bird	Cartwright	Mess cook and housekeeper
1908	Naomi Pottle		Assistant cook

Figure 9.2. Sealskin boots made by "Good Mrs. Lane" for Sir William MacGregor, 1907. Artist Mrs. Clara Lane, Port Burwell, Labrador. MacGregor Collection, Marishal Museum, University of Aberdeen, Scotland.

Figure 9.3. Fur coat with bone/ivory toggles made by "Good Mrs. Lane" for Sir William MacGregor, 1907. Artist Mrs. Clara Lane, Port Burwell, Labrador. MacGregor Collection, Marishal Museum, University of Aberdeen, Scotland.

From Fur Trade Wife to Rural Laborer

> And my mother she, well she was a hard worker too . . . she used to
> pick stones, and dig the big stones out . . . Them days was they were
> digging Seneca roots and they were good price . . . we got the new house
> by digging Seneca roots . . . I tell you it's very hard times.
> —Caroline Henry, interview #1

In 1982, Métis elder Caroline Henry remembered working with her mother picking Seneca roots, chopping and selling wood, and supplementing their family income by laboring in farm fields and houses in rural Saskatchewan (1982: 2). By the twentieth century, Aboriginal peoples in Canada were economically, legally, and socially marginalized as white settlement increased. As shown, women had been productively engaged in fur trade economies within and outside the confines of the post. But throughout the nineteenth century, the status and respect accorded that work diminished significantly. Caroline Henry's experience of hard work and marginal survival was common to an entire generation of women. By the twentieth century, Aboriginal people's place in the hierarchy of work was at the lowest, most physically demanding level, and this lowly status informed government policies and sustained public attitudes. There seemed to be a concerted effort to adapt women's manual work of the fur trade into emerging rural economies. Moreover, the residential and industrial school system adopted, without question, simplistic gendered divisions of labor by training First Nations men as laborers and tradesmen and women as domestic servants. The expectation that children be trained as manual laborers too was an essential component of residential schools and expected economic outcomes. In 1893, the girls at the Qu'Appelle Industrial School cooked for two hundred individuals, a total of six hundred meals a day (*Annual Report* 1894: 177). In 1901 the school placed a number of "girls in service . . . in the best families" (*Annual Report* 1901: 418). The following areas of instruction were catalogued under "girl's work": "[T]he girls learn all kinds of housework, cooking, dairying, laundry work, and make their own clothes and the greater part of those worn by the boys. They assist in the garden, milk the cows in the summer-time, and have entire charge of the poultry" (418). The use of women and girls as agricultural laborers continued, as evidenced by turn-of-the-century photographs of a group of women and children picking stones in a field near Davidson, Saskatchewan (figure 9.4). Women and girls were often part of family work units, and the presence of the white tent and man standing beside a team of horses suggests that the woman and children were part of a family unit hired to clear the field.

A 1910 photograph of Cree women and children picking sugar beets in Raymond, Alberta, marks the beginning of a relationship with the labor-intensive industry that continued until the closing decades of the twentieth century. As early as 1902, the Department of Indian Affairs targeted the sugar beet industry as a potential source of employment (*Annual Report* 1902: 79). Alberta's sugar beet fields relied on Aboriginal labor, and the earliest correspondence between

Figure 9.4. (Unidentified) Indian women and children picking rocks near Davidson, Saskatchewan. Photographer unknown. Photograph #S-B 1859-60, Saskatchewan Archives Board.

the Indian Agent of the Blood Reserve and the Knight Sugar Company promoted women and children as ideal laborers "who do work as good as or better than men" (Regular 1999: 215). The 1965 *Department of Citizenship and Immigration Report* declared that the sugar beet industry was "the largest single movement of seasonal [First Nations] labor, mainly from the north" (23). By 1969, the Departments of Indian Affairs and Manpower were implicated in a scandal when investigative journalism exposed poor working conditions, corruption, exploitation of workers, and the use of child labor (Laliberte 1994: 132).

Mid-twentieth-century circumstances sustained the association between Aboriginal women's bodies, hard work, and physical endurance. Aboriginal women have always worked, and their work has always been physically challenging. For European men, who had exploited female peasants and servants long before venturing to these shores, women's willingness to labor signaled sexual availability. However, from the perspective of most traditional Aboriginal ideologies, work is one of the sacred responsibilities of being a woman. As Patricia Monture-Angus declared, "I have only one right—to be a Mohawk woman. The rest are responsibilities" (Monture-Angus 1995: 87). Many Indigenous societies define "a good woman" through her work, whether it be through her artwork, or specific skills in traditional and nontraditional areas. Women interviewed by Bernadette Wabie, expressed their understanding of woman's work in straightforward Anishinaabekwe terms:

> When you look at the traditional ways, the men went out to hunt and the women had the role of getting on with it. So I think that is the main one, of getting it done (Wabie 1998: 126).

Another suggested that women's roles have not changed:

> [T]raditional teaching and ways of doing things are so durable because your human responsibilities don't change . . . the particular responsibilities that women have to take care of the family and to support the family with work and to contribute to maintaining the community . . . those things don't change (128).

The post-contact history of women's labor is inextricably tangled with colonial history, with the working body of the Aboriginal woman commonly conceived as a degraded body, degraded by her sweat and her calloused hands. But it remains true that extraordinary stories of negotiation, creativity, and survival trump colonial misconceptions to prove that women have steadfastly resisted, worked with courage and spirit, struggled to maintain the sacredness of their responsibilities, and challenged the forces that sought to confine them.

Notes

1. Derived from the local pronunciation of "live here," livyere distinguishes permanent residents from those who worked during the summer at the fishing stations. Edward Feild, *Church in the Colonies No. XIX: A visit to Labrador in the Autumn of MDCCCXLVIII by the Lord Bishop of Newfoundland* (London: The Society for the Propagation of the Gospel, 1849): 17–19.

2. The coat and boots are in the collection of the Marischal Museum in Aberdeen, Scotland (Sealskin coat ABDUA5720, Sealskin boots ABDUA6031).

3. Sir William MacGregor collection provenance, Marischal Museum.

Works Cited

Annual Report of the Department of Indian Affairs for the Year Ended 30th June 1893 (Annual Report). Ottawa, S. E. Dawson, 1894.

Annual Reports 1902, 1903.

Ballenden, John, J. McNabb, Jo. Linklater, W. Cook, G. Taylor to Hon'ble Sirs [London Committee of the Hudson's Bay Company], September 1802. *York Factory Outward Correspondence Book*, B.239/b/75 fo. 41, Hudson's Bay Company Archives.

Brown, Jennifer S. H. *Strangers in Blood: Fur Trade Company Families in Indian Country*. Vancouver: University of British Columbia Press, 1980.

Calloway, Colin. *White People, Indians and Highlanders: Tribal Peoples and Colonial Encounters in Scotland and America*. New York: Oxford University Press, 2008.

Campbell, Lydia. *Sketches of Labrador Life*. St. John's, NF: Killick Press, 2000.

Cowie, Isaac. *The Company of Adventurers: A Narrative of Seven Years in Service of the Hudson's Bay Company during 1867–1874*. Lincoln: University of Nebraska Press, 1993.

Deer, Elizabeth. Servant Contract 1881. A.32/25, folio 157. Hudson's Bay Company Archives.

Department of Citizenship and Immigration Report of Indian Affairs Branch for the Fiscal Year ended March 31, 1965. Ottawa: Queen's Printers.

Feild, Edward. *Church in the Colonies No. XIX: A Visit to Labrador in the Autumn of MDCCCXLVIII by the Lord Bishop of Newfoundland*. London: The Society for the Propagation of the Gospel, 1849.

Fitzhugh, Lynne D. *The Labradorians: Voices from the Land of Cain*. St. John's, Nfld: Breakwater Books, 1999.

Foreign Missions of the Church of Brethren's Society. *Periodical Accounts Relating to the Foreign Missions of the Church of Brethren's Society for the Furtherance of the Gospels Among the Heathen, Vol. 4*. London, U.K.: self-published, 1899.

Gough, Barry M., ed. *The Journal of Alexander Henry the Younger, 1799–1814, Vol. 1*. Toronto: Champlain Society, 1988–92.

Governor and London Committee Correspondence 1803, A.11/19:fo.1d. Hudson's Bay Company Archives (HBCA), Winnipeg, Manitoba.

Henry, Caroline. Interview #1 with Margaret Jefferson, Regina Saskatchewan, August 15, 1982. Indian History Film Project, IH-SD.77pdf. Retrieved from the University of Regina Digital Archive: http://dspace.cc.uregina.ca/dspace/handle/10294/2076 (accessed March 2012).

Houston, C. Stuart. *Arctic Artist: The Journal and Paintings of George Back, Midshipman with Franklin, 1819–1822*. Montreal: McGill-Queen's University Press, 1994.

Index to Hudson's Bay Company Servants' Contracts, 1881–1908. A.32/20–58. HBCA.

Journal of Daily Occurrences Kept at Qu'Appelle Lake, 1857–58. Hudson's Bay Company File. Saskatchewan Archives Board (SAB), Regina, Saskatchewan.

Laliberte, Ronald. *The Canadian State and Native Migrant Labour in Southern Alberta's Sugar Beet Industry*. Master's thesis, University of Saskatchewan, 1994.

Learning, Mary Jane. Abstracts of Servants' Accounts, 1877–1892, A.32/38, B.135/g/52–66 and B/235/g/14. Hudson's Bay Company Archives.

———. Biographical Sheet, 2000 update. Hudson's Bay Company Archives, Winnipeg, Manitoba.

McDonald, Ellen. Scrip affidavit, January 17, 1879. Department of the Interior, Government of Canada, RG 15, Series D-II-8-a, Volume 1322, Library and Archives Canada.

Monture-Angus, Patricia. *Thunder in My Soul: A Mohawk Woman Speaks*. Halifax: Fernwood Publishing, 1995.

Moose Factory Post Journal, 1802. B.135/c/1fo.269 HBCA.

Regular, W. Keith. "Trucking and Trading with the Outsiders: Blood Indian Reserve Integration into the Southern Alberta Economic Environment, 1884–1939." PhD dissertation, Memorial University, 1999.

Rich, Edwin E., ed. *Journal of Occurrences in the Athabasca Department by George Simpson, 1820 and 1821*. Toronto: Champlain Society, 1938.

———. *Copy-book of Letters Outward, 1679–94*. Toronto: Champlain Society, 1948.

Rompkey, Ronald. *Labrador Odyssey: The Journal and Photographs of Eliot Curwen on the Second Voyage of Wilfred Grenfell, 1893*. Montreal: McGill-Queen's University Press, 1996.

Tyrrell, Joseph B. *Journals of Samuel Hearne and Philip Turnor between the Years 1774 and 1792*. Toronto: Champlain Society, 1931.

Van Kirk, Sylvia. *"Many Tender Ties": Women in Fur Trade Society, 1670–1870*. Winnipeg: Watson and Dwyer Publishing Ltd., 1980.

Wabie, Bernadette. *Aboriginal Women and Community Development: Consistency across Time*. Master's thesis, Trent University, 1998.

Wallace, William Stewart, ed. *Documents Relating to the North West Company*. Toronto: Champlain Society, 1934.

CHAPTER 10

Northfork Mono Women's Agricultural Work, "Productive Coexistence," and Social Well-Being in the San Joaquin Valley, California, circa 1850–1950

Heather A. Howard

Introduction

This chapter examines Native women's agency in the transformation of economic life in Central California over the century that followed the establishment of American jurisdiction in 1848. I focus on Northfork Mono women's seasonal migratory labor patterns in relation to their efforts to sustain family and community physical and social well-being under the complex circumstances of land dispossession particular to California.[1] Native societies in California survived and persisted, despite overwhelming odds posed by land dispossession, in great part as a result of women's resourceful efforts to maintain the kinship structures, and to continue aspects of cultural life tied to traditional subsistence activities as they also took on roles in the non-Native economy as agricultural workers.

Market economy resource-exploitation and production arrived in California rapidly, and violently. There is no doubt that the mid-nineteenth-century influx of gold-seekers, millions of livestock, settlers, and massive irrigation projects tragically devastated Native peoples' capacity to subsist from the land. By 1900, 90 percent of the population had been devastated by disease and state-sanctioned slavery and massacre (Cook 1955). These circumstances curtailed treaty-making and largely prevented Native peoples from reserving for themselves land and rights to resources. Answering Colleen O'Neill's invitation to consider the recovery of Indigenous communities through their "creative engagement with the market" (2005: 156), I examine how women's work lives illustrate an integration of wage-labor activities into ongoing systems of Native economic life. Rather than viewing non-Native economic life as replacing Native practices, I highlight women's agency in cultural survival, social well-being, and "productive coexistence." This latter term was coined by the leadership of the North Fork Rancheria of Mono Indians, for whom I originally conducted this research, and is significant to understanding broader land claims and disputes in contemporary California.

I initially discuss the Indigenous socioeconomic complex, structured by kinship relations of rights and responsibilities, which fostered intertribal marriage and the exchange of objects and ideas. This complex operated throughout the region and it influenced the strategies adopted by the earliest non-Native gold-seekers in the area and provided the context of dispossession and gendering of labor roles generated by the invasion and occupation of California at mid–nineteenth century. Subsequently, the ethnohistorical record of Northfork Mono women's experiences is examined in relation to the Fresno River Reservation, which operated in the northern San Joaquin Valley between 1851 and 1859. Its closure represents one of several failures of the early California reservation system. Not only could Native people not rely upon resources promised at this reservation, their off-reservation labor in the harvest of their natural resources was crucial to their own survival as well as to non-Native workers, agents, and traders who occupied their lands. The labor patterns established with the Fresno River Reservation were the basis of agricultural practice in California's Central Valley, eventually a major supplier of the food consumed within the United States (Izumi 2009). After the closure of the reservation, Northfork Mono women continued to supply their labor to the changing agricultural industries occupying the San Joaquin Valley. They did so in a pattern that consciously incorporated all available resources for the survival and social well-being of their families, and in connection with their ongoing situation of landlessness and intrusions of the settler population. Lastly, I describe their work into the mid–twentieth century in terms of a continuous seasonal round by which they adapted wage labor alongside other non-Native resource activity with migratory subsistence patterns. Today, Northfork Mono women's labor is key to the tribe's effort to build community and affirmations of cultural and political sovereignty.

Gendered Labor and Status Relations

Indigenous peoples of the San Joaquin Valley and adjacent foothills of the Sierra Nevada Mountains operated within a complex requiring mobility, social and economic interaction, and intermarriage. This economy depended upon kinship to create and maintain important sociopolitical connections and to foster trade of all kinds: material, intellectual, ceremonial. The Northfork Mono held a unique standing in this complex; their dominance in the foothills positioned them as controllers of the trans-Sierra trade route connecting peoples on the eastern side of the Sierra Nevada Mountains with those in the San Joaquin Valley. Affinal ties were fundamental to this integrated and interdependent system. Northfork Mono women intermarried across moiety, tribelet, and tribal lines, and, later, with Euro-Americans, whom they initiated into their socioeconomic complex.

In precontact times marriages tended to occur between titled individuals or politically powerful families. Polygynous marriage was advantageous to a titled man, ensuring the labor to prepare feasts for the frequent visitors to whom he would be responsible (McCarthy 1993: 78). Ethnographer E. W. Gifford, who conducted research among the Northfork Mono between 1918 and 1925, observed a high frequency of intertribal marriage between the Northfork Mono and Chuk-chansi Yokuts who shared similar labor and resource-use patterns (Gifford 1996). While intertribal marriage may have been limited to the titled elite, a number of titles existed within one community. This class constituted, according to Gif-ford's estimates, a full 25 percent of the Northfork Mono population (Gifford 43). Intermarriage among the titled elite, therefore, was important to the function-ing of Indigenous society. It was "an integral part of the interregional social and ceremonial system in order to encourage and enhance trade relationships with neighbors" (McCarthy 70).

Moreover, as anthropologist Helen McCarthy argues, acorn-centered subsis-tence, based almost exclusively on women's labor in the accumulation of a surplus, was key to the larger socioeconomic system of Native peoples of the San Joaquin Valley. Located among significant supplies of highly desirable oak stands, the Northfork Mono were well-positioned within in this system. Acorns were not sim-ply stored for internal nutritional needs throughout the year but also for external trade and participation in a circuit of competitive ceremonial feasts (McCarthy 1993: 1–17, 92–106). Elite Northfork Mono men maintained their monopoly on political power within their communities and regionally largely through control and access to the surplus of acorns accumulated by women. The sex-segregated acorn harvest afforded an acorn economy that "thrived in the political-economic circumstances generated by Euro-American hegemony" (iv). Women's associa-tion with acorn production continued, whereas the political-economic complex revolving around male power eventually disappeared as Northfork Mono men integrated into the ranching and lumber industries (iv, 1–17). This continuity of women's work, although also transformed by wage labor that came with the establishment of American jurisdiction, was vital to the health and social well-being of the Northfork Mono.

After contact, the tribal kinship system incorporated Newcomers while it also persisted in its traditional forms. The few white men in the area during the early days of contact recognized that kinship governed an intertribal status system serving to connect Native peoples who spoke different languages. Kinship deter-mined rights to significant and varied resources across broad, ecologically diverse areas of shared use and occupancy. Newcomer men took Native wives as a means of integrating themselves into positions of power in the local Indigenous order, and further, to access resources. However, with gold, military might, and settler invasion, dependency on Natives lessened. As outsider male power grew, the importance of these intermarriages as a survival strategy for the Native popula-tion intensified. Native women maintained alliances with white men in order to keep peace, and to ensure a flow of goods and protection to their extended families, as well as to minimize other impacts of colonization. Through their association with non-Native men and kin ties generated by intermarriage, women assumed new roles in farming, ranching, and mining. The social role of labor is illustrated through the nurture, maintenance, and transformation of strategic intimate relations (Wolf 1982). The Aboriginal regional political-economic system was disrupted by the 1920s, yet these gendered kinship patterns and obligations continued. Women's position in the power structures of Northfork Mono society increased as androcentric formal political roles diminished. Aspects of social and ceremonial life were maintained through intertribal intermarriage, often initiated in the San Joaquin Valley floor Native labor camps.

Land Dispossession
and Labor Reconfigurations

Native peoples' history in California and with the U.S. government provides a unique context. Land dispossession brought the imperative of cultural survival and of women's agency in adaptive strategies within the colonial encounter and settler society into relief. Failed attempts at treaty- and reservation-making, in addition to horrendous uses of violence, left the majority of Native peoples landless during the latter half of the nineteenth century. Near complete dispossession occurred within a period of less than two decades between 1850 and the mid-1860s (Heizer 1993; Hurtado 1988). California contact history is characterized by slavery, violence, massacre, poverty, and neglect, beginning in the 1700s with the Spanish/Mexican mission and rancho economy, and continuing through the American gold rush, mining, timber, and ranching economy after 1848. When Americans took over jurisdiction from Mexico, the territory was inhabited by about 150,000 Native people, who were either coerced into slave-labor or fled to isolated mountain locations to escape the conditions of mission and rancho life. A legal form of Native slavery persisted under American jurisdiction into the late 1860s, accompanied by a policy of removal to labor farms on military reservations, the latter created for "protection" from the ruthless mining and settler population that arrived in droves after the discovery of gold in 1849. The Fresno River Reservation, formed in 1851, was formalized in 1853 under these circumstances of war and chaos.

In 1851, eighteen treaties were negotiated with representatives of Native tribes. These treaties recognized Native jurisdiction over the land and provided for the cession of this jurisdiction to the United States in exchange for some considerable-sized reservations in areas familiar to those who ceded the land. Although the reservation lands were located away from the mountain areas to facilitate the unfettered American exploitation of mineral resources, when the new and powerful non-Native citizens of California realized that reservations occupied other potentially resource-rich areas, they mounted a lobby against the treaties.

In 1852, a delegation to Congress successfully prevented Senate ratification of the treaties and all eighteen were placed under a fifty-year seal.

In the early twentieth century, non-Native advocacy groups exposed the cover-up of the treaties and pressured the federal government to remedy the consequential condition of landlessness among California Natives. As a result, the government purchased "Rancheria" lands for some (yet not all) Native groups and distributed to others some public domain allotments taken primarily from National Forest lands. The ancestors of citizens of the North Fork received both a small Rancheria and some allotments in the Sierra National Forest. Rancheria lands were often isolated, rocky, waterless hillsides undesirable to non-Natives. The size of Rancheria lands was generally inadequate relative to the needs of the residents. Restrictions on agricultural use and against development made allotments within National Forests little more than camping spots and grazing grounds leased by non-Native ranchers. Nonetheless, allotment and Rancheria lands constituted *Indian Country*. Ironically, it was the lack of utilization of these lands that would later be cited as the primary justification for the implementation of 1960s termination policies. The majority of California Natives have thus remained largely an off-reservation population due to this particular history of dispossession.

Northfork Mono, among others, were promised several hundred square miles of the San Joaquin Valley floor in four of the 1851 treaties.[2] They used the valley floor seasonally for hunting and gathering and intended to continue these activities on the newly treated reservation lands. They did not discontinue use or occupancy of the adjacent mountain foothills where villages were located and staples such as acorns were harvested. With increased settlement, the Northfork Mono adapted to the capitalist economy in several significant gendered ways including the integration of non-Native supplies, trade items, and labor patterns. Thereafter, a fusion of subsistence and resource acquisition was seasonally incorporated into women's labor.

The Fresno River Reservation was part of the ad hoc military reservation system formed in haste while the treaties were debated in Congress into 1852. After the failure to ratify, the Fresno River Reservation and other reservations in California suffered from Washington's reluctance to provide financial support. From inception to closure, Fresno River Reservation was plagued with food shortages, caused by a combination of drought, inhospitable growing conditions, and a lack of federally appropriated funds. Rather than remain on reservation lands where the Indian Agent was charged with turning Indians into self-sufficient farmers, the people relied upon traditional forms of subsistence and on women's work. When the reservation crops failed due to two subsequent years of drought the population survived by women's accumulation and storage of acorn, dried meat, and fish.

Subagent Adam Johnston recognized the precariousness of being unable to fulfill treaty obligations to those reserved under his jurisdiction, and expressed concern about keeping Native peoples out of the mountains away from mining operations or where they might revitalize military intentions against Newcomers. He further explained that during the previous year the people left "their principle stores of subsistence, intending to return for them as necessity required [but] the whites, in pursuing them, burnt and destroyed all that fell in their way: consequently, at the time the different treaties were entered into, the Indians . . . come from the mountains without food, depending upon the small amount allowed in their treaties, with the roots and seeds to be daily gathered by their females" (Johnston 1851). Those returning to their foothill dwellings seeking food risked violent retaliation from non-Natives; alternatively they remained at the reservation to claim treaty-brokered government food of which Agent Johnson had little to offer.

These conditions persisted after Martin B. Lewis assumed the post of Indian Agent at Fresno River where agricultural activities intensified by the mid-1850s. However, repeated droughts impeded the agent's mandate to convert the people into self-sufficient farmers and to keep them on the reservation. The Northfork Mono, as others, were compelled—and encouraged—to fuse new reservation-based agricultural activities with traditional practices of hunting, gathering, and fishing. The new cycle incorporated practices such as fishing, gathering acorns, and feasting with agriculture, irrigation, and collecting treaty provisions. The Northfork Mono developed a subsistence cycle of dual dependency spending part of the year on the reservation and others in the mountains or near rivers.

In 1856 drought was so bad that Superintendent Henley instructed Lewis to compel the Fresno River Reservation Indians to return to their habits of gathering foods from the foothills noting: "The failure of the crops, in that portion of the State under your charge, will render a return to the original modes of living, by the Indians upon the San Joaquin, and its waters, imperative" (Henley 1856). Lewis later reported that Native peoples were in the mountains harvesting acorn, and that both men and women were engaged in mining (Lewis 1856). While "income" was generated by the Northfork Mono's ongoing participation in mining, Lewis noted that it was spent in the stores of local merchants and traders on food and clothing (Lewis 1856). When drought revisited the Fresno River Reservation in 1857, Lewis proudly described how the Northfork Mono had fully incorporated the resources of the reservation with other subsistence, making them virtually self-sufficient. He needed only to supply them with garments, and they could be completely relied upon to furnish their labor on the farm when needed (Lewis August 1858). By 1858, Lewis reported as a success that the Valley's peoples moved between acorn and salmon harvests "until called for to commence the labors of another year," at the reservation (Lewis August 1858). That the government paid to build storehouses to contain acorn and dried fish processed by women reinforces the significance of their labor to survival (Lewis September 1858). Near the close of 1858, Lewis further commented on the women's contributions: "there has been a fine run of Salmon and they have taken a large quantity, all of which have been dried except the necessary consumption. The remainder . . . since the acorns have been sufficiently matured, engaged in putting up that favorite bread stuff and have procured a considerable quantity" (Lewis November 1858). Ironically, rather than recognize that subsistence practices allowed the reservation to operate, a federal investigation conducted in the late 1850s recommended the reservation's closure by concluding the agent had failed to assimilate the people.

Labor, Continuity, and Change

By 1860, after the closure of Fresno and other reservations, federal policy neglected Native peoples in California. Native people became squatters on their lands now increasingly privatized with lands originally intended as reservations expropriated for lucrative ranches and agribusinesses. As the landscape was parceled into private property Native peoples became trespassers but continued to farm, gather, and fish. They adapted to the American wage economy as laborers and consumers. As gold finds diminished, the extraction of other minerals such as silver expanded, as did the harvesting of redwood trees from the remote Sierras to supply America's urban industrialization. The city of Madera (*wood* in Spanish) sprung up in the lands of the former reservation in the 1870s. Transformed by irrigation, surrounding regions flourished with the agricultural development of wheat, barley, cotton, and grape fields, or the ranching of cattle and sheep. Nonetheless, the division of Indigenous labor between valley floor (agricultural) and mountain (ranching/herding and lumber) dovetailed with traditional gendered divisions of labor. While both men and women participated in all sectors of work, women's association with agriculture nourished traditional social life—especially intertribal relations and family integrity (figure 10.1).

In 1903, Reverend W. B. Noble established a Presbyterian Indian Mission at the town of North Fork located in the adjacent foothills. Noble observed that Natives near North Fork "live by the men working in the logging camps and in herding cattle and sheep, and the women washing gold in the creeks, and (in season) picking grapes in the San Joaquin Valley" (Lee 1998: 147–48). During the first decades of the twentieth century, this Mission was of utmost importance to the tribe's survival. Many Northfork Mono children lived and were educated, clothed, and fed at the Mission during the school year. Parents were often too poor to provide basic necessities. During part of the year, parents camped on lands at or near the Mission to be near children who boarded, and thus the Mission was incorporated into their seasonal migration. When the federal government purchased lands for homeless Native peoples, the eighty-acre North Fork Rancheria was acquired in 1916 near the Mission to accommodate more than two hundred Mono, a reservation clearly insufficient to support this size population.[3]

The Rancheria and the Northfork Mono continued to integrate seasonal subsistence with agricultural work throughout the first half of the twentieth century.

Figure 10.1. Susan Benedict, Ida Carmen, and Susie Walker working at the Minturn Vineyard Company/Sierra Vista Vineyards, circa 1910. Leona Chepo personal photograph collection. Photographer unknown. Reproduced with permission of the North Fork Rancheria of Mono Indians.

Some female citizens of the North Fork Rancheria, interviewed in 2005, described annual grape harvest labor near the small town of Minturn, located north of Madera and their former reservation lands. They also picked cotton, tomatoes, and other produce in the Clovis area, southeast of Madera. The social life of the farm labor camps included trade fairs, songs, dances, gambling games, and feasts and afforded opportunities to find marriage partners just as intertribal gatherings of the past had done, and do today. Seasonal stays in the valley were also used to collect grasses and roots for basketry and medicines.

Hunting and salmon fishing were incorporated during or between seasonal travels to the valley farms. An elder of the North Fork Rancheria, Grace Tex, aged ninety-six in 2005, recalled salmon fishing on the San Joaquin River before it was dammed in 1942. Men "went hunting in the hillsides . . . women would clean the salmon when they'd bring the salmon to shore . . . they would slice it up and dry it [on the bushes]" (Tex interview). Tex further described how diverse peoples gathered at labor camps, played hand games, and traded songs, following long-standing practices of intertribal relations.

Another elder, Gertrude Davis, recalled trips in the vicinity of Friant near cotton farms where mushrooms, wild onions, and caterpillars, dried and eaten with acorn, were collected (Davis interview). A younger Northfork Mono citizen, Claudine Martin Nunez, who was raised in Clovis, also recalled gathering trips with her grandmother with whom she spent her entire summers. Her grandmother was a basket-maker and basket materials were also collected. Her grandmother and "lady friends would all camp down there . . . gathering and fishing . . . on the San Joaquin River . . . close to 99 highway" (Martin Nunez interview). Renowned basket-maker, Ruby Pomona remembered families traveling by horse and buggy "all together with their belongings and they would camp down there . . . they used to get on the train and come to Madera and to do their shopping" (Pomona interview). Pomona's son, author Gaylen Lee, adds that his family traveled to farms located on the valley floor along the San Joaquin and Fresno Rivers, to gather basket-making materials, "Although sedge grass grows in the mountains, the roots aren't as long as those that grow in the San Joaquin Valley. Mom said her Grandma Lizzie preferred to travel there for white root" (Lee 1998: 172). Leona Chepo, also a well-known Mono basket-maker, similarly remembered when she and female relatives worked in the vineyards: "We used to go down to the river to swim and clean up after picking grapes. And they had white roots down there too." When Chepo returned there more recently to gather root materials for baskets, she could no longer find them (Chepo and Chepo interview).

Connie DeSilva, born in 1927, recollects kin working at the Minturn vineyards as a "tradition." By the late 1930s more women than men, DeSilva noted, participated in the grape harvest. This is likely because men were dispersed throughout the area in the lumber industry, construction, and military service during World War II:

> They went to pick grapes near . . . Minturn . . . we played out in the vineyards while they would pick grapes. . . . I guess it was probably my grandma, my aunts and us kids. . . . It was just always women. . . . I remember my Aunt Mina saying her sister Annie would drive the team of horses . . . and she was the driver of the horse and the wagon. . . . So, evidently it was an early thing with my aunt's generation and mother's . . . so that was kind of a tradition they did (DeSilva interview).

Another North Fork Rancheria citizen, Lou Ann Polkenhorn, born in 1921, recalled her labor:

We use to cut grapes in Clovis when I was a kid, with my mother . . . my dad, he used to come and stay with us there but he'd go back to the hills while we worked in the grapes. We slept under trees, in what you'd call big sweat boxes for beds. A little place to make the fire. My grandmother would be cooking great, big giant tortillas . . . Yes, we worked pretty hard . . . There was a lot of Indian people out there. They had camps all over the place there (Byrd and Polkenhorn interview).

By the 1930s, the labor of Northfork Mono in the vineyard and orchards near Clovis was routine. In 1937, a local chronicler wrote: "As a general rule these people go down to the valley around Clovis to work in fruit. They go down in July and return in late October" (Miller 1937). As automotive transportation became more available, Northfork Mono traveled more widely, extending their work seasons by migrating place to place and harvesting different crops as they ripened. Maggie Chepo, born in 1926, and sister-in-law, Leona, recalled grape harvesting from the late 1930s. Those who picked well, according to employers, were called back annually, "You had to be a fast picker, which I [Maggie] wasn't. The earlier [we started] the better so you could get out here before it would get hot, warm. I liked that better than cotton picking . . . Cotton picking wore out my poor fingers" (Chepo and Chepo interview). The worker had to pick and fill the collection trays with bunches of grapes quickly in order to earn even a meager wage. Estimates show that pickers earned five cents for every ten trays picked. In October 1923, the BIA Field Matron stationed at Coarsegold confirmed, "Most of Indians are back from valey [sic]. All seem to be well but did not make much money" (Landon 1923).

By the 1930s and 1940s, the rate had increased to about fifty cents per ten trays. Depending on the size of the bunches and the speed of the picker, harvesters could earn about one dollar an hour because it took about half an hour to fill ten trays. Leona recalls,

We never could keep up with the Mexicans. . . . In the old days, when my grandma and them would go pick grapes, before we went, they used to count their trays by making little notches in a stick. By the tens, that's how they counted their trays. . . . You had to fill up the pan . . . and then put it on your tray, paper trays. I think they had [board] trays though, when my grandmother worked down there. . . . They'd put a notch there. Every time they counted ten trays they would put a notch. . . . I think it was a half cent a tray when they worked. When we worked, it was two cents. . . . Or was it five cents? [Depending] on how many grapes are on the vine. If you got a good vine you got a lot of grapes. Maybe two or three minutes [to pick one tray] if you worked fast. . . . Couldn't get rich that way . . . They had those crook knives, like that, sort of a crooked knife, and if your knife was real sharp and you'd grab the grape and you miss, you could cut yourself really good. You bandage yourself up and go on. You had to do it. If you were out of school and didn't have to go back for school you could stay there and work and pick cotton. Then in the fall, I think they tie the vines or something, for the grapes to grow. It was back breaking. We had to carry our sacks too, the cotton sacks. . . . I've seen some of those Mexican girls carry over fifty pounds up the ladder to dump it in the truck. I couldn't carry mine up. I could drag it but I couldn't carry it. I don't remember how many years I worked down there, back and forth. . . . Just our mothers [went]. Our fathers worked up here [in the mountains] (Chepo and Chepo interview).

These recollections of farm work highlight the difficulties and competitiveness of the working conditions in the valley fields, as well as transformations that ended Native migrant labor in the 1950s. Increased mechanization and the influx of Mexican workers ultimately replaced Native labor. By mid–twentieth century, the Northfork Mono increasingly settled in the more urban areas in the cities of Clovis, Fresno, and Madera.

Postwar Policy Shifts and Northfork Women's Labor Today

Urbanization coincided with California's efforts to influence the federal government toward terminating its trust relationship with the Native peoples, cumulating in the passage of the California Rancheria Act of 1958. With termination came federal occupational training and relocation programs; many of the Northfork Mono moved from their rural land bases to cities where presumably they might "disappear" into mainstream society. Numerous citizens of the North Fork Rancheria participated in these programs, moving, in particular, to the San Francisco Bay Area. However, others were drawn back to Madera County by kinship and community. Some women worked their way home from Bay Area domestic jobs through the migrant labor circuit of the "lettuce sheds and the celery sheds" of the valley (Chepo and Chepo interview).

The North Fork Rancheria was terminated in 1966, removing tribal land from trust status and redistributing it to one individual. During the 1970s and into the 1980s, the Northfork Mono, and other California tribes previously terminated under the Rancheria Act, brought class action suits against the federal government to show that termination was unlawful. In 1983, the United States settled in the litigation of *Tillie Hardwick et al. vs. the United States* Civil No. C-79-1710-SW (N.D. Cal. 1983). The case demonstrated that the federal government had improperly executed termination. The status of the North Fork Rancheria and sixteen other California tribes subsequently was restored. The court also recognized that the tribes had been illegally alienated from Rancheria lands and specifically ordered the federal government to take new lands into trust for these tribes. This litigation coincided with the rise of gaming on trust lands representing yet another transformation of Native peoples' engagement with the market economy by which they stand to gain a great deal of liquid and political power.

Northfork Mono women's labor remains highly significant in the tribe's ongoing relationship with local, regional, and national non-Native communities and policies. Notably, women have dominated the tribe's leadership for decades since federal recognition has been restored.

In 2006, in compliance with the court orders described above, and as part of their endeavor to have a parcel of land placed in federal trust for a gaming project, the North Fork Rancheria have engaged public comment. The parcel is located within the reservation boundaries described in the treaties signed by their ancestors. In articles in the *Madera Times*, the Tribe publicly promoted the gaming project proposed for this land by highlighting their long-standing history of cooperation and neighborliness. Their legacy of adaptability and its application to the proposed project was emphasized:

> Despite the enormous social and economic strains placed upon our people as a result of the loss of nearly all our lands, our Northfork Mono ancestors continued a pattern of productive co-existence into modern times. Throughout the 20th century, our ancestors provided critical early labor that supported the growth of saw mills, vineyards, ranches and other defining industries of the region. Today, our connection to Madera County and reliance on collaboration remain central to our interaction with the community (Tatum 2006).

The series concluded with emphasis on the Tribe's legacy of model citizenship as one grounded in their unique history of continuity in traditional labor practices and productive adaptation to the market economy. Northfork Mono women's agricultural labor was described as equal in importance to their traditional occupational specializations in food gathering and basketry. Highlighted was the perspective that women adapted to a long-standing seasonal round of labor activity to maximize access to economic, social, and political resources. Their labor was mediated by culturally and community-defined understandings of gender rights, roles, and responsibilities within traditional kinship, political, and subsistence structures.

Conclusion

This research describes the contributions made by Northfork Mono women's labor to tribal social well-being and survival in Central California across numerous decades. Their participation and roles in the wage economy and in relation to the sociopolitical structures of their communities were particularly important in the context of land dispossession. To date, two-thirds of California Natives (the largest Native population in the United States) remain federally unrecognized as a result of dispossession. The status of the Northfork Mono women whose experiences are shared here is dependent upon federal policy, which revolves around trust land, of which Native people in California have very little. Moreover, the legal action restoring federal recognition to the Northfork Mono and other tribes ordered the federal government to place new lands in trust for these tribes; nearly three decades later this has not occurred for the most part.

As elsewhere, Northfork Mono labor was essential to the development and persistence of colonial settlement and success; yet the history of gendered labor experiences, of migration and urbanization in connection with land use and occupancy has been largely neglected. The tendency has been to focus on the processes of erasure in the face of colonization rather than on their contributions to the production and maintenance of Newcomer communities. The off-reserve struggles for California Native peoples occurred as result of colonial invasion and dispossession, with the vast majority of Native peoples federally disenfranchised from status and land. As shown, Northfork Mono women's labor was integral to the strengthening of tribal community, cultural vitality, and sovereignty, serving as a counterpoint to misinformed arguments that treat contemporary land claims as "reservation shopping," a contention that implies that tribes are more interested in land for its potential market share in a casino economy than for its tribal historical or cultural importance.

As argued elsewhere, women who relocated from reservations to cities are conventionally represented as passive, oppressed, or dependent. My prior research alternatively suggests that urban women assumed roles of leadership and strength. Women transformed themselves from providers of shelter, food, and cultural transmission, to activists and strategists (Krouse and Howard 2009; Howard-Bobiwash 2003). "Female qualities" were reaffirmed in the urban context as "traditional" roles for women, whose strategic actions with the "mainstream" tell of the significance of gender and social networking in generating a space for women to gain independence as conscious members of a growing and productive community. In this sense, Native women's work and agency contribute to the production of knowledge, identity, and community, and lay foundations not for assimilation, but for decolonization, itself defined by nonlinear movement and intersectionality. Likewise, my examination of the overlooked work of Northfork Mono women in relation to socioeconomic mobility in the production of community is valuable to understanding ongoing processes of decolonization. As Joan Sangster observed, Native culture has been crucial in accounts of Native labor history, however gender less so; "Women's work was seldom analyzed seriously and critically, though unstated assumptions about gender differences pervaded the work of many social scientists" (Sangster, this volume). Moreover, culture has most often been reified whereby Native peoples "accommodate" the market place, with cultural autonomy signifying a measure of successful "adaptation." An emphasis on agency in this approach might obscure scholarly responsibility to critique colonialism (Brownlie and Kelm 1994). Northfork Mono women's labor history presents an opportunity to not just describe cultural survival amid colonial processes, but considers women's agency in relation to economic and community survival as well as contemporary Native/non-Native power relations, and as integral to decolonizing acts of knowledge production. This research revises the historical and anthropological record of Northfork Mono identity, intertribal relations and kinship, land use and occupancy. It also validates the North Fork Rancheria's perspective of their postcontact history in the San Joaquin Valley as authentic and further serves the tribe's efforts to expand public knowledge of Indigenous history in relation to the non-Native community's new social expectations of the tribe in the era of Indian gaming.

Finally, a participatory and collaborative approach to community history, inclusive of the gendered, political, and socioeconomic engagements with the market economy, productively reconsiders the process of decolonization. Dialogues between past and present; about Native/non-Native relations; and between community and national policy in transforming people's means for survival are components of decolonization. Northfork Mono women's strategies for survival during and following invasion and dispossession of their lands historically mark important cultural and economic transitions. This experience, in the context of the economic transitions and shifts of power accompanying the current introduction of gaming, takes decolonization in yet another direction. Women's labor and its import to community is understood not simply through a lens of agency, or as cultural integrity, but as a means to negotiate power, resist assimilation, and cope with irreversible consequences of colonialism. More importantly, I think, the power of these stories resonates for current and future generations who struggle for decolonization and economic security, all recurrent themes in the affirmation of Native sovereignty and Indigenous rights to health, security. and social well-being.

Acknowledgments

I thank the Tribal Council and citizens of the North Fork Rancheria of Mono Indians, who granted the opportunity to conduct this research in connection with their efforts to restore their tribal land base and develop economic opportunity, while I was a Research Associate for James M. McClurken and Associates. I am thankful to Jim McClurken for his mentorship, support and encouragement. I am also very grateful for Carol Williams's careful, patient, and extremely helpful editorial work on this chapter, and for the commentary I received from those who attended the workshop at Trent University in 2008 in particular Sarah Carter, Sandra Faiman-Silva, Margaret Jacobs, and Cathleen Cahill.

Notes

1. Based on research conducted between 2004 and 2006 for the federally recognized North Fork Rancheria of Mono Indians located in the northern San Joaquin Valley and foothills of the Sierra Nevada Mountains, with headquarters in North Fork in Madera County, this chapter condenses information from my report for the tribe and my manu-

script, *Lineage, Land and Labor: The Northfork Mono and the San Joaquin Valley, California*. The tribe is part of a larger linguistic-cultural category referred to as Western Mono, with those inhabiting the eastern San Joaquin Valley/Sierra Nevada foothills (today Madera and Fresno counties) categorized as Northfork Mono. Many tribe members prefer *Nim* the name used in their language, although not in wide daily usage. Northfork Mono is used in this chapter. For naming history and conventions, see the Tribe's website www.northforkrancheria.com (accessed January 2012) and Lee (1998).

2. The Valley lands promised in these four treaties were intended for groups who live throughout this vast region, including Northfork Mono. The citizens of the North Fork Rancheria are descendants of signatories to the treaties. "Treaty with the Howechees, Etc., 1851" specifies, "that the mona or wild portion of the tribes herein provided for, which are still out in the mountains, shall, when they come in, be incorporated with their respective bands, and receive a fair and equal interest in the land and provisions hereinafter stipulated to be furnished for the whole reservation" (Kappler 1087–88).

3. A number of families lived simultaneously and sequentially on the Rancheria lands during its fifty-year history. Only one elderly tribe member (of several hundred) lived there by 1966, and hence when termination policy was enacted was the sole distributee of Indian land held. After a 1980s lawsuit showing the illegality of North Fork Rancheria termination, status was restored to the descendants of the distributee of the Rancheria. The descendants numbered fifty; however, the Tribe elected to extend membership to the descendants of all those for whom the reservation lands had been intended. Today membership numbers approximately 1800.

Works Cited

Brownlie, Robin, and Mary Ellen Kelm. "Desperately Seeking Absolution: Native Agency As Colonialist Alibi?" *Canadian Historical Review* 75.4 (1994): 543–56.

Cook, S. F. "The Aboriginal Population of the San Joaquin Valley, California." *Anthropological Records vol. 16, no. 2* (1955). Berkeley: University of California Press.

Gifford, Edward Winslow. "Northfork Mono Field Notes." Microfilm, Berkeley: University Archives, Bancroft Library, University of California, 1996.

Heizer, Robert, F. *The Destruction of the California Indians.* Lincoln: University of Nebraska Press, 1993.

Henley, Thomas J. Letter to George W. Manypenny. September 4, 1856, S. Exec. Doc. 5 (34-3) 875, 787–97.

Howard, Heather. Interviews: *North Fork Rancheria of Mono Indians*:
Byrd, Pauline (Polkenhorn), and Lou Ann Polkenhorn. April 20, 2005.
Chepo, Maggie, and Leona Chepo. February 13, 2005.
Davis, Gertrude. February 11, 2005.
DeSilva, Connie. Interview with James M. McClurken and Heather Howard. February 14, 2005.
Martin Nunez, Claudine. February 12, 2005.
Pomona, Ruby. February 12, 2005.
Tex, Grace. February 14, 2005.

Howard-Bobiwash, Heather. "Women's Class Strategies As Activism in Native Community Building in Toronto, 1950–1975." *American Indian Quarterly* 27.3–4 (2003): 566–82.

Hurtado, Albert L. *Indian Survival on the California Frontier*. New Haven: Yale University Press, 1988.

Izumi, April Geary, ed. *"Agricultural Statistical Review: 2007 Overview."* *California Agricultural Resource Directory 2008–2009.* Sacramento: California Department of Food and Agriculture, 2009.

Johnston, Adam. Letter to Luke Lea. June 24, 1851. *Annual Report of the Commissioner of Indian Affairs* 1851: 249–53.

Kappler, Charles J., comp. *Indian Affairs: Laws and Treaties.* Washington, D.C.: U.S. Government Printing Office, 1904–79.

Krouse, Susan A., and Heather A. Howard. "Introduction." *Keeping the Campfires Going: Native Women's Activism in Urban Areas.* Lincoln: University of Nebraska Press, 2009.

Landon, Blanche F. Weekly Report. October 6, 1923. National Archives and Records Administration, San Bruno Regional Repository, RG75, Sacramento Area Office, Coded Records, 1910–58, Of Programs and Administration, 1950–58, Code: 803.4–803.36, Box 238, Madera County, 1918–34, Closed no. 1 (2 of 2).

Lee, Gaylen D. *Walking Where We Lived: Memoirs of a Mono Indian Family.* Norman: University of Oklahoma Press, 1998.

Lewis, M. B. Letter to Thomas J. Henley. September 28, 1856. United States National Archives and Records Administration Microfilm 234 Series, Letters Received by the Office of Indian Affairs: Reel 35: 670–72.

———. Letter to Thomas J. Henley. August 18, 1858. S. Exec. Doc. 1 (35-2) 974, pp. 643–46.

———. Letter to Thomas J. Henley. November 15, 1858. United States National Archives and Records Administration, Microfilm 234 Series, Letters Received by the Office of Indian Affairs, 1824–81, Reel 36: 983–84.

———. Weekly Report to Thomas J. Henley. September 20, 1858. United States National Archives and Records Administration Microfilm6 Reel 36, Microfilm 234: 907–8.

McCarthy, Helen. "A Political Economy of Western Mono Acorn Production." PhD dissertation, University of California, 1993.

Miller, Wendell. *Report on North Fork.* Madera County, California; California Indian Legal Services, May 1937.

N. D. Cal. 1983. Hardwick, et al. v. United States, et al., Civil No, C-79-171D SW.

O'Neill, Colleen. *Working the Navajo Way: Labor and Culture in the Twentieth Century.* Lawrence: University Press of Kansas, 2005.

Tatum, Cal. "North Fork Mono Indians Historical Series." *Madera Tribune* (August 2006): 19–24.

Wolf, Eric R. *Europe and the People without History.* Berkeley: University of California Press, 1982.

CHAPTER 11

Diverted Mothering among American Indian Domestic Servants, 1920–1940

Margaret D. Jacobs

In the early twentieth century, many young Indian women took up domestic service in white women's households in urban areas of the American West such as Los Angeles and the San Francisco Bay Area. The boarding school system had trained Indian girls in domesticity and then "outed" many of them to work among white families in the vicinity of the schools. After leaving boarding schools, many Indian women found few other employment prospects and used domestic service work as part of a patchwork of seasonal economic strategies. Most women found this work tedious and their employers imperious. In particular, many intensely disliked caring for white women's children. However, despite the oppressive nature of domestic service, many Indian women gravitated to these jobs in urban areas where they formed a vibrant social network with other Indian youth and reveled in modern urban leisure pursuits.

Leisure culture—the focus of many studies by women's historians—offered greater freedom to young women who had so recently been confined to boarding schools, but it also generated new complications. While in service, many young Indian women became pregnant out of wedlock and then confronted a dilemma about how to mother their own children while earning a living as domestics and caretakers of other children. Some Indian mothers relied on extended kin while others boarded their children. Still others faced pressures by Bureau of Indian Affairs (BIA) officials, including "outing matrons," to place their children up for adoption or to institutionalize them in boarding schools. Thus, at a time when white women reformers worked to enable single mothers to stay at home with their children through mothers' pensions and Aid to Dependent Children, many Indian women domestic servants were diverted from mothering their own children to care instead for white middle-class women's children. Examining the case files of ninety-seven Indian domestic servants in the San Francisco Bay Area between 1920 and 1940, this chapter considers the ways in which Indian women's paid work as domestic servants often undermined their unpaid culturally reproductive work as mothers.

Young Indian women servants in the 1920s and 30s in the San Francisco Bay Area experienced a phenomenon that feminist scholar Sau-ling Wong calls "diverted mothering," whereby "time and energy available for mothering are diverted from those who, by kinship or communal ties, are their more rightful recipients," to care for employers' children instead (Parreñas 2001: 76). This phenomenon has often operated among working class women, particularly women of color, in the United States. The black "Mammy" in the plantation household represents the most well-known manifestation of this phenomenon, but it could be applied to every woman who has had to provide child care and perform domestic service for other women while diverting time and attention from her own home and children (Zimmerman, Litt, and Bose 2006: 193–284).

To some extent, Sau-Ling Wong's configuration presumes a universal family in which it is primarily the biological (or adoptive) mother who plays the central role in child-rearing. Within many American Indian communities, extended kin, particularly grandparents, aunts, and uncles had long helped to raise children. By the early twentieth century, however, government officials, missionaries, and reformers were promoting a nuclear family and a domestic role for women as part of assimilation policy. Prior methods of childrearing were under attack; in fact officials often justified the removal of Indian children to boarding schools based on supposedly deficient Indian child-rearing and aberrant family models. The BIA expected Indian women to conform to a middle-class model of home and family (Jacobs, 2009). Ironically, however, the promotion of "outing" and domestic service diverted young Indian women from this model.

The entrance of large numbers of American Indian women into domestic service occurred as a direct result of the assimilation policy that the BIA implemented from about 1880 to 1935. In the late nineteenth century, many reformers, including white women affiliated with the Women's National Indian Association, had called for a major overhaul of federal Indian policy. They had criticized the use of military forces to quell conflicts and the isolation and poverty of Indians on reservations. Instead, they believed that only through bringing Indian people into the American mainstream would the so-called Indian problem be solved. Consequently, as part of its assimilation policy, the federal government established a vast network of Indian boarding schools. The schools focused not only on teaching Indian children to read and write in English and to adopt Christianity but also imparted new ideas about gender and family. As part of their effort to promote domesticity among girls, the boarding schools trained them in cooking, laundry, and housekeeping. Many schools then developed outing programs in which they placed Indian girls within white families, ostensibly to practice and perfect their domesticity. Boys were placed out to do agricultural labor and other unskilled work (Adams 1995; Archuleta, Child, and Lomawaima 2000).

As boarding school scholars have argued, often outing programs grew into more elaborate enterprises that seemed to fill a demand for labor more than to meet the aim of assimilation (Lomawaima 1993). In Los Angeles and the San Francisco Bay Area, for example, the BIA hired "outing matrons," white women administrators, to link middle-class families in search of domestic servants with young Indian women—many of whom had already completed their boarding school education—to work as servants. Matrons scouted for young women from the Stewart Indian School in Carson City, Nevada; Sherman Institute in southern California; the Chemawa school in Salem, Oregon; and Indian communities in northern California, western Nevada, and southern Oregon: the Pomos, Hoopas, Shastas, Monos, Paiutes, Klamaths, Washoes, and Western Shoshones.[1]

Women, however, were not just passively herded into such jobs. Many seized the opportunity to work in urban areas, at least temporarily. Few employment opportunities existed within their home communities and many women desperately needed work to help support themselves and their families. "Daisy," for example, a Klamath Indian who had three children, wrote to the outing matron in Oakland in 1930, "I have had so much trouble . . . have left my husband, he is worthless and cruel . . . I tried to stay with him for the childrens sake but he is just impossible. . . . Must get some work to do soon as my three children and I are without shoes or clothes."[2] For others who were not saddled with such responsibilities, work in the big city seemed a grand adventure. "Irene," for example, from Salt Lake City, "was particularly interested in seeing the Golden Gate International Exposition, and to find out whether she could make Indian articles at the Exhibit."[3] Others were drawn to the prospect of earning and spending their wages on all that the city had to offer. They coveted silk stockings, high heels, romance novels, gramophones and records, and permanent wave hairstyles (Jacobs 2007).

Once they were placed within white middle-class homes in the San Francisco Bay Area, however, many young Indian women faced the stark realities of domestic service work, work that has always been notoriously demeaning and demanding (Hantzaroula 2004; Palmer 1989; Rollins 1985). As live-in servants, many women found that families expected them to be on call nearly all the time. Servants were required to cook, do laundry, iron, clean house, and in many cases, care for children. While a few women in my sample seemed to make their way with ease in this new world of work, nearly all of the case files reveal intense conflict between employers and servants. In particular, many young Indian women disliked the task of caring for white women's children. "Hannah," for example, wrote to the matron in 1932:

> I tried for 2 months to grin and take what came my way—and tell you people I was happy—up till now. I had no privacy whatever—the kids slept in my bed - used my things—sassed me back. . . . I left yesterday morning because the oldest girl was making remarks that I couldn't stand. . . . She expected me to take care of the kids and do house work at the same time—which I just could *not* do. They [the kids] wouldn't mind—then she thought I was in the wrong. I am deeply "sorry" for causing you any trouble. But I am not sorry for quitting that place.[4]

Like Hannah, many women left their employers or refused to take positions where they would have to care for children.

Despite these indignities, many women stuck with the work—at least temporarily—and still sought out such jobs. Many were drawn to the social opportunities the Bay Area afforded, particularly with other Indian youth who resided in the area, and to new leisure pursuits. Some women liked to participate in the Four Winds Club, a group sponsored by the YWCA in Oakland that met every Thursday night and held chaperoned dances once a month for the young Indians in the Bay Area (Patterson 1992: 410). Others preferred to meet friends for dancing and drinking in the city away from YWCA supervision, the matron, or their employers. Employers often complained to the outing matron that girls were "[o]ut too many nights."[5]

Young Indian women valued this social life so much that many of them avoided or sought to leave positions if they interfered with their leisure pursuits. For example, "Fern" and "Amelia" complained to the matron in 1929 about how unhappy they were working at the Mt. Diablo Country Club (inland from the San Francisco Bay). "We can't stand it here any longer," they wrote. "Too hot, lonesome, and everything. We would like to work some place else, where we can see the girls on our day off. It feels terrible not to see them, and that were [sic] way off . . . Can you please get us a better place."[6] These Indian women had discovered the lively urban social scene that had attracted many other young women workers in the first decades of the twentieth century (Alexander 1995; Kunzel 1993; Odem 1995).

In some ways these women had much in common with other young working women in the city; they, too, found greater sexual freedom—and danger—within the city. Out from under the control of the boarding schools, many Indian women reveled in the chance to flirt with young men and engage in sexual relationships. As with other young working women, their behavior alarmed many middle-class women reformers. Whereas in the late nineteenth century, such reformers characterized the "fallen woman" as a "victim of male lust and exploitation," in the Progressive era, they emphasized a new model of "female delinquency that acknowledged the sexual agency of young women" (Odem 1995: 3–4, 95–127). Indeed, one of the matrons who oversaw Indian girls in the Bay Area complained to her supervisor: "The lack of moral standards among the majority of the girls causes great social difficulties; many embarrassing moral questions have been presented during my ten years supervising Indian Welfare, in the San Francisco Bay District; unmarried girls becoming pregnant, girls leaving employment to live with men, married ones leaving wife or husband for others and the contracting of venereal diseases" (Moore 1929).

Among my sample, at least one-quarter of the servants became pregnant out of wedlock. The number might have been far greater; high incidences of runaways from domestic service may have included young, pregnant women. Some sought to terminate their pregnancies. According to an outing matron, when "Virginia" became pregnant, she "caused an abortion."[7] Those who stayed in service and went through with their pregnancies usually delivered at Oakland's Salvation Army Rescue Home, one of the two largest chains of U.S. maternity homes for unwed mothers, and took about six weeks off from their work (Moore 1929; Kunzel 1993: 6, 14–15).

Those women who bore children while in domestic service confronted a very modern dilemma; how to support themselves and care for their children. "Abby's" case illustrates the complicated dynamics that the young women faced. While working for Mrs. Tyson in Oakland, Abby became pregnant. The outing matron, Mildred Van Every, and Mrs. Tyson contacted the man named as the father, but Abby refused to marry him. In lieu of marriage, Van Every and Tyson tried un-successfully to get him to pay child support. Despite this lack of support, Abby seemed optimistic. Tyson gave her six weeks off to have her baby and reported that Abby "is very happy, not at all depressed, is extremely independent, says that she can take care of herself." However, when Abby returned to work, leaving her baby in her brother's care, the baby became ill and required surgery. The father of the child would not help pay for the operation but Tyson gave her an additional thirty dollars, three weeks off to visit the baby, and raised her wages. Abby also took out loans to cover her baby's health care. Later that year, however, according to Van Every, "Mrs. T. called to say that the heavy financial load for [Abby] was more than she could carry—that [Abby] was restless, depressed, not doing good work." The baby was getting along fine, but Abby wanted him with her. Tyson and Van Every considered a paternity suit against the father, but Abby refused.[8]

Abby's case illustrates some of the myriad ways in which Indian women sought to cope with diverted mothering. Like Abby, very few seem to have wished to marry the men who had impregnated them. Matrons often favored this option; in lieu of marriage, however, the matrons encouraged women to seek financial support from the fathers. Abby seemed to prefer to go it alone, or to turn instead to her kin and community. Like Abby, many other young Indian women sent their children home to live with grandmothers, aunts, or uncles. For many women, however, separation from their children was too painful.

Other Indian women boarded out their children in the Bay Area while they worked. In many cases, the cost of boarding an infant was as much as a young Indian woman's salary. When "Ethel" placed her baby girl in a boarding home in Oakland, the matron noted, "I do not know how we are going to pay for the baby's board, for I fear [Ethel] cannot make enough to support herself and child. The price of the baby's board is $25.00, and [Ethel] has started to work for that amount."[9] To deal with the cost of boarding their babies, other unmarried Indian women teamed up. When "Lucinda," a Pomo, was abandoned by the father of her baby, she moved in with Victoria, "also an unmarried girl."[10]

A few young Indian women found it impossible to cope with supporting a child on such meager salaries and apparently abandoned their babies. In one case, "Sharon," a young Shoshone woman, admitted to the matron, "I have been wondering what to do about [my son] who is at Mrs. Dolen's place. I know Mrs. Dolen cannot trust me any more, it is too bad as in first place I should have not neglected him." When Mrs. Dolen informed the matron that she could no longer care for Sharon's son, the matron wrote to the superintendent of the Western Shoshone Agency: "I have gone to the various agencies which are concerned with children's social welfare. The Child Placement Bureau has had Indian placements to make in the past and has found them very difficult, in fact impossible, especially when the child is of such Indian cast of features as is this little boy. . . . The Probation officer says that it is a clear case of returning the baby to the mother. . . . The feeling that [Sharon] has, that she has no responsibility for the child, cannot be accepted."[11]

Sharon's case is unusual. Most of the young women's files reveal great attachment to their children; Abby's anguish seems more common than Sharon's neglect. Moreover, the adoption of Indian children was much more frequent than the Child Placement Bureau claimed. In just one other case of an unwed Indian mother did authorities discourage the mother from giving her child up for adoption. When "Justine" went to the Salvation Army Home to have her baby, she told the officials she "expected to give her child for adoption," but an adjutant at the home "told her that if she were Indian it would be difficult to find a home for the baby."[12] Such racialized sentiments may have been common among some staff members of the Placement Bureau and Salvation Army Home staff, but the matrons strongly promoted the fostering and adoption of the Indian women's children.

In fact, the story of "Nellie" offers evidence of the great length to which the matrons went to promote fostering and adoption. While Nellie worked, she boarded her baby, "Sammy," with Mrs. Upson. By the time Sammy was twenty-two months old, Nellie had married and had had another baby. On March 1, 1934, matrons Van Every and Jeanette Traxler called on Nellie to ask her about Sammy. According to the matrons, "She says that she still wishes to have the baby with her, but that her husband has no steady work." Even though Nellie told the matrons that "she does not wish to place the child in an institution," on March 22, the matrons visited Marie White of the California Children's Home Society. White told them "that unless [Nellie] can assume the responsibility of the child or some of the girls' family can see the child thru, the child must be adopted out. The mother must give over the case of the child to the Child placing agency and sign a relinquishment or a consent before an agency can do the work need[ed] to take over the case."[13]

Subsequently, on March 26, the matrons visited Nellie again. Their efforts and economic hard times seemed to have persuaded Nellie that she had no choice but to relinquish her son. "When asked what she intended doing about [Sammy]," the matrons reported, "she said that she would have to let him be adopted out." A few weeks later, Van Every learned that "[Nellie] is expecting another baby and is quite willing to give [Sammy] up, not knowing what else to do about him. She signed the relinquishment papers."[14] The matrons' strong pressure on Nellie to put her son up for adoption suggests that they did not regard Indian women's wage work as compatible with their unwaged reproductive work. In such cases, their mothering was entirely diverted. Even when a young woman followed the ideal path—marriage—the matrons still often regarded their children as better off in an institution or in a white family.

In some ways, the fostering and adoption of children outside their tribal communities represented an abrupt departure from the past. Prior to the twentieth century, there were virtually no orphans within Indian communities. If a child's parents died, other kin readily took in the child and, according to historian Marilyn Holt, even "Indian children with living parents could be adopted, with parental consent, into another family." By the early twentieth century, many tribal communities had established their own orphanages (Holt 2001: 23, 251, 252, 255).

After World War II, the removal of Indian children and their placement within white families became an increasingly common and troubling practice. In 1969, at the request of Devils Lake Sioux Tribe of North Dakota to conduct an investigation, the Association of American Indian Affairs found that in most states with large American Indian populations, 25–35 percent of Indian children had been separated from their families (Mannes 1995).

My research into American Indian domestic servants suggests that this phenomenon has its roots in the 1920s and 1930s and stems from the irresolvable dilemma and untenable situation that the BIA created for young women. On the one hand, they had been removed from their homes to attend boarding schools, ostensibly to be trained in domestic skills and prepared to keep a home and mother children in a white, middle-class way. Yet, in the BIA's efforts to make Indians less dependent on government assistance, they were also expected to work for wages and participate in the labor market, often far from their home communities and sources of support. Interestingly, authorities often disapproved of young Indian women's decisions to stay at home with their children. A field nurse in Ukiah lamented to the outing matron about one woman, "So another effort to help her has gone wrong. I still believe the girl wants to do right. It was a lot to expect of her to leave her baby and all her relatives to go out alone to earn a living."[15]

With its expectation that an Indian woman should earn a living instead of caring for her baby, this comment contradicted prevailing attitudes toward most white single mothers at this time. Contending that white single mothers belonged with their children, Progressive women reformers lobbied for mothers' pensions to enable single mothers to remain in the home rather than work for wages. By 1921, forty states had mothers' pensions programs. Yet, such programs discriminated against single women of color; 96 percent of women who received mothers' pensions were white. In the 1930s, the Social Security Act enshrined the mothers' pensions into federal legislation, Aid to Dependent Children (later Aid to Families with Dependent Children), but this continued to follow the racialized pattern of the mothers' pension programs. Popular attitudes as well as government policies dictated that Indian women, like African American women, should work for wages, not mother their own children (Abramovitz 1988: 201, 292, 319; Gordon 1994).

The pressures Indian women experienced to give their children up for adoption seem to diverge from that of most other young non-Native women, at least before World War II. Historian Regina Kunzel found that up until the 1940s maternity homes for unwed mothers were committed to keeping mothers and their children together. It was not until the 1940s, Kunzel argues, that professional social workers pressured unwed mothers to give their babies up for adoption (Kunzel 1993: 6, 14–17, 49, 52–56, 89, 128–30, 155; Odem 1995: 52). Yet prior to World War II in contrast, many unwed Indian mothers faced intense pressures to relinquish their children for fostering, adoption, or institutionalization.

Indian single mothers in the 1920s and 1930s endured relentless interventions into their private lives, partly as a result of a new concern with "sex delinquency," but also due to racial ideologies and the unprecedented role that the federal government already played in the lives of Indian people. This intervention is illustrated most vividly in the cases of several young Indian women who fought tooth and nail against all efforts to remove their children.

When her son was taken from her, "Iris" wrote to Van Every:

> Just writing a few words to ask you if you had any thing to do with my boy Rudolph . . . I haven't seen him since last February. This Ind Welfare in Fresno refuse to help me and also said you had something to do with it. I never sign no paper. . . . I been working and trying hard to bring him up. But this last year I supposed to go threw operation. I have three other smaller children to take care and we have no regular place to stay. . . . I thought that time when you ask for the Kids Grandma you were going to help me [sic]." [16]

"Etta" also fought against her children being taken and especially to prevent her son from being sent to the boarding school she had attended. Etta had been raised at the Stewart Indian School in Carson City, Nevada. In 1931, Etta's four children "were committed by the Juvenile Court to the care of [the San Francisco Children's Agency]." The children were then placed in a foster home, "leaving [Etta] free to go to work and contribute to their support." [17] A woman at an Infant Shelter later corresponded with Matron Bonnie Royce that she was caring for Etta's two older children "until such time as they can be transferred to an Indian School for care." [18]

In 1932, a probation officer wrote of Etta, "This girl has had four illegitimate children, one of whom has reached the age of six years and is now eligible for entrance into the Stewart School." The officer lamented that "[Etta] is most unwilling for this placement, stating that she had been very unhappy there and that she could not possibly consider placing her child there."[19] All the authorities thwarted Etta's wishes to keep her oldest child from being boarded at Stewart Indian School. The Stewart School superintendent wrote to the matron, "I am surprised to learn that [Etta] states that she was very unhappy while she was a pupil at our school . . . I was not aware that she was unhappy, but on the other hand I felt that she was old enough to appreciate the protection and advantages that were given to her while here."[20] The matron asserted, "[Etta's] wishes should not be considered in this case, as she is incapable of judging what is best for her boy." She added, "You will recall that [Etta] has always been a problem. A mental test rated her mentality that of a child of 9 or 10 years. Steps are being taken now to commit her to the Sonoma State Home [for the Feebleminded, a mental institution]."[21]

This was not an isolated case; other young Indian women who had several children out of wedlock and refused to give them up also found themselves subjected to mental tests and committed to mental institutions. For example, in April 1948, Iris, who as mentioned above, had four children and fought against their removal, "was committed to Stockton Mental Hospital where she will remain for a year under treatment in the alcoholic clinic and ward."[22] "Connie," a Paiute, also faced a similar fate. Matron Royce informed an authority at her Bishop, California, reservation: "[Connie] has always been a problem. After her baby came, I thought she might settle down and care for it, but she was worse than ever. She contracted a venereal disease and was a moral degenerate. Local authorities took her in charge. She had a mental test and physical examination, the result of which placed her in the State Home for such girls in Sonoma. Her child is getting the best of care in the Ladies Relief Nursery in Oakland." Connie's parents must have been worried that their grandchild would be taken away because Royce assured the Bishop agent, "They would not send the child out without my consent, so the parents of [Connie] need have no fear of the child being given away."[23]

Finally, the case of "Marilyn" illustrates how harshly the state dealt with Indian women who flouted white, middle-class gender norms and sought to defy authorities. In 1931, when Marilyn turned up pregnant and despondent in Oakland, a field nurse reported, "She has been anything but a clean girl." She suggested that "[Marilyn] be made to nurse the baby as long as necessary for the welfare of the baby and then turn it over for the Children's Home Finding Society or the Native Daughters to find it a permanant [sic] home. The home she came from is about as bad as any I have been in. It is positively unfit for a baby to live in. She has no means of support for a baby and she has [her older] son in that unfit place at Santa Rosa rancheria. They would refuse to give up th[at] boy from the home but if the baby is never taken there perhaps we can manage to have [Marilyn] sign papers for release of the infant. She wont [sic] be able to tell who is the Father of it so there can be no trouble from that angle." The field nurse added: "[Marilyn] bragged last summer, it is said, that she was going to get another baby. This should be stopped as soon as possible. She should be put to work as soon as possible and kept under our eye as much as possible."[24] A psychological examination of sixteen-year-old Marilyn concluded that she had an IQ of 61 and was the equivalent age of a nine-year-old, and "classified [her] as [a] middle grade moran [*sic*]." Her examiner recommended: "Owing to the past history, with two illegitimate children, she should without a doubt be committed to the care and supervision of the Sanoma [*sic*] Sate Home."[25]

The testing used to determine that these young women had the mentality of a child of nine or ten years (a "moron") had been developed in the early twentieth century by psychologists Henry Goddard and Lewis Terman. Historian Wendy Kline notes that the category of "feeblemindedness" was "decidedly vague," and "allowed those with new social 'symptoms,' such as unwed mothers and prostitutes, to be diagnosed as 'feebleminded.'" In fact, because some of the girls whom authorities believed to be sexually promiscuous (thus feebleminded) tested within the normal range for intelligence, psychologists connected with the Sonoma State Home devised an "alternative scale of intelligence," that supposedly measured "social intelligence." From the 1910s on, feeblemindedness and, in particular, the 'moron' category became almost synonymous with the illicit sexual behavior of the woman adrift" (Alexander 1995: 41, 89; Kline 2001: 20–27, 29, 42; Odem 1995: 98). Alexandra Minna Stern also exposes the racialized dimensions to Terman's Stanford-Binet intelligence test; he "located the IQs of Mexicans, Indians, and 'negroes' in the borderline range of 70 to 90" (Stern 2005: 93). In other colonial contexts, Indigenous women who violated sexual norms and/or defied authorities also became subject to incarceration. Historian Victoria Haskins (2005) has found many cases of young Aboriginal women servants who were committed to mental institutions, and historian Joan Sangster (2002) has uncovered similar instances of First Nations women who were sent to reformatories and mental institutions.

In regard to Iris, Etta, Connie, and Marilyn, it appears that despite authorities' intentions, only Iris and Connie ended up in the Sonoma State Home. At the age of eighteen, in 1926, Connie was committed to the institution. Information indicates that Iris was discharged from the home in 1932. No records could be found for Etta and Marilyn, suggesting that they may have eluded authorities before they were sent to the home (Johnson 2009).

Privacy laws prevent us from knowing what happened to Connie and Iris once they were admitted.[26] However, according to Kline, the Sonoma State Home, from its founding in 1884 until the 1930s, "had become the fastest growing public institution in California and a nationwide leader in the number of eugenic sterilizations performed" (Kline 2001: 3, 32–60; Stern 2005: 6, 82–114). Both on grounds of race and sexual "immorality," the cases of these young women would assuredly have violated eugenic sensibilities and designs. Many eugenicists, including Californian Paul Popenoe, believed that American Indians were, appropriately (as an "inferior" race), becoming extinct through natural selection. Thus eugenicists would have had few or no reservations about sterilizing young Indian women (Stern 2005: 52). Though we can't be sure that these Indian women who were committed to the Sonoma State Home were sterilized, the practice of sterilizing Indian women—like that of the fostering and adoption of children—became all too common in the post–World War II era. A 1975 General Accounting Office Study, of just four of twelve Indian Health Service hospitals for a limited forty-six–month period, discovered that 3,406 Native American women had been sterilized. Many reported that they were pressured into sterilization or never gave their consent (Lawrence 2000; Torpy 2000).

The roots of widespread sterilization of Indian women as well as fostering and adoption of Indian children clearly reach back into the 1920s and 1930s when authorities generated a contradictory tangle of policies, pressures, and constraints. On the one hand, officials encouraged women to move off reservations and into cities to work for wages, but on the other, they instructed them to model themselves on nineteenth-century conceptions of white, middle-class women within the home. Many reformers and government agents considered Indian women unfit to mother but readily employed them as caregivers for white women's children. Policy makers insisted that Indian women should assimilate to middle-class white society, but not beyond the role of domestic servant. The state interventions that resulted from these contorted directives created cycles of diverted mothering. Reformers and officials justified the removal of children to boarding schools partly on the basis of Indian women's unfitness for mother-hood. Ostensibly, Indian girls were to learn the correct way to mother within the boarding schools, yet they were diverted from forming and caring for their own families by being outed to work as domestic servants in white families. When they did have their own children, authorities often pressured them to give them up, to institutions or white families.

That the BIA often undermined its stated goal of promoting domesticity for Indian women was not entirely lost on BIA officials. As Carl Moore, Supervisor of Indian Education in California in the 1920s and 1930s, lamented, "The natural and proper ambition of every Indian girl is marriage and a home of her own. The [outing] center should in every proper way promote that end. Under present conditions this is not possible to any very great extent. To those who have had the strength to withstand the temptations it apparently leads too often to a life career as a domestic servant. To a regretable [sic] number of others it leads to a life of shame" (Moore 1929). That the BIA's policies undermined its stated rhetoric leads us to wonder whether such diverted mothering was an unintended consequence of short-sighted policy makers or the underlying intent of the policy all along. Whether intentional or not, the policy created a class of unskilled laborers to fill a niche in the labor market who would have difficulty participating in the raising of their own children and thus the reproduction of Native peoples and their cultures.

Fortunately, young women such as Etta, Iris, Connie, Marilyn, were in the minority among domestic servants. Most young Indian domestic servants worked for just a short time before returning to their communities or moving on to other possibilities, rejecting a life of domestic servitude and diverted mothering. Nevertheless, the increasingly widespread practices after World War II of the fostering and adoption of Indian children and the sterilization of American Indian women derived from this era when young Indian women were outed to urban areas and in many instances diverted from mothering their children.

Notes

1. Records regarding these domestic servants contain sensitive material that may embarrass or offend the Indian women or their descendants. Therefore, to respect the identity of these Indian families, I have used pseudonyms for each young woman followed by her tribal identity, if identified in the records. The notes give the initials of each young woman.

2. M. Bl. to Royce, August 12, 1930, M. Bl. File, Box 1, Relocation Records.

3. March 5, 1939, Chronology, I. B. File, Box 1, Relocation Records.

4. F. C. to Royce, [1932], Outing Contracts.

5. M. C. File, Box 1, Relocation Records.

6. M. and A. D. to Royce, n.d. circa 1929, A. D. File, Box 2, Relocation Records.

7. Bonnie Royce to Supt Ryan, December 2, 1932, J. B. File, Box 1, Relocation Records.

8. H. B. File, Box 1, Relocation Records.

9. Royce to Holcomb, July 27, 1931, E. M. File, Box 3, Relocation Records.

10. Peterson to Royce, November 7, 1931, A. Bi. File, Box 1, Relocation Records.

11. A. H. to Traxler, March 16, 1934, Van Every to L. B. Patterson, 26 October 1934, Van Every to McNeilly, November 13, 1934, all in A. H. File, Box 2, Relocation Records.

12. Chronology: June 29, 1935, J. Q. File, Box 3, Relocation Records.

13. Notes on "outing form," March 1, 1934, March 23, 1934, and March 26, 1934, J. G. File, Box 2, Relocation Records.

14. Ibid.

15. Martin to Royce, August 8, 1932, and September 5, 1932, S. B. File, Box 1, Relocation Records.

16. V. G. to Van Every, n.d., V. G. File, Box 1, Relocation Records.

17. Miller to Director, June 10, 1932; Peterson to Royce January 24, 1931; G. W. File, Box 4, Relocation Records.

18. Paige to Royce, July 14, 1931, G. W. File, Box 4, Relocation Records.

19. Miller to Director, June 10, 1932, G. W. File, Box 4, Relocation Records.

20. Snyder to Royce, July 2, 1932, G. W. File, Box 4, Relocation Records.

21. Royce to Snyder, July 16, 1932, G. W. File, Box 4, Relocation Records.

22. V. G. to Van Every, n.d., V. G. File, Box 1, Relocation Records.

23. Royce to Goen, July 17, 1928, C. S. File, Box 5, Relocation Records.

24. Martin to Royce, March 21, 1931, R. W. File, Outing Contracts.

25. Resume of Psychological Examination of R. W., April 8, 1931, R. W. File, Outing Contracts.

26. The Health Insurance Portability and Accountability Act (1996) and California laws guarantee the confidentiality of medical records. Only family members may obtain information on past patients of the Sonoma State Home.

Works Cited

Abramovitz, Mimi. *Regulating the Lives of Women: Social Welfare Policy from Colonial Times to the Present*. Boston: South End Press, 1988.

Adams, David Wallace. *Education for Extinction: American Indians and the Boarding School Experience, 1875–1928*. Lawrence: University Press of Kansas, 1995.

Alexander, Ruth. *The "Girl Problem": Female Sexual Delinquency in New York, 1900–1930*. Ithaca: Cornell University Press, 1995.

Archuleta, Margaret, Brenda Child, and Tsianina Lomawaima, eds. *Away from Home: American Indian Boarding School Experiences, 1879–2000*. Phoenix: Heard Museum, 2000.

Gordon, Linda. *Pitied but Not Entitled: Single Mothers and the History of Welfare*. Cambridge: Harvard University Press, 1994.

Hantzaroula, Pothiti. "The Dynamics of the Mistress-Servant Relationship." *Domestic Service and the Formation of European Identity*. Ed. Fauve-Chamoux. New York: Peter Lang, 2004. 379–408.

Haskins, Victoria. *One Bright Spot*. New York: Palgrave MacMillan, 2005.

Holt, Marilyn Irvin. *Indian Orphanages*. Lawrence: University Press of Kansas, 2001.

Jacobs, Margaret. "Working on the Domestic Frontier: American Indian Servants in White Women's Households in the San Francisco Bay Area, 1920–1940." *Frontiers* 28.1–2 (2007): 165–99.

———. *White Mother to a Dark Race: Settler Colonialism, Maternalism, and the Removal of Indigenous Children in the American West and Australia, 1880–1940*. Lincoln: University of Nebraska Press, 2009.

Johnson, Linda, Archivist, California State Archives, Sacramento, California. Personal Communication. January 28, 2009 and March 4, 2009.

Kline, Wendy. *Building a Better Race: Gender, Sexuality, and Eugenics from the Turn of the Century to the Baby Boom*. Berkeley: University of California Press, 2001.

Kunzel, Regina G. *Fallen Women, Problem Girls: Unmarried Mothers and the Professionalization of Social Work, 1890–1945*. New Haven: Yale University Press, 1993.

Lawrence, Jane. "The Indian Health Service and the Sterilization of Native American Women." *American Indian Quarterly* 24.3 (Summer 2000): 400–419.

Lomawaima, K. Tsianina. "Domesticity in the Federal Indian Schools: The Power of Authority over Mind and Body." *American Ethnologist* 20.2 (May 1993): 227–40.

Mannes, Marc. "Factors and Events Leading to the Passage of the Indian Child Welfare Act." *Child Welfare* 74.1 (January/February 1995): 264–82.

Moore, Carl. Letter to Commissioner of Indian Affairs, November 21, 1929, "Miscellaneous Correspondence," Box 3, *Folder: Outing Center—Berkeley, Supervisor of Indian Education Records*. Record Group 75, Bureau of Indian Affairs, National Archives and Records Administration, Pacific Region, San Bruno, California.

Odem, Mary. *Delinquent Daughters: Protecting and Policing Adolescent Female Sexuality in the United States, 1885–1920*. Chapel Hill: University of North Carolina Press, 1995.

Outing Contracts, Outing Girls. *Records of the Berkeley Outing Matron and Placement Officer, 1916–1933*, Folder in Box 1, Record Group 75, Bureau of Indian Affairs, National Archives and Records Administration, Pacific Region, San Bruno, California, 1930.

Palmer, Phyllis. *Domesticity and Dirt: Housewives and Domestic Servants in the United States, 1920–1945*. Philadelphia: Temple University Press, 1989.

Parreñas, Rhacel Salazar. *Servants of Globalization: Women, Migration and Domestic Work.* Palo Alto: Stanford University Press, 2001.

Patterson, Victoria. "Indian Life in the City: A Glimpse of the Urban Experience of Pomo Women in the 1930s." *California History* 71 (Fall 1992): 410.

Relocation, Training, and Employment Assistance Case Records, 1933–1946. Outing Girls, California Sacramento Agency, Record Group 75, Bureau of Indian Affairs, National Archives and Records Administration, Pacific Region, San Bruno, California.

Rollins, Judith. *Between Women: Domestics and Their Employers.* Philadelphia: Temple University Press, 1985.

Sangster, Joan. "'She Is Hostile to Our Ways': First Nations Girls Sentenced to Reform School in Ontario." *Law and History Review* 20.1 (Spring 2002): 59–96.

Stern, Alexandra Minna. *Eugenic Nation: Faults and Frontiers of Better Breeding in Modern America.* Berkeley: University of California Press, 2005.

Torpy, Sally J. "Native American Women and Coerced Sterilization: On the Trail of Tears in the 1970s." *American Indian Culture and Research Journal* 24.2 (2000): 1–22.

Zimmerman, Mary K., Jacquelyn S. Litt, and Christine E. Bose, eds. *Global Dimensions of Gender and Carework.* Palo Alto: Stanford University Press, 2006.

CHAPTER 12

Charity or Industry?

American Indian Women and Work Relief in the New Deal Era

Colleen O'Neill

This chapter begins with a picture of a young Navajo woman sitting in front of a sewing machine, surrounded by mattress ticking in what looks like a semi-industrial context (figure 12.1). For her, such industrial employment within her reservation community was undoubtedly welcomed because the Navajo economy, like the rest of the United States, was in deep trouble. People suffered as they

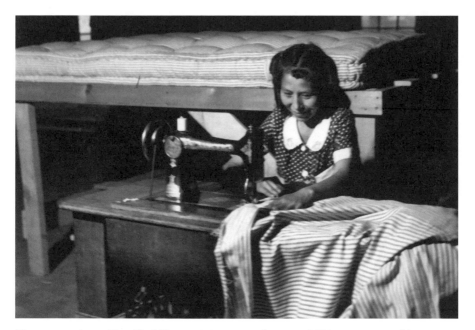

Figure 12.1. An unidentified Navajo Woman working at a WPA mattress-making project in Shiprock, New Mexico, 1940. Photographer Milton Snow. Courtesy of the Navajo Nation Museum, Window Rock, Ariz. Catalog #NO 16-378.

watched their pastoral way of life slip away; a process largely engineered by federal authorities who reduced their livestock herds in order to preserve Navajo range lands for long-term economic benefit. But, in the short term, without their sheep and goats to sustain them, many Navajos went looking for a job. Usually, in the depths of the Great Depression, that meant working in a federal work program.

We know a little about the Civilian Conservation Corps–Indian Division (CCC-ID), a New Deal–era work relief project, as well as other conservation measures. Those initiatives mostly required heavy physical labor such as building bridges, buildings, roads, and dams—jobs reserved exclusively for men (Biolsi 1992; Hall 1994; Hosmer 2004; Kelly 1968; Parman 1974; White 1983). Thanks to new, innovative scholarship, we know that such New Deal–era conservation projects such as livestock reduction and other schemes intended to draw Native peoples into the market economy, impacted men and women unevenly (Weisiger 2009; Cattelino 2004, 2008; Raibmon 2006).[1]

On a fundamental level, we know that women worked too. But, unlike their male counterparts, women's work remained marginal to the bigger story of economic transformation. BIA and county extension agents charged with developing women's relief work folded those initiatives, such as the Works Project Administration (WPA) sewing project, into domestic training programs that were already part of the federal assimilationist curriculum. Native women's labor then became "charity" work, something they did for self-improvement and community welfare, not to earn wages to support their families (even though they received wages, often on par with men). Conversely, for many Native men, working on a CCC crew provided welcomed income and their initial foray into the waged workplace. More importantly, by building roads, dams, and buildings they were literally beginning to create the infrastructure that would connect their reservations to the larger capitalist market. For some, that experience would later offer a stepping-stone into military service or jobs in the defense industry on the home front. While CCC-ID jobs pulled men into the capitalist economy, New Deal–era programs offered women a less secure future in the waged workforce. The WPA provided them with the opportunity to earn wages, even acquire vocational training. Yet, those same programs reinforced their status as non–wage earners, their work indistinguishable from the daily tasks of keeping house and caring for their families.

Indeed, working on a Works Project Administration project could be a transformative event for many Native peoples.[2] In the 1930s wage work was not a new phenomenon for American Indians. They had worked for railroad companies, commercial farmers and ranchers, and in other miscellaneous jobs since at least the mid–nineteenth century. Often seasonal, those jobs provided wages—one resource of many—which Native Americans families pooled to make a living into the mid–twentieth century. But U.S. conquest and colonization over the previous 150 years had severely weakened their communities' subsistence economies and forced many people to rely increasingly on wages to survive. New Deal–era projects, developed for reservation communities, accelerated that process to some extent, drawing Native people closer to the capitalist market economy. Previously, finding a job meant leaving home, at least temporarily. Federal relief programs provided work opportunities relatively close to home, briefly easing the burden of migrating to great distances to find a job (figure 12.2).

At different times and in different places, American Indian women's power over the production and distribution of food and the control over livestock often translated into broader cultural and economic influence in their communities. But, when those communities began to produce goods for a larger capitalist market, beyond a kinship-centered trading system, women historically lost economic ground to their male counterparts. As anthropologist Jessica Cattelino demonstrates, a federal program that distributed cattle to men exclusively created a "male gendering of Seminole tradition" (Cattelino 2004: 72) and undermined women's economic power. Conversely, as Marsha Weisiger and other scholars have shown, efforts to reduce livestock herds on the Navajo reservation (as part of a federally imposed conservation measure) impacted women disproportionally (Weisiger 2009; Lamphere 1977; M'Closkey 2002). Gendered economic change is

Figure 12.2. Navajo CCC workers building a diversion, Navajo Nation, Tuba City, Arizona. National Archives, College Park, Md. Control #75N-Nav-296CC.

not a twentieth-century phenomenon, of course. Dating back to the eighteenth and early nineteenth centuries, American Indian women saw their social status weakened as they started to lose control over agricultural production in their communities.[3]

We have seen American Indian women lose power to men in their communities, or in the larger economy as a whole when colonial markets undermined their control over livestock and crops, but we know little about them as wage earners. They too participated in federal work programs, but that history and the broader gendered implications of their incorporation into the capitalist workplace remains largely unexamined.[4] The growing literature on American Indian workers demonstrates that wage work may have brought about cultural changes, but Native communities managed to resist a complete assimilation of American social values and practices. In many instances, those jobs provided Native families with the resources they needed to maintain their cultural connections to the land and to each other. Although a picture of creative adaptation is emerging in the historical scholarship, considerations of gender remain largely unexplored. Indeed, an examination of New Deal–era programs offers important insight into the different ways that American Indian women and men engaged the waged workplace in the twentieth century.

The Mattress Project

In 1934, Mary B. Salois, a prominent member of the Blackfeet community, wrote to John Collier, the Commissioner of Indian Affairs to express her concern that work relief programs were not reaching the women of her reservation. Salois was president of Blackfeet Indian Welfare, a volunteer organization dedicated to improving educational opportunities and the general well-being of the reservation community. According to Salois, a Blackfeet delegation visited Washington D.C. a few months earlier to meet with federal officials but, because of so "many important matters pertaining to the needs of the Blackfeet, the question of employment for women was overlooked." Had Mary Salois attended those meetings in Washington, women's issues might have loomed larger on the delegation's agenda. Describing the issue as "real serious," Salois portrayed women's unemployment as a major "social and economic problem confronting us here on our Reservation." There was "no work for the girls and also the women, a great many dependent on their own efforts for a livelihood," she explained. Girls, in particular were at risk. "There is nothing with which to direct their minds in the right channels in a town like Browning, where all the 'big business' is controlled by whites and an Indian boy or girl is never given a chance to work," Salois maintained (Salois 1934; Rosier 2004, 1999).[5]

Some months earlier Salois had discussed these issues, including the possibility of creating a garment factory on the reservation, with the local Bureau of Indian

Affairs (BIA) agent. As the previous director of women's work in the Civil Works Program (CWA) on the reservation, she was convinced that Blackfeet women were ready for waged jobs. "They love to earn and use their earnings for their homes and their children," she boasted.[6] Salois' petition to Collier did not meet with immediate results, however. After briefly consulting with the BIA's Extension Division director, Collier wrote an apologetic letter to Salois, explaining that there were neither the funds nor the personnel to launch such a project (Collier 1934).

Salois was suggesting that the BIA simply extend federal work projects that employed non-Indian women elsewhere. Collier had extended conservation work to Indian men, and WPA administrators had already initiated sewing projects for unemployed women throughout the United States. Nine days after Mary Salois wrote to Collier, on August 17, 1934, Aubry Williams, the acting administrator of the Federal Emergency Relief Administration (FERA), announced the development of a mattress-making project to provide jobs to 60,000 women who were on relief roles. The mattress factory project was part of a broader scheme meant to heal the wounded U.S. economy and to solve several interlocking social problems characteristic of the Depression era: commodities without markets, people without jobs, and poor people without decent bedding. Purchasing surplus cotton would aid farmers. Turning that cotton into mattresses would provide jobs for women. Relief agencies would then distribute the product to those in need. According to Ellen S. Woodward, the Director of FERA's Women's Work Division, state relief agencies set up 410 such manufacturing units, and 233 more were on the way (FERA 1934).

Unfortunately for Woodward, the mattress project ended almost as soon as it could get off the ground. FERA administrators could not convince bedding industry leaders that the project would not cut into their market share. A month before Aubrey Williams announced plans for the mattress project, industry leaders registered their protest. H. McCain, President of the Alexandria Bedding Company, argued that such work relief schemes were "obviously impractical and instead of affording relief to labor, will in fact, be a serious detriment to both employers and employees thruout [*sic*] the country." According to McCain, the program was untenable since it would "rob thousands of mattress factory employees all over the country of what little work there is now available," in order to create a work relief program. Instead, McCain thought it was better to create plans "in every State in the Union to preach and teach the unemployed, the feeble, the backward, the timid that correct principle of self-preservation, sacrifice, hard work, how to think and the right of thinking, the development of courage, determination and will power, and demonstrate that there is no place in America for transients, incompetence, indifference, envy and selfishness" (McCain 1934). Other businessmen echoed McCain's criticism. They worried about production standards, as well as the long-term effect on their industry. It is no surprise that within a month of launching the mattress factory project, Harry Hopkins assured Robert

W. Schwab, president of the Southern Spring Bed Company, that the project was not intended to "encourage competing enterprise." In fact the production process hardly resembled modern manufacturing, since, as Hopkins noted, "mattresses are made in women's workrooms, provided with simple equipment for hand work only." Backing away from his initial goals, he promised Schwab and other bedding industry leaders, that the project would end shortly, as soon as 1 million mattresses were distributed to needy families (Burton 1941; H. L. Hopkins 1934).[7]

Hopkins faced criticism for setting up sewing rooms, in general. In a press conference in October 1934, he tried to quell criticism about such government-run "factories." Setting the record straight, he quickly asserted, "They are not factories. They are work rooms. Those people call them factories. I have not seen any that could be called factories. . . . [M]ost of them are just regular working rooms, where a woman can go in and make a dress for her youngster." (H. Hopkins 1934). WPA photographs portray sewing rooms that were closer to the industrial model than to the craft workshop image Hopkins described (figure 12.3). Indeed, industrial conditions prevailed in many sewing rooms across the country, even sparking labor unrest, such as the 1937 sewing room strike in Tampa, Florida (Green 2009).

Figure 12.3. Interior View of the Milwaukee Sewing Project. National Archives II, College Park, Md. Control #69-N-108.

The need to disguise women's work as "charity" and temporary was a rhetorical strategy that crossed reservation borders. Making clothing, gardening, and canning seemed more like a public service and less like an act of industry. Making mattresses, however, was another thing entirely. They were commodities, hardly handmade items made for personal use (Rose 1994: 110). Interestingly, while the mattress projects ended in the South and the Midwest, they continued to operate in American Indian communities through 1941. Perhaps bedding industry leaders did not feel threatened by Native women doing the work far from large, commercial markets.

The mattress project was only a small part of a much bigger plan Woodward imagined to provide employment for women. At Eleanor Roosevelt's urging, FERA administrator Harry Hopkins created a Women's Work Division, and appointed Woodward director. According to historian Martha Swain, Woodward imagined finding jobs for 500,000 women, in a variety of occupations, not simply creating the female version of ditch digging work (Swain 1983: 204–5, 207, 208). But, as Swain demonstrates, many of those programs were eliminated, in Woodward's words, in "the rush to put men to work first (207)." As a result, unemployed women had trouble finding relief work in white-collar, professional, or in other occupational categories usually reserved for men. A woman on relief who wanted a job would most likely find herself behind a sewing machine. During the week ending April 2, 1938, 56 percent of all women earning WPA wages worked on sewing and other goods production projects, 41 percent performed various white-collar jobs, and 3 percent found work on construction sites or other miscellaneous venues (Rose 1994: 108; WPA 1947: 44; Woodward 1936).

Collier had been instrumental in extending New Deal programs, including the Civilian Conservation Corps, Public Works Administration, and other Emergency Conservation Work projects to Indian Reservations. Some projects even employed entire families in various types of conservation work, including rodent control, livestock management and national park maintenance. Yet most WPA, CCC-ID, and PWA jobs were reserved for male workers. According to an official accounting, out of approximately 156 WPA projects on Indian Reservations, 11—7 percent—were designed to employ women (WPA 1947).[8]

Such a skewed gender ratio is not surprising, since non-Indian women faced a similar imbalance in work relief programs in their communities. Out of the 8,500,000 people employed in WPA projects from its inception in 1935 until the war effort absorbed the program in 1943, only 12–18 percent were women (WPA 1947: 44; Tidd 1989: 8). When World War II started to revive the industrial economy, the percentage of women working in WPA programs increased to 27 percent, more accurately reflecting their numbers in the labor market overall. As the need for labor in the defense industries increased, more women moved out of relief work and into permanent industrial jobs. In fact, the New Deal architects envisioned WPA jobs as ladders to the industrial workforce, providing women with the training and work experience to move into better paying, skilled jobs. In November 1936, Eleanor Roosevelt underscored the advantages women gained with their experience in a WPA project. After touring a WPA sewing project in Milwaukee, she reported that women in these jobs "have an opportunity to work on all types of modern machines, which is a help to future employment" (Roosevelt 1936).

Within three years after writing her letter to Collier, in 1937, Mary Salois' demands were finally addressed. Native women, Blackfeet included, found work making mattresses and in other WPA-sponsored sewing projects located in reservation communities. Responding to repeated appeals from concerned philanthropists and activists like Mary Salois, agricultural extension agents expanded the "Indian New Deal" to Native American women.

American Indian Women
and the WPA Sewing Project

Native women's work relief resembled the kinds of projects designed for women in other rural and urban areas of the country. Like poor women in Mississippi, New York, or El Paso, Native women were put to work sewing garments, mattresses, and other useful textile goods. And, like their non-Indian counterparts, they made products that would be distributed to the needy. Wages, too, would improve their buying power and stimulate the economy. In fact, the sewing rooms in rural counties, on reservations and off, were similar, employing small groups of women stitching garments by hand. Yet, the size and scope of the sewing projects varied greatly, from industrial-scale garment factories, to the more intimate room where women fashioned handcrafted linens.

What distinguished women's relief work in Cut Bank, Montana, from women's work in Brooklyn, New York, were not the products they stitched together, nor the tools they used to complete their work. The difference centered in the administrative framework itself, and the local historical dynamics out of which BIA and home extension agents interpreted and managed the relief programs and then incorporated them into a system heavily weighted by decades of paternalistic mismanagement.

Mary Salois might have imagined the development of a garment industry on the Blackfeet reservation, one that could have rivaled "big business" under white control, and perhaps a factory that would have ensured young women permanent employment. Instead, what she saw was the outgrowth of the BIA Extension division's "home improvement" program that taught American Indian women "modern" cooking, sewing, and food preservation techniques. Of course, the difference between learning to sew or to cook new recipes and this program was that that women earned $44.00 a month in WPA wages, equal to what men were making building the community centers that housed such "home improvement" programs (USDI 1937; Boyd 1937)⁹ (figure 12.4).

By the time Native women gained access to WPA jobs in reservation communities, projects directed to developing their domestic skills, such as sewing, were already in place and managed by home extension agents. Equipped with the latest research in home economics, extension agents were taking their lessons out of the Indian school classrooms and into the Native women's homes and communities. Although the boarding school curriculum may have been aimed at training Native women to become domestic workers in non-Indian residences, the extension agents seemed interested in aiding Native women in "improving," their own homes, at least according to dominant middle-class standards (Lomawaima 1994: 81–84; Jacobs 2009: 305–7; Child 1998: 81; Littlefield 1996: 111–14). Indian women were not necessarily the sole audience for these lessons. Agricultural extension agents taught canning, home economics, and scientific farming techniques to rural people in general. While canning and sewing clubs existed throughout the rural United States since at least the turn of the twentieth century, the passage of the Smith-Lever Act in 1914 helped to create systematic organization of these types of

Figure 12.4. Blackfeet women from the Browning WPA Sewing Group wearing garments they "renovated out of CCC clothing." Original photo included in the Annual Report of Extension Workers, January 1, 1936, to December 31, 1936. RG 75: Office of the Bureau of Indian Affairs. National Archives, Washington, D.C.

activities and an educational bridge between the scientific research conducted at the land grant universities to the rural peoples who could apply that information to their lives (Hurt 1994: 256–58; Jensen 1986: 201–26).

With the application of WPA funds to home extension projects, the line between homemaking and wage-work was blurred. In fact, the relief work folded into a wide range of "home improvement" lessons that extension workers were teaching. Extension agents did not make a significant distinction between working for wages sewing mattresses, or making new garments out of CCC cast-off clothing and making quilts, or making Indian crafts and handmade aprons they displayed at county fairs. Whether the women were earning wages or not, all of the work was done in the name of charity, community uplift, and the appropriate gendered instruction.

Given the kinds of raw materials, such as cast-off clothing and army surplus clothing and canvas at their disposal, the Native women were resourceful. For instance, in April of 1936, Blackfeet women received clothing from abandoned CCC camps including socks, underwear, pants, jackets, shirts, overalls, and bedding—all unwashed and undoubtedly in great need of repair. After washing the clothing at the Cut Bank Boarding School's "big laundry," the women set out to renovate the clothing into children's garments and other useful items. No piece of fabric was wasted. The Extension agent supervisor at Blackfeet, Jessie Donaldson Schulz described the transformation of the soiled CCC cast-offs:

> The women then sorted the material into piles for various uses—some to be patched and darned, others to be cut down for little children, etc. The pieces left from cutting down garments were cut into blocks for quilts, and the scraps left from the quilt blocks were used for carpet rags. What wee scraps were still unused were shipped to the Olsen Rug Company to be used by any of the women for new rugs. Hundreds of pairs of old CCC socks were darned and patched. Those unfit for renovation were raveled and dyed and made into hooked rugs with Blackfeet designs. Very attractive (USDI 1936).

One women, whom Schultz described as "ingenious," figured out a way to transform "boxes of large drawers without shirts to match," into knitted dresses. "Some are in one piece, others consist of a skirt and sweat shirt, or an over blouse." According to the extension agent, "These, when dyed are remarkably pretty. . . . The girls are enthusiastic over the dresses and want one or more if they can get them."

These sewing and other women's projects, such as canning and handicrafts, reflected the inherent tensions in Collier's Indian policy; promoting economic development collided with paternalist control over Native peoples' land and labor. And, as Donald Parman suggests, there may have been a great distance between the policy articulated by Collier and the way that agency personnel carried it out on the ground.

While some extension agents were thrilled with the new responsibility of over-seeing WPA jobs for Native women, others certainly found it an extra burden, something that undermined the goals of the extension program overall. They managed WPA programs for needy and unemployed women, giving women jobs that might eventually translate into full-time industrial work. At the same time they were teaching those women "modern" housekeeping skills. Those may not be conflicting goals, but some agents worried that WPA jobs pulled Indians away from their work on the farm. Agents wore many hats as they carried out their work and they felt that their extension mission suffered as a result. One agent summed up his nonextension responsibilities: "Issue of rations and relief; police and law and order, check distribution, reimbursable and resettlement credit, lease work census, ECW, WPA, education, employment, family quarrels, etc." (USDI 1936). Other agents expressed their opposition to WPA programs more explicitly. Reporting on his work for the Shoshone in 1935, Extension Agent Forest S. Slaugh described "make work" jobs as a quick fix; as temporary measures WPA programs redirected Native people away from the work of creating a long term solution to their poverty.

> We have the land and the water and one of the best live stock ranges in the state of Wyoming and now have a goodly supply of live stock both sheep and cattle so that independence by way of the Indians helping themselves is visible on the horizon, but this can never be realized as long as we continue to allow conditions to so shape themselves that our people will be enticed away from the farm.

Slaugh did not seem to embrace Collier's cultural pluralist vision. In fact, his goals were strictly assimilationist. In language reminiscent of late-nineteenth-century reformers, he concluded his report, "It will take many years of good persistent, hard work to remold these people and bring to them a new live [*sic*] (Slaugh 1935)."

Extension agents felt the need to defend these projects as charity, not economic development. They wrote to Collier, explaining that the project's goals did not involve turning a profit. "The manufacturing of clothing [was] for relief," stressed William Donner, the Superintendent of the Fort Apache agency. "The plan is to work up this clothing for orphan children and old people who must be taken care of," he continued. Both the products and the labor "performed by old ladies, cripples, widows," would exist outside of the market, not part of larger economic development initiatives. Donner continued: "the project will provide relief work for those providing the labor and clothing for those unable to provide for themselves" (Donner 1937). Consistently stressing the "workshop" quality of these projects, agents were careful to describe the work as charity, rather than an effort to develop textile factories that would provide permanent wage work for women on the reservations. Perhaps some of the superintendents shared commercial leaders' suspicion of New Deal programs and worried that government-run businesses might compete unfairly with private industry.

The workplace itself seemed to downplay the industrial possibilities of women's work. Agency superintendents used funds reserved for "Indian rehabilitation" to build community centers and canneries. WPA money paid wages to the male construction workers and the women who would eventually work in these facilities. But designated as "multipurpose" and for community use, these buildings were not meant for industrial manufacturing. In fact, women completed sewing projects in special sewing rooms or spread their work in general meeting areas or gymnasiums. Extension agents rarely described canneries in industrial terms. Instead, those initiatives were self-help projects, where Indian women canned surplus produce for distribution to the poor. They were also places were reservation community members could come and can produce from their own gardens, in exchange for a small percentage of their goods, which would be distributed to their needy neighbors.

By sewing mattresses and cast-off clothing women earned an income they were undoubtedly glad to receive. Yet, unlike their non-Indian counterparts, many Native women could not bring their experience into the skilled workforce. Such industries did not exist within reach of reservation communities. Later they would have to travel significant distances to find jobs in the defense industry, an option available to non-Indian women who commonly moved from sewing projects into factory work.

Or, perhaps Native women learned that their labor assembling garments, re-making cast-off clothing, or making Native crafts for the tourist market was not "work" at all. Earning wages at the sewing machine seemed to be (at least from the extension agents' perspective) more like volunteer work, a hobby or domestic training than industrial employment. Their labor in sewing workshops was not much different from the work they might do in a 4-H club. Indeed, such activity was important to their community, and significant for its altruistic achievement. Of course men's and women's relief work was temporary; sewing quilts and digging ditches were both "make-work" projects that promised minimal pay for a short period of time. But the meaning attached to men and women's work differed considerably. Building roads, dams, and economic infrastructure, the men's work drew the broader market closer to reservation communities. Women's labor, alternatively, remained defined or understood as "charity," and continued to be invisible, on the margins of the capitalist labor market in the 1930s.

Notes

1. In the Navajos' case, for example, federal initiatives threatened to undermine the material and cultural power of women in their communities. Earlier scholarship on gender and economic change for Native American women focused largely on the fur trade and women's role in subsistence agriculture from the sixteenth to early nineteenth centuries. (Perdue 1998; Van Kirk 1980; Sleeper-Smith 2001; Shoemaker 1995, Jensen 1977; Etienne and Leacock 1980).

2. Launched in 1935, as part of President Franklin Delano Roosevelt's New Deal, the WPA was a Depression-era initiative that offered state, city, and county agencies (as well as a number of charitable organizations) funding to support projects that put unemployed people to work. WPA projects included large-scale public works and scores of historical and cultural preservation efforts. Local agencies received funding from the federal government but largely retained administrative control over their projects.

3. There is extensive literature on women, colonialism, and capitalist change. In general, that scholarship shows that capitalist development impacts men and women in highly divergent ways, often favoring the former at the expense of the latter. Such change is quite variable, dependent on the historically specific conditions (including class, gender, race, culture, and type of colonial control) that ushered in new economic systems. (North American examples include Jensen, 1977; Leacock 2007; Shoemaker 1995; Lutz 2006; Kelm and Townsend 2006).

4. Historians are beginning to think about the relationship between wage work and gender in Native communities (Frances, Kealey, and Sangster 1996; Muszynski 1996; Raibmon 2005, 2006; O'Neill 2005; Kelm and Townsend 2006; Lutz 2006; Simonsen 2006; Jacobs 2007).

5. Salois noted that she had been appointed to serve as a member of the Blackfeet delegation to Washington D.C., but she had to withdraw at the last minute due to her mother's illness.

6. CWA programs were temporary federal relief measures that predate the WPA projects.

7. It is unclear when the project ended, since we have evidence of mattress projects continuing on the Fort Hall Reservation until at least July 1941. Industry leaders also worried about production standards. Ellen Woodward answered this criticism by insisting that strict quality control would be enforced and that "All mattresses must be constructed in a neat and substantial manner in conformity with the work specifications furnished by this office. Special efforts must be made to avoid lumpiness resulting from careless filling or tufting" (Woodward 1934).

8. These numbers may be somewhat skewed because the document did not include WPA projects for Arizona or New Mexico. But, given the focus on conservation projects in those regions, it is reasonable to assume a similar gendered ratio in jobs. For many American Indian men, working in lumber mills, and on conservation, road, and other construction projects represented a significant shift into the world of wage labor (Hosmer 2004; O'Neill 2005; Parman 1971).

9. Women and men earned wages standard for people employed on work relief projects throughout the United States. Wages were the same at Fort Belknap.

Works Cited

Aberle, David F. *The Peyote Religion among the Navaho*, 2nd ed. Norman: University of Oklahoma Press, 1966.

Adams, David Wallace. *Education for Extinction: American Indians and the Boarding School Experience. 1875–1928*. Lawrence: University Press of Kansas, 1995.

Biolsi, Thomas. *Organizing the Lakota: The Political Economy of the New Deal on the Pine Ridge and Rosebud Reservations*. Tucson: University of Arizona Press, 1992.

Boyce, George. *When the Navajos Had Too Many Sheep, 1940s*. San Francisco: The Indian Historian Press, 1974.

Boyd, Fred W. Superintendent of Fort Belknap agency to Commissioner of Indian Affairs. November 5, 1937. RG 75: Records of the Bureau of Indian Affairs, Records of the Rehabilitation Division, Project Records, 1935–44, Box 18, File Fort Belknap. National Archives and Records Administration, Washington, D.C.

"Burton." (no first name indicated, but possibly Henrietta). Handwritten note attached to file signed, August 15, 1934. RG 75: U.S. Department of Interior, Office of Indian Affairs, Division of Extension and Industry, Central Classified Files, Blackfeet 1907–39, File 920.

Burton, Henrietta K. Supervisor of Home Extension Work. "Supervisor's Report," U.S. Department of Interior, Office of Indian Affairs, Division of Extension and Industry, July 18, 1941. RG 75: Central Classified Files—Fort Hall, 1907–39, Box 175, File 919. National Archives and Records Administration, Washington, D.C.

Cattelino, Jessica. "Casino Roots: Cultural Production of Twentieth Century Seminole Economic Development." *Native Pathways: American Indian Culture and Economic Development in the Twentieth Century.* Eds. Brian Hosmer and Colleen O'Neill. Boulder: University Press of Colorado, 2004. 66–90.

———. *High Stakes: Florida Seminole Gaming and Sovereignty.* Durham, N.C.: Duke University Press, 2008.

Child, Brenda J. *Boarding School Seasons: American Indian Families. 1900–1940.* Lincoln: University of Nebraska Press, 1998.

Cohen, Lizbeth. *Making a New Deal: Industrial Workers in Chicago.* New York: Cambridge University Press, 1990.

Collier, John. Letter to Mary B. Salois, September 7, 1934. RG 75: Records of the Bureau of Indian Affairs, Central Classified Files, Blackfeet 1907–39, File 920. National Archives and Records Administration, Washington, D.C.

Donner, William. Superintendent, Fort Apache Agency. "Self-Help" Clothing for Relief" from "Proposal for Community Improvement Project, Indian Relief and Rehabilitation Fund. Whiteriver, Arizona, April 7, 1937." RG 75: Records of the Bureau of Indian Affairs, Records of the Rehabilitation Division, Project Records, 1935–44, Fort Apache—Fort Belknap. Box, 18, Entry 1007. National Archives and Records Administration, Washington, D.C.

Etienne, Mona, and Eleanor Leacock. *Women and Colonization: Anthropological Perspectives.* New York: Praeger, 1980.

Faue, Elizabeth. *Community of Suffering and Struggle: Women, Men and the Labor Movement in Minneapolis, 1915–1945.* Chapel Hill: University of North Carolina Press, 1991.

Federal Emergency Relief Administration (FERA). "Press Release, August 17, 1934." RG 69: Records of the Works Projects Administration, FERA Central Files 1933–36: Mattress Projects, Box 24. National Archives II, College Park, Md.

Frances, Raelene, Linda Kealey, and Joan Sangster. "Women and Wage Labour in Australia and Canada, 1880–1980." *Labour/Le Travail* 38 (Fall 1996): 54–89.

Green, Elna C. "Relief from Relief: The Tampa Sewing-Room Strike of 1937 and the Right to Welfare." *Journal of American History* 95 (March 2009): 1012–37.

Hall, Edward T. *West of the Thirties: Discoveries among the Navajo and Hopi.* New York: Doubleday, 1994.

Heaton, John W. *The Shoshone-Bannocks: Culture and Commerce at Fort Hall, 1870–1940.* Lawrence,: University Press of Kansas, 2005.

Hopkins, Harry. "Work Relief Administration Press Conference, October 8, 1934, 4:00 P.M." Record Group 69, Series 737, Box 5. Published on the New Deal Network website: http://newdeal.feri.org/workrelief/hop10.htm (accessed February 2012). Hopkins, Harry L., to

Robert W. Schwab, president of the Southern Spring Bed Company, September 19, 1934. RG 69: Records of the Works Projects Administration, FERA Central Files 1933–36: Mattress Projects, Box 24, National Archives II, College Park, Md.

Hosmer, Brian. "'Dollar a Day and Happy to Have It': New Deal Work Relief Projects As Memory." *Native Pathways: Economic Development and American Indian Culture in the Twentieth Century*. Eds. Brian Hosmer and Colleen O'Neill. Boulder: University Press of Colorado, 2004. 283–308.

Hurt, R. Douglas. *American Agriculture: A Brief History*. Ames: Iowa State University Press, 1994.

Jacobs, Margaret D. "Working on the Domestic Frontier: American Indian Domestic Servants in White Women's Households in the San Francisco Bay Area, 1920–1940." *Frontiers: A Journal of Women's Studies* 28 (2007): 165–99.

———. *White Mother to a Dark Race: Settler Colonialism. Maternalism and the Removal of Indigenous Children in the American West and Australia, 1880–1940*. Lincoln: University of Nebraska Press, 2009.

Jensen, Joan M. "Canning Comes to New Mexico: Women and the Agricultural Extension Service, 1914–1919." *New Mexico Women: Intercultural Perspectives*. Eds. Joan Jensen and Darlis Miller. Albuquerque: University of New Mexico Press, 1986. 201–26.

———. "Native American Women and Agriculture: A Seneca Case Study." *Sex Roles* 3.5 (October 1977): 423–41.

Kelly, Lawrence. *The Navajo Indians and Federal Indian Policy, 1900–1935*. Tucson: University of Arizona Press, 1968.

Kelm, Mary-Ellen, and Lorna Townsend, eds. *In the Days of Our Grandmothers: A Reader in Aboriginal Women's History in Canada*. Toronto: University of Toronto Press, 2006.

Lamphere, Louise. *To Run After Them: Cultural and Social Bases of Cooperation in a Navajo Community*. Tucson: University of Arizona Press, 1977.

Leacock, Eleanor Burke. "Women's Status in Egalitarian Society: Implications for Social Evolution." Reprinted with a new introduction by Christine Ward Gailey, in *Native Women's History in Eastern North America before 1900*. Eds. Rebecca Kugel and Lucy Eldersveld Murphy. Lincoln: University of Nebraska Press, 2007.

Littlefield, Alice. "Indian Education and the World of Work in Michigan, 1893–1933." In *Native Americans and Wage Labor: Ethnohistorical Perspectives*. Eds. Alice Littlefield and Martha C. Knack. Norman: University of Oklahoma Press, 1996. 100–121.

Lomawaima, Tsianina K. *They Called It Prairie Light: The Story of Chilocco Indian School*. Lincoln: University of Nebraska Press, 1994.

Lutz, John. "Gender and Work in Lekwammen Families, 1843–1970." In *the Days of Our Grandmothers: A Reader in Aboriginal Women's History in Canada*. Toronto: University of Toronto Press, 2006. 216–50.

McCain, J. H. President of the Alexandria Bedding Company to Harold Hopkins, July 16, 1934. RG 69: Records of the Works Projects Administration, FERA Central Files 1933–36: Mattress Projects, Box 24. National Archives II, College Park, Md.

M'Closkey, Kathy. *Swept Under the Rug: A Hidden History of Navajo Weaving*. Albuquerque: University of New Mexico Press, 2002.

Muszynski, Alicja. *Cheap Wage Labour: Race and Gender in the Fisheries of British Columbia*. Montreal: McGill-Queens University Press, 1996.

O'Neill, Colleen. Working the Navajo Way: Labor and Culture in the Twentieth Century. Lawrence: University Press of Kansas, 2005.

Parman, Donald L. "The Indian and the Civilian Conservation Corps." *Pacific Historical Review* 40 (February 1971): 39–56.

———. *Navajos and the New Deal*. New Haven: Yale University Press, 1974.

Perdue, Theda. *Cherokee Women*. Lincoln: University of Nebraska Press, 1998.

Raibmon, Paige. *Authentic Indians: Episodes of Encounter from the Late-Nineteenth-Century Northwest Coast*. Durham: Duke University Press, 2005.

———. "The Practice of Everyday Colonialism: Indigenous Women at Work in the Hop Fields and Tourist Industry of Puget Sound." *Labor: Studies in Working-Class History of the Americas* 3 (2006): 23–56.

Roosevelt, Eleanor. "My Day: November 12, 1936." Published on the New Deal Network website: http://newdeal.feri.org/dolls/md111236.htm (accessed February 2012).

Rose, Nancy E. *Put to Work: Relief Programs in the Great Depression*. New York: Monthly Review Press, 1994.

Rosier, Paul C. "'The Old System Is No Success': The Blackfeet Nation's Decision to Adopt the Indian Reorganization Act of 1934." *American Indian Culture and Research Journal* 23 (1999): 1–37.

———. *Rebirth of the Blackfeet Nation, 1912–1954*. Lincoln: University of Nebraska Press, 2004.

Salois, Mary B. Letter to John Collier, Commissioner of Indian Affairs, August 8, 1934. RG 75: Records of the Bureau of Indian Affairs, Central Classified Files, Blackfeet 1907–39, File 920. National Archives and Records Administration, Washington, D.C.

Shoemaker, Nancy. *Negotiators of Change: Historical Perspectives on Native American Women*. New York: Routledge, 1995.

Simonsen, Jane. *Making Home Work: Domesticity and American Indian Assimilation in the American West*. Chapel Hill: University of North Carolina Press, 2006.

Slaugh, Forest S. "Narrative Report of Extension Activities on the Shoshone Reservation for the year 1935." RG 75: Central Classified Files, 1907–39, Shoshone, Box 2, File 03. National Archives and Records Administration, Washington, D.C.

Sleeper-Smith, Susan. *Indian Women and French Men: Rethinking Cultural Encounter in the Western Great Lakes*. Amherst: University of Massachusetts Press, 2001.

Swain, Martha. "'The Forgotten Woman': Ellen S. Woodward and Women's Relief in the New Deal." *Prologue* 15 (Winter 1983): 201–13.

Tidd, James Francis, Jr. "Stitching and Striking: WPA Sewing Rooms and the 1937 Relief Strike in Hillsborough County." *Tampa Bay History* 11 (Spring/Summer 1989): 5–21.

Trennert, Robert A. *The Phoenix Indian School: Forced Assimilation in Arizona, 1891–1935*. Norman: University of Oklahoma Press, 1988.

U.S. Department of the Interior, Office of Indian Affairs. "Home Extension Report, 1936." RG 75: Records of the Bureau of Indian Affairs Central Classified Files, 1907–39, Fort Belknap, Box 3, File 031. National Archives and Records Administration, Washington, D.C.

U.S. Department of the Interior, Office of Indian Affairs, Division of Extension and Industry. "Annual Report of Extension Workers, January 1, 1936–December 31, 1936, Blackfeet Indian Reservation, Browning Montana." RG 75: Records of the Bureau of Indian Affairs, Central Classified Files, Blackfeet 1907–39, Box 2, File 031. National Archives and Records Administration. Washington, D.C.

———. "Annual Report of Extension Workers. January 1, 1937–December 31, 1937, Blackfeet Indian Reservation, Browning Montana." RG 75: Records of the Bureau of Indian

Affairs, Central Classified Files, Blackfeet 1907–39, Box 2, File: 031. National Archives and Records Administration. Washington, D.C.

Van Kirk, Sylvia. *Many Tender Ties: Women in Fur-Trade Society, 1670–1870*. Norman: University of Oklahoma Press, 1980.

Weisiger, Marsha. *Dreaming of Sheep in Navajo Country*. Seattle: University of Washington Press, 2009.

White, Richard. *Roots of Dependency: Subsistence, Environment, and Social Change among the Choctaws, Pawnees, and Navajos*. Lincoln: University of Nebraska Press, 1983.

Woodward, Ellen S. Director of Women's Work. Memo to all State Emergency Relief Administrators, from July 6, 1934. RG 69: Records of the Works Projects Administration, FERA Central Files 1933–36: Mattress Projects, Box 24. National Archives II, College Park, Md.

———. "Address before the Democratic Women's Regional Conference for Southeastern States." March 19, 1936. RG 69: Records of the Works Projects Administration, Series 737, Box 8. National Archives II, College Park, Md.

Works Progress Administration (WPA). *Final Report on the WPA Program, 1935–43*. Washington, D.C.: GPO, 1947.

———. "Projects sponsored by the Bureau of Indian Affairs, Federal Indian Agency or Reservations." RG 69: Records of the Works Projects Administration: General Indian Relief, Box 21, File 001, National Archives and Records Administration II, College Park, Md.

CHAPTER 13

"An Indian Teacher among Indians"

Native Women As Federal Employees

Cathleen D. Cahill

In 1913, Salena Kane (Pottawatomie) wrote to the Commissioner of Indian Affairs (CIA) asking for "protection" against the superintendent of the Shawnee Indian School in Oklahoma. Kane was furious that Superintendent Buntin had ignored her requests for employment in favor of hiring white women, in violation of Indian Office regulations. Demonstrating familiarity with Indian Service rules Kane forcefully made her case, first to Buntin and then to the commissioner:

> I went to Superintendent's office and talked to him about it and . . . told him I thought an Indian had ought to be given a position in preference to the whites and he answered yes, and yet he employed the white instead of the Indian . . . I said he had ought to protect me instead of turning me down . . . I said he was going contrary to the Government rules and he knew it and he had mistreated me enough for me to report it to you.

Anticipating a common response to the complaints of Native employees, Kane added, "he can not say we are trouble makers, for it is not so" (PF Buntin CIA, April 11, 1913, NPRC).[1]

Kane's letter emphasizes that the Office of Indian Affairs (OIA) had developed hiring policies aimed at Indian employees and built on race-based assumptions that both shaped and undercut opportunities for Native people. Like Kane, many Native women actively sought employment in the Indian Service because it offered them significant opportunities, including cash wages, employment flexibility, and the possibility of remaining in their communities. Kane's complaint also demonstrates that Native women confronted a hierarchical bureaucracy often staffed by prejudiced white employees and framed by a complicated series of rules and regulations. The women were, nonetheless, skilled at navigating its administrative structure often turning rules to their advantage.

Scholars have emphasized that policy makers designed the federal Indian school system to assimilate Native children and create a colonial labor force by training Native female students for primarily menial domestic labor (Littlefield

1996; Lomawaima 1994). Inadvertently, these policies brought thousands of Native people into the Indian Service in both the white-collar and the menial sector. However, we know very little about them, why they took those jobs, and how they strategically used their positions. Scholarship exploring Native labor primarily focuses on manual, seasonal and artistic labor, and the work experiences of Indian men (Littlefield and Knack 1996; Hosmer 1999; LaGrand 2002; Hosmer and O'Neil 2004; Rand 2008; Bauer 2009). Service work was both manual and seasonal, but it also included salaried careers in skilled positions. Indeed, many employees were part of the first generation of white-collar workers, an underanalyzed sector of Native labor.

Kane's responses reveal that women often knew a great deal about the bureaucratic structures that they were navigating. Indeed, while historians focus on "weapons of the weak" or everyday nonconfrontational forms of resistance when discussing subaltern populations, the women in this case used what might be understood as "weapons of the white collar," an informed knowledge of how to participate in a bureaucratic culture; a strategy privileging skills such as letter writing or enlisting benefactors to advocate for their goals (Scott 1987: xv–xix). Their participation in the federal workforce encourages us to think more broadly about economic survival strategies that they employed at the turn of the century. Native women adapted to the changes wrought by the modern economy; but racially marked as Indians, they also struggled for economic and cultural survival in a hostile world.

In order to access their voices, the essay draws upon fifty-five personnel files (hereafter PF) from the Indian School Service. Beginning in 1905 the OIA kept individual files for each employee that afford an intimate portrayal of the everyday work lives of female personnel. Assembling personal and professional correspondence, efficiency reports, requests for transfers or retirement, and more, the files illuminate the occupational paths of these women.

Federal Hiring Policy

The Indian Service at the turn of the century had a highly unusual workforce for its time, employing large numbers of Native men and women. This distinctive character has two sources: the government's assimilationist use of the nuclear family model and the perceived pedagogical possibilities of work for Indians. Native women fit into both categories.

Policy makers sought to destroy tribal identities and political power by replacing them with possessive individualism and free labor ideology. They believed that creating individual households would transform societies based on "tribal relations" into "civilized" middle-class households characterized by a gendered division of labor. Central to domestic ideology, women held an especially important place in these theories. Vaunted as sources of moral authority and charged with the social reproduction of the subsequent generation, they would ensure that cultural change was perpetuated. "Soften, purify, and refine the mother," insisted one official, "and the task is more than half accomplished. Her genial influence will mold and inspire the children, and will civilize and elevate the father" (ARCIA 1896: 231–32).

To transform Indians according to this model, the OIA focused on land distribution and the essential role of female employees in its education policies. In 1882, it created the Indian School Service building a network of educational institutions. Many were boarding schools that aimed at disrupting the affective bonds between Native children and their parents and substituting federal employees as surrogate parents for an entire generation. As Margaret Jacobs has demonstrated, policy makers justified child removal policies by pathologizing Native women and portraying them as unfit mothers. These ideas influenced the way white superiors later viewed Native female employees in the service (Jacobs 2009: 25–52, 87–148).

The model of federal employees as fictive kin literally shaped the service. For example, administrators often hired married men to run boarding schools and employed their wives as matrons. This strategy of creating a feeling of "the school as a home," reinforced the gender division of household labor in the curriculum with living examples (ARCIA 1896: 348). The emphasis on education and gender resulted in a dramatic increase of personnel, especially female teachers in classrooms and matrons in dormitories. Women also worked as cooks, seamstresses, and laundresses, provisioning the institutions. The service workforce grew from just over 500 in 1869 to almost 4,000 by 1897. By century's end, the School Service constituted fully half of Indian Service employees, engaging thousands of women over the years. By the 1890s, roughly 60 percent of the School Service employees were female (Stuart 1979: 130–31; ARCIA 1890: 334).

The OIA also had a policy of hiring American Indians to fill positions. Officials argued that employment was instructive, teaching adult Indians specific skills and keeping educated Indians from "returning to the blanket." Policy makers believed that an Indian workforce would undermine traditional tribal authority and held up Indian employees as lessons in "civilization" for their home communities. Finally, the policy was economically motivated as the OIA often paid Natives at lower salaries than non-Native employees (Ahern 1997; Novak 1990).

Although initial efforts prioritized male employment, the development of the school system generated work for women. When civil service reform applied to the OIA in the 1890s, Native workers received exceptions to the competitive exam system applicable to non-Native candidates. Thereafter, "Indians employed in the Service at large" were appointed without the civil service examination. For more skilled positions, including superintendent, teacher, farmer, kindergartener, physician, matron, clerk, seamstress, manual training, or industrial teacher, Indian applicants were required only to pass a noncompetitive exam (Schmeckebier 1927:

293–94). These emphases on the educational value of labor and preferential hiring policies resulted in a rising percentage of Native employees holding regular, rather than temporary or casual, positions. In 1888, the CIA reported that Indian employees constituted 15 percent of the School Service. In 1895 that proportion rose to 25 percent (ARCIA 1888: cxxx–cxci; ARCIA 1895: 511–43). By 1912, Native employees made up almost 30 percent of the 6,000 school and agency service employees (SAI 1912: 27).

Those statistics exclude the majority of Indians who worked as temporary or irregular laborers. In 1912, for example, 521 Indian women served as regular employees and 941 were hired as irregulars (ARCIA 1912: 164–65, 307). These irregular hires commonly replaced vacationing regular employees or served when there was "a necessity for special work or extra labor," such as for summer canning or sewing projects (Regulations 1904: 13, 27). Temporary federal work was often only one of many diverse economic strategies that allowed women to remain on their reservations participating in the seemingly mundane, but vitally important everyday routines of their community (Rand 2008: 7).

This essay, however, focuses on the experiences of regular employees who held the manual positions of matron, seamstress, laundress, cook, or baker. Some also worked in white-collar positions as teachers, nurses, or clerks. As such, they might become, as author Zitkala-Sa (Yankton Sioux) noted in the title of one of her short stories "an Indian teacher among Indians" (Zitkala-Sa, 1921, 1985, 90). One historian contends that 20 percent of Native employees were in the white-collar sector in 1912 (Novak 1990: 647). In my sample of personnel files, ten of the women held white-collar positions, including one who served as the Grand River Boarding School superintendent (PF Fredette Employee Blank, May 15, 1911, NPRC). They represent the first generation of professional Native workers. The remaining forty were manual laborers, including five appointed as field matron.[2]

All but two women had attended federal Indian schools that, by the early twentieth century, had turned out thousands who could fill the ranks of the service. For example, the Haskell Institute and Chilocco School both had Normal Departments supplying Native teachers. In 1907, Chilocco's journal listed sixteen female graduates who obtained employment at other Indian schools that year (Lomawaima 1994: xv, 18; ARCIA 1900: 517–18). Many women received their first positions during their enrollment in or immediately after leaving school. Matilda Kruger (Colville) noted that the first position she held was sergeant at the Chemawa School in Oregon, most likely while she was a student there.

Like other applicants, Native women constructed their application requests so as to present themselves in ways appealing to the OIA. Mary Paquette (Winnebago/French) requested a position at Black River, Wisconsin, as "a member of the Winnebago tribe [who] would like to work among my own people." When informed that it was not OIA policy to place people on their own reservations, she revised her description. "I have no relatives among the Winnebagos. I have no friends among them and I have not and never had any tribal affiliations with them" (PF Paquette CIA, October 12, 1907, and CIA, October 21, 1907, NPRC). Whatever the truth, Paquette strategically provided information in order to land the job. Some applicants also used their connections to former teachers, superintendents, or other influential contacts to support their requests. Lizzie Devine (Annishaanabe) asked her former teacher, H. B. Pearis, who had become supervisor of Indian Schools, for help in getting a transfer in 1911 (PF Devine January 21, 1911, NPRC).

Work Experiences

Once women received their appointments, their experiences varied greatly. Some chose to spend their lives in the service while others moved in and out of the bureaucracy. Some remained at one post whereas others had lifelong careers spanning the country. Julia DeCora Lukecart (Winnebago/French) sister of artist and teacher Angel DeCora, began her career in August 1898 retiring in April 1932 (figure 13.1). She worked in multiple positions—field matron, assistant matron, matron, seamstress, cook, and general laborer—at fifteen different schools and agencies (PF DeCora Lukecart Retirement Record, NPRC). The files of nine female employees contain retirement records that reveal they held an average of four different positions and worked at an average of six and a half different locations throughout their careers (figure 13.1).[3]

Native women sought jobs for many reasons, but often for financial security in the face of limited job opportunities. "I can not afford to be without work," Lucinda George (Onondaga) wrote (PF George CIA, January 22, 1913, NPRC). Lizzie Bonga (Lakota) stated, "I wish the position to earn my living" (PF Bonga Application March 27, 1909, NPRC). Some women had previously worked as private domestic laborers, a job notorious for interpersonal conflicts, long hours, and lack of privacy. Hiring on with the government may have seemed like a better option. For white-collar workers, the service offered opportunities for promotion and, afforded additional perks not available in the private sector.

The opportunity to remain in their communities or with kin was also an attractive benefit of the job. Native women's efforts to maintain kinship and community ties undermined the federal desire to disrupt Native families and destroy tribal identity. For example, Maude Peacore who self-identified as Chippewa, requested a transfer to the Seneca School in Oklahoma, explaining: "I have held the position here at Tomah School [in Wisconsin] as assistant seamstress for several years. When I came here my home was at Tomah, but now my relatives are in Oklahoma. I would like a position in an Indian school near their home" (PF Peacore Superintendent to CIA, November 1, 1909, NPRC). Their ability to supervise their children in the institutions also motivated applicants (Schmeckebier 1927: 482). Jessie Morago (Ojibwa) requested a teaching position adding, "I would like to get in a school where I could enroll my children" (PF Morago CIA, November 5,

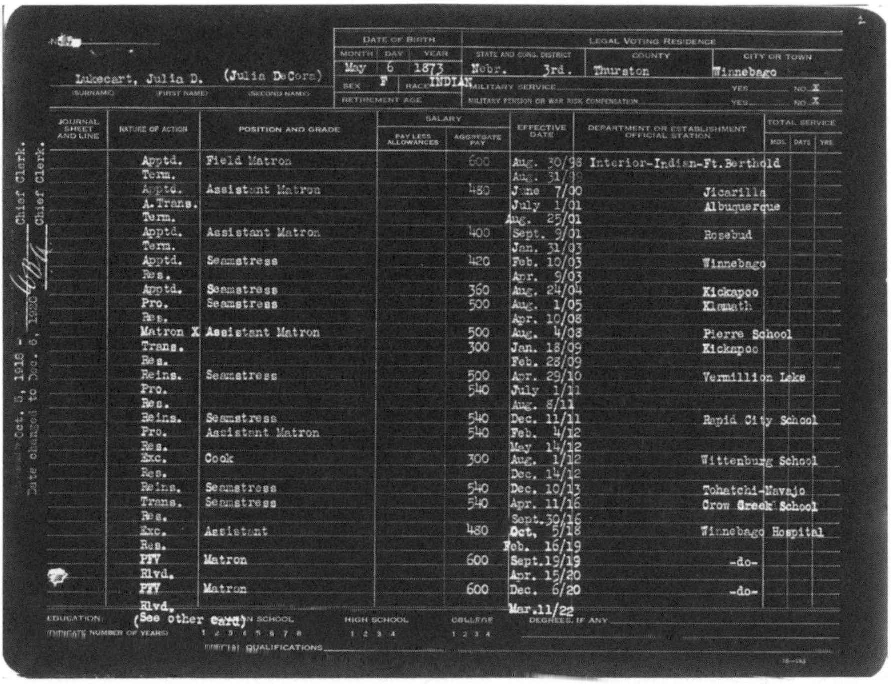

Figure 13.1. Retirement card of Julia DeCora Lukecart (Winnebago/French). One of the few Native employees to receive a pension, Lukecart's career spanned from 1892 to 1932. During that time she worked in six different positions and at fifteen different locations. Her retirement card tracked her employment to the day in determining her pension eligibility. Courtesy of the National Personnel Records Center, St. Louis, Mo.

1917, NPRC). Lottie Smith Pattee (Eastern Band Cherokee) a matron wrote "O! I can't think of giving up my little girls . . . I want to keep [Cora] in the same school with me and if possible to room with me . . . I think that I could watch over them better than a stranger." Despite fond recollections of her experiences at the Hampton Institute, Pattee rejected the premise of child removal inherent to the boarding schools insisting that she could raise her children better than any surrogate (Carney 2005: 97).

Kinship obligations also played a large role in the women's lives and the flexibility of the service was appealing. It offered its regular employees incentives that were unusual (especially for nonwhite employees) at the turn of the century, including monthlong vacations, leaves without pay, the possibility of reinstatement, and later, retirement pensions. Although many employees were unaware of these incentives upon entry into federal work, they became inducements for longevity in government employ. As with the preferential hiring policy, the requirements for these incentives varied by race, sometimes to the advantage of Native employees and sometimes to their detriment.

For instance, civil service protocol granted all employees a grace period after resignation in which they could apply for reinstatement. White employees had one year after resignation, whereas the period was indefinite for Native employees. Women often took advantage of this policy, moving back and forth between work in the service and other obligations, especially family care. Oneida Lavinia Cornelius resigned several times to care for her sick mother, dying sister, and ailing father (PF Cornelius CIA, October 11, 1907, and CIA, January 25, 1911, and CIA, July 1, 1925, NPRC). Other women used employment to weather hard times. Dollie Teabo, a Native woman from Oregon, and her husband, Joseph, resigned their posts at the Salem Indian School after having "accumulated some property." Two years later, Teabo applied for reinstatement writing, "my husband just died, leaving me alone, with debts to pay up." The flexibility to move in and out of the service helped women attend to family needs and to find economic support (PF Teabo February 5, 1912; Request for Reinstatement August 24, 1914, NPRC).

Race and Bureaucracy

As they struggled to maintain their familial and tribal ties across distances, working within a system that disparaged their cultural values, Native women confronted coworkers and administrators who often were ignorant of their cultures and history or blatantly prejudiced. Trouble with one's coworkers was not unique to Native employees; the service was notoriously divisive. The close quarters and isolation of the positions, along with a strict hierarchy of command meant that most employees encountered trouble either with each other or their superiors. Ultimately, however, Native women negotiated the service very differently than their white counterparts. They held a political stake in the outcome of federal policies and also confronted racism along with sexism.

Certainly Native and white female employees shared some common ground. They were part of the first generation of women entering heterosocial work environments and embarking on professional white-collar careers (Kwolek-Folland 1994; Gray 2008). They held the same positions and experienced similarly patronizing administrative actions. Male administrators frequently addressed them as girls, despite age or experience, and complained that they would not accommodate extra, unwaged domestic tasks for the schools. Moreover, women had to monitor their relations with the opposite sex because they were susceptible to accusations of immorality. Working side by side, they sometimes developed interracial friendships, but that was not always the case. Minnie C. King (Cherokee) wrote of her fellow white employees at Minnesota's Leech Lake School, "with the exception of one or two, who are friendly, [they] treat us with scorn and contempt, and those that are friendly receive the censure of laughter from others" (PF King CIA, July 11, 1916, NPRC).

Indeed, many of the white employees were openly racist. For example, in 1923 the CIA reprimanded Mr. Earl Place for addressing Miss Lucy Jobin, a Native woman from Michigan, "in insolent and profane terms." Place, in response, defended himself to the commissioner with "the very lame excuse" that his "language was meant for 'squaws collectively.'" Instead of firing him, the commissioner counseled: "You will be expected hereafter to refrain from cursing employees associated with you" because "the work of our Service should be free from coarse or harsh methods and the influence of its personnel should be refining and exemplary, especially so because we are in contact with a race whose moral and social elevation depends largely upon the guidance we furnish" (PF Jobin CIA to Earl Place, February 21, 1923, NPRC).

In another situation, Jobin responded to her superintendent's "ungrounded" accusations of troublemaking and disloyalty, writing "I emphatically deny that I have been disloyal to Mr. Garber. I have preformed [*sic*] my duties in a loyal and faithful manner despite the fact that Mr. Garber has shown prejudice towards me since the time of his arrival here. He is also prejudice[d] against all Indian employees, and has shown and expressed himself openly in the matter." Jobin solicited the support of the local Catholic priest who concurred with her assessment (PF Jobin CIA, June 14, 1917, and Fr. Weber, O.F.M. to Charles Lusk, January 27, 1918, NPRC).

Even when racism was less open, it persisted. The very structures and goals of the service segregated Native from non-Native employees. Hiring policies that helped Native women get positions also distinguished them. Throughout OIA records, race served as an important identifying category. An employee of Native descent, no matter how little or how much, was classified as "Indian," which informed administrative evaluations about that employee, positively and negatively.

The tension within the OIA'S desire to assimilate Native people while simultaneously marking them as different resulted in confusion, especially when the maternalist goals of teaching Indian girls gender-norms combined with the racism that characterized Native women as unfit mothers (Jacobs 2009: 42–49, 111–31). Repeatedly, superiors insisted that Native women were insufficiently "motherly" to succeed as matrons. Native matrons' efficiency reports were studded with criticisms reinforcing racial stereotypes and demonizing Indian women: They were "flitted," and were "dirty" and "clannish." They failed to keep the dormitory rooms clean; allowed children to run wild; were disheveled in appearance; and neglected the children's clothing. Such criticisms were often followed by a request to transfer the employee to the menial position of cook or laundress and to hire a white woman as replacement (PF Nash CIA, December 8, 1916, NPRC; PF Higheagle Efficiency Report, January 4, 1914, NPRC; PF George Superintendent to CIA, January 4, 1911, and Efficiency Report, October 15, 1912, NPRC;).

When filling out Emma Ledger's (Concow) Efficiency Report, the superintendent at the Round Valley reservation in California used similar tropes. The matron, he wrote, was a good employee who "serves as well as any Indian woman on this reservation would . . . but a good White Matron with a proper conception of cleanliness would have a great and beneficent influence on the Indian boys" (PF Ledger Efficiency Report, n.d., NPRC). Julia Wheelock Metoxyn's (Oneida) superintendent at the Keshena School in Wisconsin likewise complained: "Has no motherly instinct and is not fitted by nature to have charge of the small boys." Another administrator suggested that Metoxyn be demoted to laundress and "a white woman sent here to take her place" (PF Metoxyn Superintendent to CIA, November 1, 1909, and Efficiency Reports April 27, 1913, May 1, 1913, November 1, 1913, April 1, 1915, NPRC). The OIA often reinforced the explicit bias of these reports. In Ledger's case, it noted that no funds were available for a white matron's salary, so the school would have to make do with Ledger. In Metoxyn's case, the Office patronizingly responded that they were "particularly interested in assisting her to make a success of her work" because she was an Indian (PF Ledger CIA to Superintendent, August 18, 1910, NPRC; PF Metoxyn CIA to Superintendent, April 10, 1914, NPRC).

Though not always successful, Native women resisted demotion efforts. Metoxyn refused a transfer from assistant matron to cook. She "dismissed the offer of transfer lightly," her superintendent noted, "with the remark that she did not like to cook." Yet she remained stuck in her position despite correspondence expressing her wish to be a teacher (PF Metoxyn December 23, 1914, and Efficiency Report, April 1, 1911, NPRC). When Sophie Picard (Chippewa) from L'Anse, Michigan, disagreed with her superintendent at the Crow School in Montana, he charged "she has fallen back in the race" and he accused her of being "a member of the 'Indian clique.'" It is quite possible that Picard had found common cause with the people at Crow or solidarity with fellow Native employees, but her correspondence indicates that she found being replaced by a white matron and demoted to her assistant "very disagreeable" (PF Picard Efficiency Report, November 1, 1915, and Sophie Picard to the CIA, November 17, 1915, NPRC). Her superintendent's accusations rationalized her complaint into racist assumptions about Indian employees.

Tribal identity also became a contested issue. By 1912 application forms stated "it is not considered in the interest of the service or the applicants to assign him to a position among his own people" (PF Santeo Appointment Form, March 14, 1912, NPRC). Many superintendents agreed with this policy (although it was not consistently followed). The superintendent at Wisconsin's Tomah School protested Lavinia Cornelius's appointment to his school stating: "I have no doubt but that Miss Cornelius is a competent nurse but I would like to state that we have now on our school roll of employees six Oneida employees . . . [and] long experience has taught me, that for the sake of peace and harmony it is not at all advisable to get too many Indian employees of the same tribe" (PF Cornelius Superintendent to CIA, August 29, 1924, NPRC). Superintendents often recommended transferring employees to positions where they did not speak the language, had no relatives, or could not be "political troublemakers." Perceived as insiders in the system or advocates for their people, unmooring Indians from tribal identities seemed preferable to hiring educated tribal bureaucrats who might challenge white administrators.

Again, administrators met resistance. Some members of the White Earth reservation, for instance, petitioned in support of Susie McDougall, declaring her right to a teaching position. They insisted "Miss McDougall is a member of this reservation [and] has been very successful as a school teacher. . . . [W]e wish to keep her here as her services are valuable and her people want her." In another letter, Episcopal minister and tribal member Reverend C. H. Beaulieu asserted, "Miss McDougall is a member of this reservation and therefore has both treaty and moral rights to be employed in the Indian service among the Chippewas" (PF McDougall Petition to Sen. Clapp, September 16, 1910, and Rev. C. H. Beaulieu to CIA, September 20, 1910, NPRC; Densmore 1950: 451; Meyer 1994: 178).

Unofficial policies channeling women into menial positions, combined with official policies structured on race systematized economic inequality. The policy of hiring Indians without any formal civil service entry exam facilitated job opportunities for Native people, but also encouraged them to accept lower-paying positions. Even the advantage of the noncompetitive civil service exam for those seeking regular positions did not always guarantee positions for Native women. At the Phoenix Indian School, former Carlisle student Nellie Santeo (Papago) failed to pass her civil service exam for matron by less than two points out of one hundred. Despite the fact that she had been filling the matron position temporarily for several months, alongside an established record of eleven years of employment at the school, and a strong endorsement from her superintendent, the OIA denied her the position. Thereafter her employment file abruptly ends (PF Santeo February 19, 1912, and Application for Employment Form, March 14, 1912, April 25, 1912, May 31, 1912, NPRC).

Disparities from this racially structured system became glaringly apparent after the 1920 passage of the Federal Employee Retirement Act (FERA). At a time when few other jobs would do so, the federal government offered retirement provisions. FERA's provisions applied to federal employees who had served for thirty years or reached the age of seventy and who had been competitively classified civil service employees. This latter qualification affected Native employees in two ways: first, those employed in "at large" or temporary positions, as many women were, did not receive consideration; second, in allowing prospective Indian employees to take noncompetitive exams for regular positions, the OIA exempted them from the classified status, which was essential for pension eligibility (Schmeckebier 1927: 293–94).

Katie Brewer's story exemplifies how this race-based classification disadvantaged Native employees. Brewer was a Native woman of mixed heritage who was born in 1865 in Sitka, Alaska. When Oregon's Forest Grove (later Chemawa) Indian School opened in 1880, she was one of the first students, achieving sixth grade standing. There she met and married David Brewer, a Native man from Puyallup, Washington. After graduation the Brewers remained as employees; Katie served first as laundress and later as cook, baker, and matron while David worked as the school's disciplinarian until his death in 1906 (ARCIA 1900: 734; PF Brewer Personal Information Blank, March 1, 1910, and Superintendent Mc-Gregor to CIA, September 6, 1927, NPRC). Together they raised seven children while employed at the institution, though Katie and their children also appear in the Puyallup tribal census (PF Brewer Superintendent Chalcroft, June 16, 1909, and Superintendent Hall, September 27, 1921, NPRC).

Her superiors universally acknowledged Katie Brewer as an excellent and loyal employee. Administrators praised her for having "helped establish the school," and described her as "the mother of Chemawa" (PF Brewer Efficiency Report, May 1, 1914, Efficiency Report May 1, 1926, and O. H. Lipps to CIA, December 30, 1927, NPRC). Despite this, she encountered massive bureaucratic impediments in her efforts to receive a pension. In 1921, she applied to take advantage of FERA's provisions, but was denied because she was an unclassified employee. She was also informed that she was too old to take a classified exam. Her superintendent and Oregon's Senator McNary wrote to the CIA on her behalf. The commissioner acknowledged that many Native employees were outside pension eligibility, but claimed that only Congress could fix the problem. Brewer persevered and finally, in 1928, President Coolidge issued an executive order declaring "all efficient Indians now serving under a noncompetitive status will be given a classified status effective April 1, 1929" (PF Brewer Superintendent Hall to CIA, May 15, 1921, and CIA to Senator McNary, April 15, 1922; Assistant Commissioner to District. Superintendent, February 8, 1929, NPRC). Brewer's successful case was advantaged by the advocacy of a superintendent and U.S. senator (figure 13.2). Moreover, she was able to remain in the service for ten years until she qualified for a pension. All told, she served over fifty years at Chemawa.

In my sample of fifty-five Native female employees, seven women, or 12.7 percent, labored for over thirty years, eventually receiving pensions. Payments, however, were estimated as a percentage of the employee's salary, thus wage disparities between Native and white employees were reflected in pension benefits. Others were less fortunate.[4] The majority of Native employees never became eligible for pensions, and others were unable to wait until the executive order of 1928 granted them eligibility a decade after white employees. These race-based disparities contributed to ongoing economic inequalities between Native and white Americans.

The financially precarious position of Native women employed in government service is clear. Despite their hard work, they were often economically and socially marginalized. While many white female employees experienced similar

Figure 13.2. Civil service photograph of Katie Loulin Brewer. Native Alaskan Katie Brewer (right) pictured with possibly one of her daughters (left) worked for over fifty years at the Chemawa School in Oregon and earned the title "the Mother of Chemawa," but she nonetheless had to fight for ten years to receive her retirement pension because Native employees were excluded from the program until 1929. Courtesy of the National Personnel Records Center, St. Louis, Mo.

economic difficulties, the overall economic strain experienced within Native communities structurally and systemically disadvantaged Native women. These women had a very small, or nonexistent, safety net and sought federal government aid. Several women (often widowed or divorced) in my sample requested reinstatement or financial assistance in their old age. In 1929 Harriet Chapman (Maidu) inquired whether she was entitled to a pension due to her twenty-one years of employment. Her request was denied because she had been hired as a cook in the service without an exam and because her career had ended before FERA's passage. She continued to seek assistance from both the Indian Service and other federal agencies, citing her years of hard work, shouldering of family responsibilities, and efforts toward self-sufficiency but was repeatedly denied. Her correspondence illustrates the economic straits common to many older Native women, and when she was seventy-six years old, she described herself as "reduced to beggary" (PF Chapman May 11, 1929, December 9, 1929, October 14, 1934, and CIA to Chapman, March 21, 1941, NPRC). Even those who received pensions teetered on the brink of poverty. When Dollie Johnson (Chinook) died in 1932 after thirty years in the service, her "destitute" heirs received the money deducted from her salary for her pension. It amounted to $47.15. Dollie Johnson had nothing else (PF Johnson April 12, 1932, NPRC).

Conclusion

Native women's employment in the federal Indian Service was a fundamental component of their economic strategies in the early twentieth century. Federal policies appeared to provide an opportunity for upward mobility. Federal jobs afforded both training and occupational possibilities, but Native women—because of a race-based bureaucracy and incentive structure—faced obstacles and limits. Structurally, the service both benefited them—their exemption from competitive civil service exams or the flexibility of the reinstatement policy—and harmed them—the consequences that exemption had on their access to pensions. Moreover, administrators' acceptance of racial stereotypes often consigned Native women to menial lower-paying jobs.

Despite the major structural disparities Native women encountered in the Indian Service, their correspondence makes clear that they wanted these positions and aggressively asserted claims to them. They wielded their knowledge of middle-class manners, OIA protocol, and letter-writing skills to obtain and retain their positions, to defend themselves against accusations, and request promotions. Ironically, these "weapons of the white collar" were the very skills taught in the federal boarding schools that policy makers assumed would result in assimilation. Instead, the files reveal that women used their training and their employment in ways that often undermined the federal goals of rending Native families and destroying tribal identity.

Notes

1. When possible, self-identification of the individual is adopted in conformity with correspondence.

2. This includes assistant positions for these jobs.

3. The small number reflects the fact that most Native employees did not qualify for retirement until 1929.

4. Some employees, like Annie Abner, took a competitive exam before 1929 in order to qualify for a pension. A sympathetic superintendent may have been instrumental in making this happen.

Works Cited

Annual Report of the Commissioner of Indian Affairs (ARCIA). Washington, D.C., Government Printing Office (GPO).

Report of the Executive Council on the Proceedings of the First Annual Conference of the Society of American Indians (SAI).Washington, D.C., 1912.

National Personnel Record Center (NPRC), St. Louis, Missouri.
  Personnel Files (PF) for the following employees:
  Annie Abner
  Lizzie Bonga
  Katie Brewer
  John Buntin
  Harriet M. Chapman
  Lavinia Cornelius
  Lizzie Devine
  Agnes Fredette
  Lucinda George
  Louisa Higheagle
  Lucy Jobin
  Dollie Johnson
  Minnie King
  Matilda Kruger
  Emma Ledger
  Julia DeCora Lukecart
  Susie McDougall
  Julia Wheelock Metoxyn
  Addie Molzahn
  Jessie Morago
  Elizabeth Morrison
  Violetta Nash
  Mary Paquette
  Maud Peacore
  Sophie Picard
  Nellie Santeo
  Dollie Teabo

Adams, David Wallace. *Education for Extinction.* Lawrence: University Press of Kansas, 1995.

Ahern, Wilbert H. "An Experiment Aborted: Returned Indian Students in the Indian Service, 1881–1908." *Ethnohistory* 44 (1997): 263–304.

Bauer, William J., Jr. *We Were All Like Migrant Workers Here.* Chapel Hill: University of North Carolina Press, 2009.

Brown, Estelle Aubrey. *Stubborn Fool.* Caldwell, Idaho: Caxton Printers, 1952.

Cahill, Cathleen D. "Only the Home Can Found a State": Gender, Labor and Race in the United States Indian Service, 1869–1928," PhD dissertation, University of Chicago, 2004.

Carney, Virginia Moore. *Eastern Band Cherokee Women.* Knoxville: University of Tennessee Press, 2005.

Carter, Patricia A. "'Completely Discouraged': Women Teachers' Resistance in the Bureau of Indian Affairs Schools, 1900–1910." *Frontiers: A Journal of Women's Studies* 15.3 (1995): 53–86.

Child, Brenda J. *Boarding School Seasons.* Lincoln: University of Nebraska Press, 1998.

Deloria, Philip J. *Indians in Unexpected Places.* Lawrence: University Press of Kansas, 2005.

Densmore, Frances. "The Words of Indian Songs As Unwritten Literature." *The Journal of American Folklore* 63 (1950): 450–58.

Emmerich, Lisa A. "'Right in the Midst of My Own People': Native American Women and the Field Matron Program." *American Nations*. Eds. Frederick E. Hoxie, Peter C. Mancall, and James H. Merrell. New York: Routledge, 2005. 143–55.

Gray, Susan E. "Miengun's Children: Tales from a Mixed-Race Family." *Frontiers: A Journal of Women's Studies* 292–3 (2008): 146–85.

Horne, Esther Burnett. *Essie's Story*. Lincoln: University of Nebraska Press, 1998.

Hosmer, Brian. *American Indians in the Marketplace*. Lawrence: University Press of Kansas, 1999.

Hosmer, Brian and Colleen O'Neill, eds. *Native Pathways*. Boulder: University Press of Colorado, 2004.

Jacobs, Margaret D. "Working on the Domestic Frontier: American Indian Domestic Servants in White Women's Households in the San Francisco Bay Area, 1920–1940." *Frontiers: A Journal of Women Studies* 28 (2007): 165–99.

———. *White Mother to a Dark Race*. Lincoln: University of Nebraska, 2009.

Jenkins, Minnie Braithwaite. *Girl from Williamsburg*, Petersburg, Virginia: Dietz Press, 1951.

Kwolek-Folland, Angel. *Engendering Business*. Baltimore: Johns Hopkins University Press, 1994.

LaGrand, James B. *Indian Metropolis*. Champaign: University of Illinois Press, 2002.

Littlefield, Alice. "Indian Education and the World of Work in Michigan, 1893–1933." *Native Americans and Wage Labor*. Eds. Alice Littlefield and Martha C. Knack. Norman: University of Oklahoma Press, 1996. 109–14.

Lomawaima, K. Tsianina. *They Called It Prairie Light*. Lincoln: University of Nebraska Press, 1994.

McAnulty, Sarah. "Angel DeCora: American Artist and Educator." *Nebraska History* 57 (1976): 143–99.

Meeks, Eric V. "The Tohono O'Odham, Wage Labor, and Resistant Adaptation, 1900–1930." *Western Historical Quarterly* 34 (2003): 469–90.

Meyer, Melissa. *The White Earth Tragedy*. Lincoln: University of Nebraska, 1994.

Mihesuah, Devon A. *Cultivating the Rosebuds*. Champaign: University of Illinois Press, 1997.

———. *Indigenous American Women*. Lincoln: University of Nebraska Press, 2003.

Novak, Steven J. "The Real Takeover of the BIA: The Preferential Hiring of Indians." *Journal of Economic History*. 50 (1990): 639–54.

O'Neill, Colleen. *Working the Navajo Way*. Lawrence: University Press of Kansas, 2005.

Rand, Jacki Thompson. *Kiowa Humanity and the Invasion of the State*. Lincoln: University of Nebraska, 2008.

Regulations of the Indian Office. Washington: GPO, 1904.

Regulations of the Indian Office: Indian Schools. Washington: GPO, 1928.

Schmeckebier, Laurence F. *The Office of Indian Affairs*. Baltimore: The Johns Hopkins Press, 1927.

Scott, James C. *Weapons of the Weak*. New Haven: Yale, 1987.

Simonsen, Jane E. *Making Home Work*. Chapel Hill: University of North Carolina Press, 2006.

Stuart, Paul. *The Indian Office*. Ann Arbor: UMI Press, 1979.

Trennert, Robert A., Jr., *The Phoenix Indian School*. Norman: University of Oklahoma Press, 1988.

Vuckovic, Myriam. *Voices from Haskell*. Lawrence: University Press of Kansas, 2008.

Zitkala-Sa. *American Indian Stories*. Foreword by Dexter Fisher. Washington, D.C.: Hayworth Publishing House, 1921; repr., Lincoln: University of Nebraska Press, 1985.

CHAPTER 14

"Assaulting the Ears of Government"

The Indian Homemakers' Clubs and the Maori
Women's Welfare League in Their Formative Years

Aroha Harris
Mary Jane Logan McCallum

Introduction

In the summer of 1945, Indian Homemakers' Clubs from southern Ontario congregated in Tyendinaga Mohawk Territory for their first annual convention. The gathering marked eight years of the Clubs' existence in Canada and signaled a significant era of First Nations women's cultural and political activity. Six years later in September 1951, some 300 Maori women gathered in Wellington, New Zealand, to attend the inaugural conference of the Maori Women's Welfare League. The first such meeting of Maori womanhood, it was the pinnacle of many months of organizing, and many decades of Maori women's participation in women's voluntary organizations. The Clubs and the League represented new units of social and political organization—units sponsored into existence by the Department of Indian Affairs in Canada and Maori Affairs in New Zealand. The departments relied upon the Indigenous women participants to further state goals of assimilation, integration, and citizenship within Indigenous communities, urging the women to apply themselves, in the spirit of self-help, to the important role of providing happy and integrated, yet culturally distinct, home environments that produced citizens of the modern world. Meanwhile, the women involved viewed their womanhood and citizenship through the lens of Indigeneity, and from that position authoritatively discussed and debated welfare issues in their respective communities while simultaneously devoting themselves to the broad goals of Indigenous development. Consciously or not, they also shaped the social and political histories of Indigenous women in Canada and New Zealand.

This chapter aims to complicate depictions of mid-twentieth-century Indigenous women's organizations as conservative or complicit with the state.[1] We challenge common historical narratives about Indigenous women, which place them apart from the modern world, as fixed and passive objects colonial policies and systems processed and eventually exceeded. In fact, the Maori Women's Welfare League and the Indian Homemakers' Clubs are an important link between earlier Indigenous women's social and reform efforts of the late nineteenth century and Indigenous political movements of the 1960s. Our collaborative trans-Indigenous research also recognizes the women's interactions and negotiations with the state as distinctly Indigenous. While materially and practically tied to the state's policies of integration, the women involved consistently prefaced their womanhood and their citizenship with their Indigeneity.

Focusing on the formative years of the Clubs and the League (the late 1930s to the 1960s), this chapter explores some of the key activities of the two organizations. In addition to local activities, each organization coordinated efforts on a broader scale, including developing their constitutions and hosting regional conventions in Canada and national conferences in New Zealand. At all levels, members organized activities and discussion that reflected the priorities of the groups themselves including their concerns about the state. Our analysis of the constitutions and meetings shows that Indigenous women were active participants in workable (though often strained) relationships with the Departments of Indian and Maori Affairs. These government agencies were neither anonymous nor unknown and were optimally positioned to direct government resources to Indian and Maori communities. Club and League women recognized and even respected state expectations, yet reworked state goals to meet their own. They creatively navigated the tensions that existed between state expectations and the women's aspirations for themselves, their families and communities. They used the organizations to enter the public sphere and engage with what they saw as the most important and relevant Indigenous political and community issues of the mid–twentieth century.

Formation and Organizational Structures

The founding and expansion of the Indian Homemakers' Clubs hinged on a number of overlapping developments. Dr. Thomas Robertson, Inspector of Indian Agencies for Saskatchewan, is commonly cited as the founder of the Clubs, with the first Club established in 1937 in Saskatchewan (Milne 2004: 63; Magee 2009: 28). By 1940, a "large number" of Clubs had been initiated under Robertson's direction, in addition to "a number of somewhat similar groups" organized in British Columbia, Manitoba and Ontario (*DMRRIAB* 1941: 187). Regional differences in Clubs have influenced contemporary historical scholarship (for example, Milne 2004; Magee 2009; Edwards 2005; Barkaskas 2009) and the analysis of the Homemakers' here focuses primarily on Clubs located in the "Eastern Region," an area covering southeastern Quebec to southwestern Ontario.

At a local level, many Clubs evolved out of interests in sewing and in obtaining sewing equipment. The acquisition of a sewing machine and materials including piece goods, wool, and thread from the department signaled the initiation of a Club. Commonly the Clubs met around sewing projects. The Oneida Club, for example, reported in 1953: "we meet regularly the first Tuesday of each month, and every other Tuesday we have a sewing gathering" ("Oneida East Homemakers' Club Bulletin" 1954: 4). The Clubs accepted clothing from various groups, "making over" such donations for members of their communities. The department also sent the Clubs clothing and shoes discarded by the Armed Forces and the Royal Canadian Mounted Police (RCMP). The Clubs recycled and remodeled the clothing, as Mrs. Louise Rice, President of the Caughnawaga Indian Homemakers' Club in the early 1960s, recalled: "We gave out the good ones as they are, and the little damaged we ripped, washed, and made into beautiful clothing for the children. We would not have traded them for store clothes, because the material we got from the Government was much better than we could afford to buy. We were proud that the clothing was appreciated as we worked so hard to make them" (*Quebec Indian Homemakers' Clubs* 1960: 3). Another popular sewing project was making new clothing from raw materials the federal government provided. In 1950 Clubs on eleven different reserves made and shipped 4,912 garments for the Department of National Health and Welfare. Sewers were paid between 35 cents and $1 per piece for a total of $3,957.35, while the total value of the finished garments was $12,213.05 (*DCIRIAB* 1952: 21). Clubs used this work as a fund-raising activity and it continued for many Clubs into the 1960s. Funds were directed to a number of different areas. Mrs. Thelma Martin, President of the Restigouche Club, reported that earnings helped community members purchase house paint, linoleum, and sets of dishes, as well as livestock. Mrs. A. McDougall, President of the Maniwaki Club, reported that members used their "slight pay" manufacturing pajamas as a "source of revenue to unemployed heads of family" (*Quebec Indian Homemakers' Clubs* 1960: 4, 5). According to the department's Superintendent of Welfare, manufacturing clothing was best suited to reserves where the "small returns realized are regarded as a means of supplementing the family budget" (Gordon to Morris July 10, 1957).

The Department of Indian Affairs capitalized on the voluntary labor of Indigenous women, harnessing their influence for the purpose of reform in homes and communities. The federal mandate for the Clubs was to further the goals of assimilation, integration, and citizenship, yet the Clubs engaged in activities and projects meant to improve social and cultural life on reserves. For example, members discussed Canadian Indian policy including issues related to education, child welfare, family allowances, and health services. They practiced, promoted, and preserved traditional skills in Indian communities and acted as cultural ambassadors outside of them. The Maori Women's Welfare League operated similarly.

Through the League, Maori Affairs officials rallied Maori women to the central cause of welfare and home. The League's goals required members to balance the good citizenship model of Pākehā life with the most important elements of Maori culture. Yet, the Clubs and the League did not necessarily operate in complete harmony with the state. As community-based and community-influenced initiatives, they also engaged in a gendered community politics that was often quite distinct and independent from the federal departments that sponsored them.

Club activities included public lectures on topics from sanitation and health to child care and homemaking. Local nurses, provincial and federal government officials, and domestic science experts were commonly invited to speak at Club meetings. To promote fellowship, Clubs also invited neighboring non-Indigenous women's organizations to their meetings. Most Clubs' energies however, emphasized locally based community service projects including: visiting the sick and their families and providing them with gifts of money, cards, and baskets; giving flowers to bereaved families; holding bingos and socials to raise funds for youth clubs, teams, and bands; giving wedding and baby shower gifts; and caring for reserve cemeteries. Club members would also plan special events to acknowledge individuals and groups in the community, such as celebrating the oldest person on the reserve on their birthday or catering community banquets.

At annual regional conventions, Club members reported on the activities of each Club, attended lectures, and discussed topics similar to those covered at the meetings of individual Clubs. They also debated concerns common among the groups such as the care of school children and the elderly, adult education, health and welfare issues and community improvement. In 1945 the first convention in Eastern Canada included Clubs from southeastern Ontario and Quebec. Subsequent conventions saw Quebec and Maritime Clubs unite while Ontario Clubs operated two conventions, one in the north and one in the south. Ten years later, the movement had expanded to warrant five conventions held across the country. Craftwork competition was a focal part of the conventions with several categories of entry including sewing, leatherwork, beadwork, knitting, rugs, basketry, bark and quill work, paper dressmaking, and quilting.

Homemakers' Clubs complicate a conventional view that considers women's voluntary and paid labor as distinct and separate from each other. Many Club members considered labor, whether paid or voluntary, a site of expertise connected to and not separate from domestic and community activities. This convergence was evident at Kettle Point where Club members did "voluntary work in selling the baskets and novelties made by Indian women" at the reserve craft shop, as well as in the cities of Sarnia and Port Huron ("Kettle Point Report" circa 1951). Many Club members also worked for wages. In 1957, for example, Mrs. Dolson of the Lower Muncey Club reported that "most of the members are working on tobacco" (SPHC Golden Lake 1957: 19). Seasonal labor, such as tobacco, was so important that the Lower Muncey Club did not meet in the summer and Club members debated holding the next 1958 convention earlier in the month of August (47).

In many respects, Indian Homemakers' Clubs were like other women's organizations of the time, especially the Women's Institutes (WI). The Clubs were said to have been "patterned" on the WI and the two organizations shared the motto "For Home and Country." Some Clubs like Alnwick's were "affiliated" with the WI while others, such as one at Six Nations, were Women's Institutes that attended Indian Homemakers' conventions. In New Zealand, the League and the Country Women's Institutes also attempted to work cooperatively. Membership of some Institutes was wholly Maori and Maori women often enjoyed being members of both organizations (Harris 2007: 91–92). In Canada in the late 1950s, there was some interest in formal amalgamation on the part of the Federation of Women's Institutes and the Department of Indian Affairs. The Federation endeavored to contact Indian Homemakers' Clubs "in hope of eventual affiliation and integration" ("The W.I. and Indian Homemakers' Clubs" 1958: 2). Meanwhile, the department pushed for southern Ontario Clubs to be replaced by WIs. The provincial Department of Agriculture funded the WI and so an amalgamation would enable the department to relinquish its financial and personnel commitment to the Clubs. However, members at the 1961 southern Ontario Clubs Convention reported that they wished to be "identified with their own particular group, that is, Indian women who work for the good of their own reserves" (Bonnah June 29, 1962). So while there were some overlapping activities and areas of interests, the Clubs operated according to distinct realities of the modern Indigenous women who lived on reserves.

The history of Indian Homemakers' Clubs illustrates some of the operations of the Department of Indian Affairs. Although Clubs were autonomous entities, the Welfare and Training Service Branch collected information about them and recorded it alongside other branch activities in education, employment, and relief. The Clubs reflected increased postwar departmental interests in adult education that included postsecondary education and training, employment placement, urban relocation, home nursing and first aid courses, and folk schools. The expansion of Clubs also coincided with the department's increased interest and investment in "handicrafts" as an area of reserve economic development.

Another important development in Indian Affairs impacted the Clubs: the department's hiring of its own trained social workers. Officially, department social workers were to deal with the "many problems affecting the welfare of individual Indians and groups" (*DCIRIAB* 1952: 3) and in 1950, the department shifted the responsibility for initiating, encouraging, and working with the Clubs to them. Very few social workers worked for the department; five originally, each responsible for one region of the country, and eight by 1952. Significantly, all were women. Coinciding with this development was a threefold increase in Indian

Homemakers' Clubs nationwide, from 60 in 1948 to 178 in 1956 (*DMRRIAB* 1949: 219; *DCIRIAB* 1957: 48).

The features that characterized the formation and organization of Indian Homemakers' Clubs were similarly evident in the establishment of the Maori Women's Welfare League. The Department of Maori Affairs was influential; an integrationist policy pervaded its work, and it envisioned itself as engaged in the task of remedying "Maori problems." Indeed, if not problematizing a race, the department was likely racializing a problem. Unsurprisingly, League women did not see the League, its members, or Maori people as problems and were more likely to see government policy and officials as problematic.

In the League's view, it was Rangi Royal, Controller of the Welfare Division of the department, who took the initial steps toward establishing a national Maori women's organization (Brief History of the League 1965). Maori men gathered in tribal committees and deliberated on matters affecting the community but "left undone those things which impinged upon family life and upon the home" (Assistant Secretary August 17, 1955). Reflecting on the League's history Mira Szazy said Royal could see that women were excluded: "Nothing was being done with regard to one of the greatest needs of the Maori people—housing, and the conditions of the family, the women, and the children" (Szazy 1990: 19). Szazy was a welfare officer at the time the League was constituted, serving as the League's first secretary and, later, president from 1973 to 1977.

After the war, female welfare officers organized Maori women throughout the country into women's welfare committees. The department aimed to have Maori women's organizations networked nationally as "an instrument in furthering the Government's policy for the betterment of the Maori race" (Assistant Secretary December 2, 1959). By 1950 there were 160 branches of the League nationwide (Secretary March 19, 1954; Under-Secretary March 31, 1951). In June that year, Royal asked that the branches choose a name for the new organization, preferably the Maori Women's Welfare League or, alternatively, the Women's Advancement League. He also called for a motto, colors, a badge, a flag, and an ode. Once these details were completed, Royal called the first conference of delegates (Controller June 19, 1950). Meanwhile, the Minister of Maori Affairs Ernest Corbett embarked on a countrywide tour, during which he was advised to encourage the League's position in relation to the department's Welfare Division and give the women "great heart in this very important phase of our activities" (Under-Secretary 1951).

By the time of the League's inaugural conference, 187 branches had formed under 22 district councils with 2,503 paid members, and a further 30 branches were pending (Secretary 1954). The conference formalized the constitution and appointed a national executive council. Whina Cooper, a prominent leader from the Hokianga, was the League's first president. Whina was a high-profile participant at the conference: the first to respond to the welcome speeches, to answer the roll call, and to question Royal about the constitution. The buoyant congratulatory mood, and smooth running of the conference, belied the underlying complexities of relations between the League women and the officers of the department. Indeed, Whina and other League women are remembered for "assaulting the ears of Government departments" particularly on issues related to housing and mortgages (*Te Unga Waka* n.d.: 13).

Over three solid days the women finalized and adopted a constitution of 64 clauses. District council reports attested to the "versatility of the delegates." The women debated a wide range of topics including health, housing, education, and justice, producing 72 resolutions that reflected the diversity of the women and their respective concerns. Toward the end of the conference, Tipi Ropiha, Under-Secretary of Maori Affairs, encouraged the women to "go home fully charged with the responsibilities of the positions you hold in this very valuable organization . . . and stimulate the interest of those who are living in the isolated districts" (Minutes, September 25–27, 1951).

Rumatiki Wright, welfare officer and conference chair, gave the impression that the League was embarking on a grand enterprise, leading the people through a time of enormous change. Maori women, she said, "are on the march":

> May they, like their menfolk of the famed Maori Battalion, march also, to honour and glory, on the humble homefront! May they build up Racial Prestige and respect, from the humble home to the pah maraes, through the lanes and by-ways and great thoroughfares of our lovely land may their mission be blest and fruitful, not only for our brown New Zealanders but also for white as well. Then "Tatou Tatou" (we of one house) will indeed be a reality in this land of ours (Wright 1951).

Wright's "we of one house" was a telling interpretation of the League's motto, Tātou Tātou. The constitutional translation was "Let us be United" (MWWL *Constitution September* 27,1951). A more recent translation is "we are all in this together" (Byron 2002: 142). The respective translations capture the core sentiment of unity or common endeavor. Wright's version, however, reflected the political rhetoric of the day, particularly the idea promoted by conference speakers that Maori and Pākehā were "two people in one house" or "family." Though on the path to unity, Maori and Pākehā were not yet one people, and, it was thought, the League could play an important role in smoothing out any difficulties (Minutes 1951). The first of the constitution's fifteen aims was "to promote fellowship and understanding between Maori and European women." This aim echoed the Department of Maori Affairs' policy of "co-operation with the Pakeha" (Seaton December 1, 1949). The department did not explicitly require the League to serve as the country's race relations monitor or national explainer of all things Maori. However, the department did expect the League to fit with the philosophy of integration that underpinned the government's Maori policies. Urged to be shining examples of good New Zealand citizenship—clean, healthy, sober, law-abiding, family-oriented, and Christian—

the League's members were also counseled to maintain the traditions of the Maori race, to "reserve, revive and maintain the teaching of Maori arts and crafts and to perpetuate the Maori culture" (MWWL *Constitution* 1951).

Constitutions and Conceptions

Maori Women's Welfare League and Indian Homemakers' Club records present important, albeit mediated, windows into Indigenous social, political, and cultural life in the mid–twentieth century. The Clubs and the League officially organized around and often reproduced contemporary mainstream notions of gender, sexuality, and citizenship. Yet they also fashioned their objectives in ways that made dominant ideologies consistent with Indigenous women's lives. Rethinking the Clubs and the League forces a reckoning of Indigenous women's relationship with the state and their communities as they positioned themselves alongside department officials. Impeccably respectful and courteous in their correspondence with the department, Homemakers' Club members also used contemporary Indian Affairs discourse on Aboriginal people. However, interpreting these records demands a historical methodology that reflects and acknowledges the lived realities of Indigenous women in the mid–twentieth century. Alternative readings of the constitution and conventions in particular demonstrate how Homemakers' Club members so politely tolerated department officials and why they sought the ear of the state in the first place.

The Indian Homemakers' Club Constitution was drafted and approved at the Sarnia Convention in 1950 (DCIIAB *Constitution* 1951). It explains the organization's form, functions and procedures. The organization was "non-sectarian" (a standard also adopted by the League) and "open to all Indian women"—specifically, Indian women and girls sixteen years of age and over who paid their annual Club membership dues (50 cents). Monthly meetings were held with an annual general meeting in December. Each Club had an executive comprised of a president, one or more vice presidents, a secretary, and a treasurer. The Constitution also outlined how the general body appointed delegates to attend conventions.

The purpose of the Homemakers' Clubs, according to the Constitution, was to "improve living conditions in Indian communities by co-operating in all projects which have as their objectives a better way of life" (DCIIAB *Constitution*1951: 5–6). Similarly, the League's constitution urged its members to "take an active interest in all matters pertaining to the health and general well-being of women and children of the Maori race." Other Club objectives were: "To assist Indian women to acquire sound and approved practices for greater home efficiency; to help the aged and less fortunate, and improve living conditions on the Reserve; to discover, stimulate and train leadership; to sponsor and actively assist in all worthwhile projects for the betterment of the community; to develop better, happier and more useful citizens" (5–6).

Repeatedly, government officials assured Indian Homemakers' Club members that "stimulating social betterment" (*DCIRIAB* 1957: 49) or improving life on their reserves was not only a reachable goal but also their responsibility as upstanding citizens. At the 1957 convention, Assistant Regional Supervisor of Southern Ontario Indian Agencies T. L. Bonnah, advised Homemakers' Clubs accordingly:

> YOU are the ones who can elect a good Indian Council and assure them of your cooperation and support.
>
> YOU are the ones who can teach your children that respect and devotion to family, community and God runs on a two-way street without any "stop" signs to throw you out of gear.
>
> As descendents of the first people of this great country lying at the cross-roads of the world you have much of which to be proud. But you cannot rest on that alone. Nor can you look to others to solve all your problems. There is much work to be done and which only YOU can do (SPHC Golden Lake 1957: 40–41).

Bonnah's declaration captures the department's rhetoric on self-help and self-sufficiency (as well as history, pride, and place in the Canadian nation). The rhetoric contained an old message, one that conveniently and fundamentally denies colonialism, racism, and poverty ("stop" signs) in favor of the indomitable individual agency of a "can-do" Indian. Such messages were spun by Indian Agents, missionaries, school principals, the RCMP, and Indian Health Service staff. After World War II, the social worker and employment placement officer also represented the department and its objectives and addressed Indian Homemakers' Club conventions.

When invited to speak at the 1954 Indian Homemakers' convention in Tyendinaga, department social worker Jane Bartlett discussed the "Problem of the Unmarried Mother and her Child." Alarmed at the apparent increase of illegitimate births of Indian children in Canada between 1948 and 1951, Bartlett argued that this "state of affairs" was due to several "conditions": deprivation, financial want, crowded homes, underprivileged families, lack of wholesome recreation, family discord, and "a pattern in which girls repeat what their mothers do." Bartlett feared the "girls" were "unconscious of wrongdoing" and that their children would grow up "without anyone being really responsible for them and without too much extra support, except the Family Allowance." Bartlett also worried that unmarried "girls" did not seek the assistance of the health nurse, doctor, or social worker, nor did they receive "essential" prenatal or postnatal care (SPHC Tyendinaga 1954). At a time when Indian communities were about to face widespread government involvement in the fostering and adoption of Native children, Homemakers' Club members were asked by the department's social worker to respond to a variety of questions: Is it fair to the children to have only one parent? Who is to blame for these problems? Do we approve this situation? Should we enforce a curfew? What can be done?

Homemakers' Club records are in many ways evidence of colonial intervention into gender and community relations in the areas of marriage, parenting, and family. The department's perspectives were characteristic of the general interest in the 1950s in maintaining "normal" or nuclear families with marriage taken for granted. Yet it is significant that marriage per se was not the focal point of discussion at this convention. Neither did members explicitly reject living common law or otherwise. Instead, the discussion Bartlett initiated prompted members to argue for more resources for clubs for boys and girls and reserve recreation and community centers. In addition, Club women discussed trends in reserve parenting, the importance of instilling parenting skills in youth, and the impact of the absence of men in families. When asked, they identified alcohol and unemployment as more pressing problems their communities faced.

Jack Fransen, one of the department's new Indian Placement Officers was invited to the 1957 convention. After an icebreaker about how he had "forgotten to bring along his knitting," Fransen outlined the goal of the department's new Indian employment plan: "to promote educational and employment opportunities for the boys and girls living on reservations." He told the Homemakers' Clubs that, as a placement officer, his role was to "see that the Indian people get their share of jobs." Fransen urged them to help Indian boys and girls "take their places in society most advantageously" by helping them to develop "good study habits" and "good work habits." Using familiar themes of self-help and state cooperation, Fransen stated, "We at Indian Affairs . . . are in a boat travelling together with the people on the Indian reserves. We are in charge of one oar and you have the controls of the other oar. It is only as we put our greatest efforts into our work that we are able to assist the boys and girls to attain maximum success in life to which they are entitled" (SPHC Golden Lake 1957: 45–47).

Fransen's speech was more than a little misleading. The postwar Indian labor program he described was designed to funnel "suitable" individuals from reserves into postsecondary training and permanent low-paying jobs in urban areas, in an effort to stimulate and manage Indian off-reserve movement, and to promote permanent urban settlement (McCallum 2008). Department officials working for the program complained about candidates leaving their jobs at the request of parents and grandparents who wanted them to return home. Fransen's appeal for cooperation was likely an attempt at public education targeted not at potential candidates, but at their older relatives.

Aboriginal "homes" "family," and "motherhood" were rhetorically employed in policies to reform Aboriginal women. These concepts were also politicized discourses of liberation and sovereignty enlisted by Indigenous women in Canada. Homemakers' Clubs did not report about marriage or parenting "problems" on their reserves, or the "success" of individuals who found urban employment. Rather, reports focused on community service–related activities including care for the "needy" (old people, school children, the sick, and the bereaved) and raising funds for, helping out at, and hosting community events. In her 1957 annual report of the Sarnia Club, Mrs. Mildred Rodd recorded that the Club catered four community banquets, hosted a Christmas party, contributed four turkeys to the annual New Year's Feast, and held monthly Bingos. The Club celebrated birthdays, provided baby blankets for newborns and cake, flowers, fruit, and clothing for old people and the sick. The Club also materially assisted families in need and paid the church oil bill and the bill for the Sunday school bus. Money was raised for young girls for sewing, and welcoming parties were held for two women who married into the reserve (SPHC Golden Lake 1957: 20).

Like the Indian Homemakers' Clubs, the League's various activities also emphasized home, family, and motherhood. Officials who addressed the League's inaugural conference rhetorically stressed the role of mothers as homemakers. Home was the "incalculable" foundation of a happy national life, and mothers were the bedrock. Mothers, therefore, had a "profound" influence in education, sanitation, and "raising standards of living." Corbett credited "the minds of mothers" as the source of "all advances" in community life. The League's Constitutional aims included "discussion and instruction in the proper care and feeding of babies, the preparation of meals, the care and maintenance of the home, and the benefits to be derived from fresh air and sunshine" (MWWL *Constitution* 1951).

The newly adopted Constitution and the inaugural conference set up the League's platform. Written by Maori Affairs officers, the League's Constitution—like the Homemakers'—aligned the organization's work with government views on family, motherhood, and being Maori. But the apparent conservatism of the League's constitution did not accurately reflect the League's activities or its interests. Nor was the department's influence an indication of ongoing harmony or collaboration. Conference resolutions suggest the League was a complex organization that did not always toe the departmental line and was interested in far more than breast-feeding and flax-weaving.

Many inaugural conference remits debated a range of specific measures under the general headings of health, housing, education, and alcohol. Two remits that drew particular attention advocated the inclusion of Maori language, arts, and literature in schools. The first advocated that the libraries of all schools attended by Maori children include books on Maori subjects. The League considered that Maori children who attended public schools were "at a definite disadvantage" because they lacked access to such material and therefore tended "to grow up in ignorance of their own people." The second remit made a case for the teaching of Maori language in Maori schools and urged the Education Department to address the "difficulties caused by the lack of qualified teachers and reading materials." The women understood that proficiency in English was "essential in modern life," but they also felt that Maori language had a place in schools. Even children who learned Maori at home lost it because it was absent from the school curriculum (Minutes 1951).

These two education resolutions were referred to the Minister of Education. Throughout the ensuing years remits on education were fine-tuned recommending that Maori arts and crafts be incorporated into the training of teachers and Maori language be made a compulsory subject (Minister of Education June 17, 1952; MOMA April 10, 1959). Various government responses generally noted that basic support was given for Maori language, arts, and crafts in both schools and teachers' training colleges. However it was "impossible" to endorse the suggestion that language be made compulsory, although teacher trainees could be encouraged to study it (Minister of Education 1952). In 1955 the League received support from the National Committee on Maori Education: the committee formally resolved that teaching culture was "necessary for the full development of the Maori" and recommended doing "everything possible" to implement the teaching of language. Four years later, the matter was still one of the League's primary concerns, although little had changed in schools. Walter Nash, the Minister of Maori Affairs from 1957 to 1960, said Maori culture was part of "ordinary classroom teaching" at remote Maori schools; it was mainstream schools that needed the most assistance. Nash partially made the League responsible, saying that its membership included "quali-fied women who could give effective help where required" (MOMA 1959).

The constitutions and conventions of the Clubs and the League provide impor-tant insights into Indigenous women's politics of the postwar era. Batting remits back and forth with the government and undertaking a myriad of community-based, welfare-related activities, exemplified the ways in which these women's organizations expended their energy. Over the years the League made pivotal contributions to the survival of the weaving arts among Maori women, supporting workshops during a time when few, if any, government resources were applied to the task. The Homemakers' Clubs also actively maintained Indian women's arts. Since the League's inception, teaching and preserving the Maori language and culture has remained a constant in Maori development. The area of language and culture illustrates how the so-called conservatism of the League ultimately bowed to the radicalism of the Maori protest movement that flourished in the 1970s and 80s (Harris 2004: 10–31, 44–51). The apparent politics of flax-weaving (and sewing for the Clubs) illustrates what distinguished the League's social and political activities from that of Pākehā women: the importance of continuing the cultural distinctiveness of Māori. The League definitely focused on the home, but its ideas about womanhood were consistently prefaced with ideas about being Maori. Indeed, Whina Cooper's speeches during her tour of branches in 1952 were described as making "every individual more than ever conscious of his or her responsibility to family, community and race" (Comments September 1952). Indigeneity was central to the expression of the distinct politics of Maori womanhood. Indian Homemakers' Clubs may be similarly understood, as they strove to mediate state-sponsored and state-monitored activities in the particular circumstances of their individual reserves.

Conclusion

This trans-Indigenous examination of the Clubs and the League indicates much of what mattered to Indigenous women in Indigenous communities during a significant era. Analyzed in a comparative light, their histories span and challenge fields and periodizations that are usually considered separately, including social reform, formal Native women's political movements, the so-called "reserve" and "urbanization" periods, Indigenous rights movements, and community development strategies of the late twentieth century. Our research emphasizes the women's distinctly Indigenous standpoint to allow an Indigenous history to be told in a manner appreciative of the League's and the Clubs' creative and complex strategies for dealing with government departments. Women's interactions with the departments highlight the difficulties of negotiating working relationships that, at times, might be productive and cooperative despite underlying philosophical differences. The departments supported Indigenous distinctiveness, but they could not prioritize or materially support "difference" if the goals of integration, assimilation, or citizenship were undermined. Concurrently, the Clubs and the League consistently promoted Indigenous values within their communities while allowing for a degree of integration.

Our analytical frame considers Indigenous-state relations of that era as conflicted yet also sophisticated and collaborative. The very real problems that integration policies propagated were not set aside. So, even if the Indian Homemakers' Clubs and the Maori Women's Welfare League retain the mantle of complicit conservatism, they might also be cast as creative negotiators. The women might easily accept government's critical focus on home and family and the benefits offered by integration's emphasis on education, employment, and housing; but they did not forsake Indigenous autonomy. They did not explicitly reject integration; they simply built their views, their families, and their communities on their own Indigenous unintegrated ethos.

Notes

1. We acknowledge that the research on the Indian Homemakers' Clubs has been very generously supported by funding from the Canadian Institutes of Health Research—Institute of Aboriginal Health and the Manitoba First Nations—Centre for Aboriginal Health Research.

Works Cited

ABBREVIATIONS

ANZW—Archives New Zealand, Wellington
DCIIAB—Department of Citizenship and Immigration, Indian Affairs Branch
DCIRIAB—Department of Citizenship and Immigration Report of the Indian Affairs Branch
DMA—Department of Maori Affairs
DMRRIAB—Department of Mines and Resources Report of the Indian Affairs Branch
LAC—Library and Archives Canada
MA 1—Maori Affairs Series (of DMA files)

MOMA—Minister of Maori Affairs
MWWL—Maori Women's Welfare League
RG 10—Record Group 10 (Department of Indian Affairs)
SPHC—Summary of Proceedings Homemakers' Convention, Southern Ontario Region
VOL—Volume

SECONDARY SOURCES

Barkaskas, Patricia Miranda. "The Indian Voice: Centering Women in the Gendered Politics of Indigenous Nationalism in BC, 1969–1984." MA thesis, University of British Columbia, 2009.

Byron, I. *Nga Perehitini: The Presidents of the Maori Women's Welfare League 1951–2001.* Auckland: Te Ropu Wahine Maori Toko i Te Ora, 2002.

Edwards, Brendan Frederick R. *Paper Talk: A History of Libraries, Print Culture, and Aboriginal Peoples in Canada before 1960.* Lanhan, Md.: Scarecrow Press, 2005.

Harris, Aroha. "Dancing with the State: Maori Creative Energy and the Policies of Integration, 1945–1967." PhD thesis, University of Auckland, 2007.

———. *Hīkoi: Forty Years of Maori Protest.* Wellington: Huia Publishers, 2004.

Magee, Kathryn. "'For Home and Country': Agency, Activism and Education of Alberta's Native Women's Clubs, 1942–1970." *Native Studies Review* 18.2 (2009): 27–49.

McCallum, Mary Jane Logan. "Labour Modernity and the Canadian State: A History of Aboriginal Women and Work in the Mid-Twentieth Century," PhD dissertation, University of Manitoba, 2008.

Milne, Jennifer. "Cultivating Domesticity: The Homemakers' Clubs of Saskatchewan, 1911 to the Post-War Era." MA thesis, University of Saskatchewan, 2004.

No Author. *Te Unga Waka Huri Tau 25: Silver Jubilee 5th March 1966 to 1991,* n.d.

———. "The W.I. and Indian Homemakers' Clubs." *News and Eastern Townships Advocate* St. Johns PQ 111.2 (September 11, 1958): 2.

Szazy, Mira. Interview by Anne Else, "Recording the History of the Maori Women's Welfare League." *New Zealand Women's Studies Journal* 6.1 (1990).

PUBLISHED PRIMARY SOURCES

DCIIAB. *Constitution and Regulations for Indian Homemakers' Clubs.* Ottawa: King's Printer, 1951.

DCIRIAB. Fiscal Year ended March 31, 1951. Ottawa: King's Printer, 1952.

DCIRIAB. Fiscal Year ended March 31, 1956. Ottawa: Queen's Printer and Controller of Stationery, 1957.

DCIRIAB. Fiscal Year ended March 31, 1957. Ottawa: Queen's Printer and Controller of Stationery, 1957.

DMRRIAB. Fiscal Year ended March 31, 1940. Ottawa: Printer to the King's Most Excellent Majesty, 1941.

DMRRIAB. Fiscal Year ended March 31, 1948. Ottawa: King's Printer and Controller of Stationery, 1949.

UNPUBLISHED PRIMARY SOURCES

LAC RG 10 VOL 8482, File 1/24-5. Mrs. Louise Rice, President, "History of the Caughnawaga Indian Homemakers' Club since Its Foundation"; Mrs. Thelma Margin, President, "History of the Indian Homemakers' Club of Restigouche since Its Foundation";

and Mrs. A. McDougall, President, "History of the Maniwaki Indian Homemakers' Club since Its Foundation" in *Quebec Indian Homemakers' Clubs through the Years Tribute to the Jubilee Clubs Caughnawaga—Restigouche—Maniwaki 1941–1960*. Maniwaki, Août, 1960.

LAC RG 10 VOL 8482, File 379/24-5, pt. 1. J. H. Gordon (Superintendent of Welfare) to J. E. Morris (Regional Supervisor of Indian Agencies) Re: "Homemakers' Club, Georgina Island, Manufacture of Hospital Clothing." July 10, 1957.

LAC RG 10 VOL 8482, File 379/24-5, pt. 1. Miss H. Martins (Social Worker) to J. E. Morris (Regional Supervisor), Memorandum "Homemakers' Convention, Southern Ontario." August 3, 1960.

LAC RG 10 VOL 8482, File 379/24-5, pt. 1. "Oneida East Home Makers Club of Muncey." *Homemakers' Club Bulletin*. March 18, 1954.

LAC RG 10 VOL 8482, File 379/24-5, pt. 1. SPHC, Tyendinaga. August 24–26, 1954.

LAC RG 10 VOL 8482, File 379/24-5, pt. 1. SPHC, Golden Lake Reserve. August 20–22, 1957.

LAC RG 10 VOL 8482, File 401/24-5 pt. 2. T. L. Bonnah (Regional Supervisor, Toronto). "Homemakers' Convention—Southern Ontario Region." Memorandum to Chief, Welfare Division Indian Affairs Branch, Ottawa. June 29, 1962.

LAC RG 10 VOL 8483, File 471/24-5. "Kettle Point Report." n.d. [circa 1951].

ANZW, MA 1, 36/26/11 pt 1. Mary Seaton. To Under-Secretary, DMA. December 1, 1949.

ANZW, MA 1, 36/26/11 pt 1. Minister of Education to Dominion Secretary, MWWL. June 17, 1952.

ANZW, MA 1, 36/26/11 pt 2. A Brief History of the League. *Te Ropu Wahine Maori Toko i te Ora Newsletter* 1.5 (1965).

ANZW, MA 1, 36/26/18 pt 1. Minutes of the Inaugural Conference of MWWL. September 25–27, 1951.

ANZW, MA 1, 36/26/18 pt 1. MWWL. Constitution. September 27, 1951.

ANZW, MA 1, 36/26/18 pt 1. *Dominion*. "'We Are One' Chosen as Maori Women's Motto." October 3, 1951.

ANZW, MA 1, 26/26/18 pt 2. Comments of Meeting Addressed by Mrs. Whina Cooper. September 1952.

ANZW, MA 1 W2459, 1/1/41 pt 1. Secretary, DMA to MOMA. March 19, 1954.

ANZW, MA 1 W2490, 36/24. Assistant Secretary. to MOMA. December 2, 1959.

ANZW, MA 1 W2490, 36/26 pt 1. Controller, Welfare Division, DMA. To all Welfare Officers. June 19, 1950.

ANZW, MA 1 W2490, 36/26 pt 1. Under-Secretary, DMA to MOMA. March 31, 1951.

ANZW, MA 1 W2490, 36/26 pt 1. Rumatiki Wright. "The First Conference of the MWWL," 1951.

ANZW, MA 1 W2490, 36/26 pt 1. Assistant Secretary to Secretary, Public Service Commission. August 17, 1955.

ANZW, MA 1 W2490, 36/26 pt 3. MOMA to Secretary MWWL. April 10, 1959.

CHAPTER 15

Politically Purposeful Work

Ojibwe Women's Labor and
Leadership in Postwar Minneapolis

Brenda J. Child

Before there was a relocation program, the migration of Ojibwe people to the city took place in stages, sometimes separated by decades, and resulted in new journeys to familiar but changing landscapes. Milwaukee, Chicago, Toronto, Duluth, and other Great Lake cities were gathering places and fast-growing centers of urban Indian life in the postwar years. Dispossession made people hungry for new experiences. Minneapolis and Saint Paul, cities established in the Dakota homeland, were foremost destinations for tribal people moving from both the prairies and northern lake country of the upper Midwest. Wartime industries and job shortages opened doors to new opportunities for American Indians, many that had been locked shut before the challenging circumstances of World War II. Ojibwe women arrived in Minneapolis and Saint Paul along with families and friends, though some came independently in search of employment. Minneapolis became home to one of the largest Indigenous populations in the United States—with a spectacular jumble of Indian activism in the 1960s and '70s (Johnson 1997).

Ojibwe women living in major cities like Minneapolis and Saint Paul responded to growing needs in their urban community by developing new ideas about labor, but they did so in ways that linked the values of the traditional Ojibwe economy to the city. Rather than abandon cultural ideas about work, they reimagined and restructured labor in ways that were of greatest worth to the community. A starting point for this essay is an oral history project with a number of inspirational Minnesota Ojibwe women who lived and worked in Minneapolis, among them Gertrude Howard Buckanaga, Pat Bellanger, Rose Robinson, and Vikki Howard, who shared stories about their own mentors in the Indian community. The politically purposeful work at which Ojibwe women excelled allowed these women, their many colleagues, and predecessors to map an agenda for new systems of education, social service welfare reform, and laws to meet the needs of rural and urban families.[1]

Because of the tremendous importance of Ojibwe women's work in the public and urban realm, it might be easy to overlook how their politically purposeful efforts generated new ways of life for the women themselves. In postwar Minneapolis, Ojibwe women, who once entered the labor market at the lowest salaries and with only a high school degree at best or a boarding school education, invented new directions for their labor. Eventually, as Ojibwe women began to attend community meetings, participate in new activist movements, and achieve degrees in higher education, they embraced and often created distinctive patterns of white-collar labor focused on education and family and child welfare. When members of this generation are asked to reflect on their life's work, they never fail to mention the significance of an underlying value system that always made their work meaningful and deeply rooted in community life.[2]

Gertrude Howard Buckanaga, a leader within the Minneapolis Indian community and since 1986 a Director of the Upper Midwest American Indian Center, was born in the Pine Point community on the White Earth Reservation in 1935. Today, she tells grandchildren about her childhood in northern Minnesota. The Howard family gathered wild rice in late summer, and Howard Buckanaga remembers a time when Ojibwe "people would check the rice every day to see if it was ready" and "all the kids would play and have fun at the rice camp." She worked with her family "to finish the rice [them]selves" in the era right before state regulation and ricing licensing disrupted older practices of the harvest (Howard Buckanaga interview 2007).

Howard Buckanaga's memories of ricing and blueberry picking at White Earth are an important reminder that most Ojibwe women began the twentieth century in rural communities and as laborers in the traditional economy, a time when land loss and violence threatened Ojibwe survival. Even later migrants to the city had a strong foundation in traditional forms of work. Rose Robinson, an Indian Child Welfare expert, remembered her family's seasonal routines at Leech Lake. "We all grew up ricing. That was part of our routine every fall. We'd all get ready for ricing as early as we could take a boat out. So we all learned how to do that because that's how we earned our school clothes" (Robinson interview 2007). For reasons that were culturally and economically satisfying, women on rural reservations in Minnesota and Wisconsin focused their energy around seasonal labor as harvesters of many foods, especially wild fruits, maple syrup, and wild rice. In the Great Lakes, Indigenous people have harvested wild rice for a thousand years or more, and historically, the wild rice camp was a worksite organized by female collectives (Child 1998).

Ojibwe call wild rice *manoomin*, the good seed that grows in water, and the seasonal grain is sacred food and a dietary staple for many generations. Prior to harvest, women went to the rice lakes in small canoes and tied the stalks into sheaves with strips of basswood fiber, marking their territory and protecting the crop from high winds and birds. Binding rice was important economically for

Ojibwe women, who expressed prior claims to rice and a legal right to use rice beds in rivers and lakes through this system. Water was a gendered space where women held property rights. Women labored not only for material and physical sustenance but for their own empowerment and the spiritual well-being of family and community.

Ojibwe society placed extraordinary value on the collective practices associated with women's work, in addition to the actual products of their labor. Once Ojibwe people moved to the city, women did not forsake the values associated with traditional labor. Eventually they found ways to infuse and redirect the principles associated with the wild rice economy into urban living. Some, like Gertrude Howard Buckanaga, even continued to travel homeward every August for the wild rice harvest, as much for the social and cultural aspects of the harvest as for the rice itself. At first glance, the labor of harvesting wild rice and that of organizing people and new ideas in politically purposeful ways may seem to have little in common. When considering the twentieth-century movement to urban areas, it is tempting to imagine an abrupt end to one way of life, and the beginning of a modern reality for city transplants, much like the "before and after" stylizations of Carlisle school students. Even after relocation, women's labor, however, continued to be shaped by Ojibwe concepts of work, which they translated into countless inspiring projects and new directions for white-collar labor within the urban community.

American Indian women entered the world of white-collar labor as office workers, with the very first generation of Indian professional women employed by the Indian Service working in government boarding schools and agencies of the Indian Office since the late nineteenth century (Ahern 1983). Government boarding schools also trained girls for nursing positions, and some found jobs in reservation hospitals and clinics, also as employees of the government's Indian Health Service. By the mid–twentieth century, the political economy of Great Lakes reservations had few positions for women within the limited paid labor force of sawmills and tribal fisheries, though tourism had added a new variety of seasonal labor for women in scenic areas of the northern lakes. Off the reservation, potential employers viewed Indian women as suited only for domestic work, and the variety of small businesses in reservation border towns reserved white-collar opportunities for white women, simultaneously discriminating against Indians while depending on their custom for economic survival. Howard Buckanaga remembered her mother's advice when they crossed the reservation's borders into the nearby town of Park Rapids: "'You're going to run into people that don't like you . . . who don't like us. But you know what? That's their problem. That's not your problem.' . . . So that's how I viewed it all the while I was growing up. They got a problem. Not me" (Howard Buckanaga interview 2007). Ojibwe people coped with de facto segregation in stores, restaurants, and other businesses in northern Minnesota for many years. Little changed until the Red Lake Reservation's tribal chairman, Roger Jourdain, inspired by the growing civil rights and treaty rights movements, led an economic boycott of the town's businesses in the mid-1960s. Bemidji, Minnesota, thirty miles from the borders of the Red Lake Reservation, and a shorter distance from Leech Lake, was the central shopping destination for hundreds of Ojibwe by midcentury. Roberta McKenzie of the Red Lake Reservation remembered "Oh yes, Bemidji didn't like us," even at a time when her two brothers risked their lives in the military during World War II and her father toiled as a lumber grader at the reservation sawmill for long hours six days a week during the war.

In 1950, McKenzie painfully discovered the town of Bemidji shut out Indians seeking jobs. After graduating from a secretarial course, she began working Saturdays as a file clerk for a small ice cream business in town, but when the owner came into the office and discovered a young Ojibwe woman, McKenzie remembered his outrage and "didn't want me out in front in the office," consequently she lost her meager part-time job (McKenzie interview 2006). Without hope of finding work closer to home, McKenzie was accepted into the relocation program in the early 1950s and spent most of the decade as a medical secretary at the University of Minnesota.

Women who failed to find jobs and wages in reservation border towns also joined the movement to urban areas. For Ojibwe people and many other American Indians seeking employment in the 1940s through the 1960s—despite facing discrimination in the city over jobs, housing, and education—it was at least possible to secure employment in Minneapolis. In the early days, women worked primarily as domestics in hotels or as factory laborers, entering the working class of Minneapolis and Saint Paul at the lowest level of the pay scale and social ladder. Still, Ojibwe women continued to leave Red Lake, Bois Forte, Fond du Lac, Turtle Mountain, Lac Courte Oreille, and other Ojibwe reservations and communities and subsequently found new sources of employment and educational opportunities in Minneapolis.

Reservations of the mid–twentieth century notoriously lacked the infrastructure and basic amenities available in most rural communities of the Midwest. Howard Buckanaga and other Ojibwe in northern Minnesota never forgot the hardship and extra work associated with winters without running water or electricity, and summers, without refrigeration for butter and milk. During summer, everyone in the community bathed in the nearest rivers and lakes. Natural springs remained the best source of drinking water. At White Earth and other Ojibwe reservations in the 1950s and 1960s, people relied on outhouses, wood stoves, kerosene cookers, and oil lamps.

White Earth, reduced in land by over 90 percent by the postallotment scandals of dispossession, had the largest population in Minneapolis and Saint Paul. The first generation landed in Minneapolis with few job skills and frequently arrived with little experience of how to secure employment. A young widow with a four-

year-old son, Winnie Jourdain came to Minneapolis from White Earth in 1926.
Jourdain and her friends helped others gain jobs and a foothold in the city for
the next several decades, including nineteen girls who arrived directly from the
Flandreau boarding school. She recalled her first job with Custom Laundry: "I
sent eight letters. I told them I was a widow with a small child and I had no skills
but would volunteer to work free for two weeks until I learned the job. I got five
answers, and I took the closest one to save carfare . . . wages weren't much in
those days, just $12 a week" (Jourdain in Peake n.d.).[3]

Oral histories and documentary sources indicate a steady prewar migration
of women to Minneapolis from the plundered White Earth Reservation dating
from the 1920s, and possibly earlier. Like Jourdain, some were young mothers
who found jobs, switched employers, and moved frequently along with opportunities. Their participation in the urban labor force was motivated by an array
of family and community priorities. In 1924, a young mother worked long days
in the "linen room at the Ryan Hotel" in downtown Saint Paul. From the linen
room, she composed lonely and longing letters to three sons at the Flandreau
Indian School in South Dakota, where the boys attended school, as she toiled as
a housekeeper and worked toward their future together in the Twin Cities (BIA).

For young women the city offered certain freedoms as well as amenities not
found at home. Amelia Jones, Winnie Downwind, Alvina Stately, Fanny Stately,
and Melissa Tapio, teenagers from Redby on the Red Lake Reservation, together
headed for Minneapolis in 1943. Like most Ojibwe women who left home in the
1940s, they had few resources but were determined and hard-working. They
stopped to top onions at a farm and went on to Wells, Minnesota, to earn wages
in a chicken factory before landing in Minneapolis where they "went to work right
away," cleaning houses by day, getting paid every evening. The women found work
cleaning rooms at the Hampshire Arms Hotel in downtown Minneapolis, where
they lived in a basement annex with "lots of Indians." Amelia Jones remembered:
"[we] thought we were having a big adventure, we were scared to go out at night.
We were all from Redby. We rode the trolley cars to get around town" (Family
interview, 10/7/2001).[4]

Ojibwe women's personal networks with other Indian people were essential
to city survival, and their efforts were an expression of Indigenous values that
resulted in the emergence of distinctive urban Indian communities. The Indian
enclaves within Minneapolis and Saint Paul allowed for a rich social life and a
safety net in hard times, but also helped prepare members of the community for
the next stage of more formal organization. One of the first important leaders
to emerge from the early Indian community was Emily Peake. Peake's family
blended French, English, and Ojibwe ancestry, and they came to Minneapolis
from White Earth. Born in the city in 1920, Peake attended public school with the
children of Jewish, Irish, Norwegian, Swedish, and other immigrants. She liked
to refer to herself as a "thoroughly urban Indian," following the example of her

parents who were active in a very early organization known as the "Twin Cities Chippewa Tribal Council," which often met in their home (Peake n.d.).

Peake had a long career of service, beginning as a Works Projects Administration laborer in the Minneapolis Public Library and making parachutes at Honeywell during World War II before joining the Women's Coast Guard in 1944. She attended the University of Minnesota on the GI Bill, graduating in 1947 with a BA in Psychology. Peake formed an early social club for women during the 1940s, an effort that presaged later significant Indian community organizations and centers. After spending time working in Europe, Peake returned to Minneapolis and began her life's work as a community organizer in the mid-1950s, and during the termination era she coordinated programs for poor children for Eliot Park Neighborhood House.

Peake witnessed the growth of the Indian population in the Twin Cities during the postwar relocation effort and was concerned with the lack of community services. In 1961, with a small group of Dakota and Ojibwe colleagues, including Winnie Jourdain, Peake signed the incorporation papers for Minneapolis's Upper Midwest Indian Center, serving as the Executive Director intermittently from 1972 until 1986. The center served as home for a growing number of social service programs. Peake is key to the transition of Ojibwe women's leadership and their postwar urban labor. The labor Peake and other community organizers performed was often unpaid; not until the 1960s and the War on Poverty were grants established to fund the many Indian programs in Minneapolis and Saint Paul. Peake never married and worked at odd jobs and held part-time secretarial positions to support her work at the Indian Center and related social welfare activism. A community organizer for many years, she relied on steady income from her work as a history teacher in the Minneapolis Public Schools. Minneapolis's Upper Midwest American Indian Center, during the early years, was sustained by the volunteerism of Peake and her companions before county, state, and federal grants or philanthropic donations. Peake, while in her late forties, was also a driving force behind the origin and design of the Minneapolis American Indian Center, a milestone and landmark in the history of the urban community, which incorporated circular interior spaces and an exterior wooden collage by Ojibwe artist George Morrison. In 1975, with Frances Fairbanks as founding director, the center was established in an architecturally modern building facing the "urban reservation" of East Franklin Avenue. Women, like Peake and Fairbanks, founded community centers that promoted a spectacular array of social service programs, interweaving Indian values and spiritual beliefs, personal life lessons, and political agendas.

Many significant leaders in the Indian community worked alongside Peake, or followed closely in her footsteps, including Gertrude Howard Buckanaga. Gertrude's childhood near Ponsford on the White Earth Reservation was tragically interrupted in 1946 when her mother, Sadie Howard, died in a car accident, leaving behind seven children. Both parents spoke Ojibwe, and the family had always participated in traditional ceremonies in the Pine Point community. In the aftermath of the accident, five of the children, including Gertrude, were sent to the Pipestone Indian Boarding School. It was the beginning of many transitions for the family, including speaking English rather than Ojibwe. Boarding school offered some protection and her family managed to stay together and connected. She had siblings and cousins at the school, and her father, Cyril Howard, often visited them at Pipestone. Howard Buckanaga went on to graduate from high school at nearby Flandreau Indian Boarding School in South Dakota.

Howard Buckanaga's first trip to Minneapolis in 1952 was for a summer job arranged by Flandreau's school matron. She babysat for a middle-class family with a "great big house." Howard Buckanaga humorously recalled taking care of the family's nine-year-old daughter, who showed her around town. "She grew up here in Minneapolis and so she would show me where things were. She was more of a guide to me." Howard Buckanaga moved permanently to Minneapolis the summer after graduation in 1953, a time when "the Indian community wasn't as big" and most people knew one another and lived near Eliot Park in south Minneapolis or the northeast of the city (Howard Buckanaga interview 2007). She was met at the train station by her father, already working in the city, and quickly found whatever jobs came her way, including waitressing in a chow mein restaurant on west Broadway. She met her husband in Minneapolis, also from Pine Point, and they soon began raising a family (interview 2007).

A generation of women, like Howard Buckanaga, stayed in Minneapolis to attend school, find work, and raise families. Their efforts and connections developed into a complex of organizations and networks that formed the bedrock of the urban community. Already tested by growing up on reservations during the war or living in boarding schools, they brought their hard-won knowledge to urban life and forged new communities. Howard Buckanaga recalled the time in the late 1950s and early 1960s when Indian people began to organize. Informal networks, ball games, and baby showers, were nascent channels for socialization that led to more lasting efforts in community life and social services. Also significant was the incorporation of the Upper Midwest American Indian Center in 1961:

> They used to do a lot of fundraising, grass roots fundraising like raffles and stuff like that to help other people who were moving into the urban area. I remember when they incorporated because we used to come to all those meetings way back. They were different Indian people at that time that were kind of shakers and movers. I learned a lot from them because they were here and they were helping people move into the urban community. Because I remember people didn't realize how racist it was (Howard Buckanaga interview 2007).

Once her children were in elementary school, Howard Buckanaga entered Concordia College in Saint Paul, intent on an elementary teaching degree to help counter the prejudice and the failure of private and public schools in the Twin

Cities to meet the needs of Indian children. One of her first efforts was to organize a sit-in at the college. She joined forces with African American students to
confront the administration regarding the disproportionate amount of money
that went to scholarships for white students, against the public perception that
minorities had a free ride. From her part-time job in the college's financial aid
office, Howard Buckanaga knew that few scholarships went to African American,
Chicano, and American Indian students. Her concern led to a lifelong career in
education and social work in the public schools, and she eventually helped draft
the Tribally Controlled Community College Bill (1978). She gained her license
in social work and continued to assist the Indian community, especially by over-
seeing an extensive array of services for low-income tribal people in Hennepin
County as the Executive Director of the Upper Midwest American Indian Center,
beginning in 1986. Many women, like Howard Buckanaga, credit their postsecondary education significant to their achievement, pointing to the well-trained
cohort of Indian women that assumed positions of leadership.

Ojibwe women, many of whom attained secondary degrees, increasingly assumed a wider array of paid positions and developed alternative schools, innovat-
ing curriculum to incorporate American Indian history, culture, and languages.
"Survival school" projects in Minneapolis and Saint Paul, the Red School House,
and the Heart of the Earth Survival School, were organized by community leaders, including from parent groups and the American Indian Movement. Ona
Kingbird and Vikki Howard, education activists who became creative driving
forces within the new schools, also served as teachers in these new educational
experiments. Educators like Kingbird and Howard tend to regard their work in
the community as one part of a broader spiritual journey as Anishinaabe people.
Howard, who became principal of Heart of the Earth, remarked on the lessons
she was taught: in settings that ranged from countless informal meetings in the
homes of Indian elders in Minneapolis to well-known political events like the
Longest Walk or Alcatraz, "the first thing we learned was that we pray for the
people and we serve the people" (Howard interview 2007).

Women in Minneapolis and Saint Paul pursued politically purposeful white-
collar labor in the decades after World War II, and continued their work well
after the heyday of the American Indian Movement. They called for new skills,
creativity, degrees in higher education, and labor focused on the well-being of
urban and rural children and families, and they established influential educational
institutions and became leaders of significant reform movements. In the Indian
city of Minneapolis, women applied the principles and ethics of Ojibwe seasonal
labor, finding new expression through community, schools, social welfare activism, and, eventually, an innovative style of white-collar labor.

Sandra White Hawk, a Lakota activist on adoption issues, refers to the postwar
years as the "adoption era" for American Indian children. Red Lake and White
Earth had the highest rates of child removal within the state, with the "ratio of

Indian to non-Indian children in placement five to one" at the height of the crisis (White Hawk 2008). White Hawk credits women in the Twin Cities for paving the pathway for the 1978 Indian Child Welfare Act (ICWA). Women including White Earth tribal member Norby Blake and Peggy Matler, who worked in child welfare advocacy during the 1970s, gathered testimony that was used to develop the legislation, and, through Senator J. Abourezk of South Dakota, introduced the act to the Senate Committee on Indian Affairs. ICWA was an important recognition of sovereignty in the self-determination era and protected the interests of Indian families and tribal nations "to establish standards for placement of Indian children in foster or adoptive homes, to prevent the break-up of Indian families," while promoting tribal jurisdiction over child custody proceedings (White Hawk 2008).

Rose Robinson, a teacher on the Leech Lake Reservation at the time of the passage of the ICWA, began working for the Minnesota Chippewa Tribe as a social services program developer. Robinson recollects that ICWA was an "unfunded mandate," and she solicited financial support from northern Minnesota counties, entering negotiations with the state to meet the requirements of the new law. Robinson recalled a difficult time when she had to quit working for the Leech Lake Band in the 1980s, discouraged over political issues and feeling that progress on the ICWA was stalled:

> It was a lot of women that were getting projects, getting the grants . . . Indian women that were writing these grants. We were all part of a team. . . . It was a hard place to be. Even now it gets to be hard because women still aren't respected like they should be. I mean if they truly looked at the old ways, women always held that position of respect. Like my dad. Before he went to Washington, DC that time, he went and sat with my grandma for hours *before he went*. She spoke Ojibwe. She was very sharp and she knew how things should be. She wasn't mean to anybody but her husband (laughter). She was not mean. She was very firm. She'd say you can't be doing that. In Ojibwe. Tell the kids no, no, no. They'd be all scared of her. But she was trying to teach us. We have those old ways that we should really learn from. I think if we did that we'd be a stronger community (Robinson interview 2007).

Robinson left northern Minnesota to work for the Minnesota Indian Women's Resource Center. Founded in 1984 to empower women and their families by promoting good health through a comprehensive range of social services, the center was located in the Phillips neighborhood of Minneapolis, by then the third largest national urban Indian community. There, Robinson enjoyed the mentorship of her colleague and the center's founding director, Cherokee social worker Margaret Peake Raymond. With a growing resume of child welfare experience, Robinson accepted a position as field specialist with Minnesota's Department of Human Services and worked toward her master's degree in social work at the University of Minnesota. Hennepin and other counties made dramatic progress on Indian family and child welfare issues, especially after the passage of Minnesota's Indian Family Preservation Act in 1988 that afforded stable funding.

Robinson eventually returned to Leech Lake as director of the child welfare program, but acknowledged the work of a welfare agency is hard, especially with babies "born positive with drugs in their system," and harder still if one is "related to half the rez." Committed to reforming a system that "works against the tribes," Robinson regards as her "life's work" in child welfare advocacy as essential to cultural and political sovereignty: "We had a staff meeting today and I said, 'You're all doing a great job.' This is what we're here for. This is the tribe taking over this work. It's not the county saying to the community you've got to do it this way. It's the tribe. We're involved. It's about self-determination" (interview 2007).

On the Leech Lake Reservation, Robinson brought home the lessons learned in Minneapolis including at the Women's Resource Center; she opened offices and hired a staff to further the goals of child welfare and tribal sovereignty. Tribal communities in the Great Lakes became a beneficiary of women's labor in the city. Highly regarded at home and in the urban community, Robinson's work is not merely locally important. She and other advocates have helped Minnesota develop into "one of the most progressive states in working with Indian child welfare" (interview 2007).

Ojibwe women grew into important leadership positions in postwar Minneapolis and sustained community life in the city and on reservations through activism and advocacy. Incredibly, they achieved college degrees while raising children, as they simultaneously pursued meaningful jobs and cared for parents and other families members, all while mentoring other women. Robinson remembered the dedication of Gertrude Howard Buckanaga of the Upper Midwest American Indian Center, Frances Fairbanks of the Minneapolis American Indian Center, and others who shared "this passion to help our communities" (Robinson interview 2007). When the Indian Center opened in 1975 it became a distinctive hub of urban life and social services for a population that may have exceeded 14,000 American Indians. The postwar years and the experience of termination were inextricable with poverty, substandard housing, discrimination in education, and a lack of basic services in the city; these circumstances profoundly influenced the decisions of many women to meet the social welfare needs of the Indian community.

Ignatia Broker, a White Earth Ojibwe who came to Minneapolis during the World War II era, recalled a time when "No Indian family dared approach urban relief and welfare agencies. They knew that they would be given a bus ticket and be told to go back to the reservation where the government would take care of them as usual" (Broker 1983: 6). Women's activism in intertribal organizations and Indian centers, in addition to their significant roles within the American Indian Movement, can be traced to the long list of deficiencies in urban Indian life in the postwar, and termination era, cities of the Great Lakes (Krouse and Howard-Bobiwash 2003).

The American Indian Movement that emerged in 1968 was most visible and successful in its earliest years, a time that included momentous episodes such as the takeover of both Alcatraz Island and the Bureau of Indian Affairs building in Washington D.C., as well as the events surrounding Wounded Knee in 1973. Yet women's efforts have been overshadowed by the presence of highly charismatic male leaders, and women's rich and significant involvement in AIM and other organizations are hidden in the history. Many women attended the early forums organized in the summer of 1968, including Francis Fairbanks, Mary Jane Wilson, Melissa Tapio, Caroline Dickinson, Joanne Strong, Peggy Bellecourt, Ellie Banks, Bobby Jo Graves, Alberta Atkin, Pat Bellanger, and countless others. From those ranks, Fairbanks went on to establish the Minneapolis American Indian Center, and Wilson, once a national leader in AIM, became a child welfare family worker within the Indian Center.

Bellanger remained active in AIM for decades. She first moved from Leech Lake along with her mother, a nurse, and she attended the summer forums of 1968. Once again, child welfare work significantly emerged for AIM women because of pleas from parents whose children were being removed; Bellanger received countless phone calls from members of the community recalling that Ramsey and Hennepin counties "were taking Indian children from homes where they felt that the child wasn't being educated, that they were being made a failure, and so they were put into white homes . . . parents were panicking, saying, you know, "My child is good, I have a good kid," yet Indians were not succeeding in mainstream public schools (Davis 2004: 101).

Vikki Howard was still a teenager living in Minneapolis when she first learned about AIM. During the takeover of Alcatraz, Howard and classmates at North High School affiliated with AIM youth and called themselves TANS for True American Native Students. They coordinated a tour to "all the Indian boarding schools from Minnesota to southern California, to Alcatraz and back" (Howard interview 2007). Reaching Alcatraz toward the end of the occupation, Howard entered Macalester College in Saint Paul during the year of Wounded Knee. Some friends went out to South Dakota while Howard "stayed focused" in college. The later trials at the Saint Paul federal building and the formation of new survival schools left Howard feeling there was "never a dull moment." She recalled:

> As I grew into a young adult, in my twenties with the American Indian Movement, I went on the Longest Walk in 1978. I ended up going out with the Minnesota team, the group that went from Minnesota AIM. Through the movement I was exposed to my first Sun Dance and spirituality, different elders. All this came about as I started working at Heart of the Earth. And that's when I began my journey to find my way. . . . back to the Anishinaabe way of life (Howard interview 2007).

"It was a good time in history to be growing up in the Twin Cities American Indian Community," said Howard, "like the Renaissance of American Indian everything" (interview 2007). Howard spent ten years after college working at Minneapolis's Heart of the Earth Survival School, spending long days writing new curriculum in history and social studies incorporating American Indian history and culture for students from seventh through twelfth grades. She eventually accepted a post as the school's principal. AIM survival schools were sustained by a core group of dedicated women committed to the education of urban children. The careers of Kingbird, Bellanger, Howard, and others show the variety of ways in which the creative vision of activist women outlasted the early highly symbolic and renowned AIM protests of the 1970s.

Scholarship on the twentieth-century struggles for greater tribal sovereignty emphasizes the nineteen-month takeover of Alcatraz that began on November 20, 1969, as a benchmark for activism, though Vine Deloria Jr. frequently referred to formative political efforts of Indian leaders and foundational organizations from the early 1960s and before. Recently, historian Daniel Cobb has advocated precisely for a longer and broader view of Indian activism, acknowledging a variety of "politically purposeful ways" to organize political action. such as arranging community meetings, writing grants, coordinating youth programs, and testifying before local and state political bodies, in addition to militancy (Cobb 2008). When gender is brought into the longer history of Indian activism in Minneapolis, it is transparently clear that women held the majority of sustained leadership roles in the community through their participation in the less sensational but no less visionary work of organizing new schools, Indian centers, curriculum, social services, and legislation. Their body of work is a breathtaking achievement that led to increased well-being for Indians in Minnesota and greater sovereignty for Indian people nationwide.

From the earliest formation of an Indian community in postwar Minneapolis women quickly grew into significant positions of leadership and directed their efforts and labor toward the well-being of children and families. In the process, they created distinctive patterns of white-collar labor around education and social and child welfare. The women remain outspoken yet humble and often cite male leaders in the community for their ability to give good speeches or create political change. Women, including Emily Peake, Gertrude Howard Buckanaga, Rose Robinson, Frances Fairbanks, Ona Kingbird, Norby Blake, Pat Bellanger, Vikki Howard, and colleagues laid a foundation for influential and long-lived institutions and laws not only in Minneapolis but other regions. Their underlying spirituality and commitment to Ojibwe values, which they learned from mothers, fathers, and grandparents, remains a powerful influence in their working lives. As Pat Bellanger expressed, "Ojibwe women have been strong throughout everything" and "we have kept our ways," acknowledging the significance of the women's work like harvesting wild rice, which "has always gone through the women" (Bellanger interview

2007). Like their Ojibwe grandmothers, they labored as they had in the wild rice economy—not only for material sustenance, but for their own empowerment and the spiritual well-being of their families and community.

Notes

1. Transcripts of interviews conducted by Brenda J. Child and Karissa E. White in 2007 with Howard Buckanaga, Bellanger, Robinson, and Howard are in the collections of the Minnesota Historical Society, Saint Paul, Minnesota. Robert Head McKenzie was interviewed in 2006 as part of the Minnesota's Greatest Generation Project.

2. Although I refer to the individuals as a "generation," they vary in age and were born between the 1930s and the 1950s.

3. Brunette, "Early Years," and short interview in the collections of the MHS.

4. Child's Aunt Amelia (b. 1926) generously took part in this interview on October 7, 2001, two months before her death from cancer on December 10.

Works Cited

Ahern, Wilbert. "The Returned Indians: Hampton Institute and Its Indian Alumni." *Journal of Ethnic Studies* 10 (Winter 1983): 101–24.

Bellanger, Pat, Gertrude Howard Buckanaga, Vicki Howard, Roberta Head McKenzie, and Rose Robinson. Interviews by Brenda J. Child and Karissa E. White. *Minnesota's Greatest Generation Oral History Project*. Minnesota Historical Society, Saint Paul, Minnesota, 2007.

Broker, Ignatia. *Night Flying Woman*. Saint Paul: Minnesota Historical Society Press, 1983.

Brunette, Pauline. "An Urban Elder Remembers the Early Years of the Minneapolis Indian Community." *Hennepin County History* 49.1 (Winter 1989–90): 4–15.

Child, Brenda J. *Boarding School Seasons: American Indian Families, 1900–1940*. Lincoln: University of Nebraska Press, 1998.

Cobb, Daniel. *Native Activism in Cold War America*. Lawrence: University Press of Kansas, 2008.

Cobb, Daniel M., and Loretta Fowler, eds. *Beyond Red Power: American Indian Politics and Activism since 1900*. Santa Fe, N.Mex.: School for Advanced Research Press, 2007.

Davis, Julie. *American Indian Movement Survival Schools in Minneapolis and St. Paul, 1968–2002*. PhD dissertation, Arizona State University, 2004.

Deloria, Vine, Jr., and Clifford M. Lytle. *The Nations Within: The Past and Future of American Indian Sovereignty, 1984*. Austin: University of Texas Press, 1998.

———, eds. *American Indians, American Justice, 1983*. Austin: University of Texas Press, 1997.

George, Lila, Rose Robinson, and Fran Felix, eds. Minnesota. *A Minnesota Guide to Indian Child Welfare Act Compliance*. Minnesota: Department of Human Services, 1994.

Johnson, Troy R. *The Occupation of Alcatraz Island: Indian Self Determination and the Rise of Indian Activism*. Champaign: University of Illinois Press, 1997.

Krouse, Susan Applegate, and Heather Howard-Bobiwash, eds. "Special Issue: Keeping the Campfires Going: Urban American Indian Women's Community Work and Activism." *American Indian Quarterly* 2.3–4 (Summer and Fall 2003).

McKenzie, Robert Head. Interview by Brenda Child and Karissa E. White. *Minnnesota's Greatest Generation Oral History Project*. Minnesota Historical Society, Saint Paul, Minnesota, 2006.

Minnesota Indian Affairs Council. *Public Testimony Regarding "Out of Home Placement of Indian Children; Indian Child Welfare Act; Minnesota Indian Family Preservation Act."* State of Minnesota: Indian Affairs Council, 1990.

National Archives, Record Group 75, Records of the Bureau of Indian Affairs (BIA), Flandreau Indian School, April 23, 1924.

Peake, Emily. Peake Research file on Minnesota Ojibwe women, 1887, [194–?], 1990–1991. Minnesota Historical Society, Saint Paul, Minnesota.

Warrior, Robert Allen, and Paul Chaat Smith. *Like a Hurricane: The Indian Movement from Alcatraz to Wounded Knee*. New York: New Press, 1996.

White Hawk, Sandra. Personal Communication, 2008.

CHAPTER 16

Maori Sovereignty, Black Feminism, and the New Zealand Trade Union Movement

Cybèle Locke

Introduction

An incident occurred in 1982 at the Auckland Trade Union Centre in New Zealand—a small group of Maori radicals, called Black Unity, who ran the Polynesian Resource Centre were accused of antitrade unionism and racism and, consequently, were evicted from the Auckland Trade Union Centre with the assistance of the New Zealand police. This article explores the radical ideas of Maori sovereignty and Black feminism propagated by Black Unity that inflamed Auckland trade unionists, focusing on the writings of the group's spokeswomen, Ripeka Evans (known earlier as Rebecca Evans) and Donna Awatere.[1] Their key demand was that the racist New Zealand state be overthrown and Maori sovereignty, land, and fisheries be returned to Maori. The sectarian Left, the trade union movement, white feminists, and Black men were heavily criticized for prioritizing class or gender in their radical politics or assimilating into the white system. Instead, Black Unity called on Black women, as the most oppressed in society, to lead the revolutionary force for Maori sovereignty.

Black Unity was at the radical edge of the modern Maori protest movement that began in the late 1960s and matured alongside women's and gay rights movements in the 1970s and 1980s. The focus of Maori protest was the New Zealand Government's policies of assimilation (and later integration) that threatened to destroy Maori culture and the institutionalized racism that existed in New Zealand society (Harris 2004: 13–17). Maori activists explored how the history of colonization had relegated Maori to the lowest socioeconomic position in New Zealand society. They used pickets, demonstrations, occupations, and marches to demand the return of tribal lands unfairly taken, the protection of Maori language and culture, and political rights for Maori to determine their own future. New Zealand's population was small, approximately 3 million in 1981, and Maori made up 12 percent of that population (Statistics New Zealand). Maori predominantly lived in urban centers, particularly Auckland, and thus Maori radical protest action had a significant impact on mainstream New Zealand society.

Some scholarly attention has been given to Maori women who identified as feminists and worked within the Maori protest movement in the late 1970s and early 1980s, but little has been said about their interactions with the trade union movement and the sectarian Left.[2] Chris Trotter, political commentator, accused Maori nationalists (and lesbian separatist feminists) of "[s]plitting up the small communist parties, sundering decades-old alliances between the intellectual Left and the trade union movement, leaving in their wake the tragic wreckage of personal and political relationships" (Trotter 2002: 7). In contrast, this chapter examines the philosophical position that Maori nationalist members of Black Unity espoused; explores the historical context for the demand for Maori sovereignty first articulated by Black Unity in 1981; explains why the Maori sovereignty position was also a Black feminist position; asks what led Maori women to turn with such anger on the radical Left in the early 1980s; and finally, analyzes the longer-term affect of Maori sovereignty demands on the Maori protest movement, the women's movement, the sectarian Left, and the trade union movement. But first, a little context.

Maori workers had always been active in trade unions but due to their marginal position in the workforce, they remained on the periphery of the labor movement. Colonization depleted Maori-owned land in the nineteenth century and forced Maori to become rural workers in the emergent settler-capitalist economy. And once rural work declined in the 1920s and 1930s, Maori migrated away from tribal areas to join the manufacturing workforce in towns and cities in the post–World War II period; and they joined the appropriate unions. By 1980, Maori and Pacific Island workers were 10 percent of the workforce but the union movement was slow to build structures to promote Maori and Pacific Island leadership or work issues.

In 1980, Maori trade unionists established the Polynesian Resource Centre to educate Auckland-based trade unionists on the impact of racism in the workforce—for example, the segmentation of Maori into blue-collar jobs and attendant vulnerability to layoffs. Seven Maori organizations used the Centre in 1982 and they were all reputed to subscribe to the principle of Maori sovereignty (Awatere 1984: 49). This was not the dominant ideology of the Auckland Trades Council, however.

Members of the New Zealand Socialist Unity Party (SUP) had gained strategic positions in the blue-collar trade union movement, including the Auckland Trades Council, and the SUP belief in class as the primary analytic category for organizing workers had decisively infiltrated union policy.[3] For example, a section of the Northern Drivers' Union policy document read: "Race and sex discrimination is a direct reflection of the class nature of society. . . . [T]he ending of racial and sexual discrimination will only be finally tackled when the working class and their allies end the class nature of society" (*Trucker* 1986). Bill Andersen, President of the Socialist Unity Party and the Auckland Trades Council, secretary of the Northern Drivers' Union, and a member of the national executive of the New Zealand Federation of Labour (NZFoL), was a powerful advocate for class-based organizing.[4]

Ripeka Evans, an unpaid volunteer, worked full-time for the Polynesian Resource Centre between 1980 and 1982. Serious political differences developed between Bill Andersen and Ripeka Evans when Evans began to promote the separate political interests of Blacks, particularly Black women, in her work for the Polynesian Resource Centre. Andersen objected to her political philosophy. Matters came to a head when a small organization that used the Centre, called Black Unity (of whom Ripeka Evans was a member), presented a paper at a nuclear-free and independent Pacific conference in Fiji in December 1981. Andersen circulated the paper among Auckland trade unionists and used the paper's content to secure the eviction of the Polynesian Resource Centre on April 19, 1982, and HART (Halt all Racist Tours), an antiapartheid group that supported the Polynesian Resource Centre (Jesson May 1982: 4–5). So what was this "antiunion" position?

Black Unity Conference Paper

Three Maori radicals delivered the Black Unity paper at the Pacific Conference in 1981. Their key point was that only with the return of Maori sovereignty would revolutionary change be brought about in New Zealand. Black Unity sought to overthrow racism; in their eyes racism was the mechanism for imperialist conquest. To overthrow racism was to overthrow the state and capitalism (Black Unity 1982: 4–7). "Our struggle is for our sovereignty," they claimed, "[f]or New Zealand, which because the terms of the Treaty [of Waitangi] were never kept, is possessed illegally" (4–7).[5] Racism and capitalism kept Maori "superoppressed" among the working class. They were adamant that a Marxist, class-focused analysis failed to address the impact of colonization. Black Unity radicals claimed that white Marxists failed to account for the unity of economic and spiritual modes of production in precontact Maori society. Further, a Marxist analysis did not assess the impact of colonization on Maori social structures that disconnected the economic from the spiritual. A Marxist agenda would not, they argued, amend this disconnect. The white trade union movement, Labour Party, working-class, and sectarian Left were challenged to adopt a critique of racism as primary and to stop describing Maori as an oppressed section of the New Zealand working class (Jesson May 1982: 4–5).

Black Unity sought alliance with other peoples of the Pacific to bring about revolutionary change. They adopted the term "Black" rather than Brown, Maori, or Pacific. Maori radicals criticized white colonial racial hierarchies whereby Europeans described Maori as brown or noble savages due to their highly structured society and dismissed Aborigines as black and therefore hardly human. The color hierarchies of colonialism divided and ruled Indigenous Pacific peoples. By adopting the mantle of Blackness, Ripeka Evans argued, Maori radicalism declared an affinity with other Black peoples of the Pacific because "when it comes down to it you're either Black or you're white. There is no halfway, no grey, no brown. . . . What's happened in New Caledonia, Tahiti and Australia is exactly the same as what's happened here." But not all Pacific peoples were welcomed to ally with Black Unity.

Maori and Pacific Island men who held an increment of power in the white, patriarchal capitalist system were characterized as "house niggers" in the Black Unity paper: "All those big black men who act like house niggers have to be dealt to. Pacific men are showing that just like Maori men, they will sell you out, while they tell you it is for the benefit of the country. Just look around you, you will see your men going with white women, forming alliances that will rationalize them selling out Pacific women and Pacific people. Your academics, your leaders, the neocolonial elite selling you all out" (Black Unity 1982: 6). According to Evans, white colonial practices of integration created "house niggers":

> Integration is a porous process, like having a blanket over your head. . . . Before you know it you have been through the process of sitting still with a blanket over your head waiting for so long to be able to assert your identity and somewhere in the white-washing process the blanket has crept over your head and enveloped you—it's like an invisible creeper. It leaves you with a black skin and pulls an invisible white blanket over you and whitens your insides.—You come out as a "House-nigger" (Evans 1981: 18).

Black Unity opposed black-white intimacy because it bought into the white system. In this vein, white feminists were charged with failing to take racism seriously, having relationships with Black men or women, and remaining complicit with capitalists. Because the white system was patriarchal, Black Unity argued, Black women were less likely to be integrated or become "house niggers," and they called on women of the Pacific to lead the revolutionary movement; overthrow white, patriarchal capitalism; and advocate sovereignty.

This call for a radical withdrawal from white society, led by Black women, was intended for conference participants who championed an independent Pacific, not for the trade union movement. However, the most controversial sections of the conference paper—claims that the Maori struggle was "more revolutionary and more fundamental than working class struggles," that the male Left, the trade union movement and black men were collectively part of the capitalist problem, and opposition to interracial intimacy—were circulated among Auckland trade unionists (Black Unity 1982: 4–7). Trade unionists were outraged and accused Black Unity of being racist, anti–working class and antiunion, and the Polynesian

Resource Centre was evicted from the Trade Union Centre in 1982. There was no debate about Black Unity's ideas at the time. So let us ask now, what gave rise to the key demand for Maori sovereignty in 1981?

Forging a Demand for Maori Sovereignty

When Donna Awatere and Ripeka Evans participated in Black Unity's demand for sovereignty in 1981, they had been involved in Maori activism for many years. Awatere was one of a small group of young, university-educated urban Maori radicals who, in 1971, formed Ngā Tamatoa (Young Warriors) to oppose racism and champion Maori culture and identity in New Zealand (Harris 2004: 48). Ngā Tamatoa were influenced by Black Power leaders such as Rap Brown and Stokely Carmichael and employed a combination of Brown Power, Maori liberation and self-governance rhetoric, protest tactics, and self-help programs—such as job placement assistance for migrants to the city (Walker 2004: 210). The group drew attention to the broken promises of the Treaty of Waitangi declaring February 6th Waitangi Day an annual day of mourning for Maori land loss and dispossession. Ngā Tamatoa initiated a highly successful advocacy campaign demanding the inclusion of te reo Maori (Maori language) in primary and secondary schools (Harris 2004: 34–84). In 1975 when tens of thousands of Maori marched from Te Hapua in the north to Parliament in Wellington, demanding "[n]ot one acre more" to draw attention to the expropriation of land, Ngā Tamatoa was among the coalition that organized the march. They drew attention to the impact of landlessness and the long-standing social distress caused by land unfairly acquired by the government (Harris 2004: 70). By the 1970s, Ngā Tamatoa supported land occupations as important strategies for redress. They took part in occupations of Bastion Point with Ōrākei Maori in Auckland in 1977 and the Raglan Golf course with Tainui Awhiro tribal people in 1978.[6]

Reflecting on the early campaigns and land occupations staged by Ngā Tamatoa, Ripeka Evans divided protest action into two categories: "the fight for Maori Civil Rights and the fight for the Retention of Maori Land," with common ground forged on the history of Maori dispossession under British colonial rule (Evans June 1982: 1). What these protest actions lacked, she argued, was "a national movement based on the demand for Maori sovereignty" (2). Awatere and Evans both experienced a shift in their political consciousness in 1978 when they attended an international conference in Cuba and were influenced by Third World independence movements, particularly Indigenous women's activism. Indigenous peoples met regularly during the conference sharing information on Indigenous and women's issues. Evans was inspired by women from the Palestine Liberation Organization (PLO). She recalled: "Talking with the PLO women moved my political thinking on from where I thought about making piecemeal demands like at Bastion Point, Raglan, the land march and so on to sewing these together into a coherent political philosophy" (Roth 1985: 6–7). Consequently, Evans made a lifelong commitment to "the nationhood of the Maori people"—what would later be described as Maori sovereignty (Evans October 1982: 15).

Evans and Awatere returned after the Cuba conference and organized a Marxist Study group that met every Sunday to analyze political economy and to interrogate the relationship between capitalism and colonialism. Evans also consolidated international communications with other Pacific independence movements in the late 1970s (15). The Maori sovereignty position also became a Black feminist position.

Forging Black Feminism

Awatere's and Evans's Black feminist philosophy was shaped by their respective experiences with the New Zealand women's liberation movement. The (primarily white) women's movement displayed a diversity of feminist viewpoints from the outset, yet in the early 1970s was constituted by radical feminist collectives united by the common objective of "bringing down patriarchy," defined as an oppressive system of masculine domination (Dalziel 1995: 64). Radical feminists were the catalyst for the subsequent formation of more liberal feminism women's groups, who sought to reform the system for women rather than overthrow it. Collectively, these groups constituted the wider women's movement that existed into the 1980s (Dann 1985: v). Thousands of feminists, representing an extraordinary range of organizations, attended United Women's Conventions during the 1970s to debate what feminism meant, set the goals of the movement, and propose how to achieve them.

Awatere was one of two Maori members of the Auckland Women's Liberation groups when they were first established in 1970. During these early stages of development, Awatere recalled feeling very alone" (Dann 1976: 6). A visit to feminist organizations in the United States in early 1976 alerted Awatere to the movement's limitations both at home and abroad. In both countries, feminist organizations were dominated by white, middle-class women who devoted their energies to providing health centers, legal aid, and radical feminist therapy for women—but these efforts were not reaching poor black women, whose main struggle was economic. Upon return, Awatere sought innovative strategies toward consciousness-raising among Maori women in Maori organizations.

When Ngā Tamatoa was re-formed in 1976 by Hilda Halkyard and Ripeka Evans, Awatere pushed the group to fight internal sexism as well as racism (Dann 1986: 7). Evans reflected on the fact that Ngā Tamatoa women did all the organizational work while the men, as vocal leaders, claimed the glory (Evans October 1982: 12). Awatere, Halkyard, and Evans decided to reorganize the group so that political and organizational jobs were shared equally (Evans October 1982: 15; Dann 1976: 7).

Ngā Tamatoa women also took a stand against black-white intimacy. Their opposition stemmed from the fact that practically all their male comrades in Ngā Tamatoa had Pākehā (New Zealanders of European descent) girlfriends or wives, and none were active in the struggle for Maori liberation. As Evans explained: "That thing that white women are the prize and the Maori women are like the booby prize were [sic] strong. We said. No. Maori women are the prize. We stepped out to put forward a positive view of our women" (October 1982: 13). Awatere described Maori men's preference for Pākehā women over Maori women in political terms: "'the grass is greener' syndrome—Pākehā women tend to have higher status, more money, more contacts and other advantages than Maori women." Pākehā women sought Maori men out and Maori men were susceptible to the stereotype of feminine beauty—"blond hair, wide blue eyes, big bosom," and so forth. Awatere understood men's desire for Pākehā women as a manifestation of assimilation, practices that the New Zealand state had been guilty of for many years (Dann 1976: 8). The issue of interracial intimacy came to a head at the Ngā Tamatoa national hui in Wellington in 1976. Evans explained that in the end, "the contradiction between their [Black men's] stated goals for the Maori people and their actual physical, emotional, psychological and sexual alliance with the White Nation became unavoidable even for them" (Evans October 1982: 13). And from that time, she concluded, there was a real change in men's behavior. Black men were held to account for their sexist practices and challenged for selling out to the White Nation, signaled by their sexual relationships with white women.

Concurrent to their critique of interracial intimacy, Evans and Awatere began to challenge white feminists to take racism just as seriously as sexism. The United Women's Conventions of the 1970s constructed a mythology of homogenous sisterhood—proposing gender as a unifying factor across boundaries of class, race, ethnicity, sexual orientation, and religious differences. However, as the seventies progressed, discord between feminisms was a common occurrence that became more sharply defined. Maori women, who had always been a small minority in the women's movement, offered their own challenges (Vanderpyl 2004: 319–20). Awatere's and Evans's paper on Maori women at the 1979 United Women's Convention stated: "We cannot romanticise about the past or the present. Most of all we cannot exaggerate the trivial jobs which Maori women have done and are still doing, in order to make it appear as if Maori women have ever had any equal status. To equate Maori women's oppression to any facet of oppression of Pākehā women is to do Maori women grave injustice. As N.Z. society thrives from having one of the most sexist societies in the world—a society so sexist that Maori women are no longer good enough for Maori men, where Maori women only get the scraps after Pākehā women have finished choosing their jobs" (Awatere and Evans n.d.).[7]

Evans recalled examining "degrees of powerlessness under white colonial rule, and the alliances that prop up white male domination: white men and white women, white men and black men" (Evans October 1982: 14). The Women's Convention was criticized, "firstly, for its failure to recognise Maori women as the most oppressed; secondly for the failure of white women to accept responsibility to change white institutions; and thirdly for the failure to recognise the ways in which racism and sexism were intertwined within the feminist analysis dominant at the convention" (Vanderpyl 2004: 318). The women's movement, they argued, would never meet its revolutionary potential without the leadership of Maori women (Evans October 1982: 14). Their criticism was not embraced by the majority. However, a small collective of feminists took this challenge seriously and invited Evans to set up and coordinate a section of the feminist newspaper *bitches, witches & dykes* titled *Black Forum*, devoted to Black feminist issues.[8]

Within *Black Forum*, Evans's tripartite analysis of Black women's oppression evolved. She believed that the three cornerstones of oppression—racism, sexism, and capitalism—were all instigated by white men, but offered some benefits for Black men and white women. This hierarchy of oppression positioned white women above Black women and Black men above Black women due to their privilege within the sexual division of labor of the capitalist workforce. Evans further identified Pacific Island women as similar to Maori women in this hierarchy but with varied origins, because Maori women possessed status as Indigenous and true claimants to Aotearoa (Evans August 1980: 9).

In this forum, Evans also interrogated the myth that white women could "fight racism by fucking the oppressed" (Evans October 1982: 14). Influenced by Hope Landrine's theory of racist stereotyping, Evans condemned essential assumptions that held Maori women as naturally more sexualized and beliefs that intimacy with Black women somehow combated racism. Evans wrote, "Having a relationship with a person of an oppressed race does not make you any closer to us or absolve you from white racism" (Evans December 1980: 11).[9] Evans accused heterosexual and lesbian white women who bedded Maori men and women of engaging in white supremacy. There were a range of feminist responses to Evans's articles in *Black Forum*. Some accused her of antilesbianism, some defended their position of uniting as women first to combat sexism, while others found Evans's ideas stimulating and supportive of the Black women's struggle ("Letters" 1981).

In September 1980, Evans and Awatere played key roles in bringing together eighty Black women at a National Black Women's Conference to discuss ideas for revolutionary change. Young Maori women who attended brought perspectives developed from experiences in antiracist, Maori civil rights or Maori land rights movements. They were active on feminist issues—equal pay, abortion, contraception, child care and health issues, especially smoking and alcohol consumption (Awatere March 1980: 13). The Conference was organized by a wide range of women's groups: the Auckland Black Women's Group, the Otara Black Women's Group, the Black Feminist Collective, Ngā Tuahine (which included the Women in Prisons Collective), and Black Dykes. All combined the politics of feminism, antiracism and Marxism, and some, such as Black Dykes, had a long involvement with the women's movement (Awatere November 1980: 10). The first discussion paper, "Feminism, the Black Women's Revolution," presented by Donna Awatere, addressed obstacles Maori women faced with assuming leadership in the international feminist movement: "fear; lack of information, awareness and understanding of women's oppression and exploitation; initial resistance to accepting facts, developing understanding and experimenting with change; romanticism, especially Maori romanticism of pre-European culture; backlash trashing" (Maori women trashing each other) (11). Evans and Halkyard followed with their joint presentation on why black-white intimacy was politically destructive to the Black people's movement and to Black women in particular.[10] From final plenary emerged an umbrella group—the United Congress of Maori and Pacific Women—charged with organizing a conference for the following year (12). Evans accordingly focused on Black women's issues as part of her work for the Polynesian Resource Centre, holding workshops on the "political economy of Maori women" within trade unions and another on Black women's health issues. From this organizational base of vocal leadership, Maori women became critical to New Zealand's antiapartheid movement during the Springbok Rugby tour of 1981.

1981 Springbok Rugby Tour
and the Antiracism Movement

Maori women, including Evans and Awatere, played prominent organizational roles in protests against the tour of the South African rugby team to New Zealand between July and September of 1981. Many New Zealanders opposed the apartheid system in South Africa, symbolized by the exclusion of Black South Africans from the Springbok team and past refusals to permit Maori members of the New Zealand All Blacks rugby team to tour South Africa (Mohanram 1995: 58). New Zealand's middle class took to the streets for the first time in extraordinary numbers—women were especially prominent (Belich 2001: 518). *Broadsheet* reported: "New Zealanders watching the latest incredible episode of the Tour Troubles unfolding on their tellies can't have missed the fact that marshalling the marches, facing the batons, and directing the invasions of jet planes, motorways and rugby pitches are women. For women, and especially Maori women, form the backbone of the anti-tour movement" (Coney 1981: 8). Maori women forged alliances with the Workers' Communist League (League) leadership of HART who were also at the forefront of the anti-tour protest movement.[11]

Awatere and Evans mistakenly anticipated that the upsurge of people marching against racism in South Africa would stimulate antiracism activism in New Zealand. With its main directive being the opposition against South African apartheid, the antiracist movement in New Zealand was largely a Pākehā movement and thus distinct from Maori radicalism and civil and land rights movements (Jesson July 1982: 14). After the tour, many Pākehā involved in the protests abandoned the antiracist movement and League members resisted the demands of Maori radicals, such as Evans and Awatere, to sustain protest against local racism. When League members did organize in support of Maori issues, they did so with a class-based analysis rather than one based on the return of Maori sovereignty. This class preoccupation incensed Maori radicals and sparked the Black Unity paper.

After the Eviction

Despite the lack of debate about Maori sovereignty inside the Auckland Trades Council in 1982, the philosophy gathered momentum during the 1980s and had a significant effect on white feminists, Maori radicals, the sectarian Left, and the trade union movement.

Awatere took the ideas that Black Unity had first espoused in 1981 and developed a manifesto for Maori sovereignty, first published as a series of articles by the feminist magazine *Broadsheet* in 1982 and 1983, and then as a book, *Maori Sovereignty*, in 1984. She called on Maori to withdraw from white culture (including interracial intimacy) and make "all time and all space Maori." Once this had been achieved, Maori could then seek alliance with white people (1984: 52, 101). A key difference between this manifesto and the Black Unity paper was that Pacific Islanders joined white women, trade unions, and the sectarian Left on the list of those criticized for failing to ally with Maori on the issue of Maori sovereignty (35–41). It would appear to be no coincidence that in 1983, Maori women decided to meet separately from Pacific Island women and the unifying description of "Black," embracing Indigenous women, women of color, and Third World women, dropped out of use.

The Maori sovereignty articles had a significant impact on the women's movement. Kathie Irwin writes: "Women formed study groups to debate the papers, wrote responses, critiques, cancelled their subscriptions to *Broadsheet*, idolised Donna as the new revolutionary, proclaimed her ideas up and down the country, or decided that she was a lunatic and evidence that Maori nationalism should be wiped out at any cost" (Irwin, "Challenges" 1992: 83). A group of Marxist feminists, called Women for Aotearoa, meeting regularly between 1982 and 1984, embraced Awatere's ideas in her articles on Maori sovereignty. Ultimately, however, their analysis did not impact the broader women's liberation movement (Simpkin 1994: 234). Irwin reflected that Awatere's critique of the women's movement as racist also prevented Maori women from getting involved in women's issues (Irwin, "Challenges" 1992: 83).

Maori sovereignty quickly became popular in Auckland Maori radical circles. The Waitangi Action Committee, the political inheritors of Ngā Tamatoa, declared: "Maori people are a sovereign people" as early as 1981 (Walker 2004: 220). By 1983, the Maori People's Liberation Movement of Aotearoa claimed that most young Maori activists had taken up the demand for Maori sovereignty. And in 1985, Maori unemployed rights activists in the national unemployed and beneficiaries' movement demanded the Treaty of Waitangi be honored, liberation from oppression, and Maori sovereignty (Report 1986).

The sectarian Left were also influenced by Maori sovereignty ideas. While the Workers' Communist League had opposed Andersen's eviction of Maori radicals involved with the Polynesian Resource Centre (and the coterminous eviction of HART from the Trade Union Centre), League members involved with the Victoria Students' Association in Wellington attempted to ban Evans from a speaking tour of university campuses on "women and racism" in 1982. Accused of being "antiwhite" and "antistudent," Evans's writings in *bitches, witches & dykes* and her association with Black Unity were used as evidence of her bias (Coney 1982: 7). Yet political revelation followed. Once Awatere's Maori Sovereignty articles were published, the League studied the communist movement and eventually decided, in 1984, to reject a monolithic communist model "and take into account decolonisation and gender issues as well as worker's issues" (Bradford 1999).

And change occurred in the trade union movement. Under pressure from Maori trade unionists, the NZFoL established the Maori and Pacific Island Advisory Committee to give Maori members a voice in national union politics in 1983. A motion was put to the union movement that it support demands for Maori sovereignty that year, but it was soundly defeated. However, debate about Maori sovereignty reemerged in the trade union movement in 1985. Maori trade unionists had become increasingly discontent with the NZFoL's refusal to treat Maori work issues as different to working-class issues; to signal this, they voted to drop "Pacific Island" from the name of their NZFoL committee. When official channels yielded no results, some Maori trade unionists proposed setting up a separate Maori trade union movement to attend to Maori issues. The Hui a Nga Kaimahi o Aotearoa (the Meeting of Workers of New Zealand) was organized in 1986 to discuss this proposal, and over 400 Maori delegates from private and public sector unions attended to air their grievances. After lengthy debates, the Hui decided against a separate trade union movement but demanded that the NZFoL and the Combined State Unions support Maori self-determination, grow Maori representation on all union decision-making structures, encourage real consultation, and take action on Maori issues. As a result of the Hui, the Maori advisory committee won the right to be represented on the NZFoL national council, and national executive in 1986 (*Socialist Action* 1986). Significantly, Bill Andersen supported this motion. Maori representation rights were retained when the New Zealand Council of Trade Unions was formed in 1987.

Conclusion

This chapter evokes the actions of a small, outspoken circle of Maori women who developed a philosophy of Maori sovereignty in the 1970s and early 1980s. Influenced by Maori civil and land rights movements, the women's liberation movement, the antiracist movement and Third World independence movements, Donna Awatere and Ripeka Evans, and other Maori women radicals, incorporated feminist and Marxist theory into a New Zealand–based revolutionary theory. Maori sovereignty was its key demand. Socialists and communists, white feminists, Black men, and the trade unionists, although expected to be the natural allies of Maori radicals, were harshly accused of failing to take the pervasiveness of, and their own complicity in, institutionalized racism seriously. And yes, this did cause conflict and division. But for those who were goaded into engaging these ideas, it brought an opportunity for new kinds of alliances. And for others, the specter of Maori nationalists taking back political, economic, and cultural control of New Zealand made bicultural ways of working seem moderate and almost appealing.

Notes

1. Ripeka Evans grew up in rural Northland with a strong Ngāpuhi tribal identity and went to Auckland University in the mid-1970s. Donna Awatere was born in Rotorua, of Ngāti Porou and Ngāti Whakaue descent, and became active in Auckland radical groups in 1970.

2. I pay tribute here to Radhika Mohanram, Michele Dominy, and Kathie Irwin, whose discussions of Maori feminism and sovereignty activists inform my thinking.

3. The pro-Soviet, New Zealand Socialist Unity Party (SUP) was formed in 1966 and led by Bill Andersen. It was a working-class party and advocated the establishment of a socialist society.

4. Bill Andersen had been involved in the union movement since 1951 and was deeply respected by Auckland trade unionists, particularly those in the drivers, seafarers, boilermakers, laborers, and carpenters unions.

5. Britain colonized New Zealand in 1840 with the Treaty of Waitangi.

6. The Bastion Point occupation lasted for 506 days and culminated in the arrest of 222 people. In 1987, the Waitangi Tribunal found in favor of Ngāti Whātua o Ōrākei's historical claim and recommended the return of Bastion Point to its rightful owners. Tainui Awhiro successfully challenged the local council's ownership of the Raglan Golf Course (taken from Tainui Awhiro "temporarily" during World War II). The government returned the land to Tainui Awhiro in 1983 and the golf course was transformed into a Kokiri training center, farm, and marae.

7. Both Awatere and Evans wrote articles analyzing how the effects of colonization—limited job opportunities, unemployment, a racist justice system, poor health, high mortality rates, and domestic violence—were disproportionately felt by Maori and Pacific Island women.

8. *bitches, witches & dykes* was a women's liberation movement newspaper, written for a feminist audience.

9. In 2001, bell hooks constructed a similar argument (hooks 424–25).

10. Conference reports do not indicate how many Maori women attending subscribed to these views.

11. Formed in 1978, the Workers' Communist League was a covert, orthodox communist organization and committed to the vanguard view of the Communist Party, one-party government, democratic centralism, and the primacy of class above other social problems.

Works Cited

Andersen, Bill. "Facts Re Eviction of Polynesian Resource Centre." *The Republican* 41 (July 1982): 7–9.

Awatere, Donna. "Awatere at Copenhagen." *Broadsheet* 83 (October 1980): 10–13, 19.

———. "Korero-tia Wahine Ma!" *Broadsheet* 84 (November 1980): 10–14.

———. "Looking Back at the Seventies." *Broadsheet* 77 (March 1980): 12–13.

———. "Māori Sovereignty Part Two." *Broadsheet* 103 (October 1982): 24–29.

———. *Maori Sovereignty*. Auckland: Broadsheet, 1984.

Awatere, Donna, and Ripeka Evans. "Māori Women." MS 98-162-1/11, Alexander Turnbull Library.

Belich, James. *Paradise Reforged: A History of the New Zealanders from the 1880s to the Year 2000*. Auckland: Penguin, 2001.

Black Unity. "A Statement on the Attempt by White Leftists to Divide Pacific Peoples." *The Republican* 41 (July 1982): 4–7.

Bradford, Sue. Interview by Cybèle Locke. January 27, 1999, Auckland.

Coney, Sandra. "Women against the Tour." *Broadsheet* 92 (September 1981): 8–11.

———. "Evans Attacked." *Broadsheet* 100 (June 1982): 6–7.

Dalziel, R. "Political Organisations." *Women Together: A History of Women's Organisations in New Zealand. Ngā RŌpū Wāhine o te Motu*. Ed. Anne Else. Wellington: Department of Internal Affairs/Daphne Brasell Associates Press, 1993. 55–69.

Dann, Christine. "Behind the News: Māori Women on the Move." *Broadsheet* 44 (November 1976): 6–9.

———. *Up From Under: Women and Liberation in New Zealand 1970-1985*, Wellington: Allen and Unwin/Port Nicholson, 1985.

Dominy, Michele. "Māori Sovereignty: A Feminist Invention of Tradition." *Cultural Identity and Ethnicity in the Pacific*. Eds. Jocelyn Linnekin and Lin Poyer. Honolulu: University of Hawaii Press, 1990. 237–57.

Evans, Ripeka. "He aha nga mahi? Work work work!!!" *bitches, witches & dykes* (August 1980): 9, 12.

———. "Black Women Unite!!" *bitches, witches & dykes* (December 1980): 11.

———. "The Politics of Blackness and Black-White Relationships." *bitches, witches & dykes* (November 1981): 18, 22.

———. "Korerotia Wahine Ma." *bitches, witches & dykes* (June 1982): 1–3.

————. "Rebecca Evans." *Broadsheet* 103 (October 1982): 12–17.

Harris, Aroha. *Hīkoi: Forty Years of Māori Protest*. Wellington: Huia, 2004.

hooks, bell. "Eating the Other: Desire and Resistance." *Media and Cultural Studies: Keyworks*. Eds. Meenakshi Gigi Durham and Douglas M. Kellner. Oxford: Blackwell, 2001. 424–38.

Irwin, Kathie. "Towards Theories of Māori Feminism." *Feminist Voices: Women's Studies Texts for Aotearoa/New Zealand*. Ed. Rosemary Du Plessis. Auckland: Oxford University Press, 1992. 1–21.

————. "'Challenges,' to Maori Feminists." *Broadsheet: Twenty Years of Broadsheet Magazine*. Ed. Pat Rosier. Auckland: New Women's Press, 1992. 79–85.

Jesson, Bruce. "Conflict in the Anti-racist Movement." *The Republican* 40 (May 1982): 4–5.

————. "Māori Radicals and the Pakeha Left: How Much in Common?" *The Republican* 41 (July 1982): 13–14.

"Letters." *bitches, witches & dykes* (December 1980): 2; *bitches, witches & dykes* (May 1981): 3.

Mohanram, Radhika. "The Construction of Place: Maori Feminism and Nationalism in Aotearoa/New Zealand." *NWSA Journal* 8.1–2 (Spring 1996): 50–69.

Report on the National Organisation for Maori Policy Council, 1986, MS 90-180-03, Alexander Turnbull Library.

Roth, Margot. "Ripeka Evans: Analyse History and Get a Whole Vision of Society." *Women's Studies Journal* 2.1 (August 1985): 2–14.

Simpkin, Gay. "Women for Aotearoa: Feminism and Māori Sovereignty." *Hecate* 20.2 (1994): 226–38.

Socialist Action, May 23, 1986.

Statistics New Zealand. http://www.stats.govt.nz/ (accessed March 2012).

Trotter, Chris. "What's Left?" Bruce Jesson Memorial Lecture, Auckland, 2002.

Trucker, May 1986.

Vanderpyl, Jane. "Aspiring for Unity and Equality: Dynamics of Conflict and Change in the 'By Women For Women' Feminist Service Groups, Aotearoa/New Zealand (1970–1999)." Unpublished dissertation, University of Auckland, 2004.

Walker, Ranginui. *Ka Whawhai Tonu Matou*, 2nd ed. Penguin: Auckland, 2004.

CHAPTER 17

Beading Lesson

Beth H. Piatote

The first thing you do is, lay down all your hanks, like this, so the colors go from light to dark, like a rainbow. I'll start you out with something real easy, like I do with those kids over at the school, over at Cay-Uma-Wa.

How about—you want to make some earrings for your mama? Yeah, I think she would like that.

Hey niece, you remind me of those kids. That's good! That's good to be thinking of your mama.

You go ahead and pick some colors you think she would like. Maybe three or four is all, and you need to pick some of these bugle beads.

Yeah, that's good, except you got too many dark colors.

You like dark colors. Every time I see you you're wearin' something dark. Not me. I like to wear red and yellow, so people know I'm around and don't try talkin' about me behind my back, aay?

The thing is, you got to use some light colors, because you're makin' these for your mama, right, and she has dark hair, and you want 'em to stand out, and if they're all dark colors you can't see the pattern.

I got some thread for you, and this beeswax. You cut the thread about this long, a little longer than your arm, but you don't want it too long or it will tangle up or get real weak. You run it through the beeswax, like this, until it's just about straight. It makes it strong and that way it don't tangle so much.

You keep all this in your box now. I got this for you to take home with you, back to college, so you can keep doin' your beadwork.

How do you like it over there at the university? You know your cousin Rae is just about gettin' her degree, she has just has her practicum, then she'll be done. I think her boyfriend don't like her being in school, though, and that's slowing her down. It's probably a good thing you don't have a boyfriend right now. They can really make a lot of trouble for you and slow you down on things you got to do.

Now you gotta watch this part. This is how you make the knot. You make a circle like this, then you wrap the thread around the needle three times, see? You see how my hands are? If you forget later you just remember how my hands are, just like this, and remember you have to make a circle, okay? Then you pull the needle through all the way to the end—good—and clip off the little tail.

I'll show you these real easy earrings, the same thing I always start those men at the jail with. You know I go over there and give them beading lessons. You should see how artistic some of them are. They work real hard, and some of them are good at beadwork.

I guess they got a lot of time to do it, but it's hard, it's hard to do real good beadwork.

You got to go slow and pay attention.

I know this one man, William, he would be an artist if he wasn't in jail. I'll show you, he gave me a drawing he did of an eagle. It could be a photograph, except you can tell it's just pencil. But it's good, you would like it. There's a couple other Indian prisoners—I guess we're supposed to call them inmates, but I always call them prisoners—and sometimes I make designs for them for their beadwork from what they draw. The thing is, they don't get very many colors to work with.

They like the beadwork, though. They always got something to give their girl-friends when they come visit, or their mothers and aunties.

You have to hide the knot in the bead, see, like this, and that's why you got to be careful not to make the knot too big.

Maybe next time you come they will be having a powwow at the prison and you can meet my students over there, and they can show you their beadwork. I think they always have a powwow around November, around Veteran's Day. Your cousin Carlisle and his family come over from Montana last time, and the only thing is, you got to go real early because it takes a long time to get all your things through security. They have to check all your regalia and last time they almost wouldn't let Carlisle take his staff in because they said it was too dangerous or something.

What's that? Oh, that's all right. Just make it the same way on the other one and everyone will think you did it that way on purpose.

Your mama is really going to like these earrings. I think sometimes she wishes she learnt to bead, but she didn't want to when she was little. She was the young-est so I think she was a little spoiled, but don't tell her I said that. She didn't have to do things she didn't want to, she didn't even have to go to boarding school. I think she would have liked it. It wasn't bad for me at that school. Those nuns were good to me; they doted on me. I was their pet. I think your mama missed out on something, not going to St. Andrew's, because that's when you get real close with other Indians.

I like that blue. I think I'm goin' to make you a wing dress that color.

I think you'll look real good when you're ready to dance. Once you get going on your beadwork I'll get you started on your moccasins, and you know your cousin Woody is making you a belt and I know this lady who can make you a cornhusk bag. You're goin' to look just like your mama did when she was young, except I think she was younger than you the last time she put on beadwork.

I used to wonder if you would look like your dad, but now that you're grown you sure took after her. I look at you and I think my sister, she must have some strong blood.

Hey, you're doin' real good there, niece. I think you got "the gift"—good eyesight! You know, you always got to be workin' on something, because people are always needing things for weddin's and memorials and going out the first time—got to get their outfits together. Most everything I make I give away, but people pay me to make special things. And they are always askin' for my work at the gift shop. My beadwork has got me through some hard times, some years of livin' skinny.

You got to watch out for some people, though. Most people aren't like this. But some people, when they buy your beadwork, they think it should last forever. Somebody's car breaks down, he knows he got to take it to the shop, pay someone to get it goin' again. But not with beadwork—not with something an Indian made. No, they bring it back ten years later and they want you to fix it for free! They think because an Indian makes it, it's got to last forever. Just think if the Indians did that with all the things the government made for us. Hey, you got to fix it for free!

You done with that already? Let me show you how you finish. You pull the thread through this line, see, then clip it, then the bead covers it up. That's nice.

That's good. I'm proud of you, niece. You got a good heart. Just like your mama and dad.

I think your mama is really goin' to like these earrings, and maybe she'll come and ask you to teach her how you do it. You think she'll ever want to learn bead-work? Maybe she'll come and ask me, aay?

What do you think of that? You think your mama would ever want to learn something from her big sister? I got a lot of students. There's a lady who just called me the other day, she works at the health clinic and she wants to learn how. I said sure I'll teach her. I teach anyone who wants to learn. I just keep thinkin' if I stay around long enough, everyone's goin' to come back and ask me, even your mama.

CONTRIBUTORS

TRACEY BANIVANUA MAR is a senior lecturer in colonial history at La Trobe University. She teaches and researches histories of race relations and land transfer in colonies of settlement in the western Pacific. Her book *Violence and Colonial Dialogue* (2007) explores race relations in Queensland's Pacific slave trade, and she is completing a book on Indigenous forms of decolonization in the western Pacific. She has published widely on issues of race formation and law, frontiers, and colonial labor relations and has produced two edited collections, the most recent of which is *Making Settler Colonial Space: Perspectives on Race, Place and Identity* (2010), coedited with Penelope Edmonds. She has completed for UNESCO coauthored research on the slavery in the Pacific and is currently working on an Australian Research Council–funded project looking at colonial cultures of possession and dispossession in Fiji, Australia, New Zealand, and Hawaiʻi.

MARLENE BRANT CASTELLANO is a member of the Mohawk Nation and professor emerita of Trent University, Ontario, Canada. She joined the Faculty of Native Studies at Trent University in 1973 and went on to serve as department chair for three terms. From 1992 until 1995 she was Co-Director of Research of the Royal Commission on Aboriginal Peoples, where she led research and policy analysis on social and cultural affairs, including women's perspectives. Brant Castellano's research interests include policy and practice of human services, contemporary applications of Indigenous knowledge, and research ethics. She researched and wrote Volume 1 of the *Final Report of the Aboriginal Healing Foundation, A Healing Journey* (2006), presenting analysis and outcomes of community-based initiatives to heal the trauma of residential schooling. She coedited a collection of papers titled *From Truth to Reconciliation, Transforming the Legacy of Residential Schools* (2008), also published by the Aboriginal Healing Foundation. Brant Castellano's articles on traditional and contemporary roles of Aboriginal women have appeared in journals and books on women's issues, including the chapter "Heart of the Nations: Women's Contribution to Community Healing" in *Restoring the Balance, First Nations Women, Community and Culture* (2009). Her knowledge and expertise are sought after by universities, public institutions, and community organizations across Canada. She is the recipient of three honorary degrees and numerous awards including appointment as an Officer of the Order of Canada.

CATHLEEN D. CAHILL is an assistant professor of history at the University of New Mexico. Her monograph, *Federal Fathers and Mothers: A Social History of the United States Indian Service, 1869–1929* (2011) received the 2011 Labriola Center American Indian National Book Award. She also coedited the special issue on "Intermarriage in American Indian History: Explorations in Power and Intimacy in North America" for *Frontiers: A Journal of Women Studies* (2008). During 2009–10 she held a Bill and Rita Clements Research Fellowship at Southern Methodist University's Clements Center for Southwest Studies. Her essay, "An Indian Teacher among Indians: American Indian Women's Labor in the Federal Indian Service," details the history of Native women's work experiences within the U.S. Office of Indian Affairs' Indian School Service in the early twentieth century. As Cahill suggests, the Indian School Service provided Native American women an opportunity for paid employment on isolated reservations; however, sustained patterns of racism within the U.S. Office of Indian Affairs resulted in distinct experiences for these workers compared to their white counterparts.

BRENDA J. CHILD is a professor of American Indian Studies and history at the University of Minnesota and chair of the Department of American Indian Studies. Her monograph, *Boarding School Seasons: American Indian Families, 1900–1940* (1998) moves beyond an examination of federal policies relating to the boarding school system and toward an in-depth look at the lives and individual experiences of Native children and families through the use of letters to retell history. As the first study of boarding schools to use letters to document individual experiences, *Boarding School Seasons* was awarded the North American Indian Prose Award. Child also wrote *Ojibwe Women and the Survival of Indian Community* (2011) and is coediting a volume of essays on a comparative history of Indigenous education. On top of her academic pursuits, Child has earned praise for her community involvement, winning the President's Outstanding Community Service Award from the University of Minnesota. Child also serves as a board member on the executive council of the Minnesota Historical Society, on the editorial board for the Indigenous Education Series at the University of Nebraska Press, as a councillor for the American Society of Ethnohistory, and on the board of directors for the Division of Indian Work in Minneapolis. She is a citizen of the Red Lake Nation in Minnesota.

SHERRY FARRELL RACETTE, associate professor in Native Studies/Woman and Gender Studies at the University of Manitoba, is an accomplished artist and interdisciplinary scholar. Her recent publications include "Encoded Knowledge: Memory and Objects in Contemporary Native American Art" in *Manifestations: New Native Art Criticism* (2011); "Returning Fire, Pointing the Canon: Aboriginal Photography As Resistance" in *The Cultural Work of Photography in Canada* (2011); "This Fierce Love: Gender, Women and Art Making" in *Art in Our Lives: Native Women Artists in Dialogue* (2010); *Clearing a Path: New Ways of Seeing*

Traditional Indigenous Art (with Carmen Robertson, 2009); "Haunted: First Nations Children in Residential School Photography" in *Depicting Canada's Children* (2009); and "Sewing for a Living: The Commodification of Métis Women's Artistic Production" in *Contact Zones: Aboriginal and Settler Women in Canada's Colonial Past* (2005). Farrell Racette has illustrated seven books, including Maria Campbell's *Stories of the Road Allowance* (1994/2010) and the children's series *Fiddle Dancer* (2007) and its sequels *Dancing in My Bones* (2008) and *Call of the Fiddle* (2011). From 2009 to 2010, Farrell Racette was the Ann Ray Fellow at the School for Advanced Research in Santa Fe, New Mexico. She is a member of Timiskaming First Nation in northwestern Quebec.

CHRIS FRIDAY is a professor of history, former chair of the Department of History, and former director of the Center for Pacific Northwest Studies at Western Washington University, Bellingham, Washington. Friday's current scholarly and teaching areas include the histories of the Pacific Northwest, American Indians, Asian Americans, U.S. Labor, World History, and Public History. The contribution to this volume grew out of his work with the U.S. Department of Justice and the U.S. Department of the Interior on behalf of the Lummi Nation. Other relevant publications include *Don "Lelooska" Smith: A Life's Journey into Northwest Coast Indian Art* (2004) and "Performing Treaties: The Culture and Politics of Treaty Remembrance and Celebration," in *The Power of Promises* (2009). Friday is currently working on studies of trans-Pacific laborers, the relationship between Columbia River Plateau peoples, horses, and imperialism, as well as constructions of gender and subsistence patterns among Puget Sound American Indians in the reservation era.

AROHA HARRIS (Te Rarawa, Ngāpuhi) is a senior lecturer in New Zealand History at the University of Auckland. Harris's research approaches Maori history through a mix of oral and documentary sources. Her book, *Hīkoi: Forty Years of Māori Protest* (2004), presents a photographic account of Maori people's protest from the 1960s to the *Hīkoi* of 2004. Harris's other research publications include "Concurrent Narratives of Maori and Integration in the 1950s and 60s" in *Journal of New Zealand Studies* (2008); "Letty Brown, Wahine Toa" in *Shifting Centres: Women and Migration in New Zealand History* (2002); and "'I Wouldn't Say I Was a Midwife': Interviews with Violet Otene Harris" published in the *Journal of the Australian Society of the History of Medicine*, Maori Health Special Issue (1997). Harris is also a published creative writer and member of the Waitangi Tribunal.

FAYE HEAVYSHIELD (Kainai Nation) recently held the Eiteljorg Fellowship for Native American Fine Art, Eiteljorg Museum of American Indians and Western Art, Indianapolis; she is a contemporary conceptual artist from the Kainai Tribe of southern Alberta, Canada. Her art and installation work has been widely exhibited at prominent galleries across Canada and the United States, including

Canada's National Gallery, Calgary's Glenbow Museum, and Bard College in Annandale-on-Hudson, New York. Exhibitions from HeavyShield's past three decades of professional activity include *blood* a solo exhibition at the Southern Alberta Art Gallery in 2004; *A Question of Place* at the Walter Phillips Gallery in Banff, Alberta, in 2004; *Migrating Motifs* at Bard College in Annandale-on-Hudson in 2002; and *venus as torpedo* at Regina's Dunlop Art Gallery in 1995. Her work is held in private and public collections throughout North America, including the Eiteljorg; the Kelowna Art Gallery in Kelown, British Columbia; and the Heard Museum in Phoenix. HeavyShield attended the Alberta College of Art and Design and the University of Calgary from 1980 to 1986, and she is renowned for installations that are minimally constructed yet carry a powerful social message reflecting the complexities of female indigenous existence.

HEATHER A. HOWARD is an assistant professor of anthropology at Michigan State University and affiliated faculty with the Centre for Aboriginal Initiatives at the University of Toronto. Howard's research interests include Native urban community organizing, health and illness knowledge production and politics, labor and socioeconomic class, sovereignty, decolonization and social justice movements, community-based participatory research, and ethics with Native communities in Canada and the United States. Howard is the editor with Susan Applegate Krouse of *Keeping the Campfires Going: Native Women's Activism in Urban Communities* (2009) and with Craig Proulx of *Aboriginal Peoples in Canadian Cities: Transformations and Continuities* (2011). She is completing a monograph titled *Lineage, Land and Labour: The Northfork Mono and the San Joaquin Valley, California*. Other publications include *Feminist Fields: Ethnographic Insights* (1999), and *The Meeting Place: Aboriginal Life in Toronto* (1997).

MARGARET D. JACOBS is the Chancellor Professor of History at the University of Nebraska, Lincoln. Jacobs is the winner of the 2010 Bancroft Prize for her book *White Mother to a Dark Race: Settler Colonialism, Maternalism, and the Removal of Indigenous Children in the American West and Australia, 1880–1940* (2009). She focuses on comparative analyses of the removal of Indigenous children from their families and communities in Australia and the United States. Jacobs's work also includes *Engendered Encounters: Feminism and Pueblo Cultures, 1879–1934* (1999). In 2001 Jacobs was granted a Fulbright Senior Scholar Award.

ALICE LITTLEFIELD is professor emerita in the Department of Sociology, Anthropology and Social Work at Central Michigan University. Littlefield is co-editor, with Martha Knack, of *Native Americans and Wage Labor: Ethnohistorical Perspectives* (1996), an anthology of important essays exploring the centrality of wage labor to the Native American community and individual survival in North America since the seventeenth century. *Marxist Approaches in Economic Anthropology* (1991), coedited with Hill Gates, explores the complex interdependency of polities, kinship systems, and the state. This anthology examines a diversity of contexts ranging from the political economies of eighteenth-century Northern Ireland to twentieth-century China. Among other noteworthy advocacy projects, Littlefield has contributed her expertise to the creation of a federal acknowledgment petition for the Burt Lake Band of Ottawas and Chippewas and to a study of the projected impact of the expansion of Soaring Eagle Casino at the Saginaw Chippewa Tribe in Mt. Pleasant, Michigan.

CYBÈLE LOCKE most recently taught in the Department of Gender and Women's Studies at Connecticut College; she currently is a full-time parent. She teaches transnational women's history, Indigenous histories and restitution movements, and anti-sweatshop movements. She is a feminist labor historian who works on unemployed workers' movements and labor movements in New Zealand, with particular attention to Maori. She recently wrote the entry on Maori and Trade Unions for *Te Ara*, New Zealand's online encyclopedia. Publications include "'Blame the System, Not the Victim!' Organizing the Unemployed in New Zealand" in *International Labor and Working-Class History* (2007); "Fractious Factions: The Organized Unemployed and the Labour Movement in New Zealand, 1978–1990," in *Unemployment and Protest: New Perspectives on Two Centuries of Contention* (2011); and *Workers in the Margins* (Bridget Williams Books, forthcoming). She has also written three socioeconomic impact reports for Ngāti Kuia, Maratuahu, and Rotorua and Taupo iwi to support their land claims to the Waitangi Tribunal.

MARY JANE LOGAN MCCALLUM is an assistant professor in the History Department at the University of Winnipeg and is the recipient of a Canadian Institutes of Health Research New Investigator Award from the Manitoba NEAHR (Network Environments for Aboriginal Health Research). Her research interests are in the areas of twentieth-century Aboriginal history and the history of Aboriginal women, and her work deals with labor, health, and education and histories of race and imperialism in Canada. Her publications include "The Last Frontier: 'Isolation' and Aboriginal Health" in the *Canadian Bulletin of Medical History* (2005) and "Indigenous Labor and Indigenous History" in the *American Indian Quarterly* (2009). Her first monograph, a history of Aboriginal women and work in the mid–twentieth century, is forthcoming from University of Manitoba Press. She is a member of the Munsee-Delaware Nation.

KATHY M'CLOSKEY is an adjunct associate professor in the Department of Sociology, Anthropology, and Criminology at the University of Windsor, Ontario. She is also a research associate at the Southwest Center, University of Arizona, Tucson. The recipient of four substantial research grants since 1998, M'Closkey's scholarship is consistently supported by the Social Sciences and Humanities Research Council of Canada. Her most recent book, *Swept Under the Rug: A Hidden*

History of Navajo Weaving (2002, 2008), recounts how the commodification of Navajo weaving by the dominant, mainstream culture exposed stereotypical and inaccurate histories that gloss over the obvious exploitation of Navajo women weavers. *Swept Under the Rug* was awarded "Outstanding Academic Title" by the American Academic Library Association in 2003. M'Closkey served as research director of the 2008 award-winning PBS documentary *Weaving World: Navajo Tales of How the West Was Spun*, directed by Navajo Bennie Klain, cofounder of Trickster Films in Austin, Texas. She continues to forge new paths, taking her investigation into Navajo weaving to a global level, and is preparing another book-length manuscript tentatively titled *Why the Navajo Blanket Became a Rug: Excavating the Lost Heritage of Globalization.*

COLLEEN O'NEILL is an associate professor of history and coeditor of *Western Historical Quarterly* at Utah State University, where she was awarded the Researcher of the Year Award from the College of Humanities, Arts and Social Sciences in 2007. O'Neill's recent monograph, *Working the Navajo Way: Labor and Culture in the Twentieth Century* (2005), winner of the Historical Society of New Mexico's 2006 Gaspar Pérez de Villagrá Award for the best historical publication, examines the drastic economic changes Navajos faced from the New Deal era of the 1930s to the 1970s. She coedited, with Brian Hosmer, *Native Pathways: American Indian Culture and Economic Development in the Twentieth Century* (2004). O'Neill's next book is *Labor and Sovereignty: History of American Indian Workers, 1890–1990.*

BETH H. PIATOTE is an assistant professor of Native American Studies at the University of California, Berkeley, where she specializes in Native American literature and law in the United States and Canada; American cultural studies; and Niimiipuu (Nez Perce) language, literature, and culture. She is the author of *Domestic Subjects: Gender, Citizenship, and Law in Native American Literature* (2012).

MELISSA ROHDE completed her PhD at the University of Illinois. A U.S. historian, Rohde's dissertation, "Working America's Enchanted Lands: American Indian Tourism Labor, 1900–1970," focuses on labor and working class history, race and ethnic identity formation, and women's history. Rohde received a research fellowship in June 2007 from the New Mexico Office of the State Historian as well as a graduate student fellowship from the Illinois Program for Research in the Humanities in 2009–10.

SUSAN ROY is a Post-Doctoral Research Fellow in the History Department at York University. Her book, *These Mysterious People: Shaping History and Archaeology in a Northwest Coast Community* (2010), concentrates on the history of the Musqueam First Nation and develops a critique of the processes through which historical evidence and material culture have acquired authority in public history contexts, including museum displays and land claims cases. She has worked for many years as a research consultant for First Nations in British Columbia and Canada, including the Sechelt First Nation.

LYNETTE RUSSELL is the director of the Monash University Indigenous Centre. Her monograph, *Savage Imaginings* (2001) explores the historical and contemporary constructions of Australian Indigenous identities from a broad perspective, and *A Little Bird Told Me* (2002) delivers a personal account of the ways one Aboriginal woman's identity was affected by her incarceration in mental institutions in the early 1900s. She was editor for an anthology entitled *Boundary Writing: An Exploration of Race, Culture and Gender Binaries in Contemporary Australia* (2006) that investigates Western culture's propensity to categorize individuals into groups based on race, ethnicity, gender, or sexuality. Other books by Russell include *Appropriated Pasts: Indigenous Peoples and the Colonial Culture of Archaeology* (2005), coauthored with Ian McNiven; *Colonial Frontiers: Cross-Cultural Interactions in Settler Colonies* (2001); and the forthcoming *Roving Mariners: An Exploration of Indigenous Agency, Autonomy and Subjectivity in the Whaling and Sealing Industries*. Russell has served as a visiting fellow at the University of British Columbia, Cambridge University, Klagenfurt University in Austria, and Trent University. In 2011 Russell was awarded a five-year Australian Research Council Professorial Research Fellowship.

JOAN SANGSTER teaches in the History Department and in the Canadian Studies and Indigenous Studies graduate program at Trent University, Ontario, Canada. She has published five books on labor, women's, and legal history, including her most recent, *Transforming Labour: Women and Work in Postwar Canada* and *Girl Trouble: Female "Delinquency" in English Canada* (2002). She has coedited five books, including the recently released *Labouring Canada: Class, Race and Gender in Canadian History* (2010). Sangster was on the editorial board of the prominent labor history journal *Labour/Le Travail* for nine years, a recent coeditor of the *Journal of the Canadian Historical Association*, and she is currently an associate editor of *Labor: Studies in Working Class History of the Americas*. In addition to organizing workshops and conferences on Canadian history, women in the criminal justice system, and women in the workforce, Sangster has served on the local board of directors of the Elizabeth Fry Society of Canada.

RUTH TAYLOR lived in Guatemala for ten years where she worked as a journalist. Along with writing and publishing fiction, she has worked on numerous research and historical projects for Indigenous and other communities in Latin America and Canada, including the Sechelt First Nation of British Columbia.

CAROL WILLIAMS is associate professor and chair of the Women and Gender Studies Department at the University of Lethbridge, in Southern Alberta on the western plains of Canada. From 2008 to 2011 she held an interdisciplinary Tier II

Canada Research Chair at Trent University; prior to that appointment she taught at the University of Lethbridge, the University of Houston, and the University of New Mexico. For the past fifteen years, Williams has concentrated on defining questions of visual culture, the relationships between Indigenous peoples and settlers within settler nations, and women's history, as examined in *Framing the West: Race, Gender and the Photographic "Frontier" in the Pacific Northwest* (2001); "Economic Necessity, Political Incentive, and International Entrepreneurialism: The 'Frontier' Photography of Hannah Maynard" in *Cultural Work of Photography in Canada* (2011); "Beyond Illustrations: Illuminations of the Photographic 'Frontier'" in the *Journal of the West* (2007); and "Nation, Identity, Periphery, and Modernity" in *Image and Inscription* (2005) and other publications. Williams has also published widely on the cultural activism and art production of contemporary North American women artists.

INDEX

Note: Page numbers in italics indicate figures.

Abner, Annie, 222n4

Aboriginal Curatorial Collective, 4

Aborigines, Australia: multiculturalism rejected by, 16; organizations concerned with, 12–13, 82; unionists' exclusion of male workers, 10. *See also* Tasmanian Aboriginal communities

—women: post-sealing trade roles of, 64–67; sealing industry roles of, 61–64; travels and adventures of, 67–70. *See also* sealing industry

Aborigines, Canada: initiatives to secure rights, 108, 114–15; marginalization of, 159; overview of rights issues, ix–x. *See also* First Nations; Inuit people

—women: agency of, 38–39, 40n2; constructed as nonproductive and peripheral to fur industry, 149; life histories retrieved by, 32–33, 39; status rights lost in intermarriage and in citizenship, 17, 22n7

Aborigines Protection Board (NSW, Australia), 12–13

Aborigines Protection Society (Queensland), 82

Abourezk, J., 248

acculturation policy: differences across states, 36–37; gender normativity and, 28–29, 35. *See also* assimilation and integration

acorn-centered subsistence, 165, 167–69

activists. *See* Black Unity; grassroots activism; political activism; urban community activism

Adams, Elizabeth, 157, *157*

Admiral Cockburn (ship), 69

adoption: forced, 247–48; promoted for unwed mothers, 179, 184–85, 186. *See also* child removal policies, U.S.

African Americans: as labor competition, 35

agency: Aboriginal, 38–39, 40n2; attenuated in later sealing industry, 68–69; indentured women's shaped by colonization, 74, 81–84; of Northfork Mono women, 163–64,

175–76; sexual, of women, 182–83; victimization vs., 60

agricultural fairs: Ojibwe uses of, 141–43, 144; spud peeling contest at, 95, *95*–96

agriculture: of Anishinaabeg, 49–50; colonial emphasis on, for Aboriginal peoples, 88, 91, 92, 112, 142, 167; commercialization's effects on, 89; decline of labor in, 53, 56; extension agents and, 200–204; gendered notions of, 11–12, 94–96, *95*; Indian boys trained for, 28, 50, 180; local and regional markets for, 93–94; masculinization of, 88, 92; mechanization of, 79–80, 93–94, 96, 173; pest control in, 80; self-sufficiency linked to, 92–93; subsistence activities combined with reservation-based, 168–69; sugar beet growing, 159–60. *See also* livestock; potato cultivation; seasonal agricultural labor; sugar industry

Aid to Dependent Children (later Aid to Families with Dependent Children, U.S.), 179, 186

AIM (American Indian Movement), 30, 247, 249–51

Albers, Patricia, 29, 121

Alberta (Canada): women as rural laborers in, 159–60

Alcatraz Island: occupation of, 247, 250, 251

Alexandria Bedding Company, 197

allotments: effects of, in general, 93, 94–95, 120; for Northfork Mono people, 166–68; potato cultivation and, 93; women's land ownership and, 35. *See also* land issues; relocation programs

American Indian Movement (AIM), 30, 247, 249–51

American Indians. *See* Native American people

Amsden, C. A., 126

Andersen, Bill, 256, 264, 265, 265nn3–4

Anderson, Ian, 64

Anfield, Earl, 106–7

Anishinaabeg (People of the Three Fires): assimilation policies' impact on, 48, 49–50; children removed to residential schools, 50–53; cultural identities maintained by, 57–58; decline of rural communities, 53–54; industrial economic context of, 54–55; land cessions of, 138; reflections on, 56–58; subsistence strategies of, 137–39; urban migration of, 52–54, 57; women's roles in, 160–61. *See also* Anishinaabe women; Ojibwe women

Anishinaabe women: approach to, 46–47; assimilation pressures on, 49–50; occupational mobility and adaptability of, 17–18, 49–53, 56, 136–45; reflections on, 56–58; tribal jobs of, 54–55; U.S. policy environment of, summarized, 47–48. *See also* Ojibwe women

Anishinabequek (organization), 19

anthropology, approaches to, 28, 30

anti-apartheid movement (Aotearoa/New Zealand), 262–63

anticolonial movements, 29, 31

antimodernism, 141–43

Anti Slavery Society (Queensland), 82

Aotearoa/New Zealand: antiracism movement in, 262–63; bicultural discourse in, 16; colonization of, 13–14, 15, 265n5; Maori population of Auckland, 254–55; terminology in, 22n2; trade union movement of, 254–56, 257–58, 264–65; "two people in one house" idea in, 231–32; women in Parliament of, 19. *See also* Auckland Trade Union Centre; Black Unity; Maori Affairs department

Apostle Islands Indian Pageant, 144

Archdale, Agnes, 144

Arizona: CCC-Indian Division project in, *195*; Native teachers and schools in, 219; trading posts and Navajo weaving in, *121*, 128–29, 132n1

art and aesthetics: community activism linked to, 245; of Navajo weaving, 123, 129, 130; romantic depictions of labor, 82–83; socialist realism, 148–49. *See also* commodity production; craft entrepreneurialism; *and specific crafts*

Arts and Crafts Movement, 123, 129

assimilation and integration: Anishinaabeg impacted by, 48, 49–50; assumptions about wage labor and, 57–58; Black Unity's critique of, 254–55, 257–58; boarding schools' goal of, 47, 180–81, 210–11; commercialization of dance as detrimental to, 142–44; Indigenous mobility and resistance to, 19–20;

masculinization of agriculture in, 88, 92; policies designed for, 47–48; report's rejection of, 28; resisted despite wage work, 196; tourist-related activities deployed to counteract, 137–45. *See also* acculturation policy; Bureau of Indian Affairs; federal work relief projects; gender division of labor; gender normativity; Indian Homemakers' Clubs; male breadwinner/nuclear family model; Maori Women's Welfare League; mothers and motherwork

Association of American Indian Affairs, 185

Atkin, Alberta, 250

Attwood, Bain, 67

Auckland Black Women's Group, 262

Auckland Trade Union Centre (New Zealand): changing stance of, 264–65; political context of, 255–56; Polynesian Resource Center evicted from, 254, 256, 258, 264

Auckland Women's Liberation groups, 259

August, Val, 106, *106*

Australia: acculturation policy of, 36–37; boycott of hotels in, 111; child removal policies of, 12–13; colonial government's attempts to incarcerate Tasmanian Aborigines, 65–66, 67; colonization in, 13–14; motherwork regulated in, 32; multicultural discourse in, 16; penal colony established in, 60–61; sealing grounds map, *62*; whitewash of interracial past of, 67, 75, 84; wool production of, 125. *See also* Aborigines, Australia; Bass Strait region; indentured labor trade; Queensland; sealing industry; sugar industry

Awatere, Donna: activism of, 258–59, 265, 266n7; on antiapartheid movement, 262–63; background of, 265n1; Black feminist stance of, 20, 259–62; key demand of, 254; Maori sovereignty manifesto of, 263–64

Backhouse, James, 67–68

Balch, Solomon, *95*

Ballew, Mrs. Richard, 95

Balmer, James W., 140, 141

Banivanua Mar, Tracey: essay by, 73–87; references to, 8–9, 11

Banks, Ellie, 250

Bartlett, Jane, 233, 234

basket making: childcare combined with, 106, *106*; "feminization" of, 11, 107, 114; gathering materials for, 113–14, 115–16, 171; imports of, 57; logging's relation to, 107; OIA surveys of, 139–40. *See also* birch-bark goods

Bass Strait region (Australia): Aboriginal

culture's survival on, 64–66; map of, *62*; sealing contract and, 68–69; whaling station of, 66–67

Bastion Point occupation, 258, 265n6

beadwork: HeavyShield's work, 3, 5–7, 8; literacy of, 5–8; OIA surveys of, 139–40; sharing techniques of, 268–70

Beaulieu, C. H., 219

Bellanger, Pat, 240, 250, 251

Bellecourt, Peggy, 250

Bemidji (Minn.) boycott, 243

Benally, Martha, 130

Benedict, Susan, *170*

BIA. *See* Bureau of Indian Affairs

Bigelow, Erastus, 125

Biolsi, Thomas, 99n6

birch-bark goods: BIA purchases of, 52; gathering *wattap* for stitching, 151–52; OIA surveys of, 139–40

bitches, witches & dikes (*Black Forum*, newspaper), 261, 264, 266n8

Black Dykes, 262

Blackfeet Indian Welfare (organization), 196

Blackfeet women: conditions of, 196–97; garment project of, 200–204, *201*; mattress-making project of, 18, 197–200

Black feminism: Auckland trade unionists opposed to, 254; creation of, 259–62; summary of, 265. *See also* Black Unity; Maori sovereignty demands

Black Feminist Collective, 262

Black Forum (*bitches, witches & dikes*, newspaper), 261, 264, 266n8

Black men (New Zealand): Black feminist critique of, 259–62; Black Unity's critique of, 254, 257

Blackness, 256–57

Black Power (U.S.), 258

Black Unity (and related Maori radicals): Black feminist stance and, 259–62; conference paper of, 256–58; key demand of, 254; political context of, 254–56; refusal to be silent, 20; summary of, 265. *See also* Maori sovereignty demands

Black women: call for action of, 257–58; demise of use of term, 263; South African rugby team tour opposed by, 262–63. *See also* Black feminism

Blake, Norby, 248, 251

blood quantum rules, 14, 35

boarding schools. *See* residential and boarding schools

Board of Indian Commissioners (U.S.), 92, 99n4

Bonga, Lizzie, 214

Bonnah, T. L., 233

Boone, George, *94*

Borrows, John, 4

boycotts and sit-ins, 111, 243, 250

"Boys Potato Club," 88

Brant Castellano, Marlene: preface by, ix–xi; references to, 3, 4, 21

Brewer, David, 220

Brewer, Katie Loulin, 219–20, *221*

British Columbia: Aboriginal title and rights in, 108; Burrard Inlet sawmills of, 111; canneries of, 107; Indian homemakers' clubs in, 226; Sunshine Coast of, 104; timing of colonial conquest in, 36. *See also* logging by hand; logging industry; shíshálh people

British Columbia Forestry Act (1910), 112

British Empire: New Zealand as colony in, 13–14, 15, 265n5; slavery abolished in, 8–9. *See also* Aotearoa/New Zealand; Australia; colonialism; Great Britain

Broker, Ignatia, 249

Brown, Jennifer, 149

Brown, Margaret, 136

Brown, Rap, 258

Brown, William, 152–53

Brown family, 96, *97*

Brownlie, Robin Jarvis, 17, 38

Brunot, Felix R., 92

buckskin goods, 139–40

buffalo: women's roles in processing, 151, 152

Buntin (superintendent), 210

Bureau of Indian Affairs (BIA, U.S.): assimilationist compulsions of, 12; contradictory policies of, 185–86, 189, 216–17; "home improvement" goals of, 200–204; labor programs for women of, 35; limitations of, 51–52; mattress-making project and, 196–200; modernity and progress ideals of, 129–30; mother and family model of, 180–81; Native women's understanding of system, 210–11, 213–14; recognition of tribes by, 47–48, 56; reservation households surveyed by, 96; sit-in at headquarters, 250. *See also* assimilation and integration; Indian School Service; Native American people-women as federal employees; Office of Indian Affairs; outing matrons; reservations and reserves; residential and boarding schools

Burke, Charles, 142–43

Burt Lake Band (Ottawas and Chippewas), 46–47. *See also* Anishinaabe women

Bushby, A. T., 111

business interests: mattress-making project

opposed by, 197–98; San Joaquin Valley development, 169. *See also* capitalism and capitalist development; commodity production; *and specific industries*

Cahill, Cathleen D.: essay by, 210–24; references to, 19
California: confidentiality of medical records in, 190n26; unrecognized and dispossessed Natives in, 174; unwed mothers committed to mental institutions in, 187–88; violence of settler colonialism in, 163–64, 166–67. *See also* domestic "outing" program; Fresno River Reservation; Los Angeles; Northfork Mono people; San Francisco; San Joaquin Valley; seasonal agricultural labor
California Children's Home Society, 184
California Rancheria Act (1958), 173–74, 177n3
Campbell, Lydia (née Brook), 155, 156, 157
Campbell, Mary, 33
Canada: colonization in, 13–14; ethical guidelines for human subject research in, 3, 22n3; motherwork regulated in, 32; multicultural discourse in, 16; women as rural laborers in Alberta, 159–60; women's status rights lost in intermarriage and in citizenship, 17, 22n7. *See also* Aborigines, Canada; First Nations; Hawthorne Report; Indian Act; Indian Affairs Branch; Indian Homemakers' Clubs; trading posts-Canada; *and specific provinces*
Canadian Armed Forces, 227
canneries, 106–7, 113
capitalism and capitalist development: Black feminist critique of, 261–62; gendered effects of, 205n3; Navajo woolgrowers and weavers impacted by free trade, 124, 127–29. *See also* assimilation and integration; business interests; commodity production; wage labor
Carmen, Ida, *170*
Carmichael, Stokely, 258
Carrier women, 29
casinos and gaming, 48, 55, 56, 58, 173–74
Cattelino, Jessica, 195
Caughnawaga Indian Homemakers' Club, 227
CCC-ID (Civilian Conservations Corps-Indian Division), 194, *195*, 197, 199, *201*, 202
cedar tree: community-based research on, 108–9; roots of, 113–14, 115–16; shíshálh's relationship to, 104–5, 107, 116–17. *See also* coastal forest; logging by hand; shíshálh people
Celestine, Aurelia, 99

Central Valley (California): labor patterns in, 164
Chapman, Harriet, 221
Charles, Al, 91–92
Chemawa School (aka Salem Indian School, Salem, Oregon), 181, 216, 220, *221*
Chepo, Leona, 171, 172–73
Chepo, Maggie, 172
Chicago and North Western Railway, 139, 142
Child, Brenda J.: essay by, 240–53; references to, 20
Child Placement Bureau, 184
child removal policies, Australia, 12–13
child removal policies, U.S.: Anishinaabeg and, 50–53; investigation and possible roots of, 185; Native women pathologized in, 212; women's activism against, 247–48, 250–51. *See also* adoption; residential and boarding schools
children: basket making combined with care for, 106, *106*; concerns for, 248–50; indentured domestic work of, 80–81; Indians likened to, 92, 140; kin used in care for, 180, 183; potato cultivation by (boys), 88; of sugarcane workers, *73*, 73–74, 84–85. *See also* child removal policies; domestic "outing" program; education; kinship and tribal relations; residential and boarding schools
Children's Home Finding Society (U.S.), 187
Chilocco Indian School (Chilocco, Oklahoma), 213
China: sealskins imports of, 61
Chippewa. *See* Anishinaabe women; Ojibwas/Chippewas; Ojibwe women; Saginaw Chippewa women
Chowitsut (Lummi headman), 90
Chukchansi Yokuts, 165
churro sheep, 124–25, 126, 130
CIA. *See* Commissioner of Indian Affairs
citizenship: differences across nations, 35; theorization of, 21n1; women's status rights lost in, 17, 22n7
Civilian Conservations Corps-Indian Division (CCC-ID), 194, *195*, 197, 199, *201*, 202
civilizing mission: agricultural production linked to, 88, 91, 92, 112, 142, 167; labor as key to, 13, 82–84, 212–13. *See also* assimilation and integration; colonialism
Clark, William, 6
Clarke, Percy, 80
Cleveland, Grover, 120, 126
clothing production: repurposing of discarded clothing, 200–204, *201*; sealskin

boots and fur coats, 157, *158*. *See also* sewing projects

Clovis (California): seasonal agricultural labor in, 170, 171, 172, 173

coastal forest: hunting and fishing rights in, 110–11; redefinition of, 115; shíshálh rights to control of, 111–13; shíshálh's ongoing use of, 104–5, 107, 115–17. *See also* cedar tree; logging by hand; logging industry

Coast Salish: agricultural production among, 89–90; economic and cultural strategies of, 106–7; hereditary rights and kinship among, 110; potato's meanings for, 90–91. *See also* Cowichan women; Lummi women; shíshálh people

Cobb, Daniel, 251

Collier, John: contradictory policy of, 202; cultural pluralist view of, 203; mattress project and, 196, 197, 199, 200; on sheep and wool quality, 130

Collins, June M., 99

colonialism: Aboriginal kinship impacted under, 110; approach to women's work and, 27; attempts to incarcerate Aborigines, 65–66, 67; Black feminist critique of, 261–62; Black Unity's critique of, 256–57, 266n7; discipline of labor in, 82–84; external imperialism vs. internal, 37; "intellectual," 39; invisible work in, 8–13; Maori impacted by, 255; Maori protests against, 258–59, 266n7; Northfork Mono women's intermarriage as response to, 165–66; patriarchal legacies of, 31; photography and, *73*, 73–76, *76*, *77*, 78–81, 82–84; shíshálh hand logging in context of, 107, 111–13; structural view of, 29; transnational approach and, 34–35; women's organizations in context of, 225–26, 232–37. *See also* civilizing mission; gender normativity; settler colonialism

Commissioner of Indian Affairs (CIA, U.S.): on Indian employees, 213; mattress project and, 196, 197, 199, 200; Navajo textile production reported to, 122; on pension eligibility, 220. *See also* Bureau of Indian Affairs; Office of Indian Affairs

commodity production: of buckskin goods, 139–40; of Indian Homemakers' Clubs, 228; knitting, 98, 106–7; Ojibwe women's role in, 141–43; ricing as, 137, 139, 144, 241–42, 251–52; sealskin boots and fur coats and, 157, *158*; subsistence strategies combined with, 137–38, 139, 151–52. *See also* basket making; beadwork; birch-bark goods; fur industry; Navajo weaving; textile goods; weaving

Concordia College, 246–47

conquest doctrine, 14

Constitution Act (Canada, 1982), ix

contact zones concept, 17

Conte, Christine, 17–18

Coolidge, Calvin, 220

Cooper, Whina, 230–31, 236

copyright issues, 123–24

Corbett, Ernest, 230, 235

Cornelius, Lavinia, 216, 218

Cotton, Clinton N., 128, 129

cotton picking (California), 169, 170, 171, 172–73

Country Women's Institutes (New Zealand), 229

Cowichan women, 106–7

Cowie, Isaac, 153–54

craft entrepreneurialism: commodification of, 18; copyright issues and, 123–24; fairs for, 141–43. *See also* basket making; beadwork; birch-bark goods; commodity production; Navajo weaving; weaving

creative adaptation: in casinos and gaming, 57; in depression-era work projects, 196; fur trade as, 17, 157, 161; to market, in general, 13, 163; in political activism, 226, 237, 247, 251; in potato cultivation, 89; tourism work as, 145. *See also* commodity production; craft entrepreneurialism; subsistence activities; wage labor; *and specific subsistence activities*

Crocket, David, 92

Crow School (Crow Agency, Montana), 218

Crumm, E. S., 129

cultures: agency and accommodation in survival of, 175–76; economic marginalization based on, 29; feminist sensibility and, 30–31; history writing's turn to, 37–39; tourist-related activities deployed to maintain, 137–45; women's responsibility for maintaining, 235–36

Curthoys, Ann, 33, 34

Curwen, Eliot, 156

Cush, Amelia, 98

Cush, Justina and Dan, 98

Custom Laundry (Minnesota), 244

Dakota homeland. *See* Minneapolis–Saint Paul

Dakota women, 29

dance. *See* performance

Davis, Gertrude, 171

Davis Inlet (Labrador), 155

Davitt, Michael, 83, 84–85

Dawes Act (General Allotment Act, U.S., 1887), 35, 93, 120. *See also* allotments; relocation programs

decolonization: contextualization of, 34, 264; debates about, 27; process of, 175–76

DeCora, Angel, 214

Deer, Elizabeth, 156–57

Delgamuukw v. British Columbia (Canada, 1997), ix, 22n4

Deloria, Philip J., 105

Deloria, Vine, Jr., 251

Dene people, ix, 36

Denetdale, Jennifer Nez, 4

DeSilva, Connie, 171

Deur, Douglas, 92

Les Deux Charles (ship), 69

Devine, Lizzie, 214

Dickinson, Caroline, 250

dike project, 96

Diné. *See* Navajo people

Dion, Wally, *Nurse Tracy*, *148*, 148–49

Dirlik, Arif, 40

discovery doctrine, 13–14

diverted mothering: adoption promoted for, 179, 184–85, 186; concept of, 180; difficulties faced in, 183–84; sexual agency and, 182–83; treatment of unwed mothers who refuse to cooperate, 186–88

Dixon, Johnny Joe, 115, *116*

domesticity: basket production linked to, 106, *106*; BIA's promotion of, 185–86, 189; federal hiring policy and, 211–12; mattress-making and sewing projects linked to, 198, 200–204; OIA surveys of, 136; spud peeling contest as enforcing, 95, 95–96; white practices imposed, 32, 217; work relief projects tied to, 193–94. *See also* domestic service; federal work relief projects; femininity; gender normativity; maternalism; mothers and motherwork

domestic "outing" program (San Francisco): adoption as solution for workers with children, 179, 184–85, 186–87; approach to, 12, 179; assimilation policy linked to, 180–81; dilemmas of workers in, 185–86, 189; pregnancies of workers in, 182–84; realities of live-in workers, 181–82; treatment of unwed mothers who refused to cooperate, 186–88; women's short-term stay in, 189–90

domestic service: in federal agency, 211; girls trained in, at boarding schools, 159–61, *160*, 180–81, 194, 217, 242; Indigenous children apprenticed in, 12–13; Ojibwe female urban

migrants in, 244; social network underlying, 19; of women at fur trade post, 153–57, *157*. *See also* diverted mothering; domesticity; domestic "outing" program

Donner, William, 203

Downwind, Winnie, 244

drover's boys, 67, 71n5

Duffie, Mary Kay, 14

Dutton, Sarah (Renanghi), 66–67, 69

Dutton, William Pelham, 66–67

Economic Recovery Administration, 53

economy: Aboriginal women constructed as nonproductive and peripheral to, 149; attitudes toward Aboriginal integration in, 28–29; gendered changes and, 193–95; global expansion of, 48–54; Indigenous women's adaptive approaches to, 17–18, 106–7, 113–17. *See also* capitalism and capitalist development; commodity production; creative adaptation; Marxism; seasonal agricultural labor; subsistence activities; wage labor; wool and textile markets

Eden, Charles, 80

education: acculturation policy and, 35; Maori women's remit concerning, 235–36; Native urban women's activism in, 246–48, 251–52. *See also* residential and boarding schools

Edwards, Eva, 98

Eisemann Brothers (company), 127–28

Eliot Park Neighborhood House (Minneapolis), 245

Ellinghaus, Katherine, 4, 36–37

"Enchanted Summer Land," 139. *See also* Wisconsin

English language, 66

eugenic sterilization, 188–89

Evans, Ripeka (earlier, Rebecca): accusations against, 264; activism of, 256, 258–59, 265, 266n7; on antiapartheid movement, 262–63; background of, 265n1; Black feminist stance of, 20, 259–62; on Blackness, 257; key demand of, 254

exchange relations, of Aboriginal women and Newcomer men, 64–66

Fairbanks, Francis, 245, 249, 250, 251

family, "universal" ideal of, 180. *See also* children; gender normativity; kinship and tribal relations; male breadwinner/nuclear family model; mothers and motherwork; patriarchy

Farrell Racette, Sherry: essay by, 148–62; references to, 4, 16

Federal Emergency Relief Administration (FERA, U.S.), 197, 199

Federal Employee Retirement Act (FERA, 1920), 219–22

federal work relief projects (U.S.): Anishinaabeg (Michigan), 52; extended to women, 196–97, 199–204; gendered nature of, 18, 193–94; wages of, 200–201, 205n9. *See also* mattress-making project; sewing projects; Works Project Administration (WPA, U.S.)

Federation of Women's Institutes (Canada), 229

feeblemindedness category, 187–88

Feild, Edward, 155

femininity: racial "otherness" as testing, 21; white vs. Indigenous prescriptions, 11. *See also* domesticity

feminism: Aboriginal, creation of, 30–31; on agency and oppression, 39; Black feminist critique of, 259, 260–62, 263–64; Black Unity's critique of, 254, 257; exclusions of Western tradition, 2; false universalisms in, 33; homogeneous construction of, 260; on motherwork as work, 32; political economy ideas in, 29–30; stance and definitions of, 259. *See also* Black feminism

FERA (Federal Emergency Relief Administration, U.S.), 197, 199

FERA (Federal Employee Retirement Act, 1920), 219–22

Finkbonner, C. C., 90, 91

First Nations: borders imposed on, 33–34; land use issues for, 114–15; marginalization of, 159; multiculturalism and, 16; subsistence strategies of, 151–52. *See also* Aborigines, Canada; Métis men; Métis women; reservations and reserves; residential and boarding schools; shíshálh people

—women: colonialism experienced by, 27; Indian agents' control over, 17; life histories of, collected, 32–33. *See also* Métis women; shíshálh people-women

fishing: in Anishinaabeg subsistence strategies, 139; Carrier women's role in, 29; rights and privileges in, 110–11, 112; seasonal agriculture combined with, 168–71; state regulations on, 138, 140–41. *See also* gathering activities; hunting; salmon

Fiske, Jo-Anne, 29

Fitzhugh, Edmund C., 88

Flandreau Indian School (Flandreau, South Dakota), 244, 246

Florida: sewing room strike in Tampa, 198

forest. *See* cedar tree; coastal forest; logging by hand; logging industry; shíshálh people

Fort Apache, 203

Fort Hall Reservation (Montana), 205n7

Fort Vermillion, 150

Fort Wedderburn, 152–53

Four Winds Club (YWCA), 182

Franklin, John, 153

Fransen, Jack, 234

free trade. *See* capitalism and capitalist development

French language, 67–68

Fresno River Reservation (California): closure of, 169; conditions on, 167–69; establishment of, 166; period of operation, 164

Friday, Chris: essay by, 88–103; references to, 11

fur industry: characterizations of women's roles in, 149–53; competition of men and their female partners in, 153–54; expansion of potato cultivation linked to, 88; "gendered racialization" of women's bodies in, 32; interracial relationships key to, 16; on Labrador Coast, 155–57; negotiations concerning women at factories of, 150–51; short-term labor contracts for, 154–55; women's centrality to, 30, 49; women's creation of items in, 157, *158*; women's work shifted away from, 159. *See also* Hudson's Bay Company (HBC); North West Company

gaming and gambling enterprises, 48, 55, 56, 58, 173–74

Garrison, Emma, 94–95

gathering activities: acorn-centered subsistence and, 165, 167–69; agriculture combined with, 168–69; fur trade roles combined with, 151–52; state regulations on, 138, 140–41. *See also* fishing; hunting

Gauthier, Ben C., 144

gender: intersectional approach to, 1–2; racial stratification and, 11, 79–84

gender division of labor: of Anishinaabeg subsistence strategies, 137–39; appropriate jobs for male and female in, 28–29, 35; governmental policy and, 57, 112–13; masculinization of agriculture in, 88, 92; in post-fur trade Canada, 159–61, *160*; potato cultivation associated with women's gardens, 93–94; on sugar plantation, 11, 79–84

gender normativity: assumptions about male and female labor in, 9–13, 28–29, 107; deployed on federal reserves, 17; domesticity and motherwork in, 32; dualities in, 107, 114–15; in education and employment policies, 35; feminist investigations of, 30–31; treatment of unwed mothers who refuse to follow, 186–88. *See also* domesticity; male breadwinner/nuclear family model; patriarchy

George, Lucinda, 214

Gibbs, George, 89

Gifford, E. W., 165

"Girls Canning Club," 88

global anticolonial movements, 29, 31

global economy, 48–54. *See also* wool and textile markets

Goddard, Henry, 188

Gogh, Vincent Van, 82

gold-seekers (California), 163, 164, 165, 166, 169

governmental policy: gender division of labor in, 28–29; gender roles inculcated by, 35; motherwork regulated in, 32. *See also* acculturation policy; assimilation and integration; power relations

—U.S.: aid for mothers and children, 179; anthropologists as advisors on, 28; federal and tribal program expansions in, 54–55; masculinization of agriculture in, 88, 92; modernity and progress ideals in, 129–30; mothers' pensions, 179, 185–86; salience of, 57; summary of, 47–48; tourist-related activities deployed against paternalism in, 137; on wool tariff, 120, 125, 126, 128. *See also* allotments; land issues; New Deal; relocation programs; reservations and reserves; residential and boarding schools; *and specific agencies*

Graham, Alexander, 149–50

Grand River Boarding School (Dakota Territory, United States), 213

Grant, Ulysses S., 99n4

grape harvest, 169, 170, *170*, 171–72

grassroots activism: approach to, 19–20, 225–26; constitution and ideas of, 232–36; formation and organizational structures of, 226–32; summary of, 236–37. *See also* Anishinabequek; domestic "outing" program; Indian Homemakers' Clubs; Maori Women's Welfare League; political activism; urban areas; urban community activism

Graves, Bobby Jo, 250

Great Britain: penal colony of, 60–61; slavery abolished by, 74; wool production in, 125. *See also* British Empire; colonialism

Great Depression: Anishinaabe women's occupations in, 52–53; Lummi struggles in, 96; Navajo livestock reduced by government in, 130, 194; tourism work and income during, 143–44. *See also* New Deal (U.S.)

Great Lakes region: few jobs for women on reservations of, 242–43; iron ore mining in, 31; logging decline in, 52, 56, 136. *See also* Anishinaabeg; Ojibwas/Chippewas

Green, Rayna, 29–30

Grenfell, Wilfred, 156

Grimshaw, Patricia, 4

Gross-Kelly and Company (earlier, Gross-Blackwell), 128

Guard, Julie, 39

Gunew, Sneja, 15–16

Gutman, Herbert, 38

Halkyard, Hilda, 259, 262

Halt all Racist Tours (HART), 256, 262–63, 264

Hammitt (OIA superintendent), 143–44

Hampshire Arms Hotel (Minneapolis), 244

Hampton Institute, 215

Harris, Aroha: essay by, 225–39; references to, 19, 20

HART (Halt all Racist Tours), 256, 262–63, 264

Haskell Institute (earlier, Haskell Indian Industrial School; Kansas), 52, 53, 213

Haskins, Victoria, 4, 188

Hawaiians, 14

Hawthorne Report (*A Survey of the Contemporary Indians of Canada*), 9, 28

Health Insurance Portability and Accountability Act: Privacy and Security Rules (HIPPA, U.S., 1996), 190n26

Heart of the Earth Survival School (Minneapolis), 247, 251

HeavyShield, Faye: *hours* (beaded book), 3, 5–7, 8; references to, 4

Hemingway, Ernest, 56

Henley, Thomas J., 168

Henry (ship), 66

Henry, Alexander, the Younger, 150, 151–52

Henry, Caroline, 159

historical materialism, 38. *See also* Marxism

history: Aboriginal topics limited in, 30; cultural turn in, 37–39; nation and economy as shaping writing of, 36–37; politics of, 39–40; transnational approach to, 33–34; universal assumptions in, 2–3. *See also* labor history; methodology

Holt, Marilyn, 185

Homemakers' Clubs (Canada), 32

Hoopas, 181

hop industry, 91
Hopkins, Harry, 197–98, 199
Horsefall (First Nations worker), 154
Hoskins, Elias, 95
Hoskins, Te Kawehau Clea, 2, 8
"house niggers," use of term, 257
housing: Anishinaabeg, 137–38; of fur trade clerks and their partners, 153–54; status in building of, 90
Howard, Cyril, 246
Howard, Heather A.: essay by, 163–78; references to, 18
Howard, Sadie, 245
Howard, Vikki, 240, 247, 250–51
Howard Buckanaga, Gertrude: background of, 245–46; migration and education of, 246–47; mother's advice for, 242; oral history of, 240; on reservation conditions, 243; on ricing and blueberry picking, 241–42; as role model and mentor, 249, 251
Hubbell, Lorenzo, 122–24, 128, 129
Hudson's Bay Company (HBC): gender-related concerns of, 149–50; lives of men and their partners recruited by, 153; negotiations on role of women at factories of, 150–51; shíshálh attempt to sell cedar shingles to, 111; women's labor contracts with, 156–57, *157*
Huggins, Jackie, 4
Hui a Nga Kaimahi o Aotearoa (Meeting of Workers of New Zealand), 264–65
human rights discourse, 36
human subject research: ethical guidelines for, 3, 22n3
Hunt, Wanda Brown, 144
Hunter (schooner), 68–69
hunting: seasonal agricultural labor combined with, 168–69, 170–71; state regulations on, 138, 140–41. *See also* fishing; gathering activities

IAB. *See* Indian Affairs Branch
ICWA (Indian Child Welfare Act, U.S., 1978), 248
identity: of Blackness, 256–57; cultural, 57–58; self-defined vs. legislated, 2–3; states' definitions of, 17, 35; tribal, 218–19. *See also* Indigeneity
ImagineNATIVE, 4
indentured labor trade, Queensland: approach to, 8–9; colonial photography of, *73*, 73–76, *76*, *77*, 78–81, 82–84; colonization's shaping of agency in, 74, 81–84; labor law on, 75; slavery compared with, 74, 86n2;

sugar plantation labor described, 79–81; summary of, 84–85. *See also* South Sea Islanders
Indian: state definition of, 17, 35
Indian Act (Canada, 1876): appeal against "marrying out" clause, 15; gender discrimination effects of, 108, 110; gendered assumptions in, 112–13; "Indian" defined in, 17, 35; women's organizing against, 30
Indian Affairs Branch (IAB, Canada): Indian employment plan of, 234; Indian Homemakers' Clubs sponsored by, 225, 227–28, 229–30; labor programs for women of, 35, 159–61; male breadwinner defined by, 9; self-help rhetoric of, 225–26, 233
Indian Child Welfare Act (ICWA, U.S., 1978), 248
Indian Family Preservation Act (Minnesota, 1988), 249
Indian Friendship Centre (Thunder Bay, Ontario), 19
Indian Health Service (U.S.), 189, 242
Indian Homemakers' Clubs (Quebec and Ontario): activities and goals of, 227, 228–29, 232–35; approach to, 19, 225–26; colonial self-help rhetoric for, 233–34; constitution and structure of, 226–27, 232; conventions of, 228, 234; IAB workers and, 229–30; motto of, 229; summary of, 236–37
Indian Reorganization Act (U.S., 1934), 47, 144–45
Indian School Service (U.S.): hiring policy of, 211–14; Native women's understanding of system, 210–11; racism and sexism in, 216–22. *See also* Native American people-women as federal employees; residential and boarding schools
Indigeneity: blood quantum measures of, 14, 35; strategic type of, 14–15; women's organizations and, 225–26, 232–37
Indigenous people: assumed extinction of, 16; opposition to sovereignty of, 15; white Newcomers' power vs. androcentric roles among, 165–66. *See also* Aborigines; First Nations; Native American people; *and specific groups*
Indigenous socioeconomic complex concept, 164–66
Indigenous Studies, 2–4
Indigenous women: adaptive economic approaches of, 17–18; agency, politics, and, 39–40; centrality of, 40; "gendered racialization" of bodies, 32; Indigeneity and relationship to state, 225–26, 232–37;

mystification of, 27; occluded but essential to colonialism, 9–13; overview of, 1–5; as primary cultivators, 88; resiliency and versatility of, 20–21; scholarly perspectives on, 28–33; state scrutiny of white Australian, 75; strain of root gathering on, 153; in transnational context, 33–39; work as "charity" of, 194, 199, 202–4. *See also* creative adaptation; *and specific groups*
individualism: encouraged among woolgrowers and weavers, 129; federal hiring policy and, 211–12; fetishization of, 15; women's organizations in context of, 225–26, 232–36
Inkster, John, 153
intelligence tests, 187–88
intermarriage: key to Northfork Mono socioeconomic connections, 164–66; white men's insinuation through, 16; women's status rights lost in, 17, 22n7. *See also* marriage
interracial intimacy, critiqued, 257, 260
Inuit people, 36
Inuit women, labor contracts of, 157
iron ore industry, 31
Iroquois people, 5
Irwin, Kathie, 263–64
Isbister, James, 152–53

Jacobs, Margaret D.: essay by, 179–92; references to, 4, 12, 212
Jefferson, Thomas (Lummi), 93
Jeffries, Mary Anne, 104, *105*, 106, *106*, 117
Jeffries, Theresa M., 110, 114
Jeffries, Violet, 104, *105*, 117
Jervis Inlet (British Columbia), 111
Jobin, Lucy, 217
Joe, Benny, 107, 110, 114
Joe, Carrie, 104, *105*, 117
Joe, Clarence, 114, 115–16
Joe, Clarence, Sr., 113
Joe, Gilbert, 104–5, 111, 113
Joe, Grace, *121*
Joe, Madeline, 104, *105*, 110, 113–14, 117
Joe, Mary, 104, *105*, 117
Johnson, Andy, Sr., 113
Johnson, Dollie, 221–22
Johnson, Margaret, 98
Johnson, Mary, 22n4
Johnston, Adam, 167–68
Jones, Amelia, 244
Jourdain, Roger, 243
Jourdain, Winnie, 244, 245
Julian (shíshálh chief), 112
Julian, Chris, 111
Julian, Christine, 106, *106*, 117

Kahaleole Hall, Lisa, 15
Kanaka: use of term, 74, 83, 85n1. *See also* Pacific Islanders; South Sea Islanders-women
Kane, Salena, 210–11
Kangaroo Island. *See* Bass Strait region (Australia)
Kauanui, J. Kehaulani, 4
Kelly, James, 63
Keshena School (Keshena, Wisconsin), 218
Kessler-Harris, Alice, 13
Kettle Point Club (Indian Homemakers' Club), 228
King, Minnie C., 216
Kingbird, Ona, 247, 251
kinship and tribal relations: childcare shared among, 180, 183, 185; IAB rhetoric on, 233–34; knowledge based on place and, 109–11; reciprocity (*ke̓*) and, 120–21; sociopolitical and economic context of, 164–66; in women's work for federal agency, 212, 214–16; work forms linked to, 241–42. *See also* children; marriage
Klamaths, 181
Kline, Wendy, 188
Knack, Martha, 8
Knight Sugar Company (Canada), 160
knitting, 98, 106–7
knowledge systems: disruption of museum visitors' ideas about, *105*, 105–6; land use and property definitions, 114–15; place, ritual, spiritual, and kin-based, 109–11; place of song in, 22n4; traditional vs. Eurocentric, 2–3, 5–6
Kruger, Matilda, 213
Kunzel, Regina, 186

labor. *See* work
labor history: Aboriginal history entangled with, 39; feminist vs. Left's view of, 29; gaps in, 3, 8, 31–32, 78–79; intersectional approach in women's, 1–2; as male history, 9; new approaches to, 20–21; tourism work as challenge to, 137; transnational approach to, 33–34; universal assumptions in, 2–3; work-culture relation in, 38. *See also* history; methodology
labor organizing: exclusions of, 10, 11; Native women strike breakers marginalized and silenced, 39. *See also* trade union movement
Labrador Coast: women working for fur trade along, 155–57
Lac du Flambeau and Lac Courte Oreilles Ojibwe reservations: agricultural fairs of,

141–43, 144; dance and performance as work and income for, 142–44; depression-era jobs on, 144–45; economic changes on, 136–37; establishment of, 138; land sales encouraged by OIA, 140, 145; OIA industrial surveys of, 18, 136, 139–40; subsistence strategies of, 137–39; tourism and fishing on, 139

Ladies Relief Nursery (Oakland, California), 187

Ladies Sewing Guild (Cartwright, Labrador), 157

Lake, Marilyn, 9, 33

Landes, Ruth, 28

land issues: dispossession of, and labor reconfigurations, 166–69; expropriation of, 169, 258–59; Indigenous occupations of, 258, 265n6; Lummi woman and, 94–95; male head-of-household model in, 92; OIA encouragement of sales of, 140, 145; privatization of, 47; Western framework for, 108. *See also* allotments; relocation programs; reservations and reserves; *and specific peoples*

Landrine, Hope, 261

Lane, Clara, fur coat and sealskin boots created by, 157, *158*

Lane, Julius, 157

Langlois, Michel, 152

languages: Aboriginal survival linked to, 65, 66, 67–68; Maori, 235–36, 258; shásh-ishálem, 109, 111

Lawrence, Bonita, 16, 17, 35

Learning, Mary Bird, 157

Learning, Mary Jane, 156

Learning, William, 156

Ledger, Emma, 217–18

Lee, Gaylen D., 171

Leech Lake Reservation (Minnesota), 248, 249

Left political economy, 29, 38–39. *See also* sectarian Left

legibility of Indigenous women's lives: creative works in, 3, 5–8

leisure culture, 179, 181, 182

Lewis, Martin B., 168–69

Lewis, Meriwether, 6

literacies: creative works, 3, 5–8; traditional narratives vs. alphabetic-based, 5–6. *See also* knowledge systems; oral and life histories

Littlefield, Alice: essay by, 46–59; references to, 8, 17–18

lived experience: culture as, 38; Left's neglect of, 29; transnational approach linked to, 33–34. *See also* oral and life histories

livestock: Aboriginal women's pastoral work and, 67; *churro* sheep, 124–25, 126, 130; federal distribution of cattle to Seminole men, 195; government's reduction of, 130, 194

Livyeres: use of term, 155, 161n1

Locke, Cybèle: essay by, 254–67; references to, 20

logging by hand (British Columbia): demise of, 112; description of, 111–13; familial-based property in, 110; marginalized in industry, 114; "masculinization" of, 11, 107, 115, *116*; racialization of, 115; in shíshálh family economic strategies, 111, 113–17; women engaged in, 104–5, *105*, 110, 113, 115–17. *See also* shíshálh people

logging industry: alienation of lands by, 108; basketry's relation to, 107; changes in, due to environmental impact, 138; decline in Great Lakes region, 52, 56, 136; expansion of, 111–12; Ojibwas in, 50; sales of timber on reserves, 112–13; shíshálh's contributions to, 104–5

London Committee. *See* Hudson's Bay Company

Longest Walk (U.S., 1978), 247, 250

Los Angeles (California): Indian domestic workers in, 179; Indigenous mobility and, 19

Louie, Janet, 106, *106*, 117

Lovelace, Sandra, 15

Lower Muncey Club (Indian Homemakers' Club), 228–29

Lugard, Flora, 80

Lukecart, Julia DeCora, 214, *215*

lumbering. *See* logging industry

Lummi Agricultural Fair: agricultural and home economics exhibits at, 88; spud peeling contest at, 95, 95–96

Lummi Reservation, 88, 91–92, *93*, 96

Lummi women: characteristics of, 88; performing work characterized as male, 11; photographs of, *93*, *94*, *95*, *96*; potato cultivation models and families of, 97–98; potatoes cultivation of, 90–96, *94*

Macdonald, Robert, 6

MacGregor, William, 157, *158*

Madera (California): gaming debate in, 174; origins of, 169; shopping in, 171

male breadwinner/nuclear family model: assumptions about agricultural production based on, 92; concepts underlying, 9; governmental imposition of, 129–30, 211–12; IAB rhetoric on, 233–34; white imposition of, 28–29, 35. *See also* gender division of labor; gender normativity; patriarchy

"manifest domesticity" concept, 32
Maniwaki Club (Indian Homemakers' Club), 227
Maori Affairs department (Aotearoa/New Zealand): Maori Women's Welfare League sponsored by, 230–32; women's organization sponsored by, 225
Maori language (te reo Maori), 235–36, 258
Maori people: call for action of, 263–65; colonization's impact on, 255; land rights of, 6; recognized as Indigenous (*tangata whenua*), 22n5; sovereignty movement of, 16, 254–56. *See also* Aotearoa/New Zealand; Black men; Black Unity; Black women; Maori sovereignty demands
Maori People's Liberation Movement of Aotearoa, 264
Maori radicals. *See* Black Unity
Maori sovereignty demands: activism leading to, 258–59; Auckland trade unionists opposed to, 254; Black feminist stance and, 259–62; Black Unity conference paper on, 256–58; manifesto on, 263–64; political context of, 254–56; summary of, 265. *See also* Black Unity
Maori women: consciousness-raising among, 259; political leadership of, 19; status rights of, 2. *See also* Black feminism
Maori Women's Health League (Aotearoa/New Zealand), 19
Maori Women's Welfare League (Aotearoa/New Zealand): activities and goals of, 228, 232, 235–36; approach to, 19, 225–26; constitution and structure of, 231–32, 235–36; conventions of, 230–31, 235; motto of, 231; structure of, 228, 229; summary of, 236–37
maritime labor, 11. *See also* sealing industry; whaling industry
marriage: differences in expectations of, 12–13; IAB rhetoric on, 233–34; precontact Northfork Mono, 164–65; pregnant domestics' refusal of, 183–84; women's loss of rights in, 10–11. *See also* intermarriage; kinship and tribal relations
Martin, August, 95
Martin, Thelma, 227
Martin Nunez, Claudine, 171
Marxism: Black feminism's incorporation of, 265; Black Unity's critique of, 256, 257–58; study group on, 259. *See also* historical materialism
maternalism: differences in expectations of, 12–13. *See also* diverted mothering; domesticity; mothers and motherwork
maternity homes, 186. *See also* diverted mothering; Salvation Army Rescue Home (Oakland, California)
Matheson, Laurie, 3
Matler, Peggy, 248
mattress-making project: background and goals of, 196–97; as domestic in nature, 198–99; end of, 205n7; Navajo women in, *193*, 193–94; opposition to, 197–98
Mauritius: Aboriginal women's travels to area of, 67–70
Maxwell, Gilbert, 127
McCain, H., 197
McCallum, Mary Jane Logan: essay by, 225–39; references to, 19, 20, 32
McCarthy, Helen, 165
McClurken, James M., 49–50
McDonald, Archibald, 153–54
McDonald, Ellen, 153–54
McDonald, R. C., 110
McDougall, Mrs. A., 227
McDougall, Susie, 219
McEachern, Allan, 22n4
McGrath, Ann: on Aboriginal workers and wages, 10, 67; on child removal policies, 12; on gender roles, 11; as influence, 4; on knowledge systems, 2
McHalsie, Naxaxalhts'i Albert (Sonny), 6
McKenna-McBride Commission (British Columbia), 112
McKenzie, Roberta, 243
McLeay, Alex, 69
M'Closkey, Kathy: essay by, 120–35; references to, 18
McNab, Robert, 61
McNary, Charles L., 220
McNeal, Lyle, 130
McPhee, John, 122
mechanization, agricultural, 79–80, 93–94, 96, 173
Medicine, Beatrice, 30
Meeting of Workers of New Zealand (Hui a Nga Kaimahi o Aotearoa), 264–65
mental hospitals, 187–88
methodology: community-based research, 108–9; oral history sources, 46–47, 107–8; scholarly dialogue as, 27; transnational dialogue as, 3–4; women's voices recovered, 32–33, 39. *See also* oral and life histories; photography
Métis men: Hollywood depictions of, 37; work at fur trade post, 154–55. *See also* First Nations
Métis women: agricultural work of, 154–55, 159–61, *160*; contradictory characterizations of fur trade roles of, 148–53; daily activi-

ties of, 152–53; fur factory roles of, 150–51; labor contracts for, 154–57, *157*; partners of, recruited by fur companies, 153–54; recovering history of, 33; white men's marriages with, 16. *See also* First Nations–women; fur industry

Metoxyn, Julia Wheelock, 218

Meyer, Manulani Aluli, 4

Michelin, Hannah (née Brook), 156, 157

Michigan: assimilation policies in, 49–50; industrial economic decline in, 54–55; occupations in, 49; residential schools for Indian children in, 50–53; urban shift in, 53–54; U.S. policy environment in, summarized, 47–48. *See also* Anishinaabeg; Anishinaabe women

Michigan Indian Employment and Training Service, 55

migrants and migration: Anishinaabeg, 52–54, 57; Maori people, 255; Northfork Mono people, 173–74; Ojibwe, 240–41, 243–44

Mihesuah, Devon, 4

Millet, Jean-Francis, 82

Million, Dian, 4

Minneapolis American Indian Center, 245, 250

Minneapolis–Saint Paul: education in, 246–47; Native leadership in, 245–47; Ojibwe migration to, 240–41, 243–44; Ojibwe personal networks in, 244–45; Ojibwe women's politically purposeful white-collar labor in, 247–52

Minnesota: racial segregation in, 242–43. *See also* Minneapolis–Saint Paul

Minnesota Department of Human Services, 248–49

Minnesota Indian Women's Resource Center, 248–49

Minturn vineyards (California), 170, *170*, 171

miscegenation, 75, 78. *See also* racial ideologies and stratification; racism

missions: attempts to remove Indigenous women from manual labor by, 12; Northfork Mono people's strategies and, 169; Tasmanian Aborigines incarcerated at, 65–66, 67, 70. *See also* Board of Indian Commissioners

mobility: colonial permits for, 112. *See also* migrants and migration

Mohanram, Radhika, 4

Monos, 181. *See also* Northfork Mono people

Montana: Native teachers and schools in, 218; sewing project in Cut Bank, 200–204

Monture-Angus, Patricia, 4, 160

Moore, Carl, 189

Morago, Jessie, 214–15

Morrison, George, 245

mothers and motherwork: homes for unwed, 183; IAB rhetoric on, 233–34; pensions for, 179, 185–86; state regulation of, 32; treatment of unwed Indian, 186–89. *See also* diverted mothering; domesticity; maternalism

Mt. Diablo Country Club (near San Francisco), 182

Mt. Pleasant Indian School (Mt. Pleasant, Michigan), 50–52, 53–54

multiculturalism, 15–16

mythologies, national, 14, 36–37

Nahovay (Cree woman), 153

NAPT, 4

Nash, Walter, 236

National Black Women's Conference (New Zealand), 261–62

National Committee on Maori Education (Aotearoa/New Zealand), 236

Native American and Indigenous Studies Association (NAISA), 4

Native American/Native Studies programs, 32–33

Native American people: childcare among, 180; eugenicists on, 188–89; expected extinction of, 16, 188; federal wage work for, 194; sovereignty rights of, 16. *See also* Anishinaabeg; child removal policies; First Nations; Navajo people; Northfork Mono people; Ojibwas/Chippewas; Ottawas/ Odawas

—women: "charity" work of, 194, 199, 202–4; decline of power of, 195–96, 204n1; forced sterilization of, 12, 188–89; New Deal extended to, 200–204; pathologized in child removal policies, 212; political organizing by, 30; unwed mothers labeled as mentally ill, 187–88. *See also* Anishinaabe women; Blackfeet women; diverted mothering; domestic "outing" program; Lummi women; Navajo people-women; Northfork Mono people-women; Ojibwe women

—women as federal employees: agency hiring policy and, 211–14; civil service exam of, 212, 222n4; job openings for, 99; photographs of, *221*; racism and sexism faced by, 216–22; retirement benefits and, 19, 214, *215*, 219–22; summary of, 222; training for urban jobs, 242; women's understanding of system, 210–11; work experiences of, 214–16

Native Daughters (organization), 187

Native Women's Association of Canada (NWAC), 4, 30

natural resources: commodification of, 140; environmental concerns about, 138; land dispossession for settler access to, 166–67. *See also* agriculture; cedar tree; coastal forest; commodity production; fishing; hunting; gathering activities; logging industry; sealing industry; subsistence activities; whaling industry

Navajo people: *churro* sheep of, 124–25, 126, 130; gaps in scholarship on, 132n2; historical context of, 121–22; kinship and reciprocity (*kè*) among, 120–21; livestock reduced by government, 130, 194; male breadwinner model imposed on, 129–30; poverty of, 123, 126, 131

—women: adaptive economic approaches of, 17, 18; as cultural performers vs. workers, 120–21; decline of power of, 123–24, 204n1; as identified in ledger books, 132n3; male breadwinner model imposed on, 129–30; mattress-making project and, *193*, 193–94; photographs of, *121*, *193*, 193–94; on weaving, 130; weaving production of, marginalized, 126–27. *See also* Navajo weaving

Navajo weaving: blanket transformed into rug, 126; centrality of, 120–21; commodification of, 18; "domestication" of production of, 126–27; global context of, 125–26; historical context of, 121–22; photographs of, *123*; plummeting price for, 128–29; reflections on, 131; traders' coopting of, 122–24; women's voices on, 130; wool values and, 124–25. *See also* wool and textile markets

New Deal (U.S.): gendered policies of, 18, 193–94; Indian-federal relations reformed in, 47; specific programs: Civilian Conservations Corps-Indian Division, 194, *195*, 197, 199, *201*, 202; Economic Recovery Administration, 53. *See also* federal work relief projects; Great Depression; Indian Reorganization Act; Works Project Administration

New Mexico: mattress-making project in, *193*, 193–94; trading posts and Navajo weaving in, 127–29

New Zealand. *See* Aotearoa/New Zealand

New Zealand Federation of Labour (NZFoL), 256, 264–65

New Zealand Socialist Unity Party (SUP), 255–56, 265n3

Ngapuhi people, 15, 22n5

Ngā Tamatoa (Young Warriors), 258–60, 264

Ngāti Whātua o Ōrākei Maori, 258, 265n6

Ngā Tuahine, 262

Nicolson, Marianne, 7

Nixon, Richard M., 47

Noble, W. B., 169

North America: perspectives on post-WWII Aboriginal work in, 28–33; politics and research connected in, 27; politics of history in, 39–40; questions about borders in, 33–39. *See also* Canada; United States

Northern Drivers' Union (New Zealand), 255–56

Northfork Mono people: current membership of, 177n3; federal recognition of, 173–74, 175; gendered labor and status relations among, 164–66; land dispossession and labor reconfigurations of, 166–69; Rancheria of, 167, 169–70, 173–74, 176–77n1, 177nn2–3; subsistence cycle of dual dependency, 168–69; wage labor of, 168, 169, 171; website of, 177n1. *See also* Monos

—women: adaptation to land dispossession, 166–69; approach to, 18, 163–64, 175–76; current labor of, 173–74; marriage and intermarriage in socioeconomic system of, 164–66; social life of farm labor camps and, 170–73; transformation and adaptability of, 175–76; as tribal leaders, 174

North West Company, 149, 150, 153–55

Nottawaseppi Huron Band (Potawatomis), 46–47, 51–52, 55. *See also* Anishinaabe women

Nunavut (Canadian territory), 36

NWAC (Native Women's Association of Canada), 4, 30

NZFoL (New Zealand Federation of Labour), 256, 264–65

objects: narratives embedded in, 5–7

occupations of women. *See* basket making; beadwork; commodity production; craft entrepreneurialism; domestic service; fur industry; Indian School Service; logging by hand; potato cultivation; sealing industry; seasonal agricultural labor; subsistence activities; tourism; whaling industry

Office of Indian Affairs (OIA, U.S.): determined to halt dance and performance, 142–44; industrial surveys on reservations by, 18, 136, 139–40; land sales encouraged by, 140, 145; Native women's understanding of hiring policies at, 210–11, 213–14; racism and sexism in, 216–22; retirement benefit requirements of, 219–22; tourist-related

activities deployed against, 137–45. *See also*
Bureau of Indian Affairs; Commissioner of
Indian Affairs; Indian School Service
Ojibwas/Chippewas: areas of, 48; subsistence
strategies of, 137–39; urban migration of,
240–41, 243–44. *See also* Anishinaabeg;
Lac du Flambeau and Lac Courte Oreilles
Ojibwe reservations
Ojibwe women: commodity sales to tourists
by, 141–43; jobs of, in urban areas, 242–43;
as leaders, 245–47; multiple occupations of,
136; personal networks of, 244–45; politically purposeful white-collar labor of, 20,
247–52; urban migration of, 240–41, 243–
44. *See also* Anishinaabe women; Saginaw
Chippewa women
Oklahoma: Indian schools in, 210–11, 214
Oneida Club (Indian Homemakers' Club),
227
O'Neill, Colleen: essay by, 193–209; references
to, 18, 129, 163
one-story-fits-all narrative, 31
Ontario: Tyendinaga Mohawk Territory in,
225. *See also* Indian Homemakers' Clubs
Ontario Native Women's Association
(ONWA), 4
oral and life histories: avoiding Western
frameworks in, 108–9; on Navajo weaving,
120–21; politically purposeful work highlighted in, 240–52; recovery of women's,
32–33, 39, 107–8; on residential school experiences, 50–53; on seasonal agricultural
labor, 170–73; of South Sea Islanders, 75
Oregon: Indian schools in, 181, 216, 220, *221*
Orpheus (ship), 69
Otara Black Women's Group, 262
Ottawas/Odawas: areas of, 48; birch-bark
boxes made by, 52; Burt Lake Band, 46–47;
wage labor of, 49–50; WWII service and
occupations of, 52
outing matrons (BIA): adoption promoted by,
179, 184–85, 186–87; workers' complaints
to, 181–82; workers' pregnancies and, 179,
182–84

Pacific Conference, nuclear-free and indepen-
dent (1981), 256
Pacific Islanders, 9, 74–75, 81–82, 263. *See also*
South Sea Islanders
Painter, Betsy (Deer), 157
Paiutes, 181, 187
Pakeha: use of term, 22n2
Palestinian Liberation Organization (PLO),
258

Paquette, Mary, 213–14
Parman, Donald, 202
Pascoe, Peggy, 34
patriarchy: Black feminist critique of, 31,
259–62. *See also* gender division of labor;
gender normativity; male breadwinner/
nuclear family model
Pattee, Lottie Smith, 215
Paul, Elizabeth and Eugene, 97–98
Paul, Ellen, 106, *106*, 117
Paul, Mrs. Dan, 113
Peacore, Maude, 214
Peake, Emily, 244–45, 251
Peake Raymond, Margaret, 248
Pearis, H. B., 214
Pendleton Woolen Mills (U.S.), 123
pensions: civil service exam to qualify for,
222n4; denied to Native teachers, 19, 220;
files for, 214, *215*; U.S. legislation on federal,
219–22
performance: in Anishinaabeg subsistence
strategies, 139; behavior and work definitions in context of, 142–44; at men's prison,
269
Perry, Adele, 36
Philip, Arthur, 60–61
Phoenix Indian School (Phoenix, Arizona),
219
photography: civil service use of, *221*; conditions and women's work evidenced in,
73–75, 78–81; discursive representations in,
82–83; ideological composition of, 83–84;
indentured women workers, examples
of, *73*, 73–74, *76*, *77*; of Navajo woman at
mattress-making project, *193*, 193–94; portrait shots of Islanders, 85; Western ideas
disrupted by, *105*, 105–6, *106*
Piatote, Beth H.: essay by, 268–70; references
to, 3, 4, 7–8
Picard, Sophie, 218
pictographs, 110
"pin money" argument, 127
Pipestone Indian Boarding School (Pipestone,
Minnesota), 246
Place, Earl, 217
PLO (Palestinian Liberation Organization), 258
Point Elliott Treaty Council, 90, 99n1
political activism: class-based stance in,
255–56; gender incorporated into studies
of, 251–52; governmental spaces for, 32; left-
ist turn in, 29; male and female leadership
in, 249–52; transnational approach to, 33;
women's role in, 30. *See also* grassroots activism; urban community activism

Polkenhorn, Lou Ann, 171–72
Polynesian Resource Center: evicted from Trade Union Centre, 254, 256, 258, 264; goals and political activities of, 255–56; workshops for Black women in, 262
Pomona, Ruby, 171
Pomos, 181
Popenoe, Paul, 188–89
Port Jackson (Australia), 60–61
postcolonial paradigms, 37, 40
potato cultivation: characterized as male work, 11; competition in, 96; depression-era, 96–97, 97, 98–99; long-standing practices of, 88; meanings and status of cultivating, 90–91; models of, 97–98; as primary subsistence and commercial activities, 91–92; request for machines for, 93–94; on reservations, 90–91; self-sufficiency linked to, 92–93; spud peeling contest and, 95, 95–96; women as primary agents in, 89–90, 95–96, 154–55. *See also* Lummi women
Potawatomis/Bodawatomis, 48. *See also* Anishinaabeg; Nottawaseppi Huron Band
power relations: local exchanges and histories of, 34; questions about, 40; in transnational approach, 34–35. *See also* colonialism; gender normativity; governmental policy
Presbyterian Indian Mission (California), 169
production: definition of, 21
productive coexistence: use of term, 163–64
psychological testing, 187–88
public/private dichotomy, 9, 11–12, 13

Qu'Appelle Industrial School (Labret, Saskatchewan), 159
Qu'Appelle post journal, 153–54
Quarts de Lodges, 152–53
Quebec Native Women's Association, 4
Queensland (Australia): colonial photography in, 73, 73–76, 76, 77, 78–81, 82–84; legal limits on Indigenous employment in, 78–79; plantation sizes in, 79; women and children domestic workers in, 80–81. *See also* indentured labor trade

racial ideologies and stratification: blood quantum measures and, 14, 35; in civil rights discourse, 15; differences across states, 36–37; plantation field labor and, 11, 79–84; structural type of, 19. *See also* miscegenation; racism
racialization: of adoption, 184–85; of motherhood, 179, 185–86; of psychological testing, 187–88; of women's bodies, 32; of work, 115

racism: Black feminist critique of, 260–62; Black Unity conference paper on, 256–58; Black Unity's critique of, 254–55; Native American federal employees' encounters with, 216–22; Ngā Tamatoa's critique of, 258–59; South African rugby team tour and, 262–63; women's work in context of, 9–13. *See also* miscegenation; racial ideologies and stratification
Raglan Golf Course occupation, 258, 265n6
Ramirez, Renya, 4, 16, 33
Rasmussen, Birgit Brander, 5, 6
RCMP (Royal Canadian Mounted Police), 227
Red Lake Reservation (Minnesota), 243, 244, 247–48
Red Power movement, 29
Red School House (Minneapolis), 247
Reichard, Gladys, 120–21, 124, 127
relocation programs: differences across states, 35; forced, 28–29; Potawatomis from Michigan, 49; urban migration due to, 19, 53, 56, 240–41, 243–44; women's labor in aftermath, 242–43. *See also* allotments; land issues
Renanghi (Sarah Dutton), 66–67, 69
reservations and reserves: as contact zones, 17; established in Wisconsin, 138; expropriated by ranchers and agribusiness, 169; failures of, 164; federal relief programs extended to, 18, 193, 193–95, 199–200; few jobs for women on (1950s on), 242–43; infrastructure lacking on, 194, 243–44; logging income for building construction on, 111–12, 117n3; masculinization of initial agricultural attempts on, 88, 92; potato cultivation on, 90–91; shíshálh sales of timber on, 112–13; termination policy impact on, 173–74, 177n3; treaty cover-ups and, 166–67; urban relocation from, 19; women as heads of households on, 98; women living off and on, 16–18. *See also* allotments; migrants and migration; relocation programs; *and specific reservations*
reservation shopping, 175
residential and boarding schools: acculturation and gender normativity in, 28–29, 35; assimilation as goal of, 47, 180–81, 210–11; boys trained for agriculture and manual labor at, 28, 50, 180; dilemmas fostered by goals of, 185–86, 189; domestic training for girls at, 159–61, 160, 180–81, 194, 217, 242; family and kin model for, 212; Native American women teachers of, 213–14, 219–20, 221; oral histories about, 50–53;

unwed Indian mothers' children placed in, 186–87. *See also* child removal policies; domestic "outing" program; education; Indian School Service; Native American people-women as federal employees
Restigouche Club (Indian Homemakers' Club), 227
Rice, Louise, 227
rituals, "first crop," 90
Robertson, Thomas, 226
Robinson, George Augustus, 62, 65
Robinson, Rose, 240, 241, 248–49, 251
Rodd, Mildred, 234–35
Rohde, Melissa: essay by, 136–47; references to, 18
Roosevelt, Eleanor, 199, 200
Roosevelt, Franklin D. *See* New Deal
Ropiha, Topi, 231
Ross, Luana, 33
Roy, Susan: essay by, 104–19; references to, 11
Royal, Rangi, 230
Royal Canadian Mounted Police (RCMP), 227
Royce, Bonnie, 186, 187
rugby, 262–63
Ruiz, Vicki, 38
Russell, Lynette: essay by, 60–72; references to, 4, 11
Ryan Hotel (Saint Paul), 244

Saginaw Chippewa women: approach to, 46–47; occupations of, 53–54; postwar economy and occupations of, 54–55. *See also* Anishinaabe women; Burt Lake Band; Ojibwe women
Salem Indian School (aka Chemawa School, Salem, Oregon), 181, 216, 220, *221*
salmon: limitations of focus solely on, 89, 90, 99; seasonal agriculture combined with fishing for, 168–71
Salois, Mary B., 196–97, 200, 205n5
Salvation Army Rescue Home (Oakland, California), 183, 184
Sam, Susan, 98
San Francisco (California): access to leisure culture in, 179; Indian domestic workers drawn to, 181, 182; Northfork Mono people's move to, 173–74; potato sales in, 91. *See also* domestic "outing" program
San Francisco Children's Agency, 186
Sangster, Joan: essay by, 27–45; references to, 4, 5, 8, 9, 175, 188
San Joaquin Valley (California): acorn-centered subsistence in, 165, 167–69; gendered labor and status relations in, 164–66; inva-

sion and occupation of, 163–64; land dispossession and labor reconfigurations in, 166–69; Northfork Mono women's seasonal labor in, 169–73, *170*; postwar policy shifts in, 173–74; reflections on Northfork Mono women in, 174–76
Santeo, Nellie, 219
Saskatchewan (Canada): demographic shift debated in, 148–49; Indian Homemakers' Club in, 226; women as rural laborers in, 159–61, *160*; women's work at trading posts in, 153–55
Saunders, Isabella (Pottle), 157, *157*
Schulz, Jessie Donaldson, 202
Schwab, Robert W., 198
sealing industry (Australia): Aboriginal women's travels and, 67–70; accommodation to new circumstances in, 64–65; approach to, 11; historical context of, 60–61; Renanghi and Dutton as couple involved in, 66–67, 69; Southeastern Australia grounds for (map), 62; women's centrality to, 61–64. *See also* Tasmanian Aboriginal communities
seasonal agricultural labor: fur trade economies linked to, 151–52; grape harvest and cotton picking as, 169, 170, *170*, 171–73; Indian Homemakers' Club members and, 228–29; of Métis women, 154–55, 159–61, *160*; Northfork Mono women's adaptation of, 18, 169–73, *170*; urban adaptation of, 247; wages of, 172
Sechelt First Nation. *See* shíshálh people
sectarian Left (New Zealand), 254, 256, 264. *See also* Left political economy
self-help rhetoric, 225–26, 232–33. *See also* individualism
Seminole men, 195
Seneca Indian School (Wyandotte, Oklahoma), 214
service work. *See* domestic service; tourism
settler colonialism: characteristics common in, 34; colonized labor as invisible in, 8–13; differences across states, 36; doctrines of, 13–14; necessity for Indian agricultural production for, 91; pioneer "creation" myths of, 14; structural amnesia of, 75–76; violence of, in California, 163–64, 166–67. *See also* Aotearoa/New Zealand; Australia; Canada; colonialism; United States
Seweler, John, 68
sewing projects: domestic work rooms for, 198; garment projects, 200–204, *201*; Indian Homemakers' Clubs linked to, 227; unemployed women shunted into, 199–200. *See*

also clothing production; mattress-making project

sexism: Black feminist critique of, 259, 260–62; Native American federal employees' encounters with, 216–22; women's work in context of, 9–13

sexuality: delinquency attached to Indian women's, 186–89; essentialist views of, 261; urban opportunities for exploring, 182–83

sexual labor, 60–62

sháshishálem (language), 109, 111

Shastas, 181

Shawnee Indian School (Shawnee, Oklahoma), 210–11

Sherman, Paula, 4

Sherman Institute (Perris, California), 181

shíshálh people: church and school construction of, 112, 117n3; coastal forest used by, 104–5; economic and cultural strategies of, 106–7, 113–17; family connections and territory of, 109, 109–11, 114–17; gender roles among, 11, 107; land use issues for, 114–15; research program of, 108–9; territorial rights and logging of, 111–13, 114. *See also* logging by hand; tems swiya Museum —women: basket making of, 106, 106; Indian Act's discrimination effects on, 108, 110; logging by, 104–5, 105, 110, 113, 115–17; marginalization of, 114–15; as "skookum," 104, 107–8

Shoemaker, Nancy, 4

Shoshones, 181, 184, 203

Sickels (OIA superintendent), 140

Sierra Nevada Mountains, 164–65, 167

Simpson, Audra, 4

Simpson, Leanne, 4

Sinclair, Mary, 153

Sinclair, William, 153

Sioux Tribe, Devils Lake (North Dakota), 185

sit-ins and boycotts, 111, 243, 250

skookum women: use of term, 104, 107–8

Slaugh, Forest S., 203

slave: use of term, 9

slavery, 8–9, 74, 86n2

Smith, Andrea, 37

Smith-Lever Act (U.S., 1914), 201

Social Security Act (U.S.), 185–86

Sonoma State Home (California), 187–89, 190n26

South African rugby team tour, 262–63

Southern Spring Bed Company, 198

South Sea Islanders: deported from Queensland, 75; mortality rate of, 74, 81–82 —women: approach to, 9; colonial photography of, 73, 73–76, 76, 77, 78–81, 82–84; colonization's shaping of agency of, 74, 81–84; resistance of, 85; summary of, 84–85

Southwest (U.S.): wool and textile trade of, 121–22, 127–29

sovereignty: advocacy for, 249–52; definition of, 19. *See also* Maori sovereignty demands

The Sower (iconic images), 82

Springbok Rugby Tour (1981), 262–63

Squamish territory. *See* logging by hand; shíshálh people

Stasiulis, Daiva K., 2

state: conceptualization of, 21n1. *See also* citizenship; governmental policy; *and specific policies and agencies*

Stately, Alvina, 244

Stately, Fanny, 244

state multiculturalism concept, 15–16

sterilization, 12, 188–89

Stern, Alexandra Minna, 188

Stern, Bernard J., 89, 99n3

Stevens, Isaac, 90

Stevenson, Winona, 2, 12

Stewart Indian School (Carson City, Nevada), 181, 186–87

Stockton Mental Hospital (California), 187

strategic indigeneity concept, 14–15

Strong, Joanne, 250

subsistence activities: acorn-centered, 165, 167–69; commodity production combined with, 137–38, 139, 151–52; dual dependency in, 168–69; wild rice gathering, 137, 139, 144, 241–42, 251–52. *See also* commodity production; fishing; gathering activities; hunting; seasonal agricultural labor; wage labor

sugar beet growing, Canada, 159–60

sugar industry, Australia: field labor in, described, 79–81; gender and racial stratification of labor in, 11, 79–84; indentured laborers photographed, 73, 73–76, 76, 77, 78–84; summary of indentured women's work in, 84–85

SUP (New Zealand Socialist Unity Party), 255–56, 265n3

A Survey of the Contemporary Indians of Canada (Hawthorne Report), 9, 28

surveys, 9, 18, 28, 96, 136, 139–40

"surviving school" projects, 247, 250, 251

Suttles, Wayne, 92

Swain, Martha, 199

Szazy, Mira, 230

Tainui Awhiro Maori, 258, 265n6

TANS (True American Native Students), 250

Tapio, Melissa, 244, 250

Tasmanian Aboriginal communities: cultural survival of, 64–66; historical context of, 60–61; sealing industry of, 61–64; sources on, 70n2; travels of women from, 67–70; whale station operations and, 66–67. *See also* sealing industry

Taylor, Ruth: essay by, 104–19; references to, 11

Taylor, Thomas, 68

Teabo, Dollie, 216

Teabo, Joseph, 216

Tel-es-cl-wet (shíshálh woman), 110

tems swiya Museum (British Columbia), 104–6, *105*, 108

te reo Maori (Maori language), 235–36, 258

Terman, Lewis, 188

terra nullius doctrine, 13

Te Wheoro, Wiremu, 15

Tex, Grace, 170–71

textile goods: carpet manufacturing and wool classification in, 125–26. *See also* knitting; mattress-making project; Navajo weaving; sewing projects; weaving; wool and textile markets

Tillie Hardwick et al. v. United States (1983), 173–74

Tom, Elizabeth, 98

Tom, Laura and Elizabeth, 98

Tomah School (Tomah, Wisconsin), 214, 218

totems, pictographs as, 110

Tough, Frank, 38

tourism: casinos and, 48, 55, 56, 58, 173–74; decline of logging and shift to, 136–37; depression-era employment in, 144–45; ideological debates juxtaposed to, 141–44; performance labor in, 37–38; railroad advertising of, 139, 142; in subsistence strategies, 18, 50, 56, 136–45. *See also* commodity production; craft entrepreneurialism

Towns, Robert, 83

trade union movement
—Australia: Aboriginal men excluded from, 10
—New Zealand: Black Unity's critique of, 254, 256, 257–58; changing stance of, 264–65; political context of, 255–56

trading posts
—Canada: account books of, 151; companies' concerns about women at, 149–50; women's work at, 153–55. *See also* fur industry
—United States: "domestication" of Navajo weavers in structure of, 126–27; free trade context of, 127–29; historic site of, 132n1;

Hubbell's role in, 122–24; Navajo textile production and, 122; reflections on, 131. *See also* wool and textile markets

transnational approach: challenges of, 34–39; concept of, 33–34, 40n4

transportation issues: canoe construction, 152; Indian agricultural crops and, 96; seasonal agricultural labor and, 172

Trask, Haunani-Kay, 14

Traxler, Jeanette, 184

treaties: land and resource dispossession linked to, 166–68, 177nn2–3; land cessions in, 138; made and nullified, 14; oral negotiations vs. records of, 6; Point Elliott, 99n1; Waitangi, 15, 22n5, 256, 258, 264, 265n5

tribal governments: growth of enterprises of, 57–58; termination of, 47; women's jobs in, 54–55

Tribally Controlled Community College Bill (Minnesota, 1978), 247

Trotter, Chris, 255

True American Native Students (TANS), 250

Tsimshian nation, 22n4. See also *Delgamuukw v. British Columbia*

Turner, Herbert, 76, 78, 80

Turnor, Philip, 153

Twin Cities Chippewa Tribal Council, 245

Tyack, Jack, 68, 69

unemployment advice, 197

United Congress of Maori and Pacific Women, 262

United Indian Traders Association (UITA), 129

United Nations Declaration on the Rights of Indigenous Peoples, 15, 22n6

United Nations Human Rights Committee, 15

United State: women of color as workers and mothers in, 180

United States: agricultural extension agents' goals in, 200–204; blood quantum rules in, 14, 35; civil rights discourse in, 15; colonization in, 13–14; motherwork regulated in, 32; pioneer "creation" myths of, 14; recognition of tribes in, 47–48, 56; slavery and labor definitions in, 9; wool imports of, 125–26. *See also* Bureau of Indian Affairs; colonialism; Dawes Act; Native American people; New Deal; Office of Indian Affairs; trading posts-U.S.; *and specific states*

United Women's Conventions (1970s), 259, 260–61

Upper Midwest American Indian Center, 241, 245, 246, 247

urban areas: Anishinaabeg migration to, 52–
54, 57; appeal of working in, 181, 182, 244;
Northfork Mono people's move to, 173–74;
Ojibwe migration to, 240–41, 243–44;
Ojibwe women's jobs in, 242–43; representations of Native women in, 175; sexual opportunities in, 182–83, 186–89
urban community activism: approach to,
19–20, 240; formal and informal networks
in, 246–47; migration as context of, 240–41,
243–44; Native women's politically purposeful white-collar labor in, 247–52. *See
also* grassroots activism; Minneapolis-Saint
Paul; political activism
urban mobility, 19. *See also* migrants and migration; urban areas
U.S. Congress, 47–48, 56
U.S. General Accounting Office, 189
U.S. Senate, 96

Van Every, Mildred, 183, 184–85, 186
Van Gogh, Vincent, 82
Van Kirk, Sylvia, 30, 149
van Valkenburgh, Richard, 122
victimization: rejection of, 60
Victor, Winifred and Peter, 97
Victoria (queen), 15, 22n5
Victoria Students' League (Wellington), 264
vineyards. *See* grape harvest
violence: indentured women workers in
Queensland and, 80–81, 85; latent type of,
82; in name of state sovereignty, 37; in sealing industry, 64

Wabie, Bernadette, 160
wage labor: adaptation to various occupations, 168, 169, 171, 196; assumption of
assimilation and, 57–58; attitudes toward
Aboriginal, 28–29; racialized expectations
of women in, 179, 185–86; in subsistence
strategies, 138–39. *See also* creative adaptation; federal work relief projects; labor history; seasonal agricultural labor
wages: domestic workers, 12–13; "half-caste
apprenticeship scheme" for, 10; knitting
sweaters vs. cannery work, 106–7; Lummi
men vs. women, 92–93; Navajo weaving
vs. waged labor, 127; Ojibwe female urban
migrants, 244; sewing projects, 227; work
relief projects, 200–201, 205n9
Waitangi, Treaty of (Aotearoa/New Zealand,
1840), 15, 22n5, 256, 258, 264, 265n5
Waitangi Action Committee, 264
Waitangi Day (Feb. 6), 258

Waitangi Tribunal (Aotearoa/New Zealand),
22n5
Walker, George Washington, 67–68
Walker, Susie, *170*
wampum as narrative, 5
Wanhalla, Angella, 4, 17
WARN (Women of All Red Nations), 30
Washoes, 181
water as gendered space, 242
Wateripitau (Aboriginal woman), 69
weaving: Lac du Flambeau unit for, 145;
Maori, survival of, 236; OIA surveys of,
139–40. *See also* basket making; Navajo
weaving; wool and textile markets
Webb, Sarah Jane, 157, *157*
Weisiger, Marsha, 195
Weiss, Larry, 126
Western Mono. *See* Northfork Mono people
whaling industry, 61, 66–67
White, Marie, 184
White Crow (First Nations worker), 155
White Earth Reservation: childhood on, 241;
child removal from, 247–48; migration
from, 243–44, 245–46; petition to retain
teacher from, 219
White Hawk, Sandra, 247
"whiteness," 21, 37
white women: Black feminist critique of,
260–62; under colonial regime, 10–11; failure to build horizontal alliances, 21; Indian
domestic servants placed with, 180–90;
Maori rejection of relations with, 257, 260;
political enfranchisement sought by settlers, 8; womanhood and differences across
states, 37. *See also* child removal policies;
settler colonialism
WI (Women's Institutes), 229
wild rice (*manoomin*), 137, 139, 144, 241–42,
251–52
Williams, Aubry, 197
Williams, Carol: introduction by, 1–25
Williams, Jemima (Martin/Perry), 157, *157*
Wilson, Mary Jane, 250
Wisconsin: agricultural fairs in, 141–43, 144;
depression-era employment in, 144–45;
fishing, hunting, and other state regulations
in, 138, 140–41; industrial surveys on reservations in, 18, 136, 139–40; Native teachers
and schools in, 213–14, 218; sewing project
in Milwaukee, *198*, 200; tourism in, 137–45.
See also Anishinaabe women; Lac du
Flambeau and Lac Courte Oreilles Ojibwe
reservations
Wisconsin v. Morrin (1908), 138

Witherspoon, Gary, 126
wives: use of term, 151
women: regulatory regime for white vs.
  Indigenous, 10–11; reproductive labor of,
  12–13; sexual labor of, 60–62; universalized
  category of, 8. *See also* Indigenous women;
  white women; *and specific groups*
Women for Aotearoa, 263
Women in Prisons Collective, 262
Women of All Red Nations (WARN), 30
Women's Institutes (WI), 229
Women's National Indian Association, 180
women's organizations. *See* grassroots activism; urban community activism
Wong, Sau-ling, 180
Woodward, Ellen S., 197, 205n7
wool and textile markets: classification of
  wools for, 125–26; competition in, 127–29;
  Navajo pastoralists incorporated into, 120,
  122; quality of postreservation goods, 131;
  sheep breeds and, 124–25; U.S. tariff and,
  120, 125, 126, 128; volatility of, 124. *See also*
  Navajo weaving; trading posts
Woolgrowers' Associations (Arizona and New
  Mexico), 129
Woorrady (Aboriginal woman), 62
work: acculturation policy and, 35; assumptions about tropical plantation labor of
  whites, 81–82; as "charity," 194, 199, 202–4;
  collective practices of, 241–42; complexity

of paid/voluntary reality, 228–29; definitions of, 31, 137, 142–44; iconic images of,
  82–83; ideal worker characteristics, 9; invisibility of, in colonialism, 8–13; as key in
  civilizing mission, 13, 82–84, 212–13; motherwork as, 32; mystification of Indigenous
  women's, 27; permeable boundaries of domestic and manual, 11–12; racialization of,
  115. *See also* creative adaptation; economy;
  gender division of labor; labor history; subsistence activities; wage labor; *and specific
  occupations*
Workers' Communist League, 262–63, 264,
  266n11
Works Project Administration (WPA, U.S.):
  establishment of, 205n2; mattress-making
  project of, *193*, 193–94; men privileged in,
  199–200; Minneapolis project of, 245; wage
  work provided by, 194–95. *See also* federal
  work relief projects; sewing projects
World War II, 52, 240–41
Wounded Knee II (U.S.), 250
Wright, Rumatiki, 231

Young Warriors (Ngā Tamatoa), 258–60, 264
Yuval-Davis, Nira, 21n1
YWCA, Four Winds Club, 182

Zitkala-Sa (Yankton Sioux), 213

The University of Illinois Press
is a founding member of the
Association of American University Presses.

———————————————————————

Composed in 10.5/13 Adobe Minion Pro
by Barbara Evans
at the University of Illinois Press
Manufactured by Thomson-Shore, Inc.

University of Illinois Press
1325 South Oak Street
Champaign, IL 61820-6903
www.press.uillinois.edu